RENEWALS 458-4574

DATE DUE

FEB - 1			
GAYLORD			PRINTED IN U.S.A.

Reading de Man Reading

Theory and History of Literature
Edited by Wlad Godzich and Jochen Schulte-Sasse

For other books in the series, see p. 313

Reading de Man Reading

Edited by Lindsay Waters and Wlad Godzich

Theory and History of Literature, Volume 59

University of Minnesota Press, Minneapolis

Earlier versions of the two parts of "Looking Back on Paul de Man" by Geoffrey Hartman appeared in the *London Review of Books*, March 15–April 4, 1984, and in *The New Republic*, March 7, 1988. Reprinted by permission.

Published by the University of Minnesota Press
2037 University Avenue Southeast, Minneapolis MN 55414.
Published simultaneously in Canada
by Fitzhenry & Whiteside Limited, Markham.
Printed in the United States of America.

Library of Congress Cataloging-in-Publication Data
Reading de Man reading / edited by Lindsay Waters and Wlad Godzich ;
    foreword by Wlad Godzich.
        p.   cm. — (Theory and history of literature ; v. 59)
    Includes index.
        1. De Man, Paul — Contributions in criticism. 2. Criticism — 20th
    century. I. Waters, Lindsay. II. Godzich, Wlad. III. Series
    PN75.D45R43 1988
801'.95'0924 — dc19   88-4580
ISBN 0-8166-1660-4
ISBN 0-8166-1661-2 (pbk.) :

Contents

Abbreviations

References for quotations from the works of Paul de Man will be given in the body of the text, with the following abbreviations:

AR: *Allegories of Reading: Figural Language in Rousseau, Nietzsche, Rilke, and Proust.* New Haven, Conn.: Yale University Press, 1979.

BI: *Blindness and Insight: Essays in the Rhetoric of Contemporary Criticism,* 2nd ed., rev. Introduction by Wlad Godzich. Theory and History of Literature, vol. 7. Minneapolis: University of Minnesota Press, 1983.

CR: "Critical Response. Reply to Raymond Geuss." *Critical Inquiry,* 10 (1983): 383–90.

F: Foreword to Carol Jacobs, *The Dissimulating Harmony: The Image of Interpretation in Nietzsche, Rilke, Artaud, and Benjamin.* Baltimore: Johns Hopkins University Press, 1978, vii–xiii.

HS: "Hegel on the Sublime." In Mark Krupnick, ed., *Displacement: Derrida and After.* Bloomington: Indiana University Press, 1983, 139–53.

P: Paul de Man, "Pascal's Allegory of Persuasion." In Stephen Greenblatt, ed., *Allegory and Representation.* Baltimore: Johns Hopkins University Press, 1981, 1–25.

PM: "Phenomenality and Materiality in Kant." In Gary Shapiro and Anthony Sica, eds., *Hermeneutics: Questions and Prospects.* Amherst: University of Massachusetts Press, 1984, 121–44.

RR: *The Rhetoric of Romanticism.* New York: Columbia University Press, 1984.

RT: *The Resistance to Theory*, foreword by Wlad Godzich. Theory and History of Literature, vol. 33. Minneapolis: University of Minnesota Press, 1986.

SS: "Sign and Symbol in Hegel's *Aesthetics*." *Critical Inquiry*, 8 (1982): 761–75.

Prefatory Note

Paul de Man from the outset of his career concerned himself with the act of reading. This volume consists of contributions that address de Man's theory and practice of reading, what they have been and what they signify for reading in general. Paul de Man explored the operation of reading because it brings to the fore the issues of the text, the reader and writer, referentiality, language, and history.

This book has been in the works since 1984, initial discussions about it having been held with Paul de Man in 1983. The aim of this book has been to take up a set of technical matters pertaining to his work. The contents were, with one exception, written before de Man's writings from 1941 and 1942 were brought to light. Therefore, the contributors to this book have not had a chance to deal with the issues raised by that news and those texts. The one exception to this rule is the first essay.

Lindsay Waters

Reading de Man Reading

Looking Back on Paul de Man
Geoffrey Hartman

Radical Patience

The death of Paul de Man at the age of sixty-four deprives us of a literary critic
whose influence, already immense in the United States and on the Continent, was
beginning to be received elsewhere. This influence is not linked to a large body
of published work. De Man's career started late. His studies at the University of
Brussels were interrupted by the war; after the war, he emigrated to America,
taught at Bard, participated in Harvard's Society of Fellows, took his Ph.D. only
in 1960 (his thesis on Mallarmé and Yeats still awaits full publication), and served
as a teacher at Cornell, Johns Hopkins, and the University of Zurich before settling at Yale in 1970. And although his earliest essays appeared in French during
the 1950s (especially in *Critique*), they were not well known until the Minnesota
edition of *Blindness and Insight* (1983) incorporated some of them. *Blindness and
Insight* was his first collection, published in 1971; a second major book, *Allegories of Reading*, appeared in 1979.

Anyone who has read even a single essay of de Man's can gauge the quality
of his mind. Many of his early pieces circulated as if they were dangerous to the
academy, and assured him a samizdat reputation. His was an analytical temper
that preferred essay to book, and each essay left its mark. Students went to whatever university he was at. That he became a controversial and widely known
scholar only in the last years of his life was in harmony with his bearing. His
courtesy was absolute, but so was his refusal to accommodate either the text or
his thoughts. The teaching was superb because his intellect was quick and

3

penetrated always beyond the canonical aspects of the philosophical or literary works he took up. The tragedy of his passing is made more acute by the fact that he was, even in his own eyes, just starting to say what he wished to say. His past work he considered prolegomenal to a study of Hegel almost complete at the time he died. In his final years he made his mind increasingly severe; it was hard, in fact, to get him to release earlier essays. The pressure on both text and reader was heightened by a prose that stripped all pathos and uplift from its subject. Yet even as prose it often approached a strange vertigo in its reversing intellectual movement, as if already caught up in that sober revel characterizing the "absolute spirit" in Hegel's *Phenomenology.*

To gain an estimate of de Man one must first acknowledge the antagonism his work aroused. This adverse reaction had many sources. Some of it was based on vulgar error, and some was intelligent. (De Man himself points out that the piece called "The Resistance to Theory," now collected in his *The Resistance to Theory,* had been commissioned and then rejected by the Modern Language Association, a decision he accepted without rancor.) The most general charge by those unable or unwilling to read him was that his mode of exegesis, the intricate pressure he put on *parts* of a text, sinned against the direct or public meaning of the work as a whole, erecting rather than knocking down barriers between author and reader, and fascinating the seducible young by strength and ingenuity, rather than justness of mind.

This is an allegation made against intellectuals in almost every generation. They stand accused, in Dryden's phrase, of injuring the page, of making it speak whatever they please. Books shaped by commonsensical values are turned into a foil for the idiosyncratic thinker: "The text inspires not them, but they the text inspire." That the "injury" inflicted by de Man is a rigorous "deconstruction" of the text, and, far from being subjective, is curiously impersonal, does not itself calm the polemics. For the critical wars of today seem to have replaced the religious wars of Dryden's day, and intense speculation in literary matters is treated as a species of enthusiasm.

The modern polemical phase, it should be said, did not begin with de Man, Derrida, and the movement of deconstruction. The storm broke because of the surprising inroads of the New Criticism into the academy. *We* may consider the New Criticism rather tame, and appreciate it for introducing a tougher pedagogical stance, but traditional scholars feared that its exclusive emphasis on the specifically literary qualities of novel or poem would isolate these from the public. "We have been urged to investigate," Bonamy Dobrée wrote in *The Broken Cistern,* the Clark Lectures for 1953, "the recondite significance of imagery and symbol, of paradox and ambiguity, of irony and wit, and to embark on the treacherous oceans of the philosophy of language. New instruments have been thrust into our hands. . . . But haven't we perhaps . . . too exclusively pursued some ultimate, to the shouldering aside of what is most *commonly* valuable in poetry?"

Overanalyzed, the well-wrought urn becomes a broken cistern. Common humanity and even the survival of poetry are affected. "In paying as we do such attention
to matters which only the specialist can be at home with, haven't we, with great
ceremony, brought poetry, not into the wide halls of judgment, but into the academic laboratory?"

If the New Criticism academized and so isolated art, then deconstruction,
which suffers under the additional charge of turning everything into text ("pantextualism," "wall-to-wall textuality"), will obviously have an even harder time in
being read by a wide audience. Certain pronouncements like Derrida's "There is
no *hors texte*" have become notorious: they are taken out of context as statements
about reality itself rather than about the difficulty of turning texts inside out. The
assumption, now challenged, that texts have the interior/exterior structure of
worldly facts—like gloves or houses, for instance—influences a model of interpretation that is all too common: we must find the *core* of the text, unveil something hidden, or harmonize outside features like figures of speech or verbal tricks
with inside features presumed to be psychological.

De Man too, long before knowing of Derrida, began a critique of such models
of reading. While still at Harvard, and teaching with Reuben Brower (author of
the New Critical and devotedly pedagogical *The Fields of Light*), de Man insisted
that the New Criticism take the full consequences of its emphasis on the literary
qualities of a work. For in terms of a theory of literature, these deft critics
recoiled from their own discovery that texts were defined preeminently by the fact
of being texts—that is, made of language rather than ideas. They began to close
off rebellious textual complexities (what John Crowe Ransom called, tongue in
cheek, "irrelevant texture") by a species of the very "heresy of paraphrase" they
had condemned. Having found that words were not rendered less ambiguous by
being organized in a literary way—that the ambiguity, or beyond it, the ambivalence, became more complex and discomfiting—a tendency arose to distinguish
the literary from the linguistic in terms that relapsed into humanistic cant. De
Man's early essay, "The Dead-End of Formalist Criticism" on Richards, Empson,
Wheelright, and Eliot, remains authoritative on this turn toward what he calls in-
carnational or salvational criticism. Dobrée, in short, wins out; and while close
reading continues a technique, ways are found to short-circuit the contradictions
or divisions revealed by that technique.

"It may be said," Empson wrote in *Seven Types of Ambiguity*, "that the contradictions must somehow form a larger unity if the final effect is to be satisfying.
But the onus of reconciliation can be laid very heavily on the receiving end. "The
receiving end" is, of course, the reader; and rather than developing a reader-
response theory, with its subjectivist dangers, or facing clearly the problematics
of closure in the realm of literary interpretation, the New Criticism described that
"larger unity" by means of naturalized religious or metaphysical concepts: the

reconciliation of opposites, organic form, or (as in Northrop Frye) archetypal form.

The "insight" of the New Criticism, then, was accompanied by a "blindness" in direct relation to the intolerable force of that insight. Like a Blakean Giant Form, those close readers shrank back, at the level of theory, into a noncontradictory state far simpler than any text. De Man himself, in these early essays, uses not Blake but Hegel, Hölderlin, and Heidegger. He reverts to such concepts as Hegel's "unhappy consciousness" to indicate that art could never heal the split between consciousness and being, or the division within being itself.

Yet Hegel and Co. are by no means exempt from the "error" of the New Critics, who feel compelled to separate out a work as literary, only to deny that specificity by talking about an overall coherence or ideal unity or happy incarnation. De Man's essay on Heidegger, also written in the 1950s, shows that Hölderlin says exactly the opposite of what Heidegger makes him say. By treating Hölderlin as Holy Writ, by erecting him as the one Western (post-Greek) poet who "speaks Being," Heidegger substantiates the same poetics of presence or of the undissociated sensibility that the New Critics also could not give up.

De Man's lucid and unsentimental tracking of these moments of blindness has in it the obsession and chill of a good detective story. There is no plot in the ordinary sense, no pseudonarrative or definitive peripety: yet he never loses focus. A central essay in *Blindness and Insight* defines the type of reading he is after. The reader "has to undo the explicit results of a vision that is able to move toward the light only because, being already blind, it does not have to fear the power of this light." Such hermeneutic "Proverbs of Hell" have poetic force despite their doctrine, which de Man humorously called his "scorched earth" policy. Often, however, a slight ambiguity remains, either because the thought is so dense or because the style falters. What is the status of the "has to . . . have to?" What *necessity* may be implied by the auxiliary power of that modest English verb? Other sentences come at us with a hyperbolic twist, yet strike home like a curveball right over the plate. "Not only does the critic say something that the work does not say, but he even says something that he himself does not mean to say. The semantics of interpretation have no epistemological consistency and can therefore not be scientific."

The point made repeatedly, as if in danger of being blunted by the gentle reader, is that the relation between critic and text (including the critic's own) is never that of a sophisticated revision replacing a naive insight. Text and commentary live each other's life, die each other's death. Each is a monumental project, and each is a mortal thesis astonishing in its vigor and fallibility. We cannot feel superior: like a Greek chorus, the critic is part of what he exhibits, compelled to say what he sees from a vantage point that is neither above nor below, neither cosily inside nor on the envious periphery.

These brief remarks on de Man's earliest concerns indicate lines of thought he will follow to the end. His focus is, first and foremost, on the problematics of reading. By examining the "rhetoric" of critical readers he discovers a structure of revelation and recoil that he will name "misreading" and say that it can be exposed but not scientifically corrected. "Deconstruction" is not a bad label for this negative task, though de Man uses the term sparingly. The deconstructive method works with the language of each text rather than demystifying it from an authoritative, transcendent point of reference, backed up by a new terminology or metalanguage.

Closely associated with de Man's view that we read to close off rather than to open texts is a critique of literary history and traditional concepts of periodization (modernity, classicism, romanticism). Such period terms are often unanalyzed and contradictory, and serve mainly to privilege one kind of literature over another. So his essays on Rousseau, Wordsworth, Shelley, and Hölderlin are not devoted primarily to rescuing the romantics from disesteem, but to demonstrating that a later and favored generation (Mallarmé, Rilke, Yeats, Valéry) has been read even more sloppily than the romantics. *In Defense of Reading* was the title of the volume edited by Reuben Brower and Richard Poirier to which he contributed a remarkably balanced essay, "Symbolic Landscape in Wordsworth and Yeats." Ten years later, in "The Rhetoric of Temporality" (BI, 187–228), his redefinition of allegory deconstructed a poetics of the symbol that had enmeshed—even duped—literary history from Goethe and Coleridge on.

As de Man's career proceeds, it is fascinating that "reading" moves increasingly into opposition to "history" (i.e., history writing). In the preface to *Allegories of Reading* he confesses that he had intended to write a history, but without success. "I had to shift from historical definition to the problematics of reading." The cause is never stated but seems clear enough in retrospect. At first it was a matter of making us aware how often interpretation is governed by a received version of literary history rather than by a reading of the work itself. In fact, "the more ambivalent the original utterance, the more uniform and universal the pattern of consistent error in the followers and commentators." Rousseau is the exemplary victim, and de Man says amusingly: "It is as if the conspiracy that Rousseau's paranoia imagined during his lifetime came into being after his death, uniting friend and foe alike in a concerted effort to misrepresent his thought." This "concerted effort" or "consistent error" would not be possible without the insertion of the work into a history—which is really its insertion into a comforting principle of order.

That kind of history, in short, is not history at all, at least not *temporal* like the text it wishes to order. It maintains the myth, for example, of a parental structure or dialectical relation joining later and earlier authors. There is a relation, of course, but it is not edifying; de Man shows how Baudelaire remains an enigmatic stranger despite the effort of commentators (including Mallarmé) to fix his position as "the father of modern poetry." Periodization of this kind encourages a simplified notion of enlightenment, even a quasi-theological notion: it divides history into the blindness of a previous era (e.g., the Synagogue) and the *lux et veritas* of a new era (the Revealed Church). Each new movement becomes a light carrier of this kind; no wonder students of literature are skeptical about their discipline. History writing subserves the drive for "correct" or "canonical" readings. Such readings create a pseudohistory and deprive interpretation of temporal development. They are a substitute form of belief, the antihistorical inheritance of a literate community, whether it calls itself by a secular or by a religious name.

De Man's failure to pass from the activity of reading to literary history has the effect of keeping the historical dimension free. It is not foreshortened by a master theory. Yet by the time he publishes *Allegories of Reading*, the hope of converting this freedom into a positive yield (actual history writing) has faded, because the question, "Is history writing possible?" turns out to be identical to "Is reading possible?" De Man, as if the fires of consciousness had consumed too much, and are feeding on themselves, now doubts that reading can result in understanding. Perhaps that doubt was always there, but it articulates itself with new vigor. He sweeps away wordly-wise definitions of criticism that see it "constructing a form of intelligibility for our time" (Roland Barthes), as well as others that speak the language of natural desire, of psychopolitical *imposition*. That imposition occurs, and has immense influence, but it occurs precisely to the extent that pseudohistory dominates our consciousness of being-in-time, our "rhetoric of temporality."

We can glimpse this further stage as soon as de Man develops the notion of allegory, perhaps by way of Benjamin's attempt to grasp its mortifying effect. Benjamin's study of an antiquated genre, the seventeenth-century German tragic drama (*Trauerspiel*), revalues emblematic allegory. Even later times have never quite succeeded in reducing allegory to a picturesque prop. What is now displayed is its basic structure, independent of a historical period; and this is allegory's disquieting insistence on pure anteriority (on a time before time), which casts a shadow not only on the authenticity but also on the intelligibility of later, secular time. No doctrinal conclusions are drawn from this by Benjamin or de Man, though Benjamin is attracted to the linguistic version of pure anteriority: the idea of a primal, Adamic language. De Man, for his part, responds not only to the temporal predicament revealed by allegory as a rhetorical figure but also to its aberrant valuation in poetics. Allegory comes to mean a language of transparent signs (dove = peace), prosaic and disembodied, rather than poetic and embodied; yet it is precisely the possibility of this sort of allegory, of such arbitrary and contingent equations (stabilized only by the conventional memory), which de Man emphasizes in his end phase, especially his work on Hegel. Benjamin's pathos falls away entirely, as does that of Hegel (which had entered the soul of de Man's earlier work), and the difference between reading and understanding is purged of tragic overtones.

"Allegories of Reading" evokes, then, two different meanings of allegory that come together and obscure in a symptomatic way the most public part of a book: its title. First, a sense that remains close to riddle and the unreadable, and suggests how precarious reading is when confronted by literature. Reading seems relatively impotent from this perspective, or else impositional. The literary work rejects our hypotheses, showing them up as partial.

The danger of this attractively humble view is that we may forget that riddles have trivial as well as sublime solutions and so begin to view literature as secular scripture. De Man's book, moreover, is not humble; its *démarche* toward the point where Rousseau, Rilke, Proust, and Nietzsche reveal the contingent and arbitrary character of their fictions — where the linguistic penetrates the higher "aesthetic" or "literary" realm — is as elegant and ruthless (some would say mechanical) as ever. "Allegories of Reading" moves therefore toward a second meaning that emphasizes less the theme of making sense than of producing, through reading, a very basic and very ordinary rhetorical structure. The reduction of literature to such a figure is as foundational as de Man ever gets. Allegory is deconstructive, not only vis-à-vis the symbol, but vis-à-vis all tropological devices. It is itself no very secure bottom, however, because even its negative movement toward a moment of truth or epistemological certainty is undone by something outside the system itself, which de Man names irony.

If a text, engendered by these complexities, "puts an insurmountable obstacle in the way of any reading or understanding," it is only natural to wonder why the human intellect should produce so strange a result. This question, in turn, presupposes that we know what we are doing, especially in the area of language. But for de Man, as for Benjamin, truth is the death of intention; and a text is as much a machine as a modality of understanding. "The machine," writes de Man, "is like the grammar of the text when it is isolated from its rhetoric, the merely formal element without which no text can be generated." In practice, de Man discloses an asymmetry between grammar (or a metagrammar like Jakobson's), which tends to be normative, and rhetoric, which is disjunctive and figurative. It is this gap between figures of speech and "grammatical" modes of expression that allows vertiginous possibilities of interpretation.

What reading produces, then, is not so much a replica or restitution of "inner experience," as something more akin to vertigo than to understanding. This sense of vertigo had been associated in *Blindness and Insight* with the discovery of temporality: the sense of time as a process without synthesis, repetitive, unreconciling, leading to death rather than to a recognition of permanence, and therefore no more "authentic" than the more naive state it demystifies. De Man's eloquence concerning this vertigo is unsettling in a critic who renounces affect. Describing the process in Baudelaire, he writes: "It may start as a casual bit of play with a stray loose end of the fabric, but before long the entire texture of the self is unravelled and comes apart. The whole process happens at an unsettling speed. Irony possesses an inherent tendency to gain momentum and not to stop until it has run its full course; from the small and apparently innocuous exposure of a small self-deception it soon reaches the dimensions of the absolute." And he concludes with an unusually emphatic assertion. "Irony is unrelieved *vertige*, dizziness to the point of madness. Sanity can exist only because we are willing to function within the conventions of duplicity and dissimulation, just as social language dissimulates the inherent violence of the actual relationships between human beings" ("The Rhetoric of Temporality").

Scientific language is subject to the very same oscillation, the very same instability, as we read in "Criticism and Crisis," the first chapter of *Blindness and Insight*:

> Every change of the observed subject requires a subsequent change in the observer, and the oscillating process seems to be endless. Worse, as the oscillating gains in intensity and in truth, it becomes less and less clear who is in fact doing the observing and who is being observed. . . . In the case of a genuine analysis of the psyche, it means that it would no longer be clear who is analysing and who is being analysed. . . . The need to safeguard reason from what might become a dangerous *vertige*, a dizziness of the mind caught in an indefinite regression, prompts a return to a more rational methodology.

It would be cheap to infer from this a repressed existential pathos that floods back. Yet there is affective writing in de Man, and it punctuates without diverting an always complex, vigorously prosecuted argument. The analogy now is science fiction rather than the detective story. I am reminded of how science fiction moves against the grain of its plot, how it collapses its spectacular narrative into a few instances of disorientation, Wordsworth's "Blank misgivings of a creature / Moving about in worlds not realised." In Wordsworth, however, such moments are still described in the vocabulary of inner experience, of "recollection."

The return to Hegel in de Man's last essays is again a revision of the model of inner experience traced through Hegel's own development from the *Phenomenology* to the *Encyclopedia*. The vanity of human understanding is one error de Man is not tolerant of, and because he has no system of moral terms, he questions the function of certain terms in systems whose very pride of system makes him suspicious. "Understanding" becomes one of these terms, as if it had made itself too agreeable and now suggested complicity rather than rigor. "Aesthetic" is another such term, despite Kant's careful assessment of its role vis-à-vis cognition and judgment. How we view the "aesthetic understanding," therefore, is crucial to all further morality, in the personal or the public sphere. De Man's reinterpretation of Hegel's *Aesthetics* can give us a sense of his tenacious moral analysis of an unpromising philosophical text:

> The infrastructures of language, such as grammar and tropes, account for the occurrence of the poetic superstructures, such as genres, as the

devices needed for their oppression. The relentless drive of the dialectic, in the *Aesthetics*, reveals the essentially prosaic nature of art. . . . Hegel summarises his conception of the prosaic when he says: "It is in the slave that prose begins" . . . Hegel's *Aesthetics*, an essentially prosaic discourse on art, is a discourse of the slave because it is a discourse of the figure rather than of genre, of trope rather than of representation. As a result, it is also politically legitimate and effective as the undoer of usurped authority. ("Hegel on the Sublime")

De Man's reversion to Kojève's sense of the centrality of the master/slave dialectic in Hegel and the intricate transfer of that dialectic to a very different philosophical work are less important than his reversal of the canonical—and perhaps Hegel's own—reading of the *Aesthetics*. De Man chooses sections, he calls them "enslaved," which have little or no aura, as if at that point the dialectic were an emetic that had purged the master-thinker and brought him into "the light of common day." Perhaps because he himself is facing an end, there is something touching, even recklessly didactic about passages like this. Derrida's commentary on Hegel appears almost baroque compared to de Man's: the one is a juggler, the other a tightrope walker; and while both display a saturnine brilliance, Derrida's semioclastic revel, at least in *Glas*, is far less sober than de Man's dizzy footwork only an inch above the text.

Much more might be said about the issue of mastery, from a pedagogical point of view. That so many students are attracted to deconstruction (and use it modishly against whatever went before) triggers a pedagogical anxiety. Deconstruction's intellectual rather than identifiably ideological character differentiates it from other movements. To be more fair about that: By now we have historicized these movements or demystified their techniques—in short, found out their wishful and fallible ambitions. The academy might like to regard deconstruction as equally cliquish, another fashionable wave that will pass. Yet even in America the movement associated with de Man and Derrida is felt to challenge more than a particular set of institutionalized values such as nostalgia for a Common Reader or a Public Style or a Unified Sensibility. The spirit of criticism embodied by de Man seems to threaten the institutionalization of criticism itself.

A rude scholar like Leavis could see the academy as the very center and diffusion point of his discipline, and a polite scholar like Dobrée could see the incorporation of criticism into the university also from its deformative side. Neither questioned the outcome of whatever academic struggle had to ensue. Matters would be resolved, not entirely, not peaceably perhaps, but a new curriculum would evolve out of this conflict of interests. In America, however, those who oppose deconstruction as obscurantist, and those who espouse it as intellectually necessary, agree that it pushes against the limits of the academic. Lectures and books are being announced at an alarming rate that raise the question, Is is teachable? Even more subversively, is academic teaching (now itself deconstructed) any better than a worldly or pseudoreligious mode of authority? Can a teacher's relation to students free itself of seductiveness or imposition or — to sum it up in one massively bad word — pathos?

It may not be an accident, but the training procedures of psychoanalysis are undergoing the same kind of questioning, one so traumatically introduced by Jacques Lacan in the 1950s. Even in circles independent of Lacan the relation of analyst and patient, together with a notion of countertransference (the resistance, and attraction, of physician to patient, and how it may already have distorted the very system of psychoanalysis, because it was not fully acknowledged by its first physician, Freud) — these have now come forward in a disturbing way, accompanied by extreme charges and sensational publicity. The women's movement too has emphasized the "masculine, persuasive force" in Freud's remarkable assumption of authority, which he transferred to the successor institution. Thus deconstruction and psychoanalytic literary criticism often surprisingly form an alliance, despite the antipsychologistic bent of de Man's practice.

De Man was cool to such alliances. He placed himself stubbornly within a tradition he still labeled as philological, perhaps most amusingly in a *Times Literary Supplement* symposium on "Professing Literature" (reprinted in *The Resistance to Theory*). There Harvard's Reuben Brower finds himself in the company of Nietzsche and recent French theorists, even though his teaching of literature was founded on Richards's "practical criticism." The turn to theory, de Man writes, occurred as a return to philology, to an examination of the structure of language prior to the meaning it produces. Brower, from a purely teacherly and pragmatic standpoint, was able to show that "mere reading . . . prior to any theory, is able to transform critical discourse in a manner that would appear deeply subversive to those who think of the teaching of literature as a substitute for the teaching of theology, ethics, psychology, or intellectual history."

How, indeed, was de Man to situate himself? What "history" could he align himself with, given his scruples about false continuities? He forgets to mention, for example, that Reuben Brower still believed there was a "key" that would emerge from all textual bafflement to unlock a particular literary work. Or that philologists like Leo Spitzer tried to psych out the "spiritual etymon" of each writer. Or that Erich Auerbach valued historicism, and the variety of perspectives it introduced, as a Western heritage it would be tragic to lose and which had enabled him to construct the colorful narrative of *Mimesis*.

De Man, in the *TLS* symposium, was composing a little family romance, but one that had its point. He refers us to a tradition in which philosophy, including aesthetics, is an extension rather than an abrogation of philology. He invokes the shade of Brower as a humanist not deceived by fellow humanists who appropriate aesthetics as a mode of thought that circumvents both philological detail and philosophical precision. Above all, Brower serves to caution de Man's followers

about their infatuation with theory. The patience of the philologist averts the spec-
ter of mastery, and its pedagogical anxieties.

De Man's legacy is an intellectual style of remarkable purity. That purity,
moreover, seems to contain a moral quality as well as a methodological one. Undoing the illusion of mastery in others could lead to condescension, but whatever
judgment takes place is always founded on a recognition of the necessity of error,
that is, of rhetoric; and no vigilance, literary or scientific, is able to achieve an
ultimate correction. Yet if this obliges de Man to demonstrate one thing over and
again, there is no temptation to disenchant anything except, possibly, his own
style. I refer to a style marked by didactic fervor, whose undertow takes us into
strange seas of thought, but it remains analytic and prosaic, with a minimum of
semiotic play, and no mixing by montage of fiction and criticism. Though de
Man's critique of canonical reading has helped to inspire a flood of essays on
Marxist and feminist lines, his own pages note, but do not indulge in, a vocabulary of crisis. He rethinks familiar terms from the *trivium* or takes his polarities
from authors and their critics, always shifting slightly, diacritically, the value of
exemplary words. He prefers to come to a position of nonunderstanding rather
than manipulate the screen of received ideas. The effect is that of a new and
precariously impersonal diction.

His favorite authors, often called the romantics, create their illusions out of
a permanently disruptive self-consciousness. Whatever systematic unraveling
(deconstruction) occurs, or whatever vertigo threatens, de Man's writing also
continues to maintain itself, without system, afflatus, pseudohistory, or borrowed
machinery. By a hyperbolic and constitutive gesture of his own, the critic claims
a coordinate integrity for his work. Critical thought is not simply a response to
or conversational extension of a prior text. It fascinates us, rather, by a labor of
the negative so consistent that an intuitive remark of Benjamin's is confirmed.
"Unraveling an artfully wound skein with such certainty—is that not the joy of
all productivity, at least in prose?"

Radical Impatience

In December 1987, it became known that a Belgian researcher, Ortwin de Graef,
had discovered reviews of books, concerts, and conferences written by Paul de
Man in the years 1940–42. Almost all these writings date from after the fall of
Belgium in May 1940; and except for a few articles in *Les Cahiers du Libre Exa-
men*, a journal associated with the University of Brussels, and a few more in a
Flemish-language journal, *Het Vlaamsche Land*, most (close to 170) were written
for the important Belgian newspaper *Le Soir*. During the period that de Man published in *Le Soir* and *Het Vlaamsche Land*, they were under some Nazi censor-

ship. *Le Soir*, in particular, followed the Nazi line in many respects; after its takeover, it received the nickname *Le Soir Volé* (The stolen evening).

The shock of finding de Man's early articles in these journals was increased by the fact that one of them explicitly endorsed the ideology of anti-Semitism. Under the headline, "The Jews in Contemporary Literature," it argued that Jews did not have a significant influence on contemporary literature; that charges about this literature being Judaized (*enjuivé*) served merely to discredit it; that the Jews themselves helped to spread this myth of their influence; that the ability of Western intellectuals to safeguard so representative a cultural domain as literature from Jewish influence was comforting. De Man left it unclear whether it was comforting because Jewishness itself is unhealthy, or because *any* invasion of Western civilization by a foreign force, a *force étrangère*, would reflect badly on its vitality.

De Man concluded:

> By preserving, despite the Semitic intrusion [*l'ingérence sémite*] into all aspects of European life, an originality and a character that have remained intact, our civilization has shown that it is healthy in its deep nature. Moreover, we can anticipate that a solution of the Jewish problem that would envisage the creation of a Jewish colony isolated from Europe, would not result, for the literary life of the West, in regrettable consequences. The latter would lose, all in all, some people of mediocre value, and would continue as in the past to develop according to its own great laws of evolution.

This is not vulgar anti-Semitic writing by the terrible standards of the day; but however polished de Man's formulations are, they show all the marks and dangerous implications of identifying Jews as a foreign and unhealthy presence in "Western civilization." De Man's article, moreover, is framed on the page of *Le Soir* (a special page devoted to "The Jews and Us: Cultural Aspects") by a nasty cartoonlike photo, a caricature of two Jews in prayer shawls imploring God and captioned "May Jehovah confound the Goy," and by a quotation attributed to Benjamin Franklin. "A leopard can't change its spots. The Jews are Orientals [*Asiatiques*]; they are a menace for the country that lets them in, and they should be excluded by the Constitution." (The source is an *American* forgery that originated in 1934 and was refuted by Charles Beard and others. It circulated widely among German and American Nazis.)

It is hard to be dispassionate, given the anti-Semitic campaign in which *Le Soir* participated from the fall of 1940 on, and the tragic history of the persecution and final deportation of Belgian Jews. (They made up 1 percent of the country's population but accounted for a third of its civilian and military casualties.) De Man was writing in a collaborationist paper at a vulnerable period for the Jews, when the "colony isolated from Europe" was turning into sealed ghettos and concentration camps, in part because this "foreign" element could not find a home elsewhere and was treated like a disease, or a pollutant that had to be contained. In the light of history, de Man's article, and the cartoon and quotation that accompanied it (for which he was probably not responsible), become more than "theoretical" expressions of anti-Semitism. It remains important, however, to place oneself into that era and ask basic questions about motives and attitudes. What role did anti-Semitism play in de Man's thought?

His articles reveal a strong sympathy for the Flemish, who lost their independence under Napoleon and their territorial integrity in 1830. A cultural nationalist, de Man believed in the "genius" or "individual soul" of a people, in their "unanimity" attested by a shared language, a homeland, and ancestral achievement. (These qualities somehow did not apply to the Jews, who were seen as a "ghostly anti-race," in J. L. Talmon's memorable phrase.) De Man's real focus, however, is on the "New Europe" under Nazi domination, a Europe that allowed this Flemish sympathizer to take his distance from French culture and turn toward the German sphere of influence.

Nothing in this common sort of nationalism had to result in anti-Semitic attitudes. Was it youthful inexperience, then, or was it a broader acceptance of fascist ideology that made him write a piece of anti-Semitic propaganda? The Dutch historian Johann Huizinga, also acknowledging cultural (though not racial) differences between Latin, German, Anglo-Saxon, and Slavic "types," published two books, one as early as 1936 (based on 1935 lectures at Brussels), and the other as late as 1943, that look toward Europe's renewal yet refuse to accept the claim that "am deutschen Wesen wird die Welt genesen" ("the Germanic will cure the world").

The study of fascist ideology and related thought is gradually coming into its own. George Mosse and Zeev Sternhell have made essential contributions. There are textual exposés by Jeffrey Mehlman, and sensitive explorations by Alice Kaplan of the marriage between technology and fantasy in fascist publicists. The appeal of a movement that drew some very significant authors into its ranks came in part from what Mosse calls its "open-endedness . . . its ideological fluidity under authoritarian leadership." Besides the sad and demented case of Ezra Pound and the Mussolini *schwärmerei* of such figures as W. B. Yeats and Emil Ludwig, we find a large group of fascist intellectuals active in both France and Belgium. They were militant journalists and included some prestigious writers. Although they shared a political philosophy, their attitude toward collaboration (and sometimes anti-Semitism) varied greatly from suave to propagandistic. I will mention only Thierry Maulnier (proponent of a "rational anti-Semitism"), Maurice Blanchot, Bertrand de Jouvenel, Céline, Claude Mauriac, Robert Brasillach, Pierre Drieu la Rochelle (who became editor of the *Nouvelle Revue Française* during the Occupation), Robert Poulet, and Henri de Man (Paul de Man's uncle).

Let me recall what happened in Belgium at the end of April 1940. So intense was the cultural and linguistic strife between Flemish and Francophone factions that only two weeks before the German invasion the Belgian government almost fell because of a quarrel over bilingualism. Closely tied to these divided national feelings were the collaborationist careers of Robert Poulet and Henri de Man. Poulet, who initially supported strict neutrality for Belgium in the European conflict, agreed in October 1940 to become editor in chief and political director of the *Nouveau Journal*, an important Francophone publication. He accepted Nazi control in Europe and actively encouraged the war against Russia, while seeking to form a single political party for the French-speaking provinces of Belgium. Henri de Man, after the German occupation, dissolved the Labor party he headed, declaring that the European collapse was a deliverance rather than a disaster, because "sovereignty of labor" could now be realized within the framework of the New Order. The old and decrepit parliamentary democracy would be replaced by a single party in a "movement of national resurrection" encompassing "all the vital forces of the nation."[1] Poulet was condemned to death after the Liberation, but the sentence was not carried out and he continued to write against the bourgeoisie and the injustice of which he deemed himself a victim. Henri de Man failed to form his single Flanders-oriented party comprising both labor and capital, retreated in 1941 to the Alps, was condemned in absentia, but finished his life composing his autobiography and visionary blueprints for Europe.

His nephew's journalism, in this context, stands out by its refusal to engage directly with political matters. But its sympathies are clearly with Germany, and its culture politics must have furthered the cause of collaboration. Reporting in March 1941 on the first reactions of literary France to the defeat, de Man combines a dig at French intellectuals with a revealing comment about the laggard masses. "The French are not yet used to the idea that the creation of a new world organization no longer depends on them. . . . The lucidity of some [French] writers when they condemn a nefarious regime, and their determination to launch themselves on new paths is certainly a comforting symptom. But so long as this does not express itself unanimously in public opinion it is at least premature to talk about a national revival." Such "unanimity" between a nation and its leaders was stressed by fascist intellectuals. In another article de Man moves close to being explicitly collaborationist when he claims that Hitler brought about the "definite emancipation of a people called upon to exercise, in its turn, a hegemony in Europe."

De Man reviewed the writings of fascist thinkers, including Drieu, Brasillach, and Ernst Jünger. His relation to fascist ideology is not a simple matter. There is, clearly, an accommodation, but it remains very general and without recourse to the usual "virile" invective. To judge from his articles, de Man felt he was living in a revolutionary epoch where politics and a sense of collective action were essential parts of intellectual regeneration. Political militancy was displacing the *douceur* of the arts, or rather, as Walter Benjamin, and not Paul de Man, saw so clearly, aestheticizing politics for the masses. Yet with respect to the arts an admirable inconsistency crops up: not only is de Man a supporter of modern literature (including Kafka!), but he resists its political coordination. He praises Robert Poulet, the collaborationist editor of the *Nouveau Journal*, for a novel that does not subordinate "artistic sincerity" to political imperatives. And in defense of the literary review *Messages*[2] (which he may have helped to get published), de Man explicitly rejects any "brutal" targeting of art, "under the pretext that the present revolution is totalitarian . . . that it intends to modify all aspects of personal and collective existence." In most other respects de Man's themes are conformist: the renewal of Europe, the worth and dignity of national cultures, the need for roots, the spiritual unity of state and individual, of collectivity and elite.

Whether de Man's anti-Semitic strain was conventional, or an ideological reflex, does not much matter. The argument he makes presupposes a claim that efforts to emancipate the Jews had only proved that they could not be assimilated. They could adapt, to be sure, but that was only a dangerous disguise: they remained racially, essentially, a foreign body in the state. Henri de Man wrote in 1941 that he had been convinced for a long time of the need to eliminate "from our political organism the foreign body constituted by all the residues or embryos of the ghetto." This conviction could attach itself to a time-honored popular and Christian hatred, which regarded the Jews as unspiritual (materialistic) enemies of the faith, as doomed and eternal outsiders. The Jewish intellectual in particular was pictured as free-floating, cynical, subversive. The great scholar E. R. Curtius (neither a Nazi nor an anti-Semite) wrote in 1932: "We fight not Judaism but *Destruktion* [roughly: a radical questioning of traditional structures, a kind of early stage on the way to deconstruction], not a race but a negation . . . our Jews, it must regretfully be said, for the greater part and in their significant activity, are self-devoted to scepticism and *Destruktion*." (Ironically enough, *Destruktion* had gained philosophical currency through Heidegger's *Being and Time*.)

Beyond the historical context, there is the moral issue. Although I stress the anti-Semitism, it often goes with a collaborationist mentality. De Man, whose judiciousness and analytic verve are already clear in these early, routine pieces, continued his association with overtly anti-Semitic and collaborationist journals till the end of November 1942. Many French journalists and intellectuals who had pursued a policy of limited collaboration during the first year of the Nazi Occupation disengaged or joined the Resistance by the end of 1941.[3] It is also unlikely that de Man would not have known that the persecution of the Belgian Jews, begun in the fall of 1940, had taken a drastic turn.[4] The so-called spontaneous Flemish action of April 1941, in which two synagogues were sacked and burned *Kristallnacht*-style, should have made the seriousness of the situation clear. More catastrophically, the wearing of the Yellow Star was enforced in June 1942; in August systematic deportations began. Ten thousand Jews were rounded up in

Belgium by the middle of September; the "Asiatics" were sent east, that is, to their death in Auschwitz. An ideological figure of speech became literal and lethal.

That is the knowledge de Man must have faced later, and every person with a past of this kind must face. It is also the knowledge that a person like myself must face. There was no trace of anti-Semitism in the de Man I knew; we were acquainted with each other since 1961, and became colleagues and friends in 1965. But I cannot overlook that this expression of anti-Jewish sentiment, though it remained polite, was limited to suave cultural essays and never spilled over into exhortatory or demagogic rhetoric.[5]

By an irony that deserves a name of its own, the disclosure of the early articles imbeds a biographical fact in our consciousness that tends to devour all other considerations. It may not spare the later achievement, whose intellectual power we continue to feel. In de Man's own words, the "restoration of mortality by autobiography [in the present case, by biography] deprives and disfigures to the precise extent that it restores." One could argue, of course, that there is no relation between the young journalist, age twenty-one, and the distinguished theorist who published his first book at age fifty-one. Or that what relation obtains is one of reaction formation, as when he accuses Husserl of blindly privileging "European supremacy" at the very time (1935) that Europe "was about to destroy itself as center in the name of an unwarranted claim to be the center." For de Man too was a European who "escaped from the necessary self-criticism that is prior to all philosophical truth about the self."

Rereading the later work will always be troubled by the fact that de Man did not explicitly address his past. I regret his silence, which shifts a moral burden to us: are we now obliged to speak for him, to invent thoughts he might have provided? Two such thoughts have sustained themselves for me. (1) He wished to avoid confession, or any religious gesture, preferring to work out his totalitarian temptation in a purely impersonal way. (2) He may not have forgotten the purge of intellectuals in Belgium and France after Liberation. It was a time of passionate judgment that often failed to distinguish between treason and "délit d'opinion."[6] Journalist-flics abounded, and added a new opportunism to the old. It would be a further irony if de Man's silence now brought about what he feared: defamation of his work.

Yet it must be added that what we are seeing here is a special case of what happens all the time. A new fact, often a new text, makes a difference in the way we read. Although history has moved more quickly in this case, we are always in the situation of having to revise our judgment of a work, however monumental it once appeared to be. Deconstruction itself emphasizes the vanity of monumentalism. Before considering how de Man has been affected, let me take my distance from one view that has surfaced.

Those previously suspicious of deconstruction have seized on the present reve-
lations. Their sense of deconstruction as morally unsound and politically evasive
seems to stand confirmed. They condemn it as untrustworthy because it seeks to
avert the reality, and so the culpability, of error. That is how they interpret deconstruction's emphasis on the indeterminacy of meaning and the complexity of a
medium that seems to "speak" us, instead of submitting fully to our control. Such
a judgment is superficial and divorces deconstruction from its context in the history of philosophy. We may argue about whether deconstruction yields a useful
way of looking at the relation of language and meaning, but it does take up an
age-old problem. The philosopher Ernst Cassirer said that while language wished
to overcome "the curse of mediacy" it was part of the problem it tried to resolve.[7]
Our methods and media of inquiry distance the truth we seek: we get trapped in
epistemological, semantic, and interpretive hassles. One result of this perplexing
by-product of our very effort to clarify things is that philosophy has often turned
against slippery modes of expression in the name of scientific rigor. Blame is
placed squarely on the figurative or literary uses of language. "The only good
metaphor is a dead metaphor."

Deconstruction is, in this respect, a defense of literature. It shows, by close
reading, (1) that there are no dead metaphors, (2) that literature is often more self-
aware than those who attack it, and (3) that literary texts contain significant tensions that can be disclosed but not resolved by analysis. Any mode of analysis,
therefore, that sees the text as an organicist unity or uses it for a totalizing purpose
(as when the right or the left speaks for history) is blind, and the text itself will
"deconstruct" such closures.

Within the history of thought deconstruction is surely a significant critique of
German idealism ("identity philosophy"), that led to various, including fascist,
kinds of organicism. De Man in particular moves away from speculative politics.
His position is the very opposite of an idealism that confuses intellect and action,
ideology and political praxis. His emphasis, moreover, on the nonidentity of
these realms, on the asymmetry of real and ideal, does not result in a spiritualistic
or nihilistic withdrawal, tempting to many whose God has failed. Deconstruction
is neither nihilistic nor cynical when it questions whether there exists an arena
for testing ideas other than the uncontrollable one of activist politics; or when it
demonstrates that philosophy and literature express the impasse from which ideas
spring as well as those ideas themselves.

Those who see a "flight from history" in de Man—and now link it directly to
his youthful error—simplify the situation. It is true he does not put himself in
historical context, and he should have done so. But there is a philosophical scrutiny of progressive and dialectical schemes by which we organize events and identify them as historical. De Man refuses, for example, to see modernism as a
fulfillment of romanticism, and he subjects such binary concepts as symbol and
allegory to a reversing analysis that overturns the received point of view. More-

over, as de Graef has noted, de Man's reflection on the impact of the French Revolution on Hölderlin and Wordsworth may contain a self-reflection on the "revolution" in his own time, one that carried him along to a terrible defeat and raised the question of what future lay open, what mode of action might be possible.

What is neglected by those who reduce everything to biographical fact is the intellectual power in de Man's later work, the sheer power of critique, whatever its source, which he deploys against the claims of both philosophy and literary theory. It is because of this powerful analytic talent, rather than because of a peculiar theory or attitude of his own, that de Man's influence penetrated literary studies. The only peculiar thing is that a philosophical mind of this caliber should turn against the pretensions of philosophy and toward literature.

What is harder to appreciate is the standpoint from which that critique is launched. In addition to the power of deconstructive reasoning there is its purity; i.e., it does not reveal, not in de Man at least, its situatedness, its personal or ideological context. The method acts as if it had no relatives. Hegel or Heidegger or Kant or Proust are not sources but materials only: there is neither piety in this critic for their achievement nor any interest in strengthening their hold on us, consecrating their place in the canon.

To my mind it is only the purity of deconstructive thought, not its power, that can now be questioned; and though, as I said before, there is nothing of a confessional nature in de Man, it may yet turn out that here too, in the later essays, we glimpse the fragments of a great confession. The risk I will take is to link the intellectual strength of the later work to what is excluded by it, and which, in surging back, threatens to diminish its authority.

If the probity of the Paul de Man we knew, as well as his integrity as a critic, remains our focus, it is possible that the postwar writings constitute an avowal of error, a kind of repudiation in their very methodology or philosophy of reading. De Man's method of reading always asks us to look beyond natural experience or its mimesis to a specifically linguistic dilemma. He claims that the relation between meaning and language is not in our subjective control, perhaps not even human:

> The way in which I can try to mean is dependent on linguistic properties that are not only not made by me, because I depend on the language as it exists for the devices which I will be using, it is as such not made by us as historical beings, it is perhaps not even made by humans at all. Benjamin says, from the beginning, that it is not at all certain that language is in any sense human.

This is interesting and scandalous, since by "not human" de Man (interpreting Benjamin, the German Jewish critic who committed suicide in 1940 while fleeing from the Nazis) certainly does not mean divine, as if language were instituted by

God. If language were God-given, there would surely be stability; but there is stability only insofar as language is purified of ordinary referential meaning, and becomes pure speech, as in ritual or magic, or when we recite something by heart without attending to its meaning. According to de Man, we are always encountering epistemological or semantic instabilities, the incompatibility or disjunction between meaning and intent, or between what is stated and the rhetoric or mode of stating it.

De Man concludes that the language-meaning relationship is not one of stable, mutual reflection or correspondence, as when sound reinforces sense, or history seems to fall into a genealogical and progressive pattern. Oscar Wilde depreciated action in favor of imagination because it was "a thing incomplete in its essence, because limited by accident, and ignorant of its direction, being always at variance with its aim." But for de Man this description of action is *also* a description of what cannot be overcome by art, even the most imaginative kind. There is no compensation for the failure of action in the perfection of art. The fields of critical philosophy, literary theory, and history have an interlinguistic, not an extralinguistic, correlative; they are secondary in relation to the original, which is a previous text. They reveal an essential failure or disarticulation, which was already there in the original. "They kill the original, by discovering that the original was already dead. They read the original from the perspective of pure language [*reine Sprache*], a language that would be entirely freed of the illusion of meaning . . . and in doing so they bring to light a dismembrance, a de-canonization which was already there in the original from the beginning."

This talk of killing the original, and of essential failure, is strong stuff. Knowing today about the writings of the young de Man, it is not possible to evade them as merely a biographical reference point: they are an "original" to which the later writing reacts.[8] Yet de Man's method of reading insists that this relation between late and early is interlinguistic only, that the position he has abandoned, one that proved to be a failure and perhaps culpably blind, is not to be used to explain his eventual method. The biographical disclosure, in short, may occult de Man's intelligibility; that is, although his method insists on excluding the biographical ("extralinguistic") reference, I do not believe that we can read him without identifying the "original" as a language that betrayed him, as the mediated and compromised idiom of his early, journalistic writings.

De Man's assertion, for example, that "what stands under indictment is language itself and not somebody's philosophical error," all of a sudden becomes a reflection by de Man on de Man.[9] The earlier self is not off the hook, but the emphasis shifts to the way language operates. The later self acknowledges an error, yet it does not attribute it to an earlier self, to a self involved in ideas and responsible for the error, because that would perpetuate its blindness to the linguistic nature of the predicament. According to de Man's analysis, self-serving or not, and which I describe rather than endorse, enlightenment as such cannot resolve error, and even repeats it if it is deluded into thinking that the new position stands in a progressive and sounder relation to language, that it has corrected a historical mistake once and for all. Even to say, quite simply, "I was young, I made a mistake, I've changed my mind," remains blind if it overlooks the narrative closure of this or any confession.

What is at issue is the character of self-analysis. De Man's notorious example is Rousseau. In *Allegories of Reading*, he proposes that autobiography, as it was invented or modernized by Rousseau, is built on self-accusations that allow the writer to write, that is, to excuse himself, and to extend these excuses into a narrative web. It is as if de Man (so we can remark now) feared that writing would always be implicated in such an effort of exculpation. The sequence of writing, exculpation, self occurs even where there is no discernible fault or error. It originates that original fault, and with it a false genealogy or continuity based on the self. De Man therefore rejects the "pathos of history," including personal history, and insists (in his essay on Benjamin, written at a time of considerable physical suffering) on a suffering that is "specifically linguistic." This linguistic "pathos," he says, must not be confused with an "elegiac gesture, by which one looks back on the past as a period that is lost, which then gives you the hope of another future that might occur."

The personal history behind this passage was hidden to us, but we can now see more clearly de Man's attitude toward his past. He places himself beyond nostalgia yet does not say that the past can be overcome. Germans, in fact, still talk of the Nazi era as a "past that will not pass away"; it resists being worked through. De Man does not mention the exceptional Nazi years, and that is an evasion; he makes a general statement that to mourn the past as lost in order to guarantee ourselves an unencumbered future will not succeed. There cannot be, he suggests, a future that will not prove to have been a past like that.[10] His essay on Benjamin envisages a temporal repetition that subverts the hope in new beginnings, in a New Era: a hope, ultimately messianic, that always revives. I was impressed by de Man's radical patience: now the early articles show that he passed through a phase of radical impatience. One can think here of the political culture he championed in *Le Soir*, a culture that claimed to be modern and revolutionary. "Linguistic pathos," opposed to personal or historical pathos, is the painful knowledge that he had been trapped by an effect of language, an ideological verbiage that blinded critical reflection. The only activity to escape the ideological pressure was art itself, whose deeper tradition he often cites as able to resist the purely contemporary (*l'ingérence de l'actualité*).

We can accuse de Man of lacking foresight or civil courage or of underestimating the ruthlessness of the Nazi regime. And we abhor the anti-Semitism, as well as any collaboration that occurred. Once again we feel betrayed by the intellectuals. The accusations we bring, however, are a warning to ourselves. They do not justify complacency or easy judgments about the relation of political ideas to moral conduct. Many on the left also welcomed what Kenneth Burke called "sinister unifying," and succumbed to xenophobic and anti-Jewish sentiment. De Man's "dirty secret" was the dirty secret of a good part of civilized Europe. This is said not to extenuate de Man but to recall sadly that culture, intelligence, and the precise shade of politics were insufficient to guard against anti-Semitism.

That de Man concealed his past casts a shadow on our analysis of his mature criticism. To fall, however, into a pattern of either/or, of denunciation or defense, is a trap that shows the poverty of our speech when it comes to moral statement. The integrity of the later work has been questioned: it is necessary to read it again, testingly; only then can its value be clarified. The debate could be fruitful, if it leads to more than an exchange of hostilities. It does not seem excessive to ask that people at least read the essays in question rather than accepting hearsay distortions about deconstruction. It also seems appropriate to have those who were close to the Yale critic tell us what they know of his character.

Some mystery will remain: the same that always dogs us when we try to join the literary work and the life. My own attempt in that direction must remain speculative. It sees in de Man's essays not an elaborate, evasive masking of a discredited point of view but rather a severe, generalized reflection on rhetoric, spurred by the experience of totalitarianism. I do not know why de Man did not say as much directly; despite his own attitude on "excuses" such forthrightness might have been more effective, as well as morally clear. But his turn from the politics of culture to the language of art was not, I think, an escape into but an escape from aestheticism: a disenchantment with that fatal aestheticizing of politics (blatant in many of his own early pieces) that gave facism its false brilliance. De Man's critique of every tendency to totalize literature or language, to see unity where there is no unity, could be a belated, but still powerful, act of conscience.

Notes

1. "As for democracy," Dan Segre writes of his Italian fascist youth in *Memoirs of a Fortunate Jew*, "I knew it was plutocratic and decadent, and I did not understand . . . how it could continue."

2. This literary review, though nonpolitical in content, welcomed writers who did not wish to work for the collaborationist *Nouvelle Revue Française* and similar publications (see Herbert R. Lottman, *The Left Bank*, 1981).

3. There was cooperation with the Vichy regime at that time, also by many intellectuals who later joined the Resistance. The confusion is described by Sternhell in *Neither Left nor Right: Fascist Ideology in France*; he quotes from Emmanuel Mounier and Hubert Beuve-Méry to show that before they became important Resistance figures they saw in France's defeat the opening for a nationwide "spiritual" revolution. De Man's ideological position may have been the norm among a large group of French-speaking intellectuals during 1941. But after that, according to Sternhell, opportunism began to be a factor among collaborators.

4. On the difficult question of how much was known about Auschwitz, there is a growing consensus that the fall of 1942 was a "gray zone" in terms of Belgians realizing that it was not a labor camp but a death camp. By the end of the year firm evidence had replaced rumors.

5. I have found one other prejudicial reference to Jews. It occurs in a discussion of Ernst Jünger and contemporary German fiction. De Man posits a proper tradition of German art, which is marked by "deep spiritual sincerity," and then a second strain, which abused the remarkable theses of expressionism. It is not surprising, he writes, that those who went in the other direction, which he qualifies as "aberrant" and a "degeneration," "were mainly non-German, specifically Jews." Such a judgment about the degeneracy of expressionism, and about its link to the Jews, paralleled Nazi pronouncements. The *context* becomes incriminating; the argument as such is not all that different from what seems to motivate the cultural anti-Semitism of T. S. Eliot. The Jews do not fit into Christian culture (Eliot) or into the "content of the European idea" (de Man).

6. See Pierre Asseline's brief but informative *L'Épuration des Intellectuels* (1985).

7. Cassirer is constructivist, not deconstructivist: I quote him only for his acknowledgment of the problem. Philosophy has given up, according to him, the hope for an "unmediated" apprehension or reflection of reality. His magisterial introduction to *The Philosophy of Symbolic Forms* (vol. 1, on language, 1923) continues idealism's search for unity of being and unity of knowledge, though with an important use of Kant's notion of critique.

8. The other way of understanding the failure of the original remains quasi-theological: every original, like the Mosaic tablets of the law, is given, written, twice, as if it were an echo or translation of itself, with effects and derivatives that—in the perspective of faith—do not shatter an original unity but coincide with it, cohering back, as it were. In a secular or agnostic perspective, however, revelation discloses not the unity of the original but its flaw, a hairline crack that (as in de Man's own writings) could widen under the pressure of events and show ruin within the constitutive text.

9. A danger of the analysis I have undertaken is that de Man's writings could become the scene of a hunt where statements are excerpted from the author's step-by-step, rigorous sequencing, and recontextualized as displaced references to his own dilemma. This would be allegorizing him in the worst possible way; it would not be *reading*. His attempt to reverse this faulty habit of literary analysis would then have failed.

10. There is an unsentimental fatalism here that might provide the beginning of a critique of de Man's shift from history to temporality to language. His review of Luce-Fabre's *Journal de Paris* in *Le Soir*, July 21, 1942, makes a fatalistic link between the "imperious reality" of current history and "a politics of collaboration [which] results from the present situation, not as an ideal desired by the people collectively but as an irresistible necessity from which noone can escape." He praises rare and isolated (we would say, elitist) spirits like Luce-Fabre as "precursors of a unanimous will" destined to combat the inertia and hostility of the masses. Luce-Fabre's attitude, according to de Man, is not ideologically motivated (i.e., fascist) but rather "objective"; it derives from "necessities inscribed in the facts." Has the mature critic purged himself of the notion of historical necessity or has he transferred it to the necessities inscribed in language?

Psyche: Inventions of the Other
Jacques Derrida

Translated by Catherine Porter

What else am I going to be able to invent?

Here perhaps we have an inventive incipit for a lecture. Imagine, if you will, a speaker daring to address his hosts in these terms. He thus seems to appear before them without knowing what he is going to say; he declares rather insolently that he is setting out to improvise. Obliged as he is to invent on the spot, he wonders again: "Just what am I going to have to invent?" But simultaneously he seems to be implying, not without presumptuousness, that the improvised speech will constantly remain unpredictable, that is to say, as usual, "still" new, original, unique—in a word, inventive. And in fact, by having at least invented something with his very first sentence, such an orator would be breaking the rules, would be breaking with convention, etiquette, the rhetoric of modesty, in short, with all the conditions of social interaction. An invention always presupposes some illegality, the breaking of an implicit contract; it inserts a disorder into the peaceful ordering of things, it disregards the proprieties.

The Question of the Son

Cicero would certainly not have advised his son to begin this way. For, as you know, it was in responding one day to his son's request and desire that Cicero defined, on one occasion among others, oratorical invention.[1]

The reference to Cicero is indispensable here. If we are to speak of invention, we must always keep in mind the word's Latin roots, which mark the construction of the concept and the history of its problematics. Moreover, the first request of

25

Cicero's son bears on language, and on translation from Greek to Latin ("Studeo, mi pater, Latine ex te audire ea quae mihi tu de ratione dicendi Graece tradisti, si modo tibi est otium et si vis": "I am burning with a desire, father, to hear you say to me in Latin those things concerning the doctrine of speaking that you have given [dispensed, reported, delivered or translated, bequeathed] to me in Greek, at least if you have the time and want to do it").

Cicero the father answers his son. He first tells him, as if to echo his request or to restate it narcissistically, that as a father his first desire is for his son to be as knowing as possible, *doctissimum*. The son has then, with his burning desire, anticipated the father's wish. Since his desire is burning with that of his father, the latter takes satisfaction in it and reappropriates it for himself in satisfying it. Then the father offers the son this teaching: given that the orator's special power, his *vis*, consists in the things he deals with (ideas, themes, objects), as well as in the words he uses, *invention* has to be distinguished from *disposition*; invention finds or discovers things, while disposition places or localizes them, positions them while arranging them: "res et verba invenienda sunt et conlocanda." Yet invention is "properly" applied to ideas, to the things one is talking about, and not to elocution or verbal forms. As for disposition or collocation (*conlocare*), which locates words as well as things, form as well as substance, it is often linked to invention, father Cicero then explains. So disposition, furnishing places with their contents, concerns both words and things. We would then have, on the one hand, the "invention-disposition" pairing for ideas or things, and on the other hand the "elocution-disposition" pairing for words or forms.

We now have in place one of the most traditional philosophical *topoi*. Paul de Man recalls that *topos* in a beautifully wrought text entitled "Pascal's Allegory of Persuasion."[2] I should like to dedicate this essay to the memory of Paul de Man. Allow me to do so in a very simple way, by trying once more to borrow from him — from among all the things we have received from him — a bit of that serene discretion by which his thought — its force and its radiance — was marked. It was in 1967, when he directed the Cornell University program in Paris, that I first came to know him, to read him, to listen to him, and there arose between us an unfailing friendship that was to be utterly cloudless and that will remain in my life, in me, one of the rarest and most precious rays of light.

In "Pascal's Allegory of Persuasion," de Man pursues his unceasing meditation on the theme of allegory. And it is also, more or less directly, invention as allegory (invention of the other), as myth or fable, that I am concerned with here. After pointing out that allegory is "sequential and narrative," although "the topic of its narration" is "not necessarily temporal at all," de Man insists on the paradoxes in what we could call the task of allegory or the allegorical imperative: "Allegory is the purveyor of demanding truths, and thus its burden is to articulate an epistemological order of truth and deceit with a narrative or compositional order of persuasion." And in the same development he encounters the classical distinction of rhetoric as invention and rhetoric as disposition: "A large number of such texts on the relationship between truth and persuasion exist in the canon of philosophy and rhetoric, often crystallized around such traditional philosophical topoi as the relationship between analytic and synthetic judgments, between propositional and modal logic, between logic and mathematics, between logic and rhetoric, between rhetoric as *inventio* and rhetoric as *dispositio*, and so forth."

Had we had the time for it here, it would have been interesting to ask why and how, in the positive notion of rights that is established between the seventeenth and the nineteenth centuries, the view of an author's rights, or of an inventor's proprietary rights in the realm of arts and letters, takes into account only form and composition. This law thus excludes all consideration of content, thematics, meaning. All the legal texts, often at the price of considerable difficulty and confusion, stress this point: invention can display its originality only in the values of form and composition. As for "ideas," they belong to everyone; universal in their essence, they could not ground a property right. Is that a betrayal, a bad translation, or a displacement of the Ciceronian heritage? Let us leave this question hanging. I simply wanted to include in these opening remarks some praise for the father Cicero. Even if he never invented anything else, I find a great deal of *vis*, of inventive power, in someone who opens a discourse on discourse, a treatise on oratory art, and a text on invention, with what I shall call *the question of the son* as a question *de ratione dicendi*. This question happens to be a scene of *traditio* as tradition, transfer, and translation; we could also say it is an allegory of metaphor. The child who speaks, questions, zealously seeks knowledge – is he the fruit of an invention? Does one invent a child? This question will resurface later on. Does it first of all concern the *son* as the legitimate offspring and bearer of the name?

What else am I going to be able to invent?

It is certainly expected of a discourse on invention that it should fulfill its own promise or honor its contract: it will deal with invention. But it is also hoped (the letter of the contract implies this) that it will put forth something brand new – in its words or its contents, in its utterance or its enunciation – on the subject of invention. To however limited an extent, in order not to disappoint its audience, it ought to invent.

In spite of all the ambiguity of that word and concept, invention, you already have some sense of what I am trying to say.

This discourse must then be presented as an invention. Without claiming to be inventive through and through, and continually, it has to exploit a largely common stock of rule-governed resources and possibilities in order to sign, as it were, an inventive proposition, at least one, and that signed innovation will alone determine the extent to which it will be able to engage the listener's desire. But – and here is where the dramatization and the allegory begin – it will also need the signature or the countersignature of the other, let's say here that of the son who is not the invention of the father. A son will have to recognize the invention as such, as if the heir were the sole judge (hang on to the word "judgment"), as if the son's countersignature bore the legitimating authority.

But presenting an invention, presenting itself as an invention, the discourse I am talking about will have to have its invention evaluated, recognized, and legitimized by someone else, by an other who is not one of the family: the other as a member of a social community or of an institution. For an invention can never be *private* once its status as invention, let us say its patent or warrant, its manifest, open, public identification, has to be certified and conferred. Let us translate: as we speak of invention, that old grandfatherly subject we are seeking to reinvent here today, we ought to see this very speech acquire a sort of patent, the title of invention—and that presupposes a contract, consensus, promise, commitment, institution, law, legality, legitimation. There is no natural invention—and yet invention also presupposes originality, a relation to origins, generation, procreation, genealogy, that is to say, a set of values often associated with genius or geniality, thus with naturality. Hence the question of the son, of the signature, and of the name.

We can already see the unique structure of such an event—the occurrence of an invention—taking shape. Who sees it taking shape? The father, the son? Who finds himself excluded from this scene of invention? What other of invention? Father, son, daughter, wife, brother, or sister? If invention is never private, what then is its relation with all the family dramas?

So, then, the unique structure of an event, for the speech act I am speaking of must be an event. It will be so, on the one hand, insofar as it is unique, and on the other hand, inasmuch as its very uniqueness will produce the coming or the coming about of something new. It should promote or allow the coming of what is new in a "first time ever." The full weight of the enigma condenses in every word of this cluster—"new," "event," "coming," "singularity," "first time" (here the English phrase "first time" marks the temporal aspect that the French *première fois* elides). Never does an invention appear, never does an invention take place, without an inaugural event. Nor is there any invention without an advent, if we take this latter word to mean the inauguration for the future of a *possibility* or of a *power* that will remain at the disposal of everyone. *Ad*vent there must be, because the *e*vent of an invention, its act of inaugural production, once recognized, legitimized, countersigned by a social consensus according to a system of conventions, must be valid *for the future* (*a-venir*). It will only receive its status of invention, furthermore, to the extent that this socialization of the invented thing will be protected by a system of *conventions* that will ensure for it at the same time its recording in a common history, its belonging to a culture: to a heritage, a lineage, a pedagogical tradition, a discipline, a chain of generations. Invention *begins* by being susceptible to repetition, exploitation, reinscription.

We have already encountered, limiting ourselves to a network that is not solely lexical and that does not reduce to the games of a simple verbal invention, the convergence of several modes of coming or of venue, the enigmatic collusion of *invenire* and *inventio*, of event, of advent, of future or time-to-come (in French, *avenir*), of adventure, and of convention. How could one translate this lexical cluster outside the Romance languages while preserving its unity, the unity linking the *first time* of invention to the *coming*, to the arrival of the future (*avenir*), of the event, of the advent, of the convention or of the adventure? For the most part these words of Latin origin are, for example, welcomed by English (even the term "venue," in its narrow, highly coded judicial sense, and the special sense of *advent* designating the coming of Christ); they are welcome with, however, a notable exception at the center of the grouping: the verb *venir* itself. To be sure an invention amounts, says the *Oxford English Dictionary*, to "the action of coming upon or finding." But I can already imagine the inventiveness required of the translator of this lecture in those places where it exploits the institution of the Latin-based languages. Even if this verbal collusion appears adventurous or conventional, it makes us think. What does it make us think? What else? Whom else? What do we still have to invent in regard to the coming, the *venire?* What does it mean, *to come?* To come a first time? Every invention supposes that something or someone comes a *first time*, something or someone comes to someone, to someone else. But for an invention to be an invention, to be *unique* (even if the uniqueness has to be repeatable), it is also necessary for this first time, this unique moment of origin, to be a last time: archaeology and eschatology acknowledge each other here in the irony of the *one and only* instant.

So we are considering the singular structure of an event that seems to produce itself by speaking about itself, *by the act of speaking of itself* once it has begun to invent on the subject of invention, paving the way for it, inaugurating or signing its uniqueness, bringing it about, as it were; and all the while it is also, simultaneously, naming and describing the generality of its genre and the genealogy of its *topos*: *de inventione*, sustaining our memory of the tradition of a genre and its practitioners. In its claim to be inventing again, such a discourse would be stating the inventive beginning by speaking of itself in a reflexive structure that not only does not produce coincidence with or presence to itself, but which instead projects forward the advent of the self, of "speaking" or "writing" of itself as other, that is to say, what I call a trace. I shall content myself with mentioning the value of "self-reflexivity" that was often at the core of Paul de Man's analyses. Doubtless more resistant than it seems, it has occasioned some very interesting debates, notably in essays by Rodolphe Gasché and Suzanne Gearhardt. I shall try to return to these matters some other time.

But in speaking of itself, such a discourse would then be trying to gain recognition by a public community not only for the general truth value of what it is advancing on the subject of invention (the truth of invention and the invention of truth) but at the same time for the operative value of a technical apparatus hence-forth available to all.

Fables: Beyond the Speech Act

Without yet having cited it, I have been describing for a while now, with one finger pointed toward the margin of my discourse, a text by Francis Ponge. This text is quite short: six lines in *italics*, seven counting the title line — I shall come back in a moment to this figure 7 — plus a two-line parenthesis in *roman* type. The roman and italic characters, although their positions are reversed from one edition to the next, may serve to highlight the Latin linguistic heritage that I have mentioned and that Ponge has never ceased to invoke.

To what genre does this text belong? Perhaps we are dealing with one of those pieces Bach called his inventions, contrapuntal pieces in two or three voices that are developed on the basis of a brief initial cell whose rhythm and melodic contour are very clear and sometimes lend themselves to an essentially didactic writing.[3] Ponge's text arranges one such initial cell, which is the following syntagm: "*Par le mot par . . .*," i.e., "*By the word by.*" I shall designate this invention not by its genre but by its title, namely, by its proper name, *Fable.*

This text is called *Fable.*[4] This proper name embraces, so to speak, the name of a genre. A title, always unique, like a signature, is confused here with a genre name; an apt comparison would be a novel entitled *Novel*, or an invention called "Invention." And we can bet that this fable entitled *Fable*, and constructed like a fable right through to its concluding "lesson" (*moralité*), will treat the subject of the fable. The fable, the essence of the fabulous about which it will claim to be stating the truth, will also be its general subject. *Topos*: fable.

So I am reading *Fable*, the fable *Fable.*

Fable	*Fable*
Par le mot par commence donc ce texte	*/By the word by commences then this text*
Dont la première ligne dit la vérité,	*/Of which the first line states the truth*
Mais ce tain sous l'une et l'autre	*/But this silvering under the one and other*
Peut-il être toléré?	*/Can it be tolerated?*
Cher lecteur déjà tu juges	*/Dear reader already you judge*
Là de nos difficultés . . .	*/There as to our difficulties . . .*
(APRÈS sept ans de malheurs	/(AFTER seven years of misfortune
Elle brisa son miroir.)	/She broke her mirror.)

Why did I wish to dedicate the reading of this fable to the memory of Paul de Man? First of all because it deals with a text by Francis Ponge. I am thus recalling a beginning. The first seminar that I gave at Yale, at the invitation of Paul de Man who introduced me there, was on Francis Ponge. *La Chose* was the title of this ongoing seminar; it continued for three years, touching upon a number of related subjects: the debt, the signature, the countersignature, the proper name, and death. To remember this starting point is, for me, to mime a starting over; I take consolation in calling that beginning back to life through the grace of a fable that is also a myth of impossible origins. In addition, I wish to dedicate this reading to Paul de Man because of the resemblance Ponge's fable, bespeaking a unique intersection of irony and allegory, bears to a poem of truth. It presents itself ironically as an allegory "of which the first line states the truth": truth of allegory and allegory of truth, truth as allegory. Both are fabulous inventions, by which we mean inventions of language (at the root of fable/fabulous is *fari* or *phanai*: to speak) as the invention of language as the same and the other, of oneself as (of) the other.

The allegorical is marked here both in the fable's theme and in its structure. *Fable* tells of allegory, of one word's move to cross over to the other, to the other side of the mirror. Of the desperate effort of an unhappy speech to move beyond the specularity that it constitutes itself. We might say in another code that *Fable* puts *into action* the question of reference, of the specularity of language *or* of literature, and of the possibility of stating the other or speaking *to* the other. We shall see how it does so; but already we know the issue is unmistakably that of death, of this moment of mourning when the breaking of the mirror is the most necessary and also the most difficult. The most difficult because everything we say or do or cry, however outstretched toward the other we may be, remains *within us*. A part of us is wounded and it is with ourselves that we are conversing in the travail of mourning and of *Erinnerung*. Even if this metonymy of the other in ourselves already constituted the truth and the possibility of our relation to the living other, death brings it out into more abundant light. So we see why the breaking of the mirror is still more necessary, because at the instant of death, the limit of narcissistic reappropriation becomes terribly sharp, it increases and neutralizes suffering: let us weep no longer over ourselves alas when we *must* no longer be concerned with the other *in ourselves*, we *can* no longer be concerned with anyone except the other *in ourselves*. The narcissistic wound enlarges infinitely for want of being able to be narcissistic any longer, for no longer even finding appeasement in that *Erinnerung* we call the work of mourning. Beyond internalizing memory, it is then necessary to *think*, which is another way of remembering. Beyond *Erinnerung*, it is then a question of *Gedächtnis*, to use a Hegelian distinction that Paul de Man was wont to recall in his recent work for the purpose of presenting Hegelian philosophy as an allegory of a certain number of dissociations, for example, between philosophy and history, between literary experience and literary theory.[5]

Allegory, before it is a theme, before it relates to us the other, the discourse of the other or toward the other, is here, in *Fable*, the structure of an event. This stems first of all from its narrative form.[6] The "moral" or "lesson" of the fable, as one says, resembles the ending of a story. In the first line the *donc* appears merely as the conclusive seal of a beginning, as a logical and temporal scansion that sets up a singular consequentiality; the word *APRÈS* ("AFTER") in capital letters brings it into sequential order. The parenthesis that comes *after* marks the end of the story, but in a while we shall observe the inversion of these times.

This fable, this allegory of allegory, presents itself then as an invention. First of all because this fable is called *Fable*. Before venturing any other semantic analysis, let me state a hypothesis here—leaving its justification for later. Within an area of discourse that has been fairly well stabilized since the end of the seventeenth century in Europe, there are only two major types of *authorized* examples for invention. On the one hand, people invent *stories* (fictional or fabulous), and on the other hand they invent *machines*, technical devices or mechanisms, in the broadest sense of the word. Someone may invent by fabulation, by producing narratives to which there is no corresponding reality outside the narrative (an alibi, for example), or else one may invent by producing a new operational possibility (such as printing or nuclear weaponry, and I am purposely associating these two examples, since the politics of invention is always at one and the same time a politics of culture and a politics of war). Invention as *production* in both cases—and for the moment I leave to the term "production" a certain indeterminacy. *Fabula* or *fictio* on the one hand, and on the other *tekhnè, epistémè, istoria, methodos*, i.e., art or know-how, knowledge and research, information, procedure, etc. There, I would say for the moment in a somewhat elliptical and dogmatic fashion, are the only two possible, and rigorously specific, registers of all invention today. I am indeed saying "today," stressing the relative modernity of this semantic categorization. Whatever else may resemble invention will not be recognized as such. Our aim here is to grasp the unity or invisible harmony of these two registers.

Fable, Francis Ponge's fable, is inventing itself as fable. It tells an apparently fictional story, which seems to last seven years, as the eighth line notes. But first *Fable* is the tale of an invention, it recites and describes itself, it presents itself from the start as a beginning, the inauguration of a discourse or of a textual mechanism. It does what it says, not being content with announcing, as did Valéry, I believe, "In the beginning was the fable." This latter phrase, miming but also translating the first words of John's gospel ("In the beginning was the *logos*," the word) is perhaps also a performative demonstration of the very thing it is saying. And "fable," like *logos*, does indeed say the saying, speak of speech. But Ponge's *Fable*, while locating itself ironically in this evangelical tradition, reveals and perverts, or rather brings to light by means of a slight perturbation, the strange structure of the foreword (*envoi*) or of the evangelical message, in any case of that incipit which says that in the incipit, at the inception, there is the *logos*, the word. *Fable*, owing to a turn of syntax, is a sort of poetic performative that simultaneously describes and carries out, on the same line, its own generation. Not all performatives are somehow reflexive, certainly; they do not all describe themselves, they do not designate themselves as performatives while they take place. This one does so, but its constative description is nothing other than the performative itself. "*Par le mot* par *commence donc ce texte.*" Its beginning, its invention or its first coming does not come about before the sentence that recounts precisely this event. The narrative is nothing other than the coming of what it cites, recites, points out, or describes. It is hard to distinguish the telling and the told faces of this sentence that invents itself while inventing the tale of its invention; in truth, telling and told are undecidable here. The tale is given to be read; it is a legend since what the tale narrates does not occur before it or outside of it, of this tale producing the event it narrates; but it is a legendary fable or a fiction in a single line of verse with two versions or two versings of the same. Invention of the other in the same—in verse, the same from all sides of a mirror whose silvering could (should) not be tolerated. By its very typography, the second occurrence of the word *par* reminds us that the first *par*—the absolute incipit of the fable—is being quoted. The quote institutes a repetition or an originary reflexivity that, even as it divides the inaugural act, at once the inventive event and the relation or archive of an invention, also allows it to unfold in order to say nothing but the same, itself, the dehiscent and refolded invention of the same, at the very instant when it takes place. And already heralded here, expectantly, is the desire for the other—and to break a mirror. But the first *par*, quoted by the second, actually belongs to the same sentence as the latter one, i.e., to the sentence that points out the operation or event, which nonetheless takes place only through the descriptive quotation and neither before it nor anywhere else. Borrowing terms employed by some proponents of speech-act theory, we could say that the first *par* is used, the second quoted or mentioned. This distinction seems pertinent when it is applied to the word *par*. Is it still pertinent on the scale of the sentence as a whole? The *used par* belongs to the mentioning sentence, but also to the mentioned sentence; it is a moment of quotation, and it is as such that it is used. What the sentence cites integrally, from *par* to *par*, is nothing other than itself in the process of citing, and the use values within it are only subsets of the mentioned values. The inventive event is the quotation and the narrative. In the body of a single line, on the same divided line, the event of an utterance mixes up two absolutely heterogeneous functions, "use" and "mention," but also heteroreference and self-reference, allegory and tautegory. Is that not precisely the inventive force, the masterstroke of this fable? But this *vis inventiva*, this inventive power, is inseparable from a certain syntactic play with the places in language, it is also an art of *disposition*.

If *Fable* is both performative and constative from its very first line, this effect extends across the whole of the text. By a process of poetic generation we shall have to verify, the concept of invention distributes its two essential values between these two poles: the constative—discovering or unveiling, pointing out or saying what is—and the performative—producing, instituting, transforming. But the sticking point here has to do with the figure of coimplication, with the configuration, of these two values. In this regard *Fable* is exemplary from its very first line. That line's inventiveness results from the single act of enunciation that performs and describes, operates and states. Here the conjunction "and" does not link two different activities. The constative statement is the performative itself since it points out nothing that is prior or foreign to itself. Its performance consists in the "constatation" of the constative—and nothing else. A quite unique relation to itself, a reflection that produces the self of self-reflection by producing the event in the very act of recounting it. An infinitely rapid circulation—such are the *irony* and the temporality of this text—*all at once* shunts the performative into the constative, and vice versa. De Man has written of undecidability as an infinite and thus untenable acceleration. It is significant for our reading of *Fable* that he says this about the impossible distinction between fiction and autobiography:[7] the play of our fable also lies between fiction and the implicit intervention of a certain *I* that I shall bring up shortly. As for irony, Paul de Man always describes its particular temporality as a structure of the instant, of what becomes "shorter and shorter and always climaxes in the single brief moment of a final *pointe*."[8] "Irony is a synchronic structure,"[9] but we shall soon see how it can be merely the other face of an allegory that always seems to be unfolded in the diachronic dimension of narrative. And there again *Fable* would be exemplary. Its first line speaks only of itself, it is immediately metalingual, but its metalanguage has nothing to set it off; it is an inevitable and impossible metalanguage since *there is no language before it*, since it has no prior object beneath or outside itself. So that in this first line, which states the truth of (the) *Fable*, everything is put simultaneously in a first language and in a second metalanguage—and nothing is. There is no metalanguage, the first line repeats; there is only that, says the echo, or Narcissus. The property of language whereby it always can and cannot speak of itself is thus graphically enacted, in accord with a paradigm account de Man elaborated. Here I refer you to a passage from *Allegories of Reading* where de Man returns to the question of metaphor and the role of Narcissus in Rousseau. I shall simply extract a few propositions that will allow you to recall the thrust of his full demonstration: "To the extent that all language is conceptual, it already speaks about language and not about things. . . . All language is language about denomination, that is, a conceptual, figural, metaphorical language. . . . If all language is about language, then the paradigmatic linguistic model is that of an entity that confronts itself."[10]

The infinitely rapid oscillation between the performative and the constative, between language and metalanguage, fiction and nonfiction, autoreference and heteroreference, etc., does not just produce an essential instability. This instability constitutes that very event—let us say, the work—whose invention disturbs normally, as it were, the norms, the statutes, and the rules. It calls for a new theory and for the constitution of new statutes and conventions that, capable of recording the possibility of such events, would be able to account for them. I am not sure that *speech-act theory*, in its present state and dominant form, is capable of this, nor, for that matter, do I think the need could be met by literary theories either of a formalist variety or of a hermeneutic inspiration (i.e., semanticist, thematicist, intentionalist, etc.).

The fabulatory economy of a very simple little sentence, perfectly normal in its grammar, spontaneously *deconstructs* the oppositional logic that relies on an untouchable distinction between the performative and the constative and so many other related distinctions; it deconstructs that logic without disabling it totally, to be sure, since it also needs it in order to detonate the speech event. Now in this case does the deconstructive effect depend on the force of a literary event? What is there of literature, and what of philosophy, here, in this fabulous staging of deconstruction? I shall not attack this enormous problem head on. I shall merely venture a few remarks that have some bearing upon it.

1. Suppose we knew what literature is, and that in accord with prevailing conventions we classified *Fable* as literature: we still could not be sure that it is integrally literary (it is hardly certain, for example, that this poem, as soon as it speaks of the truth and expressly claims to state it, is nonphilosophical). Nor could we be sure that its deconstructive structure cannot be found in other texts that we would not dream of considering as literary. I am convinced that the same structure, however paradoxical it may seem, also turns up in scientific and especially in judicial utterances, and indeed can be found in the most foundational or institutive of these utterances, thus in the most inventive ones.

2. On this subject I shall quote and comment briefly on another text by de Man that meets up in a very dense fashion with all the motifs that concern us at this point: performative and constative, literature and philosophy, possibility or impossibility of deconstruction. This is the conclusion of the essay "Rhetoric of Persuasion" (Nietzsche) in *Allegories of Reading*.

> If the critique of metaphysics is structured as an aporia between performative and constative language, this is the same as saying that it is structured as rhetoric. And since, if one wants to conserve the term "literature," one should hesitate to assimilate it with rhetoric, then it would follow that the deconstruction of metaphysics, or "philosophy," is an impossibility to the precise extent that it is "literary." This by no means resolves the problem of the relationship between literature and philosophy in Nietzsche, but it at least establishes a somewhat more reliable point of "reference" from which to ask the question.

This paragraph shelters too many nuances, shadings, and reserves for us to be able, in the short time we have here, to lay open all the issues it raises. I hope to deal with it more patiently some other time. For now I shall make do with a somewhat elliptical gloss. In the suggestion that a deconstruction of metaphysics is impossible "to the precise extent that it is 'literary,' " I suspect there may be more irony than first appears. At least for this reason, among others, the most rigorous deconstruction has never claimed to be foreign to literature, nor above all to be *possible*. And I would say that deconstruction loses nothing from admitting that it is impossible; also that those who would rush to delight in that admission lose nothing from having to wait. For a deconstructive operation *possibility* would rather be the danger, the danger of becoming an available set of rule-governed procedures, methods, accessible approaches. The interest of deconstruction, of such force and desire as it may have, is a certain experience of the impossible: that is, as I shall insist in my conclusion, of the other—the experience of the other as the invention of the impossible, in other words, as the only possible invention. Where, in relation to this, might we place that unplaceable we call "literature"? That, too, is a question I shall leave aside for the moment.

Fable gives itself then, by itself, by herself, a patent of invention. And its double strike is its invention. This singular duplication, from *par* to *par*, is destined for an infinite speculation, and the specularization first seems to seize or freeze the text. It paralyzes it, or makes it spin in place at an imperceptible or infinite speed. It captivates it in a mirror of misfortune. The breaking of a mirror, according to the superstitious saying, announces seven years of misfortune. Here, in typographically different letters and in parentheses, it is *after* seven years of misfortune that she broke the mirror. *APRÈS*—"after"—is in capital letters in the text. This strange inversion, is it also a mirror effect, a sort of reflection of time? But if the initial effect of this fall of *Fable*, which in parentheses assumes the classic role of a sort of "moral" or lesson, retains an element of forceful *reversal*, it is not only because of this paradox, not just because it inverts the meaning or direction of the superstitious proverb. In an *inversion* of the classical fable form, this "moral" is the only element that is explicitly narrative, and thus, let us say, allegorical. A fable of La Fontaine's usually does just the opposite: there is a narrative, then a moral in the form of a maxim or aphorism. But reading the narrative we get here in parentheses and in conclusion, in the place of the "moral," we do not know where to locate the inverted time to which it refers. Is it recounting what would have happened before or what happens after the "first line"? Or again, what happens throughout the whole poem, of which it would be the very temporality. The difference in the grammatical tenses (the simple past of the allegorical "moral" following a continuous present) does not allow us to answer. And there will be no way of knowing whether the "misfortune," the seven years of misfortune that we are tempted to synchronize with the seven preceding lines, are being recounted by the fable or simply get confused with the misfortune of the narrative, this distress of a fabulous discourse able only to reflect itself without ever moving out of itself. In this case, the misfortune would be the mirror itself. Far from being expressible in the breaking of a mirror, it would consist—so as to ground the infinity of reflection—in the very presence and possibility of the mirror, in the specular play for which language provides. And upon playing a bit with these misfortunes of performatives or constatives that are never quite themselves because they are parasites of one another, we might be tempted to say that this misfortune is also the essential "infelicity" of these speech acts.

In any case, through all these inversions and perversions, through this fabulous revolution, we have come to the crossroads of what Paul de Man calls allegory and irony. Although unable to undertake the analytic work here, I shall indicate three moments or motifs to be pursued, for example, in the vitally necessary rereading of "The Rhetoric of Temporality":

1. A "provisional conclusion" (p. 222) links allegory and irony in the discovery—we can say the invention—"of a truly temporal predicament." Here are some lines that seem to have been written for *Fable*:

> The act of irony, as we now understand it, reveals the existence of a temporality that is definitely *not organic*, in that it relates to its source only in terms of distance and difference and allows for *no end, for no totality* [this is indeed the mirror, a technical and nonorganic structure]. Irony divides the flow of temporal experience into a past that is pure mystification and a future that remains harassed forever by a relapse within the inauthentic. It can know this inauthenticity but can never overcome it. It can only restate and repeat it on an increasingly conscious level, but it remains endlessly caught in the impossibility of making this knowledge applicable to the empirical world. It dissolves in the narrowing spiral of a linguistic sign that becomes more and more remote from its meaning, and it can find no escape from this spiral. The temporal void that it reveals is the same void we encountered when we found *allegory always implying an unreachable anteriority. Allegory and irony are linked in their common discovery of a truly temporal predicament.*" (118, my emphasis)

Suppose we let the word "predicament" (and the word *is* a predicament) keep all its connotations, including the most adventitious ones. Here the mirror is the *predicament*: a necessary or fateful situation, a quasi-nature; we can give a neutral formulation of its predicate or category, and we can state the menacing danger of such a situation, the technical machinery, the artifice that constitutes it. We are caught in the mirror's trap. Here I am fond of the French word *piège*, meaning trap: it was, a few years ago, a favorite theme in elliptical and lighthearted discussions between Paul de Man and myself.

2. A bit later, Paul de Man presents irony as the inverted specular image of allegory: "The fundamental structure of allegory reappears here [in one of Words-

worth's Lucy Gray poems] in the tendency of the language towards narrative, the spreading out along the axis of an imaginary time in order to give duration to what is, in fact, simultaneous within the subject. *The structure of irony, however, is the reversed mirror-image of this form*" (225, my emphasis).

3. And finally, a passage bringing these two inverted mirror images together in their sameness: "Irony is a synchronic structure, while allegory appears as a successive mode capable of engendering duration as the illusion of a continuity that it knows to be illusionary. *Yet the two modes, for all their profound distinction in mood and structure, are the two faces of the same fundamental experience of time*" (226, my emphasis).

Fable, then: an allegory stating ironically the truth of allegory that it is in the present, and doing so while stating it through a play of persons and masks. The first four lines are in the third person of the present indicative (the evident mode of the constative, although the "I," about which Austin tells us that it has, in the present, the privilege of the performative, can be implicit there). In these four lines, the first two are indicative, the next two interrogative. Lines five and six could make the implicit intervention of an "I" explicit insofar as they address the reader; they dramatize the scene by means of a detour into apostrophe or parabasis. Paul de Man gives much attention to parabasis, notably as it is evoked by Schlegel in relation to irony. He brings it up again in "The Rhetoric of Temporality" (222) and elsewhere. Now the *tu juges* (you judge, line 6) is also *both* performative and constative; and *nos difficultés* (line 7) are as well the difficulties of the author, those of the implicit "I" of a signatory, those of the fable that presents itself, and those of the community fable-author-readers. For everyone gets tangled up in the same difficulties, all reflect them, and all can judge them.

But who is *elle* (the "she" of the last line)? Who "broke her mirror?" Perhaps *Fable*, the fable itself (feminine in French), which is here, really, the subject. Perhaps the allegory of truth, indeed Truth itself, and it is often, in the realm of allegory, a Woman. But the feminine can also countersign the author's irony. She would speak of the author, she would state or show the author himself in her mirror. One would then say of Ponge what Paul de Man says of Wordsworth. Reflecting upon the "she" of a Lucy Gray poem ("She seemed a thing that could not feel"), he writes: "Wordsworth is one of the few poets who can write proleptically about their own death and speak, as it were, from beyond their own graves. The 'she' in the poem is in fact large enough to encompass Wordsworth as well" (225).

The she, in this fable, I shall call Psyche. You know that Pysche, who was loved by Cupid, disappears when she sees Eros, the rising sun. You are familiar with the fable of Psyche painted by Raphael and found in the Farnese villa. Of Psyche it is also said that she lost her husband for giving in to her wish to contemplate him when that had been forbidden to her. But in French a psyche, a homonym and common noun, is also a large double mirror installed on a rotating stand. The woman, let us say Psyche, her beauty or her truth, can be reflected there, can admire or adorn herself from head to foot. Psyche is not named by Ponge, who could well have given his fable an ironic dedication to La Fontaine, who is celebrated in French literature both for his fables and his retelling of the Psyche myth. Ponge has often expressed his admiration for La Fontaine: "If I prefer La Fontaine – the slightest fable – to Schopenhauer or Hegel, I do know why." This Ponge writes in *Promêmes* (Part II, "Poges Bis," V, 167).

As for Paul de Man, he does name Psyche, not the mirror, but the mythical character. And he does so in a passage that matters much to us since it also points up the distance between the two "selves," the subject's two selves, the impossibility of seeing oneself and touching oneself at the same time, the "permanent parabasis" and the "allegory of irony":

> This successful combination of allegory and irony also determines the thematic substance of the novel as a whole [*La Chartreuse de Parme*], the underlying *mythos* of the allegory. This novel tells the story of two lovers who, like Eros and Psyche, are never allowed to come into full contact with each other. When they can touch, it has to be in a darkness imposed by a total arbitrary and irrational decision, an act of the gods. The myth is that of the unovercomable distance which must always prevail between the selves, and it thematizes the ironic distance that Stendhal the writer always believed prevailed between his pseudonymous and nominal identities. As such, it reaffirms Schlegel's definition of irony as a "permanent parabasis" and singles out this novel as one of the few novels of novels, as the allegory of irony.

These are the last words of "The Rhetoric of Temporality" (*BI*, 228).

Thus, in the same strike, but a double strike, a fabulous invention becomes the invention of truth: of its truth as fable, of the fable of truth, of the truth of truth as fable. And of that which in the fable depends on language (*fari*, fable). It is the impossible mourning of truth in and through the word. For you have seen it well, if the mourning is not announced by the breaking of the mirror, but consists in the mirror, if it comes with the specularization, well then, the mirror comes to be itself solely through the intercession of the word. It is an invention and an intervention of the word, and here even of the word meaning "word," *mot*. The word itself is reflected in the word *mot* as it is in the name "name." The silvering (*tain*), which excludes transparency and authorizes the invention of the mirror, is a trace of language (langue):

> Par le mot *par* commence donc ce texte
> Dont la première ligne dit la vérité,
> Mais ce tain sous l'une et l'autre
> Peut-il être toléré?

Between the two *par* the silvering that is deposited between two lines is the language itself; it depends on the word, and the word *word*; it is *le mot*, the word;

it distributes, separates, on each side of itself, the two appearances of *par*. It opposes them, puts them opposite or vis-à-vis each other, links them indissociably yet also dissociates them forever. This process does an unbearable violence that the law should prohibit (can this silvering be tolerated under the two lines or between the lines?); it should prohibit it as a perversion of usage, an overturning of linguistic convention. Yet it happens that this perversion obeys the law of language, it is a quite normal proposition, no grammar has anything to object to this rhetoric. We have to get along without that prohibition, such is both the observation and the command conveyed by the *igitur* of this fable — the simultaneously logical, narrative, and fictive *donc* of the first line: "*Par le mot par commence donc ce texte . . .* "

This *igitur* speaks for a psyche, to it/her and before it/her, about it/her as well, and psyche would be only the rotating speculum that has come to relate the same to the other. Of this relation of the same to the other, we could say, playfully: It is *only* an invention, a mirage, or an admirable mirror effect, its status remains that of an invention, of a simple invention, by which is meant a technical mechanism. The question remains; Is the psyche an invention?

The analysis of this fable would be endless. I abandon it here. *Fable* in speaking of the fable does not only invent insofar as it tells a story that does not take place, that has no place outside itself and is nothing other than itself in its own inaugural in(ter)vention. This invention is not only that of a poetic fiction, a work whose production becomes the occasion for a signature, for a patent, for the recognition of its status as a literary work by its author and also by its reader. The reader, the other who judges ("*Cher lecteur déjà tu juges . . .* ") — but who judges from the point of his inscription in the text, from the place that, although first assigned to the addressee, becomes that of a countersigning. *Fable* has this status as an invention only insofar as, from the double position of the author and the reader, of the signatory and the countersignatory, it also puts out a machine, a technical mechanism that one must be able, under certain conditions and limitations, to reproduce, repeat, reuse, transpose, set within a public tradition and heritage. It thus has the value of a procedure, model, or method, furnishing rules for exportation, for manipulation, for variations. Taking into account other linguistic variables, a syntactic invariable can, recurringly, give rise to other poems of the same type. And this *typed* construction, which presupposes a first instrumentalization of the language, is indeed a sort of *tekhnè*. Between art and the fine arts. This hybrid of the performative and the constative that, from the first line (*premier vers* or first line) at once says the truth ("*dont la première ligne dit la vérité*," according to the description and reminder of the second line), a truth that is nothing other than its own truth producing itself, this is indeed a unique event; but it is also a machine and a general truth. While appealing to a preexistent linguistic background (syntactic rules and the fabulous treasure of language), it furnishes a rule-governed mechanism or regulator capable of generating other poetic utterances of the same type, a sort of printing matrix. So we can propose the following example: "*Avec le mot* avec *s'inaugure donc cette fable,*" i.e., with the word "with" begins then this fable; there would be other regulated variants, at greater or lesser distances from the model, that I do not have the time to note here. Then again, think of the problems of quotability, both inevitable and impossible, that are occasioned by a self-quoting invention. If, for example, I say, as I have done already, "By the word "by" commences then this text by Ponge entitled *Fable*, for it commences as follows: 'By the word *by*' . . . " and so forth. This is a process without beginning or end that nonetheless is only beginning, but without ever being able to do so since its sentence or its initiatory phase is already secondary, already the sequel of a first one that it describes even before it has properly taken place, in a sort of exergue as impossible as it is necessary. It is always necessary to begin again in order finally to arrive at the beginning, and reinvent invention. Let us try, here in the margin of the exergue, to begin.

It was understood that we would address here the status of invention. You are well aware than an element of disequilibrium is at work in that contract of ours, and that there is thus something provocative about it. We have to speak of the status of invention, but it is better to invent something on this subject. However, we are authorized to invent only within the statutory limits assigned by the contract and by the title (status of invention or inventions of the other). An invention refusing to be dictated, ordered, programmed by these conventions would be out of place, out of phase, out of order, impertinent, transgressive. And yet, some eagerly impatient listeners might be tempted to retort that indeed there will be no invention here today unless that break with convention, into impropriety, is made; in other words, that there will be invention only on condition that the invention transgress, in order to be inventive, the status and the programs with which it was supposed to comply.

As you have already suspected, things are not so simple. No matter how little we retain of the semantic load of the word "invention," no matter what indeterminacy we leave to it for the moment, we have at least the feeling that an invention ought not, as such and as it first emerges, have a status. At the moment when it erupts, the inaugural invention ought to overflow, overlook, transgress, negate, (or, at least—this is a supplementary complication—deny) the status that people would have wanted to assign to it or grant it in advance; indeed it ought to overstep the space in which that status itself takes on its meaning and its legitimacy—in short, the whole environment of *reception* that by definition ought never be ready to welcome an authentic innovation. On this hypothesis (which is not mine, for the time being) it is here that a theory of reception should either encounter its essential limit or else complicate its claims with a theory of transgressive gaps. About the latter we can no longer tell whether it would still be theory and whether it would be a theory of something like reception. Let's stick with this common-sense hypothesis a while longer. It would add that an invention ought to produce a disordering mechanism, that when it makes its appearance it ought to open up a space of unrest or turbulence for every status assignable to it. Is it not then spontaneously destabilizing, even deconstructive? The question would then be the following: what can be the deconstructive effects of an invention? Or, conversely, in what respect can a movement of deconstruction, far from being limited to the negative or destructuring forms that are often naively attributed to it, be inventive in itself, or be the signal of an inventiveness at work in a sociohistorical field? And finally, how can a deconstruction of the very concept of invention, moving through all the complex and organized wealth of its semantic field, still invent? Invent over and beyond the concept and the very language of invention, beyond its rhetoric and its axiomatics?

I am not trying to conflate the problematics of invention with that of deconstruction. Moreover, for fundamental reasons, there could be no *problematics* of deconstruction. My question lies elsewhere: why is the word "invention," that tired, worn-out classical word, today experiencing a revival, a new fashionableness, and a new way of life? A statistical analysis of the occidental *doxa* would, I am sure, bring it to light: in vocabulary, book titles,[11] the rhetoric of advertising, literary criticism, political oratory, and even in the passwords of art, morality, and religion. A strange return of a desire for invention. "One must invent": Not so much create, imagine, produce, institute, but rather invent; and it is precisely in the interval between these meanings (invent/create, invent/imagine, invent/produce, invent/institute, etc.) that the uniqueness of this desire to invent dwells. To invent not this or that, some *tekhnè* or some fable, but to invent the world—a world, not America, the New World, but a novel world, another habitat, another person, another desire even. A closer analysis should show why it is then the word "invention" that imposes itself, more quickly and more often than other neighboring words ("discover," "create," "imagine," "produce," and so on). And why this desire for invention, which goes so far as to dream of inventing a new desire, on the one hand remains contemporary with a certain experience of fatigue, of weariness, of exhaustion, but on the other hand accompanies a desire for deconstruction, going so far as to lift the apparent contradiction that might exist between deconstruction and invention.

Deconstruction is inventive or it is nothing at all; it does not settle for methodical procedures, it opens up a passageway, it marches ahead and marks a trail; its writing is not only performative, it produces rules—other conventions—for new performativities and never installs itself in the theoretical assurance of a simple opposition between performative and constative. Its *process* involves an affirmation, this latter being linked to the coming—the *venire*—in event, advent, invention. But it can only make it by deconstructing a conceptual and institutional structure of invention that would neutralize by putting the stamp of reason on some aspect of invention, of inventive power: as if it were necessary, over and beyond a certain traditional status of invention, to reinvent the future.

Coming, Inventing, Finding, Finding Oneself

A strange proposition. We have said that every invention tends to unsettle the status that one would like to assign it at the moment when it takes place. We are saying now that deconstruction must assume the task of calling into question the traditional status of invention itself. What does this mean?

What is an invention? What does it do? It *finds* something for the first time. And the ambiguity lies in the word "find." To find is to invent when the experience of finding takes place for the first time. An event without precedent whose novelty may be either that of the (invented) thing found (for example, a technical apparatus that did not exist before: printing, a vaccine, nuclear weapons, a musical form, an institution—good or bad—and so on), or else the act and not the object of "finding" or "discovering" (for example, in a now dated sense, the invention of the Cross[12] or the invention of the body of Saint Mark of Tintoretto). But in both cases, from both points of view (object or act), invention does not create an existence or a world as a set of existents, it does not have the theological meaning of a veritable creation of existence *ex nihilo*. It discovers for the first time, it unveils what was already *found* there, or produces what, as *tekhnè*, was not already found there but is still not created, in the strong sense of the word, is only put together, starting with a stock of existing and available elements, in a given configuration. This configuration, this ordered totality that makes an invention and its legitimation possible, raises all the problems you know about, whether we refer to cultural totality, *Weltanschauung*, epoch, *epistémè*, paradigm, or what have you. However important and difficult these problems may be, they all call for an elucidation of what inventing means and implies. In any event, Ponge's *Fable* creates nothing, in the theological sense of the word (at least this is apparently the case); it invents only by taking recourse to a lexicon and to syntactic rules, to a prevailing code, to conventions to which in a certain fashion it subjects itself. But it gives rise to an event, tells a fictional story and produces a machine by introducing a disparity or gap into the customary use of discourse, by upsetting to some extent the mind-set of expectation and reception that it nevertheless needs; it forms a beginning and speaks of that beginning, and in this double, indivisible movement, it inaugurates. This double movement harbors that uniqueness and novelty without which there would be no invention.

In every case and through all the semantic displacements of the word "invention," this latter remains the "coming," the *venire*, the event of a novelty that must surprise, because at the moment when it comes about, there could be no statute, no status, ready and waiting to reduce it to the same.

But this coming about (*survenue*) of the new must be due to an operation of the human subject. Invention always belongs to man as the inventing subject. This is a defining feature of very great stability, a semantic quasi-invariant that we must take rigorously into account. For whatever may be the history or the polysemy of the concept of invention as it is inscribed in the workings (*mouvance*) of Latin culture, even if not in the Latin language itself, never, it seems to me, has anyone assumed the authority to speak of invention without implying in the term the technical initiative of the being called man.[13] Man himself, and the human world, is defined by the human subject's aptitude for invention, in the double sense of narrative fiction or historical fabulation and of technical or technoepistemic innovation (just as I am linking *tekhnè* and *fabula*, I am recalling here the link between *historia* and *epistémè*). No one has ever *authorized* himself—it is indeed a question of status and convention—to say of God that he invents, even if, as people have thought, divine creation provides the ground and support for human invention; and no one has ever authorized himself to say of animals that they invent, even if, as it is sometimes said, their production and manipulation of instruments resemble human invention. On the other hand, men can invent gods, animals, and especially divine animals.

This technoepistemic-anthropocentric dimension inscribes the value of invention in the set of structures that binds differentially the technical order and metaphysical humanism. (By value of invention I mean its dominant sense, governed by conventions.) If today it is necessary to reinvent invention, it will have to be done through questions and deconstructive performances bearing upon this traditional and dominant value of invention, upon its very status, and upon the enigmatic history that links, within a system of conventions, a metaphysics to technoscience and to humanism.

Let us turn away from these general propositions and take up again the question of invention's legal or institutional status. If an invention seems to have to surprise or unsettle statutory conditions, it must in turn imply or produce other statutory conditions; these are necessary not only for it to be recognized, identified, legitimized, institutionalized as invention (to be patented, we might say), but for invention even to occur, or, let us say, for it to *come about* [*survenir*]. And here we have the context of the great debate, which is not limited to the historians of science or of ideas in general, over the conditions of emergence and legitimation of inventions. How can we sort out and name the cultural groupings that make a given invention possible and admissible once the invention in question has in its turn modified the structure of the context itself? Here again I have to make do with mentioning many discussions pursued in recent decades concerning such concepts as paradigm, episteme, epistemological break, and themata. Ponge's *Fable*, however inventive it may be, and in order to be so, is like any fable in that it calls for linguistic rules, social modes of reading, and reception, stabilized competences, a historical configuration of the poetic domain and of literary tradition, and so forth.

What is a statute? Like "invention," the word "statute," and this is not insignificant, is first defined in the Latin code of law and thus also that of juridicopolitical rhetoric. Before belonging to this code, it designates the stance or standing (cf.

status in English) of that which, holding itself upright in a stable way, stays erect and causes or attains stability. In this sense it is essentially *institutional*. It defines while prescribing; depending on the concept and language, it determines what is stabilizable in institutional form, within a system and an order that are those of a human society, culture, and law, even if this humanity conceives of itself on the basis of something other than itself—God, for example. A statute (or concomitantly, a status) is always human; as such, it cannot be animal or theological. Like invention, as we said a while ago. So the paradox gets sharper: every invention should make fun of the statutory, but without a prevailing statutory context there would be no invention. In any case neither the inventive nor the statutory belongs to nature, in the usual sense of the term, that is, in the sense statutorily established by the dominant tradition of metaphysics.

What are we asking when we raise questions about the status of invention? We are first asking what is an invention, and what concept is appropriate to its essence. More precisely, we are asking about the essence we agree *to recognize for it*: what concept is guaranteed, what concept is held to be legitimate for invention? This moment of recognition is essential to the move from essence to status. The status is the essence considered as stable, established, and legitimated by a social or symbolic order in an institutionalizable code, discourse, or text. The moment proper to status is social and discursive; it supposes that a group arrives, by what is at least an implicit contract, at the following agreement: (1) given that invention *in general* is this or that, can be recognized by given criteria, and is accorded a given status, then (2) this singular event is indeed an invention, a given individual or group deserves the status of inventor, will have achieved invention. That can take the form of a Pulitzer or a Nobel prize.

Patents: Invention of the Title

Status is thus understood at two levels, the one concerning invention in general, the other concerning some particular invention whose status or value is determined in relation to the general status. The juridicopolitical dimension is essential; thus the most useful index here would perhaps be what we call the patent of an invention, or the *brevet* in French. A brevet was first of all a brief text, a "brief," a written act by which royal or public authority accorded a reward or a title, indeed a diploma; it is significant that today we still speak in French of an engineer's or technician's brevet to designate an established competency. The brevet is then the act whereby political authorities confer a public title, that is, a status. The patent of an invention creates a status or an author's right, a title—and that is why our problematics should reckon with the very rich and complex problematics of the positive law of written works, both its origins and its current history, which is visibly affected by all sorts of disturbances, especially those resulting from new techniques of reproduction and telecommunication. The inventor's patent, *strictu sensu*, sanctions only technical inventions that give rise to reproducible instruments, but we can extend it to any author's right. The meaning of the expression "status of invention" is presupposed in the idea of "patent" but cannot be reduced to it.

Why have I insisted on the matter of patents? Because it may be the best index of our present-day situation. If the word "invention" is going through a rebirth, on a ground of anguished exhaustion but also out of a desire to reinvent invention itself, including its very status, this is perhaps because, on a scale incommensurable with that of the past, what is called a patentable "invention" is now *programmed*, that is, subjected to powerful movements of authoritarian prescription and anticipation of the widest variety. And that is as true in the domains of art or the fine arts as in the technoscientific domain. Everywhere the enterprise of knowledge and research is first of all a programmatics of inventions. We could evoke the politics of publishing, the orders of booksellers or art merchants, studies of the market, cultural policies, whether state promoted or not, and the politics of research and, as one now says, the "orientations" that this politics imposes throughout our institutions of higher education; we could also evoke all the institutions, private or public, capitalist or not, that declare themselves to be organs for producing and orienting invention. But let us consider again, as a symptom, just the politics of patents. Today we have comparative statistics on the subject of inventions patented each year by all the countries of the world. The competition that rages, for obvious politicoeconomic reasons, determines the decisions taken at the governmental level. At the moment when France, for example, believes it must progress in this race for patents on inventions, the government decides to beef up a given budgetary position and to pour public funds, through a given ministry, into an effort to orient, stimulate, or regulate patented inventions. We know that such programming efforts, following trajectories that may be more subtle or more heavily overdetermined, can infuse the dynamics of inventions that are said to be the "freest," the most primitively "poetic" and inaugural. This programming, the general design of which, if there were one, would not necessarily be that of conscious representations, claims—and it sometimes succeeds up to a point—to extend its determinations all the way to the margin of chance—a chance it has to reckon with and that it integrates into its probabilistic calculations. A few centuries ago, invention was represented as an erratic occurrence, the effect of an individual stroke of genius or of unpredictable luck. That was often so because of a misunderstanding, unequally shared, of the real constraints on invention. Today, perhaps because we are too familiar with at least the existence, if not the operation, of machines for programming invention, we dream of reinventing invention on the far side of the programmed matrices. For is a programmed invention still an invention? Is it an event through which the future (*l'avenir*) comes to us?

Let's now recall briefly the ground we have covered so far. The status of invention in general, like that of a particular invention, presupposes the public recognition of an origin, more precisely of an originality. The latter has to be assignable to a *human subject*, individual or collective, who is responsible for the *discovery* or the *production* of something new that is henceforth *available* to everyone. Discovery or production? This is a first hesitation, at least if we refrain from reducing the *producere* to the sense of bringing to light by the action of putting forward or advancing, which would amount to unveiling or discovering. In any case, discovery or production, but not creation. To invent is to reach the point of finding, discovering, unveiling, producing *for the first time* a thing, which can be an artifact but which in any case could already be there existing in a virtual or invisible state. The first time of invention never creates an existence, and underlying the present-day desire to reinvent invention there is doubtless a certain reserve with respect to a creationist theology. This reserve is not necessarily atheistic; it can on the contrary insist precisely on reserving creation to God and invention to human beings. So it could no longer be said that God invented the world as the totality of existences. It can be said that God invented the laws, the procedures or the calculations for the creation ("dum calculat fit mundus"), but not that he invented the world. Likewise, today one would no longer say that Christopher Columbus invented America, except in a sense that has become archaic, as in the expression "the invention of the Cross," which amounts simply to the discovery of an existence that was already there. But the use or the system of modern conventions — relatively modern ones — would prohibit us from speaking of invention that would have as its object an existence as such. If we spoke today of the invention of America or of the New World, that would rather designate the discovery or production of new *modes* of existence, of new ways of seeing things, of imagining or inhabiting the world, but not the creation or discovery of the very existence of the territory named America.[14]

You can see then some segments of a dividing line or shift in the semantic development or regulated use of the word "invention." In describing it I shall not make the distinction hard and fast, and I shall respect its position within the great and fundamental reference to the human *tekhnè*, to this mythopoetic power that associates the fable with historical and epistemic narrative. What is this dividing line? To invent has always signified "come to find for the first time," but until the dawn of what we might call technoscientific and philosophical "modernity" (as a very rough and inadequate empirical marker, let us say in the seventeenth century), it was still possible to speak of invention in regard to existences or truths that, without of course being created by invention, were discovered or unveiled by it for the first time — were found to be there. Example: the invention of the body of Saint Mark, again, but also the invention of truths, of true things. Such is Cicero's definition in *De inventione* (1, VII). As the first part of oratorical art, invention is "excogitatio rerum verarum, aut verisimilium, quae causam probabilem reddant." The cause in question here is the juridical cause, debate, or controversy between specified persons. It belongs to the status of invention that it *also always* concerns juridical questions about statutes.

Subsequently, in the light of a displacement already under way that, it seems to me, is stabilized in the seventeenth century, perhaps between Descartes and Leibniz, invention is almost never regarded as an unveiling discovery of what was already there (an existence or truth), but is more and more, if not solely the productive discovery of an apparatus that we can call technical in the broad sense, technoscientific or technopoetic. It is not simply that invention gets technologized. It was always tied to the intervention of a *tekhnè*, but in this *tekhnè* it is henceforth the production—and not only the unveiling—of a relatively independent mechanical apparatus, which itself is capable of a certain self-reproductive recurrence and even of a certain reiterative simulation, that will dominate the use of the word "invention."

The Invention of Truth

Against this background, we can envisage the work of deconstructing the rules of this use and thus of deconstructing the concept of invention, if this deconstruction also wishes to be a reinvention of invention: it would be grounded in a prudent analysis of the double determination at the core of the hypothesis I have been elaborating here. This double definition or double inscription, broad and narrow in its purview, also offers a sort of scansion that I hesitate to qualify as "historical" and especially, for obvious reasons, hesitate to date. The hypothesis I am advancing cannot fail to have ramifications for the concept and practice of history itself.

The "first" dividing line would cut across the *truth*: the relation to truth and the use of the word "truth." This is the place of decision, where the full weight of the ambivalence is gathered.

Thanks to certain contextual constraints, it is easy enough to master a certain polysemy of the word "invention." For example, in French the word designates at least three things, according to the context and syntax of the proposition in which it is used. But each of these three senses can in turn be affected, indeed split, by an ambivalence that is harder to break down because it is essential.

So what are these first three meanings that shift fairly innocuously from one place to another? In the first place we can call "invention" the capacity to invent, the supposedly natural genius for inventing, inventiveness. One can say of a scientist or a novelist that he "has invention" in him. Next we can call "invention" the moment, act or experience, the "first time" of the new event, the novelty of this newness (I note in passing that this newness is not necessarily the other). Then, in the third place, we can take "invention" as referring to the content of this novelty, the invented thing. I now recapitulate these references that the word "invention" can convey with an example: (1) Leibniz is a man of invention, was born with invention; (2) his invention of the *characteristica universalis* took place at a certain time and had certain effects; (3) the *characteristica universalis* was his invention, the content and not just the act of that invention.

If these three meanings are easily discerned from context to context, the general semantic structure of "invention," even before this triple capacity is considered, is much harder to elucidate. Prior to the division I have just mentioned, two competing meanings seem to have coexisted: (1) "first time," the event of a *discovery*, the invention of what was already there and came into view as an existence or as meaning and truth; (2) the productive invention of a technical apparatus that was not already there as such. In this case the inventor gave it a *place* upon *finding it*, whereas in the former case its place was found there where it was already *located*. And the relation of invention to the question of place—in all senses of the word—is obviously essential. Now if, in accord with my hypothesis, the first meaning of invention, which we might term "veritative," has tended to disappear since the seventeenth century to the benefit of the second one, we must still find the place where this division begins to function, a place that is not empirical or historicochronological. How does it happen that we no longer speak of the invention of the Cross or the invention of truth (in a certain sense of the truth) while we speak more and more, if not exclusively, of the invention of printing, of steam-powered shipping, of a logico-mathematical apparatus, that is, of another form of relation to truth? You see that, despite this shift in orientation, it is still in both cases the truth that is at issue. A fold or a juncture separates while joining these two senses of the meaning, which are also two forces or two tendencies, relating to each other, the one settling over the other, in their very difference. We may have in these texts a momentary bridging, a furtive and unsure instance of "invention" still meaning the invention of truth in the sense of a discovery unveiling what is already there, while also meaning already the invention of another type of truth and another sense of the word "truth": that of a judicial proposition, thus of a logico-linguistic mechanism. Then the concern is with production, that of the most appropriate *tekhnè*, with the construction of a machinery that was not previously there, even if this new mechanism of truth must in principle still be modeled on the first type. The two meanings remain very close, to the point of being confused in the relatively common expression "invention of the truth." Yet I believe they are heterogeneous. It seems to me that they have never stopped accentuating what separates them, and that the tendency of the second one, since its appearance, has been to assert its undivided supremacy. It is true that it has always shadowed and thus magnetized the first meaning. The whole question of the difference between the premodern *tekhnè* and the modern *tekhnè* lies at the heart of what I have just referred to hastily as a shadowing or magnetization. I do not have time to open up this immense topic here.

In the examples I am going to recall, it may seem that the first meaning alone (unveiling discovery and not productive discovery) is still operative. But it is never so simple. Initially I shall consider a passage from the *Logic or Art of Think-*

ing of Port Royal. This text, written in French, played a major role in the spread of Cartesian thought. I have selected it because it refers extensively to a whole tradition that interests us here, notably that of Cicero's *De inventione*. In the chapter entitled "Of Places, or of the Method of Finding Arguments" (111, XVII), we read the following:

> What the Rhetoricians and Logicians call Places, *loci argumentorum*, are certain general headings, to which all the proofs one uses in the various subjects treated can be related: and the part of Logic that they call invention, is nothing other than what they teach about these Places. Ramus quarrels with Aristotle and the academic philosophers about this, because they deal with the Places after having given the rules for argument, and in opposition to them he claims that it is necessary to explain the Places and matters relating to invention before dealing with these rules. Ramus's reason is that one should have found the subject matter before thinking about how to arrange it. The explanation of Places teaches how to find this subject matter, whereas the rules for argument can only teach about its disposition. But this reasoning is very weak, for while it may be necessary for the subject matter to be found for it to be arranged, it is nonetheless not necessary to learn to find the subject matter before learning to arrange it.

Here we encounter a debate about whether disposition ought to precede the moment of *finding the subject matter* (or that of finding the truth of the thing, the idea, the content, etc.). If we had time to examine it closely, we would see better how the question of disposition or *collocatio* is nothing other than that of the two truths to be invented: the truth of unveiling, and the truth as a propositional mechanism.

But the question is always one of *finding*, a word of a powerful and enigmatic obscurity, especially in the constellation of its relations to places, to the place where one finds something, to the place one finds, to the place found (located) somewhere or in which something is located. What does the verb *trouver* — to find — mean? However interesting the etymology of the word may be, the answer is not to be found in it. For the time being let us leave this question, which also has to do with the particularity of a given tongue, in abeyance.[15]

The *ars inveniendi* or *ordo inveniendi* concerns the *searching* as well as the *finding* in the analytic discovery of a truth that is already there. In order not to find the truth already there through a chance encounter or a lucky find, one needs a research program, a method — an analytic method that is called the method of invention. It follows the *ordo inveniendi* or analytical order (as opposed to the *ordo exponandi*). The *Logic* of Port Royal puts it as follows: "There are two sorts of method: one is for discovering the truth, called *analysis*, or *method of resolution*, that can also be called the *method of invention*; and the other, which is for conveying truth to others when it has been found, is called *synthesis*, or *method of composition*, and can also be called *method of doctrine*" (IV, 11). Now, transposing the distinctions of this discourse on invention, let us ask what we can say of a fable like that of Francis Ponge? Does its first line discover, does it invent something? Or does it expose, does it teach what it has just invented? Is its mode resolution or composition? Invention or doctrine?

In the *Logic* of Port Royal, as in Descartes or Leibniz, we observe a common approach to the truth: even if it must be based upon a truth "that has to be found in the thing itself independently of our desires" (111, XX, a, 1–2), the truth that we must *find* there where it *is found*, the truth to be invented, is first of all the nature of our *relation* to the thing itself and not the nature of the thing itself. And this relation has to be stabilized in a proposition. It is usually to the proposition that the name "truth" is given, especially when it is a matter of truths in the plural. The truths are true propositions (11, IX; 111, X; 111, xx, b, 1; IV, IX; V, XIII), mechanisms of predication. When Leibniz speaks of the "inventors of truth," we must recall, as does Heidegger in *Der Satz vom Grund*, that he means producers of propositions and not just sources of revelation. The truth qualifies the connection of subject and predicate. A person has never invented something, that is, a thing. In short, no one has ever invented anything. Nor has anyone invented an essence of things in this new universe of discourse, but only truth as a proposition. And this logico-discursive mechanism can be named *tekhnè* in the broad sense. Why? For there to be invention, the condition of a certain generality must be met, and the production of a certain objective ideality (or ideal objectivity) must occasion recurrent operations, thus a utilizable apparatus. If the act of invention can take place only once, the invented artifact must be essentially repeatable, transmissible, and transposable. The two extreme types of invented things, the mechanical apparatus on the one hand, the fictional or poetic narrative on the other, imply both a first time and every time, the inaugural event and iterability. Once invented, so to speak, invention is invented only if repetition, generality, common availability, and thus publicity are introduced or promised in the structure of the first time. Hence the problem of institutional status. If we could first think that invention put all status back into question, we also see that there could be no invention without status. To invent is to produce iterability and the machine for reproduction and simulation, in an indefinite number of copies, utilizable outside the place of invention, available to multiple subjects in various contexts. These mechanisms can be simple or complex instruments, but just as well can be discursive procedures, methods, rhetorical forms, poetic genres, artistic styles, and so forth. And in all cases there are "stories": a certain sequentiality must be able to take a narrative form, be subject to repetition, citation, re-citation. We must be able to recount and to render an account in accord with the principle of reason. This iterability is marked, and thus remarked, in the origin of the inventive foundation, it constitutes it, it lines it with a pocket in the first instant, a sort of retroverted anticipation: *par le mot par*, by the word by . . . "

The structure of language – or as I prefer to say here for crucial reasons, the structure of the mark or of the trace – is not at all foreign or inessential to all this. It is not fortuitous that the articulation joining the two meanings of the word "invention" in the expression "invention of truth" is more readily perceptible than anywhere else in Descartes or Leibniz when each of them speaks of the invention of a language[16] or a universal characteristics (a system of marks independent of any natural language). Both justify this invention by grounding the technological or technosemiotic aspect in the "veritative" or truthful aspect, in truths that are discovered truths *and* predicative connections in true propositions. But this common recourse to the philosophical truth of technical invention does not work in Descartes and in Leibniz in the same way. This difference should be important to us here. Both speak of the invention of a language or a universal characteristic. Both think about a new machinery that remains to be *forged* even if the logic of this artifact has to be based and indeed to be *found* in that of an analytic invention. Descartes twice uses the word "invention" in his famous letter to Mersenne of November 20, 1629, in regard to his project of a universal language and writing:

> The *invention* of this language depends on the true philosophy; for it is otherwise impossible to enumerate all the thoughts of men, and to record them in order, or even to distinguish them so that they are clear and simple, which in my opinion is the great *secret* one must have in order to *acquire the good knowledge.* . . . Now I hold that this language is possible, and that one can *find* the knowledge on which it depends, by means of which peasants could better *judge the truth* of things than philosophers do now. (my emphasis)

The invention of the language depends on the knowledge of truths; but it is still necessary to find this knowledge or science through which everyone, including peasants, would be able to judge the truth of things, thanks to the invention of the language it would make possible. The invention of the language presupposes and produces the new science, it intervenes between two states of knowledge as a methodic or technoscientific procedure. On this point Leibniz does follow Descartes, but he recognizes that the invention of this language depends on "the true philosophy"; "it does not depend," he adds, "on its perfection." This language can be "established, although the philosophy is not perfected: and as the knowledge of men will grow, this language will grow as well. In the interim it will be a marvelous aid for the utilization of what we know, and for the perception of what is missing in our knowledge, and for the invention of the means to find it, but most of all for the extermination of controversy in those areas where knowledge depends on reasoning. For then to reason and to calculate will be the same thing."[17]

The artificial language is not only located at the arrival point of an invention from which it would proceed, it also proceeds to foster invention, its invention serves to invent. The new language is itself an *ars inveniendi* or the idiomatic code of this art, the space of its signature. In the manner of an artificial intelligence, owing to the independence of a certain automatism, it will anticipate the development and precede the completion of philosophical knowledge. The invention comes all at once and comes in advance (*survient et previent*); it exceeds existing knowledge or science, at least in its present state and status. This difference in rhythm confers on the time of invention a capacity of productive facilitation, even if the inaugural adventure has to be kept under an ultimately teleological surveillance by a fundamental analytic bias.

The Signature: Art of Inventing, Art of Forwarding

Inventors, says Leibniz, "proceed to the truth;" they invent the way, the method, the technique, the propositional apparatus; in other words, they *posit* and they institute. They are persons of status as much as they are persons of action when the path they open becomes a method. And that never occurs without the possibility of reiterated application, thus without a certain generality. In this sense the inventor always invents a general truth, that is, the connection of a subject to a predicate. In the *New Essays Concerning Human Understanding*, Theophilus stresses this point: "If the inventor finds only a particular truth, he is but a half-inventor. If Pythagoras had only observed that a property of the triangle with sides of 3, 4, and 5 is to have the square of its hypotenuse equal to the sum of the squares of its sides (i.e., that $9 + 16 = 25$), would he then have been the inventor of this great truth that includes all right triangles and that has become a theorem in geometry?" (IV, 7).

Universality is also the ideal objectivity, thus unlimited recurrence. This recurrence lodged in the unique occurrence of invention is what blurs, as it were, the signature of inventors. The name of an individual or of a unique empirical entity cannot be associated with it except in an inessential, extrinsic, accidental way. We should even say aleatory. This gives rise to the enormous problem of property rights over inventions, a problem that, in its legislative form, dates from a relatively recent moment in the history of the West and then of the entire world. We have recently celebrated a centennial. It was in 1883 that the Convention of Paris, the first great international convention legislating rights of industrial property, was signed. It was countersigned by the Soviet Union only in 1964 and since World War II has been evolving rapidly. Its complexity, the intricacy of its casuistry as well as of its philosophical presuppositions, make it a redoubtable and intriguing object of inquiry. It is unfortunately impossible to attempt here a painstaking analysis of its juridical mechanisms, which are themselves inventions, conventions instituted by performative acts. At this point in our discussion of invention, I will focus mainly on two essential distinctions that belong to the axioms underlying this legislation: (1) the distinction between the author's right and the patent, (2) the distinction between the scientific idea (that is, the theoretical discovery of a truth) and the idea of its industrial exploitation. Only in the case of an exploitation of the industrial type can one lay claim to a patent. And that condition presupposes that literary or artistic invention, when an origin or an author can be assigned to it, does not occasion an industrial exploitation, it also supposes that we should be able to discern in theoretical discoveries the technoindustrial mechanisms that can be derived from them. These distinctions are not just hard to put into practice (hence they spawn a very refined casuistry); their authority is grounded in "philosophemes" that have in general received little criticism, but above all they belong to a new interpretation of technique as industrial technique. And it is the advent of this new regime of invention, the one that opens technoscientific or technoindustrial "modernity," that we shall try to locate here by reading Descartes and Leibniz.

I spoke a moment ago of an aleatory signature. The term "aleatory" was certainly not used by chance. The modern politics of invention tends to integrate the aleatory into its programmatic calculations. This is equally true for the politics of scientific research and for the politics of culture. Moreover, an attempt is made to weld the two together and to associate both with an industrial politics of "patents." This attempt would allow them both to support the economy (as a notion like "overcoming the crisis by means of culture" or by means of the culture industry suggests) and to be supported by it. Appearances notwithstanding, that present-day trend does not run counter to the Leibnizian project: the aim is to take the aleatory into account, to master it by integrating it as a calculable margin. Although conceding that chance can, by chance, serve the invention of a general idea, Leibniz does not see it as the best approach:

> It is true that often an example, envisaged by chance, serves as the *occasion* that prompts an *ingenious* [I underscore this word at the borderline of natural genius and technical cunning] man to *search* for general truth, but it is very often quite another matter to *find* it; aside from the fact that this path of invention is not the best or the most used by those who proceed by order and method, and that they make use of it only on those *occasions* where better methods come up short. While some have believed that Archimedes found the quadrature of the parabola by weighing a piece of wood hewn into parabolic shape, and that this particular experiment led him to find the general truth, those who know the penetration of this great man see well enough that he had no need of such an *aid*. However, even if this empirical path of particular truths had been the *occasion* of all discoveries, it would not have been sufficient to give rise to them. . . . Moreover, I admit that there is often a difference between the method we use to *teach* bodies of knowledge and the one by which they were *found*. . . . Sometimes . . . *chance has occasioned* inventions. If all these occasions had been noted

and their memory preserved for posterity (which would have been very useful), this detail would have been a very considerable part of the *history of the arts*, but it would not have been adequate for producing their *systems*. Sometimes the inventors have proceeded rationally to the truth, but along circuitous paths.[17]

(Here I would like insert a parenthetical note. If a deconstructive activity were to arise from this account of invention, if what it invented were to belong to the order of "general truths" and systematic knowledge, one should continue to apply to it this system of distinctions, notably those between chance and method, and between the method of invention and the method of pedagogical exposition. But it is exactly this logic of invention that calls for deconstructive questioning. Precisely to this extent deconstructive questions and invention are no longer subject to this logic or to its axiomatics. "*Par le mot par . . .* " teaches, describes, and performs all at once exactly what it seems to record.)

Let us now move on with our retracing of Leibniz's thought. If hazard, chance, or occasion has no essential relation to the system of invention, only to its history as the "history of art," the chance occurrence fosters invention only insofar as necessity is revealed in it, is found there. The role of the inventor (genial or ingenius) is precisely to have that chance—and in order to do so, not to fall upon the truth by chance, but, as it were, to know chance, to know how to be lucky, to recognize the chance for chance, to anticipate a chance, decipher it, grasp it, inscribe it on the chart of the necessary and turn a throw of the dice into work. This transfiguration, which both preserves and nullifies chance as such, goes so far as to affect the very status of the aleatory event.

Such is what all governmental policies on modern science and culture and war attempt when they try—and how could they do otherwise?—to program invention. The aleatory margin that they seek to integrate remains homogeneous with calculation, within the order of the calculable; it devolves from a probabilistic quantification and still resides, we could say, in the same order and in the order of the same. An order where there is no absolute surprise, the order of what I shall call the invention of the same. This invention comprises *all* invention, or almost. And I will not oppose it to invention of the other (indeed I shall oppose nothing to it), for the opposition, dialectical or not, still belongs to this regimen of the same. The invention of the other is not opposed to that of the same, its difference beckons toward another coming about, toward this other invention of which we dream, the invention of the entirely other, the one that allows the coming of a still unanticipatable alterity and for which no horizon of waiting as yet seems ready, in place, available. Yet it is necessary to prepare for it; for to allow the coming of the entirely other, passivity, a certain kind of resigned passivity for which everything comes down to the same, is not suitable. Letting the other come is not inertia open to anything whatever. No doubt the coming of the other, if it has to remain incalculable and in a certain way aleatory (one happens onto the other in the encounter), escapes from all programming. But this aleatory aspect of the other has to be heterogeneous in relation to the integrable aleatory factor of a calculus, and likewise to the form of undecidable that theories of formal systems have to cope with. This invention of the entirely other is beyond any possible status; I still call it invention because one gets ready for it, one makes this step destined to let the other come, *come in*. The invention of the other, the incoming *of* the other, certainly does not take the form of a subjective genitive, and just as assuredly not of an objective genitive either, even if the invention comes from the other — for this other is thenceforth neither subject nor object, neither a self nor a consciousness nor an unconscious. To get ready for this coming of the other is what I call the deconstruction that deconstructs this double genitive and that, as deconstructive invention, comes back in the step — and also as the step — of the other. To invent would then be to "know" how to say "come" and to answer the "come" of the other. Does that ever come about? Of this event one is never sure.

But I am getting ahead of myself.

Let's return to the *New Essays Concerning Human Understanding*. Between the integration of the aleatory under the authority of the principle of reason and the modern politics of invention, there is a deep continuum of homogeneity, whether we are considering civil or military technoscientific research (and how can the civil and military be distinguished any longer?), or programming, private or governmental, of the sciences and arts (and all these distinctions are disappearing today). This homogeneity is homogeneity itself, the law of the same, the assimilatory power that neutralizes novelty as much as chance. This power is at work even before the integration of the aleatory other, of the other chance event, actually occurs; it suffices that it be possible, projected, potentially significant. It suffices that it acquire meaning on the ground of an *economic* horizon (the domestic law of the *oikos* and the reign of productivity or profitability). The political economy of modern invention, the one that dominates or regulates its present status, belongs to the recent tradition of what Leibniz called in his time "a new species of logic":

> We would need a *new species* of *logic*, which would deal with the degrees of probability, since Aristotle in his *Topics* did no such thing as that, and satisfied himself with putting in some order certain popular rules, distributed according to the commonplaces, that may be of use on some occasion in which it is a matter of amplifying the discourse and giving it credibility, without taking pains to give us a necessary scale for weighing the probabilities and for forming a solid judgment. He who would wish to treat this question would be well advised to pursue the examination of *games of chance*; and in general I would wish that a clever mathematician would produce a substantial work, well detailed and well reasoned, on all sorts of games, as that would be very useful

for perfecting the art of invention, the human mind coming better into view in games than in more serious matters. (IV, 16; "Of the Degrees of Assent," English trans., 541)

These games are mirror games: the human mind "appears" there better than elsewhere, such is Leibniz's argument. The game here occupies the place of a psyche that would send back to man's inventiveness the best image of his truth. As through a fable in images, the game states or reveals a truth. That does not contradict the principle of programmatic rationality or of the *ars inveniendi* as the enactment of the principle of reason, but illustrates its "new species of logic," the one that integrates the calculation of probabilities.

One of the paradoxes of this new *ars inveniendi* is that it both liberates the imagination and liberates *from* it. It passes beyond the imagination and passes through it. Such is the case of the *characteristica universalis*, which is not just one example among others. It

saves the mind and the imagination, the use of which must above all be controlled. That is the principal aim of this great science that I have come to call *Characteristics*, in which what we call algebra or analysis is only a very small branch, since it is this science that gives words to the languages, numbers to arithmetic, notes to music, and that teaches us the secret of determining rational argument, and compelling it to leave something like a modest amount of visible traces on paper to be examined at leisure; and it is finally this science that causes us to reason at little cost, by putting written characters in place of things, so as to disencumber the imagination. (*Opuscules et fragments inédits*, ed. Couturat, 98–99)

The Invention of God: Politics of Research, Politics of Culture

There we have an economy of the imagination whose history we should trace. The status of the imagination shifts, we know, in and after Kant, and that cannot fail to affect the status of invention. Here I refer to what we can call, albeit hastily and superficially, a rehabilitation of the transcendental imagination or the productive imagination from Kant[19] to Schelling and Hegel. Can one say that this productive imagination (*Einbildungskraft*, like *produktive Vermögen*, that Schelling and Hegel distinguish from the reproductive *Imagination*) liberates philosophical inventiveness and the status of the invention from their subjection to an order of theological truth or to an order of infinite reason, that is, to what is *always found there already*? Can one say that it interrupts the invention of the same in accord with the same, and that it exposes the status of invention to the interruption of the other? I think not. An attentive reading would show that the argument that passes by way of the finite, as it is implied by this rehabilitation of the imagination, remains a *passage*, a required passage, to be sure, but a passage. Nonetheless we cannot say that nothing happens there and that the event of the other is absent from it. For example, when in 1803 Schelling called for a philosophical poetics, for an "artistic drive in the philosopher," for productive imagination as a vital necessity for philosophy; when, turning the Kantian heritage against Kant, he declared that the philosopher must invent forms and that "every so-called new philosophy must have taken a new step forward in the formal sphere" (*einen neuen Schritt in der Form*), or that a philosopher "can be original"[20] — that was something very new in the history of philosophy. It was an event and a sort of invention, a reinvention of invention. No one had said before that a philosopher could and should, as a philosopher, display originality by creating new forms. It was original to say that the philosopher must be original, that he is an artist and must innovate in the use of form, in a language and a writing that are henceforth inseparable from the truth as it shows itself. No one had said that philosophical invention was an *ars inveniendi* poetically and organically supported by the life of a natural language. Descartes himself had not said it at the moment when he was recommending the return to the French tongue as a philosophical language.

If I had had the time to develop this analysis here, I would have tried both to state more sharply the originality of Schelling's point and to point out as well what nevertheless keeps him within the paradoxical limits of an invention of the same in the guise of a *supplement of invention*. For invention is always supplementary for Schelling; it adds on, and thus inaugurates, it is an addition that serves to complete a whole, to fill in where there is a gap and thus to carry out a program. A program that is still theological, still the program of an "original knowledge" (*Ur-wissen*) that is also an "absolute knowledge," a total "organism" that must articulate but also represent and *reflect* itself in all the regions of the world or of the encyclopedia. And even in the state, the modern state, despite the apparently liberal conception of the philosophical institutions in the texts of Schelling. One could bring out, in the *Vorlesungen* to which I have just been referring, this logic of the picture (*Bild*) and of specular reflection[21] between the real and the ideal. Total knowledge has the unity of an absolute manifestation (*absolute Er-scheinung*, invention as unveiling or discovery) — a showing that is finite in reality but ideally infinite, necessary in its reality, free in its ideality. The invention of the other, which is both the limit and the chance of a finite being, thus gets caught up in an infinite amortization. And here we meet up again with the law of ration-alistic humanism[22] that has from the start held us inside the spectacularly *sup-plementary* logic of an anthropo-theocentrism:

> Man, the rational being in general, is destined by his position [*hinein-gestellt*] to be a complement [*Ergänzung*] of the manifestation of the world: it is out of man, from his activity, that what is missing in the to-tality of God's revelation [*zur Totalität der Offenbarung Gottes fehlt*] must develop since nature is of course the bearer of divine essence in

its entirety, but only in reality; the rational being must then express the image [*Bild*] of this same divine nature, as it is in itself and consequently in the ideal. (ibid., 49–50)

Invention manifests, it is the revelation of God, but it completes that revelation as it carries it out, it reflects revelation as it supplements it. Man is the *psyche* of God, but this mirror captures the whole only by supplying for a lack. A *psyche* is this total mirror that cannot be reduced to what is called a "soul supplement" (*un supplément d'âme*); it is the soul as a supplement, the mirror of human invention as the desire of God, in the place where something is missing from God's truth, from his revelation: "*zur Totalität der Offenbarung Gottes fehlt.*" By allowing the new to emerge, by inventing the other, the psyche reflects the same, it offers itself as a mirror for God. It also carries out, in this speculation, a program.

This logic of the *supplement of invention* could be verified, after Schelling, in every philosophy of invention, indeed in every account of philosophical invention, in all the political economies, all the programmings of invention, in the implicit or explicit jurisdiction that evaluates and legislates today each time we speak of invention. How is it possible? Is it possible?

Invention amounts to the same, and it is always possible, as soon as it can receive a status and thereby be legitimized by an institution that it then becomes in its turn. For always the objects we invent in this way are institutions. The institutions are inventions and the inventions to which a status is conferred are in turn institutions. How can an invention *come back* to being the same, how can the *invenire*, the advent of time-to-come, come to come back, to fold back toward the past a movement always said to be innovative? For that to happen it suffices that invention be possible and that it invent what is possible. Then, right from its origin ("par le mot par commence donc ce texte"), it envelops in itself a repetition, it unfolds only the dynamics of what was already *found there*, a set of comprehensible possibilities that come into view as ontological or theological truth, a program of cultural or technoscientific politics (civil or military), and so forth. By inventing the possible on the basis of the possible, we relate the new—that is, something quite other that can also be quite ancient—to a set of present possibilities, to the present time and state of the order of possibility that provides for the new the conditions of its status. This statutory economy of public invention does not break the psyche, does not pass beyond the mirror. And yet the logic of supplementarity introduces into the very structure of the psyche a fabulous complication, the complication of a fable that does more than it says and invents something other than what it offers for copyrighting. The very movement of this fabulous repetition can, through a merging of chance and necessity, produce the new of an event. Not only with the singular invention of a performative, since every performative presupposes conventions and institutional rules—but by bending these rules with respect for the rules themselves in order to allow the other to come or to announce its coming in the opening of this dehiscence. That is perhaps what we call deconstruction. The performance of the Fable respects the rules, but does so with a strange move—one that others would adjudge perverse, although it is thereby complying faithfully and lucidly with the very conditions of its own poetics. This move consists in defying and exhibiting the precarious structure of its rules, even while respecting them, and through the mark of respect that it invents.

A unique situation. Invention is always possible, it is the invention of the possible, the *tekhnè* of a human subject in an ontotheological horizon, the invention in truth of the subject and of this horizon; it is the invention of the law, invention in accord with the law that confers status; invention of and in accord with the institutions that socialize, recognize, guarantee, legitimize; the programmed invention of programs; the invention of the same through which the other amounts to the same when its event is again reflected in the fable of a *psyche*. Thus it is that invention would be in conformity with its concept, with the dominant feature of the word and concept "invention," only insofar as, paradoxically, invention invents nothing, when in invention the other does not come, and when nothing comes to the other or from the other. For the other is not the possible. So it would be necessary to say that the only possible invention would be the invention of the impossible. But an invention of the impossible is impossible, the other would say. Indeed. But it is the only possible invention: an invention has to declare itself to be the invention of that which did not appear to be possible; otherwise it only makes explicit a program of possibilities within the economy of the same.[23]

It is in this paradoxical predicament that a deconstruction gets under way. Our current tiredness results from the invention of the same and from the possible, from the invention that is always possible. It is not against it but beyond it that we are trying to reinvent invention itself, another invention, or rather an invention of the other that would come, through the economy of the same, indeed while miming or repeating it ("*par le mot par . . .* "), to offer a place for the other, would let the other come. I am careful to say "let it come" because if the other is precisely what is not invented, the initiative or deconstructive inventiveness can consist only in opening, in uncloseting, destabilizing foreclusionary structures so as to allow for the passage toward the other. But one does not make the other come, one lets it come by preparing for its coming. The coming of the other or its coming back is the only possible arrival, but it is not invented, even if the most genial inventiveness is needed to prepare to welcome it: to affirm the chance of an encounter that not only is no longer calculable but is not even an incalculable factor still homogeneous with the calculable, not even an undecidable still caught up in the process of decision making. Is this possible? Of course it is not, and that is why it is the only possible invention.

A moment ago, I said we were searching to reinvent invention. No, that search cannot be an outgrowth of *research* as such, whatever Greek or Latin tradition we may find behind the politics and the modern programs of research. Nor is it any longer possible for us to say that *we* are searching: what is promised here is not, is no longer or not yet, the identifiable "we" of a community of human subjects, with all those familiar features we wrap up in the names society, contract, institution, and so forth. All these traits are linked to that concept of invention that remains to be deconstructed. It is another "we" that is offered to this inventiveness, after seven years of misfortune, with the mirror broken and the *tain* crossed, a "we" that does not find *itself* anywhere, does not invent itself: it can be invented only by the other who says "come" and to whom a response with another "come" seems to me to be the only invention that is desirable and worthy of interest. The other is indeed what is not inventable, and it is then the only invention in the world, the only invention of the world, our invention, the invention that invents us. For the other is always another origin of the world and we are (always) (still) to be invented. And the being of the we, and being itself. Beyond being.

By the other, beyond the performance and the *psyche* of *"par le mot par."* Performativity is necessary but not sufficient. In the strict sense, a performative still presupposes too much conventional institution to break the mirror. The deconstruction I am invoking only invents or affirms, lets the other come insofar as, in the performative, it is not only performative but also continues to unsettle the conditions of the performative and of whatever distinguishes it comfortably from the constative. This writing is liable to the other, opened to and by the other, to the work of the other; it is writing working at not letting itself be enclosed or dominated by this economy of the same in its totality, which guarantees both the irrefutable power and the closure of the classical concept of invention, its politics, its technoscience, its institutions. These are not to be rejected, criticized, or combated, far from it—and all the less so since the economic circle of invention is only a movement for reappropriating exactly what sets it in motion, the *difference* of the other. And that movement cannot be recast as meaning, existence, or truth.

Passing beyond the possible, this *differance* or writing is without status, without law, without a horizon of reappropriation, programmation, institutional legitimation, it passes beyond the order of demand, of the market for art or science, it asks for no patent and will never have one. In that respect it remains very gentle, foreign to threats and wars. But for that it is felt as something all the more dangerous.

Like the future. For the time to come is its only concern: allowing the adventure or the event of the entirely other to come. Of an entirely other that can no longer be confused with the God or the Man of ontotheology or with any of the figures of the configuration (the subject, consciousness, the unconscious, the self, man or woman, and so on). To say that this is the only future is not to advocate amnesia. The coming of invention cannot make itself foreign to repetition and memory. For the other is not the new. But its coming extends beyond this past present that once was able to construct—to invent, we must say—the techno-onto-anthropo-theological concept of invention, its very convention and status, the status of invention and the statue of the inventor.

What am I going to be able to invent again, you wondered at the beginning, when it was the fable.

And to be sure you have seen nothing come.

The other, that's no longer inventable.

"What do you mean by that? That the other will have been only an invention, the invention of the other?"

"No, that the other is what is never inventable and will never have waited for your invention. The call of the other is a call to come, and that happens only in multiple voices."

Notes

1. Cf. *Partitiones oratoriae*,1–3, and *De inventione*, I, 7.

2. In Stephen Greenblatt (ed.), *Allegory and Representation* (Baltimore: Johns Hopkins University Press, 1981), 1–25.

3. We may also recall Clément Jannequin's *Inventions musicales* (circa 1545). Bach's inventions were not merely didactic, even though they were also intended to teach counterpoint technique. They may be (and often are) treated as composition exercises (exposition of the theme in its principal key, reexposition in the dominant, new developments, supplementary or final exposition in the key indicated in the signature). There are inventions in A-major, in F-minor, in G-minor, and so one. And as soon as one gives the title "inventions" in the plural, as I am doing here, one invites thoughts of technical virtuosity, didactic exercise, instrumental variations. But is one obliged to accept the invitation to think what one is thus invited to think?

4. In *Proêmes*, part I, "Natare piscem doces" (Paris: Gallimard, 1948), 45. The term *proême*, in the didactic sense that is emphasized by the learned *doces*, says something about invention, about the inventive moment of a discourse: beginning, inauguration, incipit, introduction. Cf. the second edition of "Fable," with roman and italic type inverted, in Ponge's *Oeuvres*, vol. I (Paris: Gallimard, 1965), 114.

Fable finds and states the truth that it finds in finding it, that is, in stating it. Philosopheme, theorem, poem. A very sober *Eureka*, reduced to the greatest possible economy in its operation. In Poe's fictive preface to *Eureka* we read: "I offer this book of Truths, not in its character of Truth-Teller, but for the Beauty that abounds in its Truth, constituting it true. To these I present the composition as an Art-Product alone, — let us say as a Romance; or if I be not urging too lofty a claim, as a Poem. *What I here propound is true*: — therefore it cannot die" (*The Works of Edgar Allan Poe*, vol. 9, *Eureka* and *Miscellanies* [Chicago: Stone and Kimball, 1895], 4). "Fable" may be called a spongism, for here truth signs its own name, if *Eureka* is a poem.

This is perhaps the place to ask, since we are speaking of *Eureka*, what happens when one translates *eurema* as *inventio, euretes* as *inventor, euriskô* as "I encounter, I find by looking or by chance, upon reflection or by accident, I discover or obtain it."

5. Paul de Man,"Sign and Symbol in Hegel's Aesthetics," *Critical Inquiry*, 8 (1982): 761–75.

6. "Allegory is sequential and narrative" ("Pascal's Allegory of Persuasion," 1). And again: "Allegory appears as a successive mode" ("The Rhetoric of Temporality," in *Blindness and Insight*, 2nd ed. [Minneapolis: University of Minnesota Press, 1983], 226).

7. Cf. "Autobiography as De-facement," *MLN*, 94 (1979): 921.

8. "The Rhetoric of Temporality," 225–26.

9. Ibid.

10. Ibid., 152–53. A note appended to this sentence begins as follows: "The implication that the self-reflective moment of the *cogito*, the self-reflection of what Rilke calls 'le narcisse exhaucé,' is not an original event but itself an allegorical (or metaphorical) version of an intralinguistic structure, with all the negative epistemological consequences it entails." The equation between allegory and metaphor, in this context, poses problems to which I shall attempt to return elsewhere.

11. In the space of a few weeks I received Gerald Holton's *L'Invention scientifique* (Paris: PUF, 1982), Judith Schlanger's *L'Invention intellectuelle* (Paris: Fayard, 1983), and Christian Delacampagne's *L'Invention du racisme* (Paris: Fayard, 1983). I am naturally referring to these three books and to many others (such as *L'Invention d'Athènes* by Nicole Loraux and *L'Invention de la démocratie* by Claude Lefort). Delacampagne's book reminds us that there is an invention of evil. Like all inventions, that one has to do with culture, language, institutions, history, and technology. In the case of racism in the strict sense, it is doubtless a very recent invention in spite of its ancient roots. Delacampagne connects the signifier at least to *reason* and *razza*. Racism is also an invention of the other, but in order to exclude it and tighten the circle of the same. A logic of the psyche, the topic of its identifications and projections warrants a lengthy discussion.

12. By Saint Helena, mother of Constantine the Great, in Jerusalem in 326 A.D.

13. Find *or* invent, find *and* invent. Man can invent by finding, by finding invention, or he can invent beyond what he finds and what is already found. Two examples: (1) Bossuet–"Les sourds et les muets trouvent l'invention de se parler avec les doigts" ("the deaf and the dumb find the invention of communicating with their fingers"); (2) Fénelon: "Les hommes trouvant le monde tel qu'il est, ont eu l'invention de le tourner à leurs usages" ("Finding the world as it is, men have had the inventiveness to adapt it to their own uses").

14. Here we ought to study all of part 1, "Anthropological Didactics," and especially paragraphs 56 and 57, in Kant's *Anthropology from a Pragmatic Point of View*, trans. Mary J. Gregor (The Hague: Martinus Nijhoff, 1974). We shall simply cite one fragment:

"*Invention* [*erfinden*] is quite different from *discovery* [*entdecken*]. When we say that someone *discovered* a thing, we mean that it already existed beforehand: it was just not well-known—for example, America before Columbus. But when someone *invents* a thing—gunpowder, for example—that thing was not known at all before the artist who made it. Both of these can be meritorious. But we can find something we were not looking for (as the alchemist discovered phosphor), and there is no merit at all in such a discovery. —Talent for inventing things is called *genius*. But we apply this term only to *artists* [*Künstler*], and so to people who know how to make things, not to those who merely have experiential and *scientific* knowledge of many things. Moreover, we do not apply it to mere imitators: we reserve it for artists who are disposed to produce their works *originally*, and finally, for them only when their work is *exemplary*—that is, when it serves as a model [*Beispiel*] (*exemplar*) to be imitated. So a man's genius is 'the exemplary originality of his talent' [*die musterhafte Originalität seines Talents*] (with respect to this or that kind of artistic work [*Kunstproducten*]). We also call a mind with this ability a genius, in which case the term refers not merely to a person's natural talent [*Naturgabe*] but also to the person himself. A man who is a genius in many fields is a *vast* genius (like Leonardo de Vinci)" (92–93).

I have included the German words in order to emphasize in the original language the oppositions that are important for our argument, and in particular to make it clear that the word "creator" here does not designate someone who produces an existence *ex nihilo*; it is not the inventor who can do this, as we have stressed, but rather the artist [*Künstler*]. We shall look at the remainder of this passage later on. It deals with the relation between genius and truth, the productive imagination and exemplarity.

15. It is not merely difficult to translate the entire configuration that is clustered around the word *trouver*. It is virtually impossible to reconstitute in a few words all the uses of the French *se trouver* in a non-Latin language ("il se trouve que . . . ," "je me trouve bien ici," "la lettre se trouve entre les jambes de la cheminée," and so on). No solution of translation will be completely adequate. Is

translation invention? And the purloined letter, wherever it is found, and if one finds it right there where it is found: will one have discovered, unveiled, or invented it? Invented as the body of Christ, there where it *was already (to be) found*, or as a fable? As a meaning or as an existence? As a truth or as a simulacrum? In its place or as a place? From its very incipit, "Le facteur de la vérité" (in *La Carte postale* [Paris: Aubier-Flammarion, 1980]) is linked in an irreducible, thus an untranslatable, manner with the French idiom *se trouver* and with the *si ça se trouve* in all states of its syntax (441, 448). The question of whether the purloined letter is an invention (and then, in what sense?) does not entirely cover, or at least does not completely exhaust, the question of whether "The Purloined Letter" is an invention.

16. The invention of language and of writing – of the mark – is always, for fundamental reasons, the very paradigm of intention, as if one were witnessing the invention of invention. Countless examples come to mind, but since we have been concerned with Port Royal, let us consider the view of Arnauld and Lancelot in the *Grammaire générale et raisonnée* (1660): "Grammar is the art of speaking. To speak is to explain one's thoughts by signs that men have invented to this end. It has been found that the most useful of these signs are sounds and voices. But because these sounds fade away, other signs have been invented to make sounds durable and visible: these are the characters of writing, which the Greeks call *grammata*, from which the word Grammar has come." As always, invention is at the junction of nature and institutions: "The various sounds used for speaking, called *letters*, have been found in a perfectly natural way, which it is useful to note."

If I prefer to say "invention of the mark or trace," rather than of language or writing, to designate the paradigm of all invention, it is in order to situate it at the junction of nature and culture, as any presumed originarity would have it, as well as to stop accrediting a priori the opposition between animals and men that serves as the basis for the construction of the current values of invention. If every invention, as invention of the trace, then becomes a movement of *differance* or sending, *envoi*, as I have attempted to show elsewhere, the postal framework is thereby privileged, as I should like simply to stress here once again. And to illustrate according to Montaigne, from whose writings I shall quote here, as a detached supplement to *La Carte postale*, the following fragment from *Des postes* (II, 22) which names "invention" and situates it between the animal *socius* and the human *socius*: "In the war of the Romans against King Antiochus, T. Sempronius Gracchus, says Livy, *by relays of horses, with almost incredible speed, reached Pella from Amphissa on the third day*; and it appears, when you look at the location, that they were established posts, not freshly ordered for this ride.

"Cecinna's invention for sending back news to his household was much swifter; he took swallows along with him, and released them toward their nests when he wanted to send back news of himself, marking them with some color to signify his meaning, according as he had prearranged with his people. At the theater in Rome the heads of families kept pigeons in their bosoms, to which they attached letters when they wanted to send instructions to their people at home, and these were trained to bring back an answer" (*The Complete Essays of Montaigne*, trans. Donald Frame [Stanford: Stanford University Press, 1948], 516; translation modified).

17. Gottfried Wilhelm Leibniz, *Opuscules et fragments inédits*, ed. Louis Couturat (Paris: Alcan, 1903), 27–28.

18. The remainder of this text must be cited in order to situate what might be a Leibnizian theory of *aphorism*, to be sure, but also of teaching and of a genre that might be called "an inventor's autobiographical memoirs," the workshop, the manufacture, the genesis or the history of invention. "I find that in *encounters* of importance authors would have rendered the public a service if they had been willing to mark sincerely in their writings the *traces* of their attempts; but if *the system of science has to be constructed* on that basis, it would be as if in a completed house one wanted to keep all the scaffolding the architect needed in order to build it. The good *teaching methods* are all such that science ought to have been found surely by their *path*; and then if they are not empirical, that is if truths are taught by reasons or proofs drawn from ideas, it will always be through axioms, theorems,

canons and other general propositions. It is something else again when truths are *aphorisms*, like those of Hippocrates, that is general or experiential truths, or at least most often true, learned through observation or based on experiences, and for which one does not have entirely convincing reasons. But that is not what is involved here, for these truths are not known through the connecting of ideas" (*New Essays Concerning Human Understanding*, trans. Alfred G. Langley [New York: Macmillan, 1896], 476–77; translation modified).

Leibniz stresses only the word "aphorism." "General or experiential truths", in this context, are obviously opposed to "necessary truths," truths that are universal and known a priori.

19. Cf. the remainder of the passage from the *Anthropology of the Pragmatic Point of View* cited earlier (n. 14):

"The realm of imagination is the proper domain of genius because imagination is creative [*schöpferisch*] and, being less subject than other powers to the constraint of rules, more apt for originality. —Since the mechanism of teaching always forces the pupil to imitate, it undoubtedly interferes with the budding of a genius—that is, as far as his originality is concerned. Yet every art [*Kunst*] needs certain mechanical basic rules—rules, namely, for making the work suit the Idea underlying it, for portraying *truthfully* the object that the artist has in mind. This must be studied in strict academic fashion, and is certainly an imitative process. To free imagination from even this constraint and let individual talent carry on without rules and revel in itself, even against nature, might produce original folly. But this would not be exemplary [*musterhaft*] and so could not be considered genius.

"Spirit is the *animating* principle [*das belebende Pincip*] in man. In the French language, spirit and wit have the same name, *esprit*. It is different in the German language. We say that a speech, a text, a lady at a social gathering etc, is beautiful but without spirit [*abert ohne Geist*]. Their stock of wit [*Witz*] makes no difference here: it can even repel us, because its action leaves nothing permanent behind (*nichts Bleibendes*)" (93).

20. F. W. J. Schelling, *Studium Generale: Vorlesungen über die Methode des akademischen Studiums* (Stuttgart: Alfred Kroner Verlag, 1954), lesson V, p. 79.

21. For example: "Thus Poetry and Philosophy, which another kind of dilettantism sets in contrast, are similar in that each one of them requires a self-engendered picture [*Bild*] of the world that comes into being spontaneously" (lesson VI, p. 98). "Mathematics belongs to the world consisting simply of reflected image [*abgebildete Welt*] in so far as it manifests foundational knowledge and absolute identity only in a reflection" (lesson IV, p. 69). "Without intellectual intuition, no philosophy. Even pure intuition of space and time is not present as such in common consciousness; for it is also intellectual intuition, but only as reflected [*reflektierte*] in sense-perception" (p. 70).

22. On the subject of that "humanist" or "anthropological" invariant in the concept of invention, it is perhaps time to quote Bergson (as the affinity with Schelling obliges): "Invention is the essential undertaking of the human mind, the one that distinguishes men from animals."

23. This economy is obviously not limited to any conscious representation and to the calculations that appear there. And if there is no invention without the intervention of what was once called genius, or even without the illumination of a *Witz* through which everything begins, still that generosity must no longer respond to a principle of savings and to a restricted economy of *différance*. The aleatory advent of the entirely other, beyond the incalculable as a still possible calculus—there is "true" invention, which is no longer invention of truth and can only come about for a finite being: the very *opportunity* (*chance*) of finitude. It invents and appears to itself only on the basis of what *happens* thus.

A Defence of Rhetoric /
The Triumph of Reading
Deborah Esch

> *Errichtet keinen Denkstein.*
> — Rilke, *Die Sonette an Orpheus*, I, v

What do "The Triumph of Life" and Paul de Man's programmatic reading of Shelley's unfinished poem have to tell us about theory?[1] Writing in his preface to *The Rhetoric of Romanticism*, which reprints "Shelley Disfigured" in a theoretical context distinct from that of its prior publication in the collective volume *Deconstruction and Criticism*, de Man singles out this essay as "the only place where I come close to facing some of these questions" about the fragmentary and interrupted character not only of so many pivotal romantic texts, but of his own critical corpus as well.[2] In his account of "The Triumph of Life," de Man asks, however, whether the structure of this enigmatic poem is properly one of question and answer (a structure he elsewhere terms hermeneutic),[3] or rather of "a question whose meaning, as question, is effaced from the moment it is asked. The answer to the question is another question, asking what and why one asked" (RR, 98).[4] If we can acknowledge what and why we ask when we ask the question of theory, in light of our positions (historical, institutional, ideological) as readers and theorists, we might rewrite the initial question in a way that inscribes our self-interest in plainer terms, to ask: what do these texts tell us about the theorist? One answer (though not necessarily a privileged or paradigmatic one) suggests itself toward the end of Shelley's poem, where the theorist makes a brief appearance, under doubtful circumstances. In an unsettling sequence that owes a metrical as well as a thematic debt to Dante, the figure called Rousseau is swept along in the wake of the swift advance of the chariot of Life,[5] to find himself in a mysterious dell whose air is said to be peopled with forms, benighted by phantoms dizzily dancing in a thousand unimagined shapes, hovering like vampire bats and vultures; or again like the small gnats and flies that "throng[] about the brow / Of lawyer, statesman, priest and theorist" (line 510). The theorist, then, brings up the rear in a train of shady company, beset by these ghostly shapes, these "shadows of shadows" (line 488).

The next question on our part, consequently, might well be: what are these forms that pester the theorist, and where do they come from? Or, to echo the poem's terms of direct address, "And what is this?" "Whence camest thou . . . and why?" (lines 177, 296–97) — for, as de Man notes, these questions posed in the poem (as well as in Shelley's earlier "Essay on Life") "can easily be referred back to the enigmatic text they punctuate and they are characteristic of the interpretive labor associated with romanticism" (RR, 94).[6] Rousseau recounts a tentative version of the origin of these busy phantoms:

> — I became aware
>
> Of whence those forms proceeded which thus stained
>   The track in which we moved; after brief space
> From every form the beauty slowly waned,
>
>   From every firmest limb and fairest face
> The strength and freshness fell like dust, and left
>   The action and the shape without the grace
>
> Of life; the marble brow of youth was cleft
>   With care, and in the eyes where once hope shone
> Desire . . .
>   . . . glared ere it died; each one
> Of that great crowd sent forth incessantly
>   These shadows . . .
>
> (lines 516–28)

The genesis of these forms that beleaguer the theorist makes for a narrative that is hardly reassuring; it shares with the question whose only answer is another question a self-receding structure, for the origins of the phantoms can be traced no further than to "obscure clouds moulded by the casual air" (line 532). Moreover, it is a story of waning beauty and strength that leaves "the action and the shape without the grace of life," recalling, for de Man's reader, the exemplary fate of the young man in Kleist's essay on the marionette theater, who suffers an analogous loss of grace as he tries to recover his reflection in a mirror, only to

68 ☐ DEBORAH ESCH

find himself "sentenced to narcissistic paralysis by critical self-consciousness" (RR, 275).

The theorist attempting to locate himself or herself in relation to these shadows thus encounters a certain resistance:

> Questions of origin, of direction, and of identity punctuate the text without ever receiving a clear answer. They always lead back to a new scene of questioning. . . . Whenever this self-receding scene occurs, the syntax and the imagery of the poem tie themselves into a knot which arrests the process of understanding. The resistance of these passages is such that the reader soon forgets the dramatic situation and is left with only these unresolved riddles to haunt him: the text becomes the successive and cumulative experience of these tangles of meaning and of figuration. (RR, 97–99)

In de Man's text, the reader, perhaps through a mechanism that represses some self-threatening knowledge, forgets the dramatic situation and his or her role in it—in this case, forgets what the poem has to say about theory and theorists, even in the act of asking the question. For "to question is to forget" (RR, 118), and it is this "coercive 'forgetting' that Shelley's poem analytically thematizes" (RR, 122).[7] De Man's account of the tangles of meaning and of figuration that make up "The Triumph of Life" does not so much resolve the haunting riddles posed by the text as it identifies and analytically thematizes them, and thereby, as he admits, tries to avoid them in the most effective way possible. His claim, in brief, is that the poem adumbrates a specifiably rhetorical theory of language. The claim of the present reading is twofold: first, that the theory of language (and the concomitant theory of reading) that de Man generates out of "The Triumph of Life" stands in a position of instructive interrelation to Shelley's own explicit theorizing, notably in *A Defence of Poetry*; more particularly, de Man's terminology and his critical procedures are to a telling extent prefigured in Shelley's reflections on the nature and function of poetic language. Moreover, I would argue that "Shelley Disfigured" is not only a programmatic essay (as its position in *Deconstruction and Criticism* attests), but one that, in its recontextualization in *The Rhetoric of Romanticism*, enables us to read both the force and the failings of the de Manian corpus.

I

To explicate, summarily, an intricate reading operation: de Man's essay traces the rhetorical function of language in "The Triumph of Life" in a way that might be outlined as follows. He reads the enigmatic shape encountered by Rousseau as a figure for figure (the poem's "Figures ever new," line 248), for "the figurality of all signification" (RR, 116). Figuration, in de Man's terms, may be understood as the alignment of a signification with any principle of linguistic articulation. It marks, further, the element in language that "allows for the reiteration of meaning by substitution."[8] This notion of the figure as a structure of substitution is then extended (in Shelley's term, "transfigured," line 476) from an initial model of language as a system of tropes (among which de Man here enumerates, with specific reference to the poem, metaphor, synecdoche, and prosopopoeia), a model that necessarily involves a sensory (or "aesthetic") element, to allow passage to a more complex if still figural scheme that includes such principles of linguistic organization as grammar and syntax.[9] These operate on what he calls "the level of the letter," without the intervention of an iconic or sensory factor. De Man's theory of figuration is associated at each stage with the cognitive function of language as a structure of sense making, an alignment of meaning with articulation.

This ramified notion of the figure is able to account, at least in part, for such difficult aspects of Shelley's poem as the relation of the narrator's itinerary to Rousseau's (understood as one of repetition with a difference), or the crucial metaphor of the rainbow, which uncritically figures a unity of perception and cognition without taking into consideration the potentially disruptive mediation of its own rhetoricity. It seems adequate as well to the elusive term "measure," with which the text departs from the sensory aspect of signification to stress instead the nonsignifying properties of language. Nonetheless, even this comprehensive theory of figuration does not suffice to read "The Triumph of Life" in its full complexity. No elaboration of the tropological model can explain, for example, the two events that frame the poem's narrative sequence: the sun's overcoming the light of the stars, and its being quenched, in turn, by the light of life. Only retrospectively, argues de Man, can such an event be mistaken for a structure of substitution, or for a dialectical relationship between the morning star and the evening, between one order of light and another. The sun that masters the starlight, and the light that subsequently masters the sun, are not in this account phenomenally given or produced. They do not appear in conjunction with or in reaction to anything, but with an unmediated violence and "of their own unrelated power," the sheer power of utterance. In the vocabulary of the poem, deployed in turn by de Man, these events occur as an "imposition," in the emphatic mode of positing, of *Setzung*:

And in succession due, did Continent,

> Isle, Ocean, and all things that in them wear
> The form and character of mortal mould
> Rise as the Sun their father rose, to bear

> Their portion of the toil which he of old
> Took as his own and then *imposed* on them.
> (lines 15–20, emphasis added)[10]

Hence the need for a supplementary model of language that stands heterogeneously to the tropological and substitutive, and that takes into account the positional power of language as act.[11] This further function is associated not with cognition, with the epistemological criteria of truth and falsehood (for, in the poem's
terms, "none seemed to know," line 47), but with an order of "power" (line 292)
and of "force" (line 285), an order evoked in the poem's explicit politics, its
thematics of imperialism, patriarchy, and enslavement.[12]

For de Man, reading "The Triumph of Life" thus requires a twofold theory of
the rhetorical operation of language—as trope and as positing (or what he elsewhere, appropriating Austin's vocabulary, calls performance—a performance
whose potential violence is suggested in the poem's deployment of the term: "And
frost in these performs what fire in those," line 175).[13] The two functions do not
stand in opposition, nor indeed in any symmetrical relation to one another in his
analysis. To do justice to the complexities of their interarticulation—"to keep the
actual performance of speech acts, which is conventional rather than cognitive,
separate from its causes and effects" (RT, 18)—is one objective of his critical
practice. But what then is the relation of the theory that emerges here, as well
as the methodological claims de Man makes on the basis of this fragmentary
poem, to the theory of poetic language advanced in Shelley's prose? To proceed,
once again, all too schematically, it is possible to outline the conceptual framework of *A Defence of Poetry* by way of a number of key terms in Shelley's argument that anticipate the models elaborated by de Man.

Early in the *Defence*, another unfinished text, Shelley asserts the fundamental
rhetoricity of his medium:

> [The poets'] language is vitally metaphorical; that is, it marks the before
> unapprehended relations of things and perpetuates their apprehen-
> sion. . . . These similitudes or relations are finely said by Lord Bacon
> to be "the same footsteps of nature impressed upon the various subjects
> of the world," and he considers the faculty which perceives them as the
> storehouse of axioms common to all knowledge. (SP, 278-79)

For Shelley, poetic language is first of all metaphorical, or figural, and the allusion to Bacon both anticipates the metaphor of the tracks imprinted in the sand
in "The Triumph of Life" and situates figuration in the realm of the cognitive.[14]
Synecdoche, analogy, and personification all find a place in Shelley's analysis of
poetic language, which, as he writes, "subdues to union, under its light yoke, all
irreconcilable things" (SP, 295).

But this articulation or "yoking" (accomplished in the poem largely through
figures of light) does not exhaust Shelley's theory. Like de Man, the poet
elaborates his model of language as a "figured curtain," to account for such elements as syntax and grammatical scansion, and for temporally complex narrative
figures like allegory. These latter structures, which call for a more comprehen-

sive theory of figuration, Shelley considers under the double rubric of measure and of order, as "combinations" or "arrangements" of language (SP, 278, 279) that distinguish poetry from other forms and, incidentally, render translation an exercise in "vanity" (SP, 280).[15] The poet, then, works to approximate that order from which the "highest delight" results (SP, 278). Still, the poet has a more practical and prosaic task as well, for in Shelley's scheme the "poets, or those who imagine and express this indestructible order, are not only the authors of language . . . they are the institutors of laws and the founders of civil society and the inventors of the arts of life and the teachers" (SP, 279). Shelleyan legislation—"the manner in which poetry acts to produce the moral improvement of man" (SP, 282)—is readable above all as an institution of and in language, as an exercise of positional "power" (SP, 293, 296–97). The law (*Gesetz*) functions as such by virtue of position (*Setzung*), of an act whose arbitrariness Shelley emphasizes in the *Defence*: "For language is arbitrarily produced . . . " (SP, 279).[16] Poetic language thus comprises both figure and force, that "sword of lightning, ever unsheathed, which consumes the scabbard that would contain it" (SP, 285); it is to be read as substitution on the one hand, and as institution on the other. The "light yoke" of the figure that "subdues to union all irreconcilable things" is, as the variorum edition of "The Triumph of Life" indicates, "imposed":

> From senatehouse & prison & theatre
> When Freedom left those who upon the free
> Imposed a yoke which soon they stooped to bear
> (lines 114–116, TL, 151)

In Shelley's terms as well as de Man's, then,

> The positing power of language is both entirely arbitrary, in having a
> strength that cannot be reduced to necessity, and entirely inexorable in
> that there is no alternative to it. It stands beyond the polarities of
> chance and determination and can therefore not be part of a temporal
> sequence of events. The sequence has to be punctuated by acts that can-
> not be made a part of it. (RR, 116)

Such positional acts resist inscription into a sequential narrative (or a logical argument)[17] until the reader, inconsistently but inevitably, imposes upon them the authority of sense and of meaning.[18]

Reread in the light of de Man's theoretical position, both Shelley's texts make explicit the violence of this latter imposition of meaning upon the senseless positional act—the necessary but erroneous gesture on the reader's part that de Man terms disfiguration. This delusive performance depends upon the moment of forgetting alluded to earlier, which must itself be forgotten in order that language's arbitrary power plays can be re-membered, reinscribed in a historical or aesthetic system like the one we call romanticism.[19] De Man's critical insights, which enable us to return to Shelley's prose as well as his poetry with a renewed sense of their theoretical rigor, are arguably the poet's own, forgotten in the wake of historicizing and aestheticizing interpretations of his work.[20] For, as de Man writes in the late essay "Anthropomorphism and Trope in the Lyric," "Such a historicizing pattern, a commonplace of aesthetic theory, is a function of the aesthetic ideologization of linguistic structures rather than an empirical historical event" (RR, 253). In these terms, the disfigured Shelleyan corpus is exemplary in its resistance to such recuperative monumentalizations, unavoidable as they ultimately prove to be. For the reader of de Man's own corpus, a further question remains: to what extent do his readings (of Shelley, and of other romantic texts) themselves partake of this exemplary resistance?

II

It may be that a partial answer is afforded by de Man in his preface to *The Rhetoric of Romanticism*, where he takes on the role of his own reader and critic. His tone is one of dismay as he confesses "some misgivings" about this volume that collects essays written over a span of roughly twenty-five years; like "The Triumph of Life," the body of work that presents itself to his retrospection is fragmentary to an extent that threatens the coherence of the whole:

> Such massive evidence of the failure to make the various individual
> readings coalesce is a somewhat melancholy spectacle. The fragmentary
> aspect of the whole is made more obvious still by the hypotactic man-
> ner that prevails in each of the essays taken in isolation, by the con-
> tinued attempt, however ironized, to present a closed and linear argu-
> ment. The apparent coherence *within* each essay is not matched by a
> corresponding coherence *between* them. (RR, viii)

Except insofar as it gives fair warning to the reader who requires coherence of such a volume, however, de Man's disclaimer is more properly a postface, an afterword, since the full force of his self-indictment can be brought home only to the reader who has traveled the itinerary of the book. For the failure of the corpus to coalesce is neither accidental nor remediable; it is rather a strict consequence of the theory of language elaborated in reading after reading. "Laid out diachronically in a roughly chronological sequence," he observes, the essays "do not evolve in a manner that easily allows for a dialectical progression or, ultimately, for historical totalization. Rather, it seems that they always start again from scratch and that their conclusions fail to add up to anything" (RR, viii). This retrospective judgment that the readings "always start again from scratch" — that they sound, to recall a recurring figure in de Man's teaching, like a broken record — is anticipated in the volume's opening essay, "Intentional Structure of the Romantic Image," first published in 1960. In the context of an analysis of Hölderlin's "Brot und

Wein," de Man writes that poetic language "can do nothing but originate anew over and over again; it is always constitutive, able to posit regardless of presence but, by the same token, unable to give foundation to what it posits" (RR, 6).[21] The failure to add up to anything, the need always again to start over, is already bound up with the positional power of language; positing, as understood in the essay that inaugurates *The Rhetoric of Romanticism*, is not a beginning but a repetition, a kind of embarrassing stammer.[22]

In another resigned admission in the preface, de Man contrasts his own inelegant prose with that of historians and theorists who, like Auerbach or Adorno, "have made the fragmentary nature of post-romantic literature a stylistic principle of their own critical discourse." He finds himself unable to take their recourse, for reasons that have specifically to do with romantic texts and the aesthetic ideology that marks their study:[23]

> I feel myself compelled to repeated frustration in a persistent attempt to write as if a dialectical summation were possible beyond the breaks and interruptions that the readings disclose. By stating the inevitability of fragmentation in a mode that is itself fragmented, one restores the aesthetic unity of manner and substance that may well be what is in question in the historical study of romanticism. Such is the cost of discursive elegance, a small price to pay, perhaps, compared to the burden of constantly falling back to nought. (RR, ix)

The figure of a fall is one that de Man analyzes repeatedly, from the early essay on Blanchot's reading of Mallarmé, to the treatment of Baudelairean irony in "The Rhetoric of Temporality," to his preoccupation with the title of Keats's "The Fall of Hyperion" in "The Resistance to Theory," to his reading of Kleist's "Über das Marionettentheater" in *The Rhetoric of Romanticism*'s final chapter, where "fall" surfaces as a troublesome syllable attended, in German even more than in English, by a "disjunctive plurality of meanings" (RR, 289).[24] In a context that is yet again one of irony, de Man offers an analogy, in the latter essay, for the "breaks and interruptions" in the dance, which are not part of the choreography but which afford the brief periods of repose required by human dancers (if not by the puppets): "They are like the parabases of the ironic consciousness which has to recover its energy after each failure by reinscribing the failure into the ongoing process of a dialectic. But a dialectic, segmented by repeated negations, can never be a dance; at the very most, it can be a funeral march" (RR, 287).

In this context, it is no accident that the reading of "The Triumph of Life" — a work that Hazlitt, in his review of Shelley's *Posthumous Poems*, called "a new and terrific *Dance of Death*"[25] — is isolated in the continuation of the passage from the preface: "The only place where I come close to facing some of these questions about history and fragmentation is in the essay on *The Triumph of Life*. How and where one goes on from there is far from clear" (RR, ix). In the face of these questions, "Shelley Disfigured" becomes pivotal for a reading of de Man's critical corpus, much as *A Defence of Poetry* has been for an analysis of Shelley's poetic production. The essay, first of all, can tell us why the gathering of de Man's readings into the diachrony of *The Rhetoric of Romanticism* is, as he writes of the attempt to historicize Baudelaire's sonnets, "more convenient than it is legitimate" (RR, 254). More specifically, it is analogous to the gesture that de Man, in the essay on Shelley, calls disfiguration: it amounts to the erroneous inscription into a sequential narrative of a series of positional acts (of reading)—convenient but finally illegitimate, inconsistent but finally unavoidable. Again, this editorial reinscription of the "individual readings" (initiated by William P. Germano, then editor at Columbia University Press, as de Man twice recalls in the preface) performs the inevitable forgetting of the theory that the readings work to establish—a theory that reflects on its own itinerary in no uncertain terms: "The power that takes one from one text to another is not just a power of displacement, be it understood as recollection or interiorization or any other 'transport,' but the sheer blind violence that Nietzsche, concerned with the same enigma, domesticated by calling it, metaphorically, an *army* . . . " (RR, 262).[26] The "domestication" of de Man's readings entailed in their inscription in *The Rhetoric of Romanticism* is predicated on such a (Nietzschean) forgetting—or, as he specifies in "Aesthetic Formalization in Kleist," a "forgetting that the possibility of such a transaction is precisely the burden of the proposition in the first place" (RR, 276): the burden, in other words, of the position, of reading as imposition.

If an analysis of Wordsworth's *Essays Upon Epitaphs* like that undertaken in "Autobiography as De-Facement" can disclose that "the text counsels against the use of its own main figure," indicating "the threat of a deeper logical disturbance" (RR, 78), this essay and each of the others collected in *The Rhetoric of Romanticism* resist their own disfiguration, their inscription in a sequential narrative. The critical and ideological stakes of this gesture (whether editorially or self-imposed) become apparent in the reading of Wordsworth. For de Man, the "latent threat" that inhabits the rhetoric of the *Essays Upon Epitaphs* (and of "The Triumph of Life") is that of a "monumentalization" of Wordsworth (and Shelley) and of romanticism. Likewise, in the case of *The Rhetoric of Romanticism*, it is not fragmentation or interruption, but rather monumentalization that menaces de Man's own corpus, to the extent that the volume (or its reader) seeks to impart an aesthetic unity, a pseudohistorical totalization, to an enumeration of positional acts of reading.

"Shelley Disfigured," as has been suggested, outlines the way in which the Shelleyan oeuvre is for de Man exemplary of romanticism's resistance to monumentalizing interpretation. Geoffrey Hartman concurs in his account of the essay that the "history of reception, in Shelley's case, shows how disruptive his poetry has been to monumentalizing and religious . . . perspectives" (CW, 106). This resistance has to do not only with the fragmentary status of so many of the texts in question, but also, as de Man writes in "Wordsworth and Hölderlin," with the specific temporality that structures our relation to romanticism:[27]

> In the case of romanticism it is a matter of the interpretation of a phenomenon that we can only consider from the temporal perspective of a period of time that we have ourselves experienced. . . . We carry it within ourselves as the experience of an *act* in which, up to a certain point, we ourselves have participated. . . . To interpret romanticism means quite literally to interpret the past as such, *our* past precisely to the extent that we are beings who want to be defined and, as such, interpreted in relation to a totality of experiences that slip into the past. The content of this experience is perhaps less important than the fact that we have experienced it in its passing away, and that it thereby has contributed in an unmediated way (that is, in the form of an act) to the constitution of our own consciousness of temporality. Now it is precisely this experience of the temporal relation between the act and its interpretation that is one of the main themes of romantic poetry. (RR, 49–50)

Romanticism, in other words, *imposes* itself on us, as an act incapable of dialectical mediation—an act, one might argue, of translation in the radical sense in which Walter Benjamin understood it, at the furthest remove from paraphrase.[28] In so doing, it constitutes the consciousness of temporality that we in turn bring to bear in our reading of romantic texts.

What, then, of the temporal relation of de Man's own critical acts or impositions to their interpretation, by him, in his preface? What about his own attempt at self-reading with respect to his textual past?[29] For the preface to *The Rhetoric of Romanticism* is as sustained an autobiographical account as de Man allows himself anywhere. It is, moreover, less an attempt to save face than a confession of failure, an *Aufgabe* in the sense of "the defeat, the giving up" that he reads into the title of Benjamin's "Die Aufgabe des Übersetzers" (RT, 80). But if, as de Man acknowledges, "one is all too easily tempted to rationalize personal shortcoming as theoretical impossibility," one is perhaps as readily led to rationalize exigencies of publishing (or of an academic "career") as a diachrony, or as a theoretical system. In other words, one can also explain away theoretical impossibility as a personal (or an impersonal, a critical) shortcoming. A question, then, remains: if *The Rhetoric of Romanticism* can indeed be counted a failure, is it a monumental failure?[30]

An answer (or perhaps yet another self-receding question) is afforded by a return to the reading of "The Triumph of Life," Shelley's incomplete and indeterminate swan song. In the widely reprinted version first published in 1824 in the *Posthumous Poems*, the text breaks off with a question: "Then what is Life? I cried . . . " The figure for Shelley in the poem, as well as its reader, are thus left hanging, the latter with recourse to the poet's "Essay on Life."[31] But in the variorum edition, "The Triumph" does not quite conclude at this point (though where it goes from here, to allude to de Man, is difficult to say), but "rolls onward." In the Bodleian manuscript (Shelley Adds. c-4, folder 5), the final words appear on a foolscap sheet (p. 53), which, according to Shelley's biographer Richard Holmes, "has been roughly folded in two."[32] The forgotten lines read:

> "Then, what is Life?" I said . . . the cripple cast
> His eye upon the car which now had rolled
> Onward, as if that look must be the last,
>
> And answered . . . "Happy those for whom the fold
> Of
>
> (lines 544–58, TL, 210)

The foolscap sheet unfolds the last word: "Of." The poem's end, then, reiterates its beginning, the pivotal genitive of its title, which allows for the same grammatical indetermination that de Man analyzes in "The Fall of Hyperion":

> Do we have to interpret the genitive in the title of Keats's unfinished epic *The Fall of Hyperion* as meaning "Hyperion's fall," the case story of the defeat of an older by a newer power, the very recognizable story from which Keats indeed started out but from which he increasingly strayed away, or as "Hyperion falling," the much less specific but more disquieting evocation of an actual process of falling. . . . ? Both readings are grammatically correct, but it is impossible to decide from the context (the ensuing narrative) which version is the right one. The narrative context suits neither and both at the same time, and one is tempted to suggest that the fact that Keats was unable to complete either version manifests the impossibility, for him as for us, of reading his own title. (RT, 16)

In this light, one is also tempted to suggest that Shelley's inability to finish "The Triumph of Life" (and, for that matter, *A Defence of Poetry*) has to do with the impossibility, for him as for us, of reading his title.[33] And since *The Rhetoric of Romanticism* is in an important respect unfinished — the note on permissions tells the reader that the concluding essays on Baudelaire and Kleist "did not receive final correction by the author" (RR, 322), that work on the volume was incomplete at the time of de Man's death — couldn't one argue that the partial, fragmentary, untotalizable character of the book marks the impossibility, for him as for us, of unfolding its "of" to read its title?

> And it matters a great deal how we read the title, as an exercise not only in semantics but in what the text actually does to us. Faced with the ineluctable necessity to come to a decision, no grammatical or logical analysis can help us out. Just as Keats had to break off his narra-

tive, the reader has to break off his understanding at the very moment when he is most directly engaged and summoned by the text. One could hardly expect to find solace in this "fearful symmetry" between the author's and the reader's plight since, at this point, the symmetry is no longer a formal but an actual trap, and the question no longer "merely" theoretical. (RT, 17)

The reader of *The Rhetoric of Romanticism* can expect to find little solace, then, in the fact that de Man's self-reading breaks off at the moment when he is most directly engaged and summoned: in the writing of a prefatory postface to a book he never finished. "De Man's own position," as Hartman writes of "Shelley Disfigured," has (like Shelley's) become "too absolute" (CW, 108). What, then, can such a failed text succeed in "doing" to us? How can it "help us out"? The question is indeed no longer "merely" theoretical.

It may be that the least *we* can do (and the most we have done) is to rewrite yet again the question with which we began: what do these texts have to tell us about theory? If this formulation is no longer adequate, however, it is not because theory (or the theorist) is, like the drowning poet, "in danger of going under; it cannot help but flourish, and the more it is resisted, the more it flourishes, since the language it speaks is the language of self-resistance. What remains impossible to decide is whether this flourishing is a triumph or a fall" (RT, 19-20). But can a question that is no longer "merely" theoretical—in this case, a question of a practice of reading—remain impossible to decide? If this possibility is denied to de Man in the retrospect of his preface, a practical decision is still open to his reader, in the possibility of a future act: a future re-membering of a broken project of reading.

The moment of active projection into the future . . . lies for the imagination in a past from which it is separated by the experience of a failure (*Scheitern*). The interpretation is possible only from a standpoint that lies on the far side of this failure, and that has escaped destruction thanks to an effort of consciousness to make sure of itself once again. But this consciousness can be had only by one who has very extensively partaken of the danger and failure. (RR, 58)

The failed project of *The Rhetoric of Romanticism* lies in a reading of texts by Rousseau, Wordsworth, Hölderlin, Kleist, Keats, Shelley, Baudelaire, Yeats—figures who, like de Man, have "partaken of the danger and failure." We commemorate (and fail to commemorate) them not by erecting monuments—the very "terms of resistance and nostalgia," the "defensive motions of understanding" (RR, 261-262) that their texts serve to undo—but by reading, and rereading. We "mourn" them otherwise, by remembering and remarking, however prosaically, the difference between a funeral march and a triumph of reading.[34]

Notes

1. This essay began as a contribution to a panel on "Romantic Language Theory: Modern Critical Applications," organized by Margaret Higonnet for the MLA convention in December 1984; without the encouragement of Pat Parker, it might well have remained in that fragmentary form. Ian Balfour, David Bromwich, Victoria Kahn, Tom Keenan, and Andrzej Warminski read earlier versions of the text and made helpful suggestions. No attempt has been made here to take account of the early journalistic writings that have come to light since this essay was completed.

2. Paul de Man, *The Rhetoric of Romanticism* (New York: Columbia University Press, 1984), ix. "Shelley Disfigured," like the poem it interprets, is riddled with questions, among them: "What is the meaning of *The Triumph of Life*, of Shelley, and of romanticism? What shape does it have, how did its course begin and why?" (RR, 94).

3. See in particular de Man's introduction to Hans Robert Jauss, *Toward an Aesthetic of Reception*, trans. Timothy Bahti (Minneapolis: University of Minnesota Press, 1982), vii–xxv (now collected under the title "Reading and History" in *The Resistance to Theory* [Minneapolis: University of Minnesota Press, 1986], 54–72).

4. Cf. Kenneth Neill Cameron, *Shelley: The Golden Years* (Cambridge, Mass.: Harvard University Press, 1974), 115: "Many of the questions [Shelley] raises in regard to religion, politics, ethics and literary history are precisely those that are still unanswered."

5. Rousseau is said to be "forgetful of the chariot's swift advance" (line 450). Richard Holmes notes that Shelley found the figure of the triumphal chariot carved on the arches of Titus and Constantine in the Roman forum, and first used it in the second act of *Prometheus Unbound*. See his *Shelley: The Pursuit* (New York: Dutton, 1975), 717–18.

6. The "Essay on Life" anticipates the poem's obsessive questioning, in asking "What is life? . . . For what are we? Whence do we come? And whither do we go? Is birth the commencement, is death the conclusion of our being? What is birth and death?" (in David Lee Clark [ed.], *Shelley's Prose* [Albuquerque: University of New Mexico Press], 1954, 172. Cited hereafter in the text as SP.)

7. Forgetting is thematized repeatedly in the poem, which speaks, for example, of a sound "which all who hear must needs forget / All pleasure and all pain, all hate and love" (lines 318–19); or again,

> Thou wouldst forget thus vainly to deplore
>
> Ills, which if ills, can find no cure from thee,
> The thought of which no other sleep will quell
> Nor other music blot from memory –
>
> So sweet and deep is the oblivious spell. (lines 327–31)

8. Reiteration is a key concept in both the *Defence* (SP, 280) and in the "Essay on Life" (SP, 174).

9. The problematic relation between rhetoric and grammar is analyzed more fully in "The Resistance to Theory," in RT, esp. 13–20. See also the opening chapter of *Allegories of Reading* (New Haven, Conn.: Yale University Press, 1979), 3–19.

10. See also the variant reading of line 116 in the text established by Donald Reiman: *Shelley's "The Triumph of Life": A Critical Study* (Urbana: University of Illinois Press, 1965; cited hereafter in the text as TL). Geoffrey Hartman reflects on the vocabulary of "position" in *Criticism in the Wilderness: The Study of Literature Today* (New Haven, Conn.: Yale University Press, 1980; cited hereafter as CW): " 'Positional' includes 'positing' and 'impositional': the word reflects an old distinction between 'natural' and 'positive' law. Extending de Man one could say that when Shelley claims that poets are unacknowledged legislators, he means that they promulgate laws that cannot be recog-

nized as having positive (human and subjective) force because they act on us like natural (unconsciously or inescapably suffered) events. In language, what seems natural is always positive or the effect of a 'positional power' " (107). Hartman rightly notes (107n.) that " 'positional' is a loaded word: it may participate in the effort to overcome falsely progressive (Hegelian or dialectical) theories of art." This is certainly the effort in which de Man enlists the term; it plays a pivotal role in his critique of the category of the "aesthetic" as the problematic articulation between pure and practical reason, between epistemology and ethics.

11. In Shelley's poem, Rousseau compares the effects of words and acts: "And so my words were seeds of misery— / Even as the deeds of others" (lines 280–81). Yet to speak, with Shelley and de Man, of language as an (arbitrary) act is not to construct an analogy, to say that language is *like* an act; it is emphatically to claim (with Austin) that language *is* the act in question.

12. The poem concerns itself with questions of "empire" (lines 211, 498) and with patriarchy (with the exception of Catherine the Great, the public figures it parades are uniformly male: Napoléon, the Roman emperors, the popes, Plato, Bacon, Voltaire, and Kant—the latter superimposed on Pitt, according to the variorum for line 236). These are also issues in the *Defence*, where Shelley advocates the "abolition of personal and domestic slavery" as "the basis of the highest political hope that it can enter into the mind of man to conceive" (SP, 289). In a forthcoming essay, Tres Pyle offers a rigorous analysis of the poem's thematics of power, history, and empire ("The 'Triumph' of Ideology").

13. Cf., for example, RT, 19: "The performative power of language can be called positional."

14. In this connection, see the note to the "Essay on Love" (SP, 170): "These words are ineffectual and metaphorical—most words so—No help!" See also the figure of the imprinted trace in the *Defence*: "[poetry's] footsteps are like those of a wind over the sea, which the coming calm erases, and whose traces remain only as on the wrinkled sand which paves it" (SP, 294).

15. Cf. Earl Wasserman's chapter on the *Defence* (in *Shelley: A Critical Reading* [Baltimore: Johns Hopkins University Press, 1971], 204–20): "the recurrent key words of the *Defence* are 'order,' 'organization,' 'combination,' 'arrangement,' 'union,' 'relation,' 'harmony,' and 'rhythm' (that is, order in a temporal sequence)" (208).

16. In this connection, see Rodolphe Gasché, " 'Setzung' and 'Übersetzung': Notes on Paul de Man," *Diacritics*, 11 (Winter 1981): 36–57.

17. Cf. Shelley, in the *Defence*: "Poetry, as has been said, . . . differs from logic, that it is not subject to the control of the active powers of the mind, and that its birth and recurrence have no necessary connection" (SP, 296).

18. Notable in this connection is Shelley's analogy, in *A Philosophical View of Reform*, for modern society, which he calls "an engine assumed to be for useful purposes, whose force is by a system of subtle mechanism augmented to the highest pitch, but which . . . acts against itself and is perpetually wearing away or breaking to pieces the wheels of which it is composed."

19. As Tres Pyle notes, the figure of "what was once Rousseau," as figure for the "origins" of romanticism, is itself broken, blind, and deluded.

20. Cf. Hartman's assessment of Shelley: "A politics of the spirit . . . is so closely identified with the peculiar alchemy of his language that it often does not seem to require a precise historical placement" (106).

21. In an essay on Blanchot that appeared in *Critique* in 1966 and was subsequently included in *Blindness and Insight*, de Man writes of the "difficulty of renouncing the belief that all literature is a new beginning, that a work is a sequence of beginnings. . . . The poet can only start his work because he is willing to forget that this presumed beginning is, in fact, the repetition of a previous failure, resulting precisely from an inability to begin anew. When we think that we are perceiving the assertion of a new origin, we are in fact witnessing the reassertion of a failure to originate" (BI, 65–66). The language here anticipates that of the preface to *The Rhetoric of Romanticism*.

22. See the treatment of a related impediment in Carol Jacobs's chapter on Nietzsche in *The Dissimulating Harmony* (Baltimore: Johns Hopkins University Press, 1978), 1–22, and in de Man's fore-

word to that volume. The "failure to add up to anything" and the "constantly falling back to nought" remarked in the preface to *The Rhetoric of Romanticism* recall de Man's analysis of the Pascalian "zero" in "Pascal's Allegory of Persuasion" (in *Allegory and Representation*, ed. Stephen Greenblatt. [Baltimore: Johns Hopkins University Press, 1981], 1–25).

23. Tres Pyle argues persuasively that "in Shelley's last poem we find ourselves confronted with forms of oppression and delusion which . . . belong to the ideological nature of representation itself." David Quint takes up these questions in "Representation and Ideology in 'The Triumph of Life,' " *Studies in English Literature*, 17 (Autumn 1978): 639–57. De Man would dispute the shape given to "romantic ideology" in Jerome McGann's volume of that title (*The Romantic Ideology: A Critical Investigation* [Chicago: University of Chicago Press, 1983]). For a review of McGann that takes account of de Man see that of Ian Balfour in *Critical Texts: A Review of Theory and Criticism*, 2 (July 1984): 36–38; Balfour's claim is that McGann does not finally question the ideology of the aesthetic that de Man seeks to problematize, particularly in the essays collected in *Aesthetic Ideology* (forthcoming from University of Minnesota Press). On this question see also Adorno's *Aesthetische Theorie*, ed. Gretel Adorno and Rolf Tiedemann (Frankfurt: Suhrkamp, 1974; translated as *Aesthetic Theory*, trans. C. Lenhardt [London and Boston: Routledge & Kegan Paul, 1984]). Adorno writes: "Das Fragment ist der Eingriff des Todes ins Werk. Indem er es zerstört, nimmt er den Makel des Scheins von ihm" (537); elliptically translated by Lenhardt: "A fragment is a work that has been tampered with by death" [493]). The editors of Adorno's unfinished opus theorize some of the questions raised by de Man in his preface to *The Rhetoric of Romanticism*: "The problems of a paratactical mode of presentation inherent in the last draft version of *Aesthetic Theory* are objectively determined: they reflect the *position* of thought to objectivity. Adorno's philosophical parataxis hopes to realize what is only a promise in Hegel: the pure inspection of things without any violent *disfiguration* by the subject—a form of thought that helps them articulate their muteness and non-identical essence. What it means to work in earnest with a serial method, Adorno had shown in his analysis of Hölderlin" (497–98; my emphasis). De Man notes in his preface that Hölderlin is the "obvious stumbling block" of his own enterprise (RR, ix).

24. In the context of Blanchot's reading, which argues finally against dialectical or progressive models of consciousness and temporality, de Man writes: "The various forms of negation that had been 'surmounted' as [Mallarmé's] work progressed . . . turn out to be particular expressions of a persistent negative movement that resides in being. We try to protect ourselves against this negative power by inventing stratagems, ruses of language and of thought that hide an irrevocable fall" (BI, 73).

25. Hazlitt's review takes note as well of the arbitrariness, and concomitant violence, of Shelleyan language: "The poem entitled the *Triumph of Life* is in fact a new and terrific *Dance of Death*; but it is thus that Mr. Shelley transposes the appellations of the commonest things, and subsists only in the violence of the contrast" (*The Complete Works of William Hazlitt*, ed. P. P. Howe [London: J. M. Dent, 1933], 273).

26. On the blindness of this violence, cf. the foreword to the first edition of *Blindness and Insight*: "The recurrent pattern that emerges was established in retrospect and any resemblance to preestablished theories of literary interpretation is entirely coincidental or, in the terminology of the book, blind" (vii).

27. On the problematics of the fragment in the literary theory of German romanticism, see Maurice Blanchot, "L'Athenaeum" in *L'Entretien infini* (Paris: Gallimard, 1969), 515–27; translated by Deborah Esch and Ian Balfour in *Studies in Romanticism*, 22 (Summer 1983): 163–72. See also Philippe Lacoue-Labarthe and Jean-Luc Nancy, *L'Absolue littéraire* (Paris: Seuil, 1978).

28. See the account of paraphrase in de Man's foreword to Jacobs, ix. De Man's reading of Benjamin assesses the essay on translation in its polemical context (" 'Conclusions': Walter Benjamin's 'The Task of the Translator' " in RT).

29. De Man indicates the critical importance of Blanchot's argument to the effect that the "act of reading . . . can never be performed by the author on his own writings" (BI, 65).

30. It is, at any rate, a "failure" that defaces the monument, the "monumental dignity of aesthetic values" (RR, 68).

31. Although the "Essay," as noted above, replies not with an answer, but with another posing of the question.

32. Holmes, *Shelley: The Pursuit*, 724. The biographer's account of Shelley's composition of the poem yields to a characterization of its language similar to that often made of de Man's prose: "He wrote it partly on the boat, and partly in his study at night. It is not, like his other poems, in a notebook, but written on a series of loose foolscap sheets, some much folded from being thrust in his pocket. . . . But the motley collection of Italian foolscap suggests that Shelley did not even want to think of himself as writing another serious work: he was just trying out a few ideas. . . . In one sense the poem is like nothing else he had previously written. It has a hardness of style and a lack of personal emotion which is unique among his writings: it is aloof and almost disparaging, and falls on the reader's imagination with a cold, clear light like moonlight" (717).

33. For a reading of "the *double* affirmation seen (and remarked upon) in the syntax of triumph as *triomphe-de*, triumph *of* and triumph *over*," see Jacques Derrida, "Living On," trans. James Hulbert, in *Deconstruction and Criticism* (New York: Seabury, 1979), 75–176.

34. See the conclusion to the late essay on "Anthropomorphism and Trope in the Lyric": "True 'mourning' is less deluded. The most *it* can do is to allow for non-comprehension and enumerate non-anthropomorphic, non-elegiac, non-celebratory, non-lyrical, non-poetic, that is to say, prosaic, or, better, *historical* modes of language power" (RR, 262).

Lurid Figures
Neil Hertz

This essay is about a characteristic — and characteristically unsettling — aspect of Paul de Man's writing, his particular way of combining analysis and pathos, of blending technical arguments about operations of rhetoric (often presented in an abstract, seemingly affectless idiom) with language — his own and that of the texts he cites — whose recurrent figures are strongly marked and whose themes are emotively charged, not to say melodramatic.

Take, as an initial example, the concluding paragraphs of his discussion of Kleist (RR, 288–90). De Man has been commenting on the description of the puppets in "Über das Marionettentheater," treating it as a "model . . . of the text as a system of turns and deviations, as a system of tropes" (RR, 285), and stressing the "machinelike, mechanical predictability" of the puppets' (or tropes') motion. De Man had begun his essay by quoting Schiller's "image of a beautiful society [as] a well-executed English dance, composed of many complicated figures and turns" (RR, 263); now he recalls that opening citation, contrasting its edifying talk of the harmonious integration of individuals, each respecting the freedom of the others, with what he finds in Kleist's text: a mechanical dance "which is also a dance of death and mutilation," puppets "suspended in dead passivity," "an English technician able to build such perfect mechanical legs that a mutilated man will be able to dance with them in Schiller-like perfection." This in turn reminds de Man of the "sheer monstrosity" of "the eyeless philosopher Saunderson in Diderot's *Lettre sur les aveugles*," who is himself, de Man notes, like Kleist's dancing invalid, "one more victim in a long series of mutilated bodies that attend on the progress of enlightened self-knowledge, a series that includes Wordsworth's mute country-dwellers and blind city-beggars." At this point, having culled and clustered this lurid bouquet, not willfully and not without textual justification, but certainly deliberately, de Man draws himself and his readers up short:

> But one should avoid the pathos of an imagery of bodily mutilation and not forget that we are dealing with textual models, not with the historical and political systems that are their correlate. The disarticulation produced by tropes is primarily a disarticulation of meaning; it attacks semantic units such as words and sentences.

We are warned, too late, to avoid a pathos that has been placed, unavoidable, in our paths. Moreoever, should we vow to be more alert in the future, the task is made no easier by the remaining sentences of de Man's essay, in which the grim connotations of words like "dismemberment," "trap," and "deadly" are inextricable from de Man's own concluding formulations. When he writes of "the dismemberment of language by the power of the letter," one cannot say, "But of course he means 'dismemberment' only figuratively"; nor can one say, reassuringly, of the essay's last phrase, that the dance it speaks of as "the ultimate trap, as unavoidable as it is deadly" isn't *really* "deadly." The prose has been working precisely to forestall any such assurance. It is that textual work—the forms it takes and its consequences—that I propose to explore in these pages.

I shall organize my remarks around a reading of the ten pages in *The Rhetoric of Romanticism* entitled "Wordsworth and the Victorians," a text that seems to have been intended to serve as a preface to a reissue of F. W. H. Myers's 1881 volume in the English Men of Letters series.[1] A brief occasional piece, it stands in something of the same relation to the essays that surround it ("Autobiography As De-Facement" and "Shelley Disfigured") as the talk called "Kant's Materialism" does to the longer and more polished "Phenomenality and Materiality in Kant,"[2] that is, it reads like either an intense trial run or a rapid glance over hard-won ground, both sketchier and more abrupt than the other two essays in its deployment of similar arguments and figures. It is an intriguing text, and I intend to move through it slowly, glossing its language by juxtaposing it with other writings of de Man's. I chose it partly for its brevity and informality, partly because it focuses on two key "figural terms" (RR, 92) in Wordsworth's poetry—"hangs" and "face"—commonplace words that, along with their more abstract synonyms—"suspends" and "figure"—are also persistent and central in de Man's work. "Wordsworth and the Victorians" thus offers an economical way of engaging the problem of the relation of technical and pathetic language in de Man, for the problem inheres in his recurrent use of concepts like "suspension" and "disfiguration" in puzzling (and sometimes disturbing) proximity to images of hanging or of physical defacement such as those we've just noticed in the Kleist essay. We shall want to look into the necessity behind this idiosyncratic punning.

"Wordsworth and the Victorians" falls conveniently into two halves. Its first five pages present, in highly condensed form, what de Man takes to be "the canonical reading which has dominated the interpretation of Wordsworth from Victorian to modern times" (RR, 85). De Man is prepared to acknowledge the differences between the ethically oriented commentaries of nineteenth-century critics and the phenomenologically informed close readings of contemporary Wordsworthians, but he would minimize the effect of these differences, stressing instead the ways in which accounts of Wordsworth continue to be dominated by moral and religious categories. De Man presents the contemporary version of the canonical sympathetically, but adds a decisive reservation ("And yet, the very alacrity with which Wordsworth's major texts respond to this approach should make one wary" (RR, 88), then goes on in the essay's last five pages to offer an alternative reading, centered on the "Blessed Babe" lines in *The Prelude*.

Before looking at the alternative, however, it is worth pausing at certain points in de Man's characterization of the canonical reading and noticing his way of positioning his own work in relation to it. He grants the Victorians at least an oblique awareness of what he calls "a certain enigmatic aspect of Wordsworth" or "the truly puzzling element in Wordsworth," and he locates that awareness in their worrying the question of whether what Wordsworth wrote was to be thought of as poetry or philosophy, a concern he believes is prompted by their wish to keep the two modes of discourse clearly distinct. Why should they be kept apart? Because, de Man explains, "to couple such power of seduction with such authority is to tempt fate itself":

> Hence the urge to protect, as the most pressing of moral imperatives, this borderline between both modes of discourse. Many poets can easily be enlisted in the service of this cause but others are more recalcitrant, though not necessarily because they are formally involved with philosophical systems. Wordsworth, rather than Coleridge, is a case in point. It is as if his language came from a region in which the most carefully drawn distinctions between analytic rigor and poetic persuasion are no longer preserved, at no small risk to either. Trying to state why this is so is to suggest an alternative to the canonical reading which has dominated the interpretation of Wordsworth from Victorian to modern times. Some contemporary writing on Wordsworth begins to break with this tradition or, to be more precise, begins to reveal the break that has always been hidden in it. (RR, 85)

Notice that these lines are about an epistemological threat figured in spatial terms, the possibility that the "borderline between [two] modes of discourse" will be blurred, a threat that is carried, like a virus, by language issuing from a "region" where those borderlines, certain "most carefully drawn distinctions," do not exist. But notice, too, that there is a whiff of the oedipal triangle in that image of the dangers readers face when confronting poetry's "power of seduction" coupled with the "authority" of philosophy: the danger that prompts the urge to reestablish clear demarcating lines would seem to be the threatened collapse of that triangle into a more archaic structure, at once cognitively unsettling and menacing to the integrity of the preoedipal subject. But is it the subject who is being threatened here? Not explicitly: What is at risk is the integrity of modes of discourse, the analytic rigor of the one, the persuasive power of the other. I have exaggerated the salience (and the immediate pertinence) of a psychoanalytic reading in order to point out the brief appearance of a drama of subjectivity within a discourse, de Man's, which is committed to questioning its privilege as an interpretive category.

I call attention to these shifts in idiom and connotation because the question of finding appropriate language is precisely what de Man is discussing here, just as he is necessarily engaged in the business of finding appropriate language himself. His account of the tradition of Wordsworth criticism is a story of repeated attempts to define that "enigmatic aspect" of his poetry, a dangerous "something" that philosophy, presumably, "is supposed to shelter us from." This remained "unnamed and undefined" by the Victorians, but the "effort of all subsequent Wordsworth interpreters has been, often with the poet's own assistance, to domesticate it by giving it at least a recognizable content" (RR, 86). The climax of de Man's summary of contemporary criticism—a climax followed immediately by that deflating "And yet . . . "—is his tribute to a powerfully apt, if recuperative, act of identification: "The threat from which we were to be sheltered and consoled is now identified as a condition of consciousness. Maiming, death, the wear and tear of mutability are the predicaments of 'the unimaginable touch of time' and time, in this version of Wordsworth, is the very substance of the self-reflecting, recollecting mind." A lurid thematics, to be sure, but once conceived as a subject's response to the real, to the "touch of time" rather than to "a disarticulation of meaning," it loses the added sting of incomprehensibility and becomes strangely consoling, a "triumph of consciousness over its ever-threatening undoing" (RR, 87).

What would it mean to "break with this tradition"? First, it would mean resisting the "urge" to name "the threat" at any cost. More specifically, it would mean acknowledging the provenance of Wordsworth's language as a region of *verbal* indistinction, but it would also mean, de Man insists, in an effort to "be more precise," revealing "the break that has always been hidden" within the canonical reading. That juxtaposition of figures is slightly puzzling: on the one hand, de Man would confront "a region in which the most carefully drawn distinctions between analytic rigor and poetic persuasion are no longer preserved," that is, he would risk a dissolution of difference; on the other hand, his break with the canonical would "reveal the break that has always been hidden in it," a residual, if minimal, difference in what had appeared to be a seamlessly coherent critical position. But where exactly does the threat lie: in the loss of clear distinctions? Or in the discovery of a hidden and irreducible difference? The puzzle is not to be brushed aside by insisting that, in context, these apparently contradictory figures apply to quite different critical acts: that one is about reading Wordsworth, the other about aligning oneself with previous readings. De Man's prose works to conflate those activities into one thing called "reading," and to characterize reading as invariably entangling the reader in alternating apprehensions of difference and indifference.

We would do better by looking at some other places in de Man's writing where the image of a hidden break or flaw appears, in "Shelley Disfigured," for example, where de Man claims that a reading of *The Triumph of Life* "exposes the wound of a fracture that lies hidden in all texts" (RR, 120), or in the essay entitled "The Task of the Translator," where, interpreting Walter Benjamin, de Man writes:

> All these activities—critical philosophy, literary theory, history—
> resemble each other in the fact that they do not resemble that from
> which they derive. But they are all intralinguistic: they relate to what in
> the original belongs to language, and not to meaning as an extralinguis-
> tic correlate susceptible of paraphrase and imitation. They disarticulate,
> they undo the original, they reveal that the original was always already
> disarticulated. They reveal that their failure, which seems to be due to
> the fact that they are secondary in relation to the original, reveals an es-
> sential failure, an essential disarticulation which was already there in
> the original. They kill the original by discovering that the original was
> already dead. They read the original from the perspective of a pure lan-
> guage (*reine Sprache*), a language that would be entirely freed of the il-
> lusion of meaning—pure form if you want; and in doing so they bring
> to light a dismembrance, a de-canonization which was already there in
> the original from the beginning. (RT, 84)

Here the force of "dismembrance" (like the disarticulation of Kleist's puppets or his amputees) or of "de-canonization" (like the effort to break with a tradition of criticism) is given a familiar deconstructive turn: its activity discovers a disarticulation always already there. What these lines add to that (by now) reassuring notion—for anything heard often enough is a comfort—is the discomfiting, because seemingly gratuitous, violence of construing "disarticulation" as murder and murder as, paradoxically, "discovering that the original was already dead." That is, what they add is, fleetingly, the pathos of uncertain agency. A subject is conjured up—perhaps a killer, perhaps only the discoverer of the corpse—who can serve as a locus of vacillation: did I do it? Or had it already been done? This particular version of undecidability—between the activity or passivity, the guilt or innocence of a subject—must be added to those already adduced, between the original and the secondary, the totalized and the fragmented, between difference and indistinctness, if the "threat" associated with Wordsworth's poetry, or the necessity of breaking with its canonical reading, is to be understood.

When de Man refers to Wordsworth as "a poet of sheer language" (RR, 92), the phrase combines one of his preferred honorific adjectives[3] with an echo of Benjamin's "*reine Sprache.*" And de Man's further remarks on that expression are helpful in characterizing the "region" he associates with Wordsworth's poetry. After noting how, in "The Task of the Translator," Benjamin "put[s] the original in motion, to de-canonize [it]," de Man adds:

This movement of the original is a wandering, an *errance*, a kind of permanent exile if you wish, but it is not really an exile, for there is no homeland, nothing from which one has been exiled. Least of all is there something like a *reine Sprache*, a pure language, which does not exist except as a permanent disjunction which inhabits all languages as such, including and especially the language one calls one's own. (RT, 92)

In Kenneth Burke's terms, this is the Scene that serves as background, or container, for the Agent we have just observed, a subject ambivalently guilty and innocent, alternately present in and absent from de Man's discourse. Because of a "permanent disjunction which inhabits all languages as such"—the "enigmatic aspect" or "puzzling element" interpreters of Wordsworth seek to come to terms with—we are led to figures like "homeland" or "pure language" or to a notion like that of a language to "call one's own," a mother tongue, in an effort to delineate the contour and sketch in the contents of that "region." But container and thing contained are unstable figures here: language would seem to "come from" a region at one moment (RR, 85); at another it is language that serves as the space "inhabited" by a disjunction (RT, 92). What is clear is that the "region" is sometimes registered as a "shelter," sometimes as a "threat," and, as de Man points out, it is common to confuse the two: "The strategy of denegation which calls a threat a shelter in the hope of thus laying it to rest is all too familiar" (RR, 86). Given this "predicament," we can perhaps best approach the nature of the "threat" by dwelling for a while on the word "shelter."

"We think we are at ease in our own language," de Man remarks, still glossing Benjamin on translation. "We feel a coziness, a familiarity, a shelter in the language we call our own, in which we think we are not alienated" (RT, 84). "Shelter" may have entered de Man's lexicon by way of Heidegger or Wordsworth, or both;[4] it remained there as a constant resource, recurring throughout *Allegories of Reading* and *The Rhetoric of Romanticism*. Often, for obvious reasons, it is paired with "threat." More interesting, for our purposes, are two other linkages, implicit in the sentence I've just quoted, one bringing "shelter" into relation with language, particularly figural language, the other drawing its connotations of "coziness" and "familiarity" off in the direction of the erotic or seductive. "All remains implicit, inward, sheltered in the unsuspected nuances of common speech" (RR, 87): de Man is here characterizing "the miracle of Wordsworth's figural diction." A more surprising, because unidiomatic, usage occurs in a discussion of

Rousseau: "The threat remains sheltered behind its metaphoricity" (AR, 297). One would have expected a threat to be "hidden," and its potential victim to be the one who was or was not "sheltered" from it. But the possibility of a reversal of the menacing and the menaced is precisely de Man's point: we may wish now to look back at those "unsuspected nuances of common speech" with a more apprehensive glance: why that suspicious word "unsuspected"? Have we been led to mistake a threat for a shelter there, too? If we have, it was because we have been lured or "tempted" or "seduced" by Wordsworth's figural use of common speech into a scene of familiarity, a family scene. "Shelter," for de Man, always blends the architectonic with the "familial."[5] Reading *The Birth of Tragedy*, for example, he can call attention to the combined attractiveness of "the seductive power of a genetic narrative," with its promise of rendering things intelligible by means of a model of natural descent, and the "rhetorical complicity" generated by the narrator's manner: "we are guaranteed intellectual safety as long as we remain within the sheltering reach of his voice. The same seductive tone safeguards the genetic continuity throughout the text" (AR, 94). Nor is it fortuitous that a mode of explanation (a genetic narrative) and a mode of address (a seductive tone) should be found working in tandem here: both draw their force from the pathos of the familial.

But it is not your average family that de Man is concerned with, either in the texts he chooses to discuss or in his own figurative language. Or rather, it is not an oedipally triangulated family, with child, mother, and father occupying relatively stable positions. Instead, the configurations that interest him, and which he associates with all acts of reading and understanding, are variations of the specular.[6] In privileged texts like the "Blessed Babe" lines in *The Prelude*, or in phrases like that describing the merging of poetry and philosophy into a daunting combination of seduction and authority, he would seem to be attending to narcissistic or "borderline" structures of the sort Julia Kristeva has recently explored, structures that play out the earliest exchanges between infant and mother.[7] Hence the pathos of the familial, when it appears in de Man's writing, is often concerned with the maternal. The central argument of "Wordsworth and the Victorians" takes as its text lines celebrating "the Babe, / Nurs'd in his Mother's arms . . . ," a passage that provides de Man with an occasion for some of his own boldest statements. But before engaging that "alternative reading" I want to look at a much earlier reference to the maternal, a bizarre footnote de Man appended to a discussion of Yeats in his dissertation.

In a reading of Yeats's career that was startling in 1960 and has, if anything, gained in persuasive power in the years since, de Man sees the poet's development as generated by the tension between two kinds of figurative language, mimetic images of natural things and what Yeats came to call emblems, that is, images that had their meaning, in Yeat's phrase, "by a traditional and not by a natural right" (RR, 165). Yeats's mature manner, in this account, "is a tenuous equilibrium, in itself an extraordinary feat of style and rhetoric, but no reconciliation [of image with emblem], not even a dialectic." But such an equilibrium was bound to be short-lived, and the poet's "fundamental bewilderment," according to de Man, prompted a thematic crisis in his late work, a crisis played out primarily around the theme of erotic love (RR, 204–6). De Man's understanding of this crisis requires him to dispute the canonical reading of Yeats as a celebrator of Eros and to document instead the poet's "most negative conception of the pleasures of sex" (RR, 217), a valorization that extends to the "natural seduction" of images as well: the devaluation of sexual love is the thematic sign of the drive to realize an unequivocally emblematic poetry. In the course of establishing this reading, de Man cites a number of poems that render desire not as a natural craving for satisfaction but as a desire for the destruction of desire, for postcoital stillness or death, then comments:

> One begins to understand, perhaps all too well (though one should beware not to confuse ontology and psychoanalysis), Yeats's interest in the castration myth of Attis. The rejection of all feminine and maternal elements of sex,[115] brings to mind Mallarmé's *Hérodiade*. (RR, 231)[8]

Note 115, in its entirety, reads as follows:

> 115. To the point of a kind of matricidal indifference:
>
> > What matter if the knave
> > That most could pleasure you,
> > The children that he gave,
> > Are somewhere sleeping like a top
> > Under a marble flag?
> >   ("Those Dancing Days are Gone," *Var.*, p. 525)

The initial problem is that it is hard to read those lines — or the rest of the ballad — as "matricidal." The singer is certainly indifferent to the old woman's displeasure: this stanza begins "Curse as you may I sing it through; / What matter if the knave . . . etc." And the woman is old, and her lover and her children are dead. But is it obvious that being forced to listen to these bitter truths will be the death of her as well? Still more puzzling is the expression itself, "matricidal indifference": it sounds at once crabbed and hyperbolical, and it arrives in this text with the same air of gratuitous violence (and some of the same thematic resonance) as the sentence in de Man's Benjamin essay I remarked on earlier: "They kill the original by discovering that the original was already dead." I took that sentence to be expressive of a pathos of agency, signaling the appearance in de Man's text (for however brief a stay) of a fantasmic subject, ambivalently active and passive, guilty and innocent, murderous and/or bereft. Something similar seems at work here: a passage to the limit, a rejection of the maternal carried "to the point of a kind of" matricide, produces a lurid figure—the dead mother—who functions as the disfigured specular double of the subject of a pathos, the poet as Attis, "castrated before he can return to Cybele, the mother of the gods" (RR, 201). How might this have come about? By what necessity would a subject, lurid or not, appear in this text?

De Man's mention of Attis here alludes to a moment in his argument some thirty pages earlier where he is considering Yeats's attempts to resolve the tension between image and emblem in his poetry. One recurrent figure, the tree, would seem to emblematize the tension itself; de Man quotes a stanza from the aptly named "Vacillation":

> A tree there is that from its topmost bough
> Is half all glittering flame and half all green
> Abounding foliage moistened with the dew;
> And half is half and yet is all the scene;
> And half and half consume what they renew,
> And he that Attis' image hangs between
> That staring fury and the blind lush leaf
> May not know what he knows, but knows not grief.

Aligning "foliage" with the natural image, "flame" with the emblem, de Man notes that "a synthesis is suggested by Attis' image or, more precisely, by the poetic act of hanging Attis' image between the two halves," then goes on to show how the synthesis is only apparent: what we have instead is "one more veiled statement of the absolute superiority of the emblem over the image" (RR, 201). The slight fine-tuning of his observation, his noting that it is not Attis's image but ("more precisely") the poetic act of hanging it on the tree that makes the difference, prefigures de Man's later explicit (and explicitly theorized) interest in the distinction between the meaning and the performance of a text. But it also exhibits how slippery the category of performance is, how easily "the poetic act" can be displaced, by an anthropomorphizing gesture, into the poet's act. De Man might even have pointed out an ambiguity in Yeats's stanza that goes along with the general drift of his argument: the phrasing of "he that Attis' image hangs between" rearranges the normal sequence of subject, transitive verb, and direct object so that the line allows a glimpse of the poet hanging on the tree: "he that, Attis' image, hangs between . . . " Is the stanza about an image or an action or a poet, a figure or a performance or a "figure"?

Moreover, de Man's most general statement about what it is like to read Yeats locates "the reader," that figure, in a similarly dangling position. Faced with the "tenuous equilibrium" of Yeats's style, "the reader vacillates between two extremes . . . the tendency to give in to the natural seduction of the images . . . or, on the other hand, the tendency to read them as if they were esoteric puzzles" (RR, 204). But the natural seduction of images is, as de Man will argue years later, a seduction into identification, into the positing of a specular subject as the reader's double, a "poet" behind the "poetic action."[9] Once Attis's image, the poetic act, and the vacillating reader are thus aligned, it is possible for the "threat" of Attis's castration to be communicated down the line to the poet and on to the reader, in this case de Man. The pathos of matricide would then mark the excess of force with which one reader is swung away from "the natural seduction" of Yeats's figurative language and released from suspended vacillation. In the vocabulary de Man would later adopt, it is a gesture of disfiguration, at once an insight into the transferential dynamics of reading and a conjuring up of what is, in one sense, an unmotivated pathos.

De Man would have us register this pathos but not be quite taken in by it: hence the parenthetical warning not to confuse ontology and psychoanalysis.[10] But, like the admonition to "avoid the pathos of an imagery of bodily mutilation" we began by noticing in the Kleist essay, this warning is hard to heed: at best—and this is, if not de Man's point in issuing such warnings, at least one consequence of our reading them—we can acknowledge the "predicament" they place us in. That is, we can acknowledge that a tug-of-war between "analytic rigor" and "poetic persuasion" is unavoidable in each act of reading/writing—in Yeats's, in de Man's, in our own—and acknowledge it all the more readily when the felt pressure of some other reader's pathos, here the imposition of the words "matricidal indifference," seems at once so palpable and so gratuitous. Whatever else "matricidal indifference" represents it is certainly, and to begin with, a forced reading of "Those Dancing Days are Gone," and it is by no means the only moment of interpretive violence a reader of de Man will encounter.[11] It is this question of forcing that I would like to engage now, in returning to "Wordsworth and the Victorians."

De Man bases his "alternative reading" (RR, 88–92) on the results of two exceptional earlier investigations of Wordsworthian "key words," Empson's account of "sense," which showed that "it is impossible . . . to make sense out of" the ways "sense" functions in *The Prelude*, and Wordsworth's own "technical rhetorical analysis" of "hangs," which displayed "a remarkably consistent pattern" of meaning in uses of that term. De Man notes the difference between the two analyses, one ending, to its credit, in "near-total chaos," the other in a "perfectly coherent" account of a semantic field, and, noting too that " 'hangs' is, by Wordsworth's own avowal, *the* exemplary metaphor for metaphor, for figuration in general," he is led to conclude that "the figural scheme that a philosophy of consciousness allows one to reach" is insufficient to account for all operations of Wordsworth's language.

The linking of hanging to figuration to intelligibility,[12] as well as a drive to exhaust and move beyond that cluster of concepts, is characteristic of de Man's work in and after *Allegories of Reading*. It is nowhere more explicit than in the essay that reads as a more developed companion piece to "Wordsworth and the Victorians," "Shelley Disfigured," most particularly in de Man's analysis of the sequence in *The Triumph of Life* that narrates Rousseau's encounter with the feminine "shape all light." In this poem, de Man observes, it is the shape that serves as "the model of figuration in general," for the ways in which "the seduction of the figure . . . creates an illusion of meaning." Hence it allows itself to be read, finally, as figuring "the figurality of all signification" (RR, 115–16). It is represented as "hovering" or "glimmering" with "seductive grace" in "near-miraculous suspension" (RR, 108–9) throughout a scene that, as it unfolds, "makes this knot, by which knowledge, oblivion and desire hang suspended, into an articulated sequence of events that demands interpretation" (RR, 106–7).

De Man's response is twofold: he will read the sequence rhetorically, as an allegory of figuration, and offer conceptual formulations of the sort I have just cited; but he is bound to respond in another idiom as well, as he blends citation and interpretive paraphrase into a narration of the action and pathos of Shelley's lines. So he will gloss the "disfiguration" of the shape as the active forgetting, within the language of the poem, of "the events this language in fact performs" (RR, 118). But he will also find "disfiguration" exemplified within the poem's narrative as a "drowning" of the shape when it "traverses the mirror [of the stream's surface] and goes under" (RR, 114), "to finally sink away 'below the watery floor' " (RR, 119). De Man is unaccustomedly emphatic in his insistence on this version of the shape's disappearance or death: "There is no doubt that, when we again meet the shape (ll. 425ff.) it is no longer gliding along the river but drowned, Ophelia-like, below the surface of the water" (RR, 111). Yet just such a doubt may persist: de Man has imposed his interpretation on lines that contain no demonstrable images of drowning; rather they offer Rousseau's account of the gradual fading of the "shape all light," overwhelmed by the blaze of a "new Vision":

> "so on my sight
> Burst a new Vision never seen before. –
>
> "And the fair shape waned in the coming light
> As veil by veil the silent splendour drops
> From Lucifer, amid the chrysolite
>
> "Of sunrise. . . .
>
> "So knew I in that light's severe excess
> The presence of that shape which on the stream
> Moved, as I moved along the wilderness,
>
> "More dimly than a day appearing dream,
> The ghost of a forgotten form of sleep,
> A light from Heaven whose half extinguished beam

"Through the sick day in which we wake to weep
Glimmers, forever sought, forever lost. —
So did that shape its obscure tenour keep

"Beside my path, as silent as a ghost;
But the new Vision, and its cold bright car,
With savage music, stunning music, crost

"The forest . . . [13]

If we ask how de Man could have read a drowning into these lines, and ask it not rhetorically, as if to deplore a blatant error ("How could he?!") but ask it seriously, we are led to the drowned body of the poet himself, which if it cannot be located within Shelley's lines nevertheless "is present in the margin of the last manuscript page and has become an inseparable part of the poem" (RR, 120). "Shelley Disfigured" concludes by insisting that our knowledge of the poet's death is not knowledge of an irrelevant anecdote, whose poignancy can be surreptitiously counted on while ostensibly ignored in our dealings with the poem. Rather, de Man would include the death in the series of disfigurations he finds both within the poem and, necessarily, in any subsequent writing about it. The argument is strong and unsentimental, and depends on a subtly articulated meditation that has been developing throughout the essay, a progressive raising of the stakes of interpretation that turns on the question of how we are to understand the disappearance of the "shape all light." I can't hope to reproduce either the analytic care or the persuasive force of that argument, but I need to roughly indicate its path and some of its turns, for it is backward along that path that what de Man would call the disfiguring figure of drowning is communicated from Shelley to the shape.

The moment when de Man declares that "there is no doubt" that the shape is drowned, is, as it happens, precisely the moment when he is about to stop taking Shelley's images at face value: the "chain of metaphorical transformations can be understood, up to this point," he writes, "without transposition into a vocabulary that would not be that of their own referents." But if we are to understand why the shape is "allowed to wane," he argues, we are obliged to "read in a non-phenomenal way," that is, to resist the seductions of the "representational code of the text" (RR, 115) and instead to construe Shelley's language as offering, allegorically, an account of its own workings (RR, 111–13). That account, as de Man reconstructs it in the last dozen pages of his essay, has about it the intellectual excitement of a compressed survey of the path his own research had taken him on: from a concern with the ways figurative language can unite "perception and cognition undisturbed by the possibly disruptive mediation of its own figuration" (RR, 112) to a deepened understanding of two other disruptive instances — that of the "play of the signifier" (the "literal and material aspects of language") with its power to "undo the representational and iconic function of figuration" (RR, 113–14), and that of the performative aspect of language, which he refers to as "the positional power of language considered by and in itself," or again as "the senseless power of positional language" (RR, 115–17). It is this latter power alone, the power of the performative, that de Man finds capable of accounting for the disappearance of the shape. He notes the abruptness with which one visionary scene replaces another in *The Triumph of Life*, as though the "previous occupants of the narrative space [were] expelled by decree, by the sheer power of utterance, and consequently at once forgotten," and reads the poem as a fragment of a potentially endless story of disfiguration, "since the knowledge of the language's performative power is itself a figure in its own right and, as such, bound to repeat the disfiguration of metaphor as Shelley is bound to repeat the aberration of Rousseau in what appears to be a more violent mode" (RR, 120).

That last sentence offers a clue to de Man's conversion of the shape's waning into a drowning: it is his repetition of the poem's disfigurations "in what appears to be a more violent mode." But how would that play itself out? The language with which de Man works Shelley's "actual death" into his reading is instructive:

> At this point, figuration and cognition are actually interrupted by an event which shapes the text but which is not present in its represented or articulated meaning. It may seem a freak of chance to have a text thus molded by an actual occurrence, yet the reading of *The Triumph of Life* establishes that this mutilated textual model exposes the wound of a fracture that lies hidden in all texts. If anything, this text is more rather than less typical than texts that have not been thus truncated. The rhythmical interruptions that mark off the successive episodes of the narrative are not new moments of cognition but literal events textually reinscribed by a delusive act of figuration or forgetting.
>
> In Shelley's absence, the task of thus reinscribing the disfiguration now devolves entirely on the reader. The final test of reading, in *The Triumph of Life*, depends on how one reads the textuality of this event, how one disposes of Shelley's body. (RR, 121)

How has de Man, as reader, performed "the task of . . . reinscribing the disfiguration"; that is, what has he done with Shelley's body? He has indeed, as he says all readers are bound to do, "monumentalized" it by burying it in its own text, but with a difference. His discussion of the performative power of language has allowed him to name as "events" interruptions within the poem as well as the "actual" event that interrupted the writing of the poem. He can then not merely analogize these events in general, but insist on the particular analogy of the extratextual drowning with another interruption, the disappearance of the shape, by delusively figuring the latter *as a drowning*. This act has the effect of repositioning Shelley's body at the point in the poem where the shape "goes under," where meaning yields to "sheer" performance, at the site of "the wound of a fracture that lies hidden in all texts." Shelley's death thus can serve as a means of "exposing" a death that has been there all along: it is like saying that one kills the original by discovering that the original is already dead. The difficult but powerful argument of the essay, which allows de Man to read the shape's disappearance as an allegorical gesture unmasking the "figurality of all signification," is accomplished in language that reinscribes the drowned shape and the drowned Shelley in a specular structure, paired with each other like the imagined victim of Yeats's matricidal indifference and the figure of the castrated Attis. Another way of putting this would be to say that de Man has shown how and why readers cannot help forcing their texts, but (or rather: *and*) this awareness in no way prevents him from forcing his text.

"Wordsworth and the Victorians" follows the same trajectory, and exhibits the same bifurcation, once de Man moves beyond the word "hangs" and turns his attention to another key Wordsworthian term, "face." By dwelling on the meaning of "face," in Wordsworth's text and in his own, he will produce, in brief, the alternative reading he had promised, as well as a compelling sketch of the alternative poetics he lays out more fully in "Shelley Disfigured." But he will do so by means of a series of interpretations that culminate in another strange, delusive act of figuration, a surfacing of the specular figures buried in the longer essay.

The difficulty of de Man's discussion of "face," and of the analysis of the "Blessed Babe" lines that it draws on, lies partly in the way the word itself shifts, in de Man's usage, between its ordinary meaning and an idiosyncratic, non-phenomenal sense, partly in the puzzles about priority and dependency that any speculation on beginnings is bound to raise. De Man takes the lines as "Wordsworth's essay on the origins of language as poetic language" (RR, 90); that is, he takes them as seeking to map that "region" where poetry originates by offering a genetic narrative of its birth, a narrative that de Man must then read allegorically. Wordsworth presents a sequence of causes and effects, claiming that they are merely his "best conjectures," acknowledging that what he would describe has, properly speaking, "no beginning"; and de Man retells Wordsworth's story within the frame of his own poetics, his own understanding of what comes before what, what depends on what. The two stories both sustain and interfere with one another.

"Face," for de Man, can only be thought in relation to "language": for "face" is not just "the locus of speech, the necessary condition for the existence of articulated language" (RR, 89), it is also the product of language, ineluctably figurative. "Man can address and face other men, within life or beyond the grave, because he has a face, but he has a face only because he partakes of a mode of discourse that is neither entirely natural nor entirely human." When Wordsworth writes "my mind hath look'd / Upon the speaking face of earth and heaven," de Man glosses that as designating a "prior encounter," a visual exchange that underwrites later verbal exchanges: "one can speak only because one can look upon a mode of speech which is not quite our own" (RR, 90). It is important to notice that the encounter is with a speaking face that is not, however, that of another human: it is with a face that figures "language."[14] The difficulty of the interpretation arises from the fact that the lines de Man goes on to consider, and which must bear on this encounter if they don't exactly illustrate it, are about what we may take to be the commonplace, if highly charged, face-to-face encounter of mother and infant. I cite them in full, before turning back to de Man's reading:

> Bless'd the infant Babe,
> (For with my best conjecture I would trace
> The progress of our being) blest the Babe,
> Nurs'd in his Mother's arms, the Babe who sleeps
> Upon his Mother's breast, who, when his soul
> Claims manifest kindred with an earthly soul,
> Doth gather passion from his Mother's eye!
> Such feelings pass into his torpid life
> Like an awakening breeze, and hence his mind
> Even in the first trial of its powers
> Is prompt and watchful, eager to combine
> In one appearance, all the elements
> And parts of the same object, else detach'd
> And loth to coalesce.
>
> (1805 *Prelude*, 2.237–50)

Is the child looking at "language" or at his mother? At both, de Man would say; or rather he would point out that the question was badly put: "language" is not an object; "language" is already there in the looking. Hence he stresses the child's "claim of manifest kindred" as a moment of abrupt performance, an "active verbal deed . . . not given in the nature of things" that initiates the subsequent process of exchange, an exchange that allows the child to construct a widening and increasingly meaningful perceptual field through successive acts of figuration. The first of these acts is the imposition of a figure, the producing of a "face," the coordination of visual details into "a larger, total entity," which serves as the model for all further processes of totalization. I shall quote de Man's analysis of this sequence at length, because it has its own abruptnesses that are worth attending to:

> The power and the structure of this act are described in sufficient detail
> to give meaning to the by itself enigmatic phrase: to "gather passion."
> The "gathering" is a process of exchange by which the eye is "com-
> bin[d] / In one appearance . . . " with "all the elements / And parts of
> the same object, else detach'd / and loth to coalesce. . . . " Without
> having to evoke the technical vocabulary of associationist psychology
> which is used here, *it is clear* that what is being described is the possi-
> bility of inscribing the eye, which is nothing by itself, into a larger, to-

tal entity, the "same object" which, *in the internal logic of the text, can only be the face*, the face as the combination of parts which the mind, working like a synecdochical trope, can lay claim to—thus opening the way to a process of totalization which, in the span of a few lines, can grow to encompass everything, "*All* objects through *all* intercourse of sense." Language originates with the ability of the eye to establish the contour, the borderline, the surface which allows things to exist in the identity of the kinship of their distinction from other things. (RR, 91; my emphasis except for the *alls*)

The phrases I've italicized indicate the urgency with which de Man would insist on this reading, even though its central claim is an intuitively plausible one: that the "object" constructed by the child "in the first trial of its powers" should be the mother's face, and that its own having a face will be an effect of that construction, would suit contemporary gestalt theorists, or partisans of the mirror stage, as well as eighteenth-century associationists. Nevertheless there is a tension between the canonical reading and de Man's nonphenomenal alternative: the signs of strain can be located in his gloss on "gathering." The image of an eye "gathering passion" need not be as enigmatic as he would have it. Earlier in *The Prelude* one can find a similar figure, one that resonates with these lines on the babe at the breast, for it links seeing and sucking:

> yet I have stood,
> Even while my eye has mov'd o'er three long leagues
> Of shining water, gathering, as it seem'd,
> Through every hair-breadth of that field of light,
> New pleasure, like a bee among the flowers.
> (1805 *Prelude*, 1.604–608)

De Man had remarked on how, in the "Blessed Babe" passage, the word " 'eye' . . . is prominent enough to displace 'breast' where one would most naturally expect it" (RR, 90), and it is precisely the reader's natural expectation that he would thwart, by insisting on the displacement and suppressing the possibility that the eye's "gathering passion," like its "gathering pleasure," is a scopic analogue of nursing. Hence he comments on "gather" but not on "passion," and, by eliding the next lines ("Such feelings pass into his torpid life / Like an awakening breeze, and hence his mind . . . ") he can telescope Wordsworth's account of the progress of consciousness. The totalizing activity, as Wordsworth describes it, is a *result* of the passage of feelings into the child's torpid life: de Man omits the "hence" and relocates synecdochical totalization back at the onset of the process, almost contemporaneous with the initiating "claim." That interpretation is what allows him to conclude in this fashion:

"Face" then, in this passage, not unlike the earlier "hangs," designates the dependence of any perception or "eye" on the totalizing power of language. It heralds this dependency as "the first / Poetic spirit of our human life." The possibility of any contact between mind and nature depends on this spirit manifested by and in language.

The child hangs at the mother's breast, the child depends on her, its sense of having a face depends on her having a face: but it is not that "dependency" that is being repeatedly evoked in these sentences. It is rather the logical dependence of perception and cognition on figurative language—on the figure of an outlined surface, a field or a face—that is stressed, and stressed at the expense of a more conventional intersubjective reading of the passage: the words "Mother" and- "Babe" (which until now have only appeared within quotation marks in de Man's text) now disappear altogether. The characters in de Man's story of origins are named "eye" and "face" and "language."

By insisting so forcibly on the difference between the two readings, by endorsing whatever it was that led Wordsworth to substitute "eye" for "breast," for example, de Man is pointing to a differentiating force already at work, a "wound of a fracture" in the text of *The Prelude*. He is also, we should note, performing the work of that force in suppressing the figure of the maternal as he does. The displacement from "breast" to"eye" is a gentle one, however, barely indicting the naturalness of the nurturing activity it describes. But the same force is responsible for more violent declensions in *The Prelude*: de Man goes on to relate how, later in the poem, "this same face-making, totalizing power is shown at work in a process of endless differentiation correctly called perpetual 'logic,' of which it is said that it [i.e., the poet's eye] 'Could find no surface where its power might sleep.' " And here, as he is glossing that line, dwelling on the words "surface" and "power," something peculiar happens to de Man's text. He writes:

> The face, which is the power to surface from the sea of infinite distinctions in which we risk to drown, can find no surface. How are we to reconcile the *meaning* of face, with its promise of sense and of filial preservation, with its *function* as the relentless undoer of its own claims?

The noun "surface"—which had, in the previous paragraph, indicated the bounded area of an intelligible "face," enclosed within a "contour" or "borderline"—has here turned into a verb for coming-up-for-air, and the reader is back in the thematics of drowning, made more plangent by the pathos of the first person plural: "the sea of infinite distinctions in which we risk to drown." Moreover, the phrase "in which we risk to drown"—not so much its words as the tune they make up—sounds suddenly familiar:

Like this harsh world in which I wake to weep . . .

Through the sick day in which we wake to weep . . .

Those are lines from *The Triumph of Life*, spoken by "Rousseau" and cited by de Man in his discussion of the "shape all light"; both cited and, in the case of the latter line, recited as "the *sad* day in which we wake to weep" (RR, 104, 106). It is as if "Rousseau" (defaced) and the "shape" (drowned) were linked in that phrase, both surfacing together at this moment in an essay about an altogether different poem. And behind that mediating Shelleyan couple we can glimpse the most heavily invested pair in de Man's own writing, de Man's Rousseau and Rousseau's Julie.[15]

What can be made of this strange irruption? Why should these figures surface just here? Consider the second of the sentences just cited: "How are we to reconcile the *meaning* of face, with its promise of sense and of filial preservation, with its *function* as the relentless undoer of its own claims?" It draws together the conceptual threads of the essay into an aporetic formulation familiar to de Man's readers, the impossibility of reconciling language as signification with language as performance. But it does so in a syntax that is familiar in another way: for it is the syntax of "How can we know the dancer from the dance?" the line de Man has taught us to read not only as a (celebratory) rhetorical question but also as a genuine and genuinely "anguished question" (AR, 11; RR, 201–2). And in fact a note of anxiety clings to the question as it is formulated here—a tone created by words like "filial" and "relentless." The effect is of still another surfacing, in this case of the pathos that had been suppressed in de Man's reading of the "Blessed Babe" passage. It returns here as another specular pairing, mother and child, but equivocally charged. It can be read as an attempt to align "meaning" with the mother's preserving (read: sheltering) tenderness, "function" with the child's aggressive (read: both positing and undoing) "claims." But the ambiguity of "filial preservation"—the child could be taken as either the beneficiary or the agent of that saving act of sense making—keeps the sentence from stabilizing itself in any clear-cut fashion: it remains open to the unsettling shifts of position characteristic of specular structures, and haunted by the pathos of intimacy and loss (that is, of seduction and threat) such structures generate, here indeterminately that of Wordsworth's Babe and its Mother, of the Drowned Man in *The Prelude*, whom de Man had earlier coupled with the poet's own dead mother (RR, 73), of the drowned Shelley and the shape that "goes under" (RR, 114),[16] of "Rousseau" and the shape, etc.

This is a moment of madness, that "madness of words" that de Man names as such in "Shelley Disfigured" (RR, 122): figuration turns hallucinatory in an attempt to render intelligible what, according to de Man, cannot be rendered intelligible, the "radical estrangement between the meaning and the performance of any text" (AR, 298). Or, again in the language of *Allegories of Reading*, it is the moment in which "the writer severs himself from the intelligibility of his own text," one that "has to be thematized as a sacrifice" (AR, 205–7)[17] or that, "from the point of view of the subject . . . can only be experienced as a dismemberment, a beheading or a castration" (AR, 296). Or as a drowning, we could add, if we would include the particular obsessive figure encountered here. For the form this madness adopts is that of obsession, of the repeated filling-in of unavoidable structures with images drawn from a limited set of anxieties. The attempt to dwell, speculatively, on the difference between language as meaning and language as performance cannot issue in a coolly univocal discourse: instead, the effort will trigger what I earlier called a pathos of uncertain agency, in which questions of intelligibility will be reinscribed as questions of activity or passivity, guilt or innocence and play themselves out in compulsively repeated figures.[18] De Man has to warn himself and his readers against this pathos, for it will always appear as a distraction: it will never be quite what he is talking about. But he can neither avoid falling into it, nor — and this is a stronger claim — can he or any other reader make do without it.

A final word about gender, since that has been one of the concerns of this paper from the start. Unlike Jacques Derrida, de Man has little to say, explicitly, about gender; it has been left to his readers to begin the work of articulating his implicit positions with those of other discourses, Derrida's, for example, or Lacan's or Kristeva's.[19] But we have seen how de Man has been drawn to analyze — and sometimes led to construct — scenarios in which characters face off against each other, and in which sexual difference is strongly marked. We need to ask in what ways, and at what point, the rhetorical operations he is concerned to track engage questions of gender. Of the various pairings I have been considering, the most illuminating of this issue is the confrontation of Rousseau and Marion in the last chapter of *Allegories of Reading*.

The tale of the "Purloined Ribbon," as de Man reconstructs it from the *Confessions* and the *Fourth Rêverie*, condenses the violent themes we have been examining: the "abjection" of a woman, the "castration" of a man. Rousseau imagines ("with some relish," de Man notes [AR, 279]) that his slander has almost certainly driven Marion to prostitution and an early grave; in (partial and belated) compensation, he associates her story with stories of his own near mutilation and near beheading (AR, 297). De Man presents this narrative of "desire, shame, guilt, exposure and repression" (AR, 289) in all its pathos but, in a characteristic move, questions its primacy. He cites Rousseau's explanation of how he was led to accuse Marion in the first place ("it is bizarre but it is true that my friendship for her was the cause of the accusation. She was present to my mind, I excused myself on the first thing that offered itself"), and acknowledges the possibility of a psychoanalytically informed reading ("her name is pronounced almost unconsciously, as if it were a slip, a segment of the discourse of the other"). In this account Marion is the "object of a desire" whose presence within the discursive chain is "motivated as the target of the entire action" (AR, 288–89); here her gender makes a difference: it is no accident that what can be considered the "hidden center" of the story is "Marion" and not, say, "Jules" or "Jim." But de Man does not stop there. After sketching this reading he goes on to offer an alternative, by stressing the element of contingency in Rousseau's use of the odd phrase *le premier objet qui s'offrit* and then, by a passage to the limit, absolutizing that contingency: "Marion just happened to be the first thing that came to mind; any other name, any other word, any other sound or noise could have done just as well and Marion's entry into the discourse is a mere effect of chance" (AR, 288). At this point de Man adds a variant of the warning we have encountered at other points in his work:

> In the spirit of the text, one should resist all temptation to give any significance whatever to the sound "Marion." For it is only if the act that initiated the entire chain, the utterance of the sound "Marion," is truly without any conceivable motive that the total arbitrariness of the action becomes the most effective, the most efficaciously performative excuse of all. The estrangement between subject and utterance is then so radical that it escapes any mode of comprehension. When everything else fails, one can always plead insanity. (AR, 289)

This is a warning with a difference, for the temptation we are being asked to resist is not that of being seduced by the pathos of Marion's plight, but rather that of giving "any significance whatever to the sound 'Marion,' " and thus putting oneself in a position to either enjoy or condemn Rousseau's misogynistically tinged speculations on what must have become of his victim. That is, we are being asked to resist, in Cynthia Chase's phrase, "giving a face to a name," or, still more puzzlingly, we are being asked to resist conferring the status of "name" at all on the phonemes that make up the utterance "Marion." Is this a case of de Man's adding the insult of depersonalization to the injuries Marion had already received, in reality and in lingering fantasy, at Rousseau's hands? Is a deconstructive reading here in complicity with the misogyny of its text? I think not, although the reading serves to reveal the forces at work behind the misogyny. Most explicitly, de Man's insistence on the in-significance of "Marion" asks to be taken, rather, as a counterirritant to Rousseau's lurid narrative, draining it of its misogynistic pathos by attributing the utterance "Marion" to chance, to "the absolute randomness of language, prior to any figuration or meaning" (AR, 299). At that radically "prior" moment (or, we could say, drawing on another of de Man's figures, in that puzzling "region") "Marion" is neither gendered nor otherwise determined. De Man grants that to take the enunciation of the sound "Marion" in this fashion, as an assertion of the "radical irresponsibility of fiction," no doubt "appears paradoxical and far-fetched to the point of absurdity":

It seems impossible to isolate the moment in which the fiction stands free of any signification; in the very moment at which it is posited, as well as in the context it generates, it gets at once misinterpreted into a determination which is *ipso facto*, overdetermined. Yet without this moment, never allowed to exist as such, no such thing as a text is conceivable. (AR, 293)

What is this moment whose half-life is zero, and which never exists "as such" but only as necessarily misinterpreted in (more or less) lurid figuration? It is not, as some of de Man's critics have imagined, a mystified conjuring up of a moment of "pure language." De Man is quite explicit on that point, as the passage quoted earlier from his essay on Walter Benjamin makes clear: "Least of all is there something like a *reine Sprache*, a pure language, which does not exist except as a permanent disjunction which inhabits all languages as such" (RT, 92). That "permanent disjunction," we have seen, is neither a moment nor a region but a construction of the theorist's, arrived at in the process of coming to terms with the "radical estrangement between the meaning and the performance of any text,"[20] and imaged variously as a "dismembrance" or as a "hidden break" or as "the wound of a flaw" or, in the discussion of the *Fourth Rêverie*, as "the almost imperceptible crack of the purely gratuitous" (AR, 291). This means not just that the "radical estrangement" that is the object of the theorist's attention can only be addressed in further figures, but also that it can only be experienced by the theorist as an "estrangement between subject and utterance" (AR, 289) — that is, as a sense of uncertain agency. But we have seen that the elective embodiment of the pathos of uncertain agency is the specular structure, one that locates the subject in a vacillating relation to the flawed or dismembered or disfigured (but invariably gendered) object of its attention. Here questions of sexual difference, desire, and misogyny come back into play. They are, in de Man's writing, both recurrent and judged nevertheless to be derivative. What he liked to call "rigor" meant, among other things, adopting the (necessarily unstable) position from which that judgment could be made.

December 1986

Notes

1. According to Tom Keenan, who is responsible for the bibliography of de Man's writings in RT, the reissue never appeared, so "Wordsworth and the Victorians" was published for the first time in RR. Judging from its placement in that volume, between "Autobiography As De-Facement" and "Shelley Disfigured," and from the concerns and idiom it shares with those essays, it was probably written during the same year, 1979.

2. Both papers, written in the early 1980s, will be included in a forthcoming collection of de Man's essays on philosophical texts edited by Andrzej Warminski: *Aesthetic Ideology* (Minneapolis: University of Minnesota Press). "Phenomenality and Materiality in Kant" was first published in G.

Shapiro and A. Sica (eds.), *Hermeneutics: Questions and Prospects* (Amherst: University of Massachusetts Press, 1984).

3. "Sheer" adds a note of admiring insistence to the various nouns that designate the unanalyzable, disruptive instance at work in a particular text or at a particular point in de Man's argument. For example, from "Hypogram and Inscription": "Do these readings cope with the sheer strength of figuration, that is to say master [tropes'] power to confer, to usurp, and to take away significance from grammatical universals?" (RT, 45). Cf. also "sheer metonymic enumeration" (AR, 152), "sheer imposition" (RR, 118), etc. Sometimes the rhyme "mere" will serve the same function, particularly where unexpected aleatory effects ("mere chance," "mere coincidence" [AR, 288–89]) are operating to undo the intelligibility of a text.

4. Cf. Wordsworth's "And in the sheltered and the sheltering grove / A perfect stillness" (1850 *Prelude* lines 69–70). In "Phenomenality and Materiality in Kant," a distinction is made between the "sheltering" sky of Wordsworth and Heidegger, under which man can "dwell," and a figure of the sky in Kant's Third Critique which is not "associated in any way with shelter." That would be, although de Man does not use the term here, an instance of "sheer sky." The two sh- words are brought together effectively in the last sentences of "Wordsworth and the Victorians": "It would be naive to believe that we could ever face Wordsworth, a poet of sheer language, outright. But it would be more naive still to think that we can take shelter from what he knew by means of the very evasions which this knowledge renders impossible" (RR, 92).

5. Cf. "Hegel on the Sublime," in Mark Krupnick (ed.), *Displacement: Derrida and After* (Bloomington: Indiana University Press, 1983), 139–53. Here the characterization of the "American interpretation of Romanticism" as a "closely familial romance" (144) is followed by a comment on Hegel's rejection of a genetic or "familial" reading of the *fiat lux* (146).

6. Cf. in particular "Autobiography As De-Facement," RR, 70–71.

7. Cf. Julia Kristeva, *Histoires d'Amour* (Paris: Denoël, 1984) esp. 27–58, and the chapter entitled "Something to Be Scared Of" in Kristeva's *Powers of Horror: An Essay on Abjection*, trans. Leon S. Roudiez (New York: Columbia University Press, 1982), 32–55.

8. The allusion is to a discussion in an earlier chapter of the dissertation, one never published. Hérodiade is described as turning away from the "element of natural, maternal affection": "The heroine rejects it with all the determination of one who knows its seductiveness." "Mallarmé, Yeats and the Post-Romantic Predicament," Harvard University dissertation, May 1960, 23. My thanks to Barbara Johnson for supplying me with a photocopy of these chapters, and to the Harvard University Library for allowing her to do so.

9. RR, 70. On the "seductions of identification," see Minae Mizumura, "Renunciation," in *The Lesson of Paul de Man, Yale French Studies*, 69 (1985): 91–97.

10. On the same page on which de Man notes Hérodiade's rejection of the seductiveness of the maternal (see note 8 above) one can find a similar fending off of psychoanalysis. Commenting on Mallarmé's revising an early poem, changing an apostrophic "Notre *Père*" to "Notre *Dame*," he writes: "This change adds a world of meaning (of which psychoanalytic criticism has eagerly and all too literally taken advantage)." The allusion, a footnote indicates, is to Charles Mauron's work.

11. Illuminating discussions of de Man's forcing of his texts can be found in Hans-Jost Frey's "Undecidability," in *The Lesson of Paul de Man, Yale French Studies*, 69 (1985): 124–33, and in Rodolphe Gasché's contribution to this volume. The most notorious instance, de Man's reading of Rousseau's story of Marion and the purloined ribbon (AR, 278–301) is discussed below. But one could look, too, at the last essay in *The Rhetoric of Romanticism*, in which the sequence of anecdotes in Kleist's text on puppets is read in jumbled fashion, as though the discussion of marionettes were the culminating, rather than the first, episode. One effect of this rearrangement is a puzzling symmetry: *Allegories of Reading* concludes with "Marion," *The Rhetoric of Romanticism* with "marionettes." Moreover, the two nouns are brought together at a critical juncture of the earlier essay, where de Man is considering Rousseau's claim that the lie he told about Marion was not voluntary

but rather the *effet machinal* of his embarrassment: "The machinelike quality of the text of the lie is more remarkable still when, as in the Marion episode, the disproportion between the crime that is to be confessed and the crime performed by the lie adds a delirious element to the situation. By saying that the excuse is not only a fiction but also a machine one adds to the connotations of referential detachment, of gratuitous improvisation, that of the implacable repetition of a preordained pattern. Like Kleist's marionettes, the machine is both 'anti-grav,' the anamorphosis of a form detached from meaning and capable of taking on any structure whatever, yet entirely ruthless in its inability to modify its own structural design for nonstructural reasons" (AR, 294).

The conceptual articulation de Man is proposing here—between the "referential detachment" of fiction and the "implacable repetition" of formal patterns—is allegorically read out of two lurid episodes, that of Marion, the disfigured victim of Rousseau's lie, and that of the marionettes, "suspended in dead passivity." I believe de Man would acknowledge the appearance of such figures in his own writing as involuntary illustrations of his thesis—that one is "bound to repeat the disfiguration of metaphor . . . in what appears to be a more violent mode" (RR, 120). This formulation is considered at greater length below, pp. 93–95.

12. The most haunting exemplification of this theme comes in de Man's reading of the Rilke poem "Quai du Rosaire" (AR, 40–43), which focuses on the "seductive but funereal image" of houses reflected, upside down, in the canals of Bruges while, above, the sounds of a carillon can be heard, "suspended in the skies." Rilke's characteristic "synthesis of rising and falling" is alluded to in de Man's discussion of Kleist's marionettes, "hanging and suspended like dead bodies" (RR, 287).

13. Donald H. Reiman, *Shelley's "The Triumph of Life: A Critical Study* (Urbana: University of Illinois Pr., 1965) pp. 192–95. The lines quoted are 410–15 and 424–36 of Reiman's variorum text.

14. For especially lucid discussions of the problem of "face," in Wordsworth and in de Man, see Catherine Caruth, "Past Recognition: Narrative Origins in Wordsworth and Freud," *MLN*, 100 (Dec. 1985): 935–48, and Cynthia Chase, "Giving a Face to a Name: De Man's Figures," in *Decomposing Figures: Rhetorical Readings in the Romantic Tradition* (Baltimore and London: Johns Hopkins University Press, 1986), 82–112. This is a good place to acknowledge a long-standing debt to Cynthia Chase, whose writings and conversation have been a challenge and a source of encouragement.

15. Reiman, *Shelley's "The Triumph of Life*," 60, takes the "shape all light" as an allusion to Julie; de Man, I believe, would not quarrel with that, although in other respects his reading of *The Triumph of Life* is at odds with Reiman's. De Man's persistent reference to *La Nouvelle Héloïse* is, as he liked to say, well known: it can be documented in the indexes to BI, AR, RR, and RT.

16. In the concluding sentences of "Resistance to Theory," written two or three years after "Shelley Disfigured," that "going under" itself surfaces, this time as a way of characterizing the weirdly persistent life-in-death of a quasi-personified "literary theory": "The loftier the aims and the better the methods of literary theory, the less possible it becomes. Yet literary theory is not in danger of going under; it cannot help but flourish, and the more it is resisted, the more it flourishes, since the language it speaks is the language of self-resistance. What remains impossible to decide is whether this flourishing is a triumph or a fall" (RT, 19–20).

17. A sustained and acute reading of the movement of these pages can be found in Werner Hamacher's remarkable essay "Lectio," included in this volume.

18. On obsession as a mode of intelligibility, see de Man's pairing of Baudelaire's sonnets "Correspondences" and "Obsession" in "Anthropomorphism and Trope in the Lyric" (RR, 252–62).

19. See Barbara Johnson's "Gender Theory and the Yale School" in Robert Con Davis and Ronald Schleifer (eds.), *Rhetoric and Form: Deconstruction at Yale* (Norman: University of Oklahoma Press, 1985), 101–12, and Cynthia Chase's "The Witty Butcher's Wife: Freud, Lacan, and the Conversion of Resistance to Theory," *MLN*, 102 (December 1987): 989–1013.

20. For a brief but exemplary reading of these pages see William Ray's fine study *Literary Meaning: From Phenomenology to Deconstruction* (Oxford: Basil Blackwell, 1984), 198–205.

Allegories of Reading Paul de Man
Carol Jacobs

There is no way to say adequately what the significance of de Man might be. It could not be otherwise, for he himself linked death to the impossibility of defining man as presence and with man's perpetual transgression of his own sense of self as totalized. And, given that the transgression is perpetual, it took no literal death to both upset and set the task, that of reading the man, which is to say, of writing about him.

"We write," as the essay entitled "Allegory" reminds us, "in order to forget our foreknowledge of the total opacity of [de Man's] words . . . or, perhaps worse, because we do not know whether . . . [his writings] have or do not have to be understood" (AR, 203). Let us forget, then, both this foreknowledge and this ignorance and the constant warning against the mystification of adopting a privileged viewpoint forever unable to understand its own genealogy. For the question that this reading will first raise is apparently one of origins and teleology: how does de Man's critical narrative move in the second part of *Allegories of Reading*, the essays on Rousseau? How does it move from the first chapter, on "Metaphor," to the last, entitled "Excuses"? How does it cross the borders from one essay to the next, and do the provisional syntheses that take place along the way mark a genuine progression in our understanding of Rousseau's text and de Man's?

There is much in these texts that would lead us to believe so. Almost all of the essays begin with a reference to the conclusions reached by the previous reading, giving us, at the very least, a parodic sense of traditional critical progress. Within the essays there are constant reminders of what we have learned earlier in such phrases as "As we know from the reading of *Narcisse* and *Pygmalion*"

(AR, 210), "as we know from *Julie*" (AR 283), "As we know from the 'Préface dialoguée' " (AR, 296). More compelling than these phrases that one could write off as exercises in the stylistic conventions of critical rhetoric, the texts on Rousseau repeatedly suggest a movement within each essay of moving from error to understanding. Thus, to take just one example, the essay on "Self" first presents a reading of *Narcisse* as the straightforward, mimetic representation of Valère's vanity in which his consciousness apparently moves from an inital bad faith to a triumphant good faith at the end of the play. De Man rejects this interpretation by reading a number of linguistic effects that such an interpretation fails to account for, effects that perform a suspension between self and other. He then counters this, his second interpretation, or suggests its containment, by pointing to the *Préface* to *Narcisse* that might be read as proof that Rousseau, as author, was definitely beyond the errors of his character. De Man comments on this interpretation by reading another text of Rousseau, *Pygmalion*, and, as one might expect, reverses his previous reading with the vacillation of a fourth interpretation.

More crucial than this sense of progress[1] that could be traced within each essay is the sense de Man gives his reader of a hierarchical schema of different critical levels of understanding. Thus he distinguishes between tropological narratives such as the *Second Discourse* on the one hand and allegorical narratives such as *La Nouvelle Héloïse* that tell the story of the failure to read:

> The rhetorical mode of such structures can no longer be summarized by the single term of metaphor or any substitutive trope or figure in general, although the deconstruction of metaphorical figures remains a necessary moment in their production. They take into account the fact that the resulting narratives can be folded back upon themselves and become self-referential. By *refusing*, for reasons of epistemological rigor, to confirm the authority, though not the necessity, of this juxtaposition, Rousseau unsettles the metaphor of reading as deconstructive narrative and replaces it by a more complex structure. The paradigm for all texts consists of a figure (or a system of figures) and its deconstruction. But since this model cannot be closed off by a final reading, it engenders, in its turn, a supplementary figural superposition which narrates the unreadability of the prior narration. As distinguished from primary deconstructive narratives centered on figures and ultimately always on metaphor, we can call such narratives to the second (or the third) degree *allegories*. (AR, 205)[2]

Side by side with these various modes of suggesting linear progress through time one finds, equally prevalent, a disconcerting insistence on the text as "a series of repetitive reversals" (AR, 162), as a "repetition of . . . [the tropological system's] aberration" (AR, 301), as a repetition of a pattern that ruptures dialectical progress (AR, 187). How can we account for this seeming contradiction?[3]

To put the question another way, how does time play its role in the performance of de Man's narrative? Already in the first essay on "Metaphor" we read "the discovery of temporality coincides with the acts of transgressive freedom" (AR, 140) that necessarily take place when the boundaries of man's attempts at self-totalization or naming are seen to fail. Time is that which marks the realization of the impossibility of self-definition. In the essay entitled "Promises," de Man speaks of time as "the phenomenal category produced by the discrepancy" between the "theoretical statement" of the law and its "phenomenal manifestation" that is necessarily delayed to a future moment (AR, 273). This is made clearer, if more unthinkable, in the essay on "Self":

> And just as the indeterminacy of reference generates the illusion of a subject, a narrator, and a reader, it also generates the metaphor of temporality. A narrative endlessly tells the story of its own denominational aberration and it can only repeat this aberration on various levels of rhetorical complexity. Texts engender texts as a result of their necessarily aberrant semantic structure; hence the fact that they consist of a series of repetitive reversals that engenders the semblance of temporal sequence. (AR, 162)

Temporality is a metaphor. It is generated out of a series of repetitions that give the illusion of sequence or linear temporal order. One begins to suspect that the distinction between linear dialectical progression and its disruption may not be all that clear since, as we have just read, the semblance of sequence and therefore the semblance of time seems to coincide with the endless repetition of reversals.

If we return to the passage just cited, taken as it is from an essay in which the entire problematic is that of delineating the difference between self and other, one is struck by the juxtaposition of two sentences that begin: "A narrative endlessly tells the story of its *own* denominational aberration," and a second sentence, "Texts engender [other] *texts* as a result of . . . " (emphasis mine). At stake here is not only the narrative line of an individual text but the relation between one text and another, a text and its other, the critical text that it necessarily engenders. For this reason, in reading de Man one is woven into the texture of the narrative to the point of making his text and ours into the dramatization of their own confusions.

Allegories of Reading moves like a dialectic that has no point of origin and no point of telos. Vacillation and progress cannot cancel each other out, since the text of these critical essays is, per definition, in a state of unpredictable change. Their mode of existence is necessarily temporal and historical, though in a strictly nonteleological sense. All critical progress takes place in the mode of asserting a series of irresolvable vacillations of nonpolar incompatabilities from which it implicitly exempts itself, locating these, as it does, elsewhere, in the text of Rousseau: such vacillations as those between denomination and conceptualization, self and other, self and God, mind and nature, personal and public happiness, promise and fulfillment. And just as each of Rousseau's allegorical narratives invariably "resorts to the principles of authority that it undermines" (AR, 275), so de Man's allegorical performance necessarily "relapses into the figure it deconstructs" (AR, 275), "reintroduc[ing] the metaphorical model whose deconstruction had been the reason for its own elaboration" (AR, 257), time. It "perform[s] what it has shown to be impossible to do" (AR, 275), to deconstruct. Like the author of the preface to *Narcisse* in relation to the protagonist of that play de Man might be seen to claim for himself the authority he negates in the text at hand, speaking in a "voice that, by the rigor of its negativity, finally coincides with what it asserts" (AR, 172). Like Galathea, Rousseau, and the reader in relation to Pygmalion, figures who merely *seem* able to separate themselves from the errors of the artist, de Man's text implicitly performs its blindness to the illusions of negative authority and is taken in by a vacillation it cannot coincidentally assert and perform.[4]

Yet what is it that seems, if only momentarily, to allow the critical text to escape the irresolution of the texts it deconstructs, if not its belatedness, its coming after. If time is the phenomenal category engendered out of the noncoincidence between a text's theoretical statement and its phenomenal manifestation, then de Man's critical text plays the role of that temporal passage, a temporal discrepancy that could be equally located within the text read or between the critical text and its object, for who after reading de Man could distinguish between that particular pair of self and other? *Allegories of Reading* is an elaborate allegory of the impossibility of the fundamental condition of allegory, of the illusory nature of time and of the misreading it engenders when it operates as critical progress. Its time is, coincidentally, an act of transgressive freedom, a rupture, that marks the impossibility of textual definition and self-definition. It performs this deception with respect to the texts it reads and also with respect to the text it cannot and yet inevitably does read, itself. It acts out, then, both the promise of progress and its failure, making promises it cannot fulfill in the present, making excuses rather than confessions for that which it might rather expose than hide, narrating endless fictions.

It is thus impossible to speak of this text as either knowledge or ignorance, although as long as one assumes a rhetoric of linear temporality one seems bound to such distinctions. Perhaps it is time to read a particular passage from *Allegories of Reading* rather than simply citing it (openly and surreptitiously), an exemplary moment in which de Man's maddening irony is at play.

In the chapter entitled "Self," de Man follows the vacillating evolution of the relationship of Pygmalion as artist and author to his creation, Galathea. At first Pygmalion treats Galathea as an object of sexual aggression, desiring her "unmediated possession" (AR, 182). But this moment of literality gives way to another gesture in which he reads the body of Galathea as symbolic of the beauty of her soul. When he rejects this interpretation he regards her in turn as a *general* model for a particular being, and since Pygmalion has in fact created Galathea, she becomes a general Self who might well include the particular self of Pygmalion. In the play's central moment the temptation of a "totalizing identification" (AR, 184) offers itself to Pygmalion, but, de Man maintains, no sooner does Pygmalion contemplate immolating himself so that artist and work might be one, than he withdraws from any synthesis of self and other that would put the vacillations of the text to rest. When, de Man goes on to argue, shortly thereafter, the statue comes to life and approaches Pygmalion, the final exchange between the two reiterates their antagonism, for no teleological closure of the general Self with the particular Self—in fact, no teleological closure of any kind—can take place.[5]

> And there can be no doubt about their continued confrontation, in endless repetition, in the apparent conclusion of the text. The final exchange between Galathea and Pygmalion reiterates the situation that existed in the central passage when Pygmalion withdraws from ultimate identification with the most generalized form of selfhood. (AR, 185)

But on what does he base his judgment, his justification for his positive assertion of the play's vacillation, the imbalance of final exchange between the two characters? "The play," he writes,

> could, in principle, have come to a stop in the identifying echo of the two "moi's" uttered by the protagonists: *Galathea* (touches herself and says): Moi. *Pygmalion* (transported): Moi!" (l. 1230). The supplementary exclamation mark records the imbalance acted out in the final exchanges. (AR, 185)

What is it that de Man reads in these last lines but an exclamation point?

Things get worse, or, perhaps, de Man's play, his performance of critical assertion and vacillation, becomes better. For just after assuring us that Galathea's utterance on touching Pygmalion has all the ambiguity of the enigmatic "Ach!" that closes Kleist's play *Amphytrion*, de Man cites that statement and then insists on the absolutely univocal intention of Galathea.

> "*Galathea* (with a sigh): Ah! encore moi" (l. 1230–31). The tone is hardly one of ecstatic union, rather of resigned tolerance towards an overassiduous admirer. Since Galathea is the Self as such, she has to contain all particular selves including Pygmalion; as a statement of identity in which "encore moi" means "aussi moi" ("me as well"), it is a true enough affirmation. This is certainly how Pygmalion understands it. . . . But the line "Ah! encore moi" spoken with a sigh that suggests disappointment rather than satisfaction can also mean "de nouveau moi" ("me again"), a persisting, repeated distinction between the general Self and the self as other. Indeed, the separation between Galathea's coldness and Pygmalion's impetuousness could not be greater. (AR, 185–86)

How does de Man "know" that the separation could not be greater? What can he possibly be interpreting in Galathea's "(with a sigh): Ah! encore moi"? He reads a series of singularly resistant signs, the "Ah," along with the exclamation point that follows it and a sigh, the difference between Ah! and Ah!, a tonality of voice that can nowhere be located in Rousseau's text, but only in the ironical gesture of de Man's commentary. He reads, moreover, "encore," the sign of the very critical doubling that one might claim de Man's writings to be about (in both senses of the word), "encore," which suggests both the temporal or spatial continuity of "still" and the rupturing discontinuity of "again." He reads that sign of doubling and fixes on one of its meanings, identifying it in a gesture of apparent critical certainty and progress as the sign of a rift between the artist (Pygmalion) and that which he has produced or, tellingly, between the author and that which he has written. Needless to say, the same is performed with respect to the last term of the phrase, with respect to that sign of the self (moi) which has been the titular concern of the entire essay.[6]

But, perhaps, nowhere is de Man's irony more open to view than when he reads rhetorical figures of his own making. The question he raises in the following lines is that we raised earlier in relation to de Man's own text. How compatible are rhetorical resources with selfhood and to what extent does the deconstructor unlock the rhetoric of another self and expose the delusions of the concept of self, only to establish "the authority of a [deconstructive] self at the far end of its most radical negation" (AR, 172)?

> Rhetoric all too easily appears as the tool of the self, hence its pervading association, in the everyday use of the term, with persuasion, eloquence, the manipulation of the self and of others. Hence also the naïvely pejorative sense in which the term is commonly used, in opposition to a literal use of language that would not allow the subject to conceal its desires. The attitude is by no means confined to the popular use of "rhetoric" but is in fact a recurrent philosophical topos, a philosopheme that may well be constitutive of philosophical language itself. In all these instances, rhetoric functions as a key to the discovery of the self. (AR, 173)

The passage is not yet lost in what de Man will soon speak of as "the epistemological labyrinth of figural structures" (AR, 173). So far we see the way in. The door is not locked, since our sense of direction has not yet been frustrated. We read here of a first self that has used eloquence as a means to conceal. That same tool can, in the hand of the interpreter, serve as a key to open the passageway to the self.

> In all these instances, rhetoric functions as a key to the discovery of the self, and it functions with such ease that one may well begin to wonder whether the lock indeed shapes the key or whether it is not the other way round, that a lock (and a secret room or box behind it) had to be invented in order to give a function to the key. For what could be more

distressing than a bunch of highly refined keys just lying around without any corresponding locks worthy of being opened? (AR, 173)

As unsettling as this statement may be—and we will get to its content soon
enough, but it is impossible to think what it is saying and how it is saying it all
at once—as disorienting as this statement may be, its rhetorical mode is absolutely
straightforward. It is not what de Man would call figural or metaphorical in Rousseau's sense, for its referential status is totally unproblematic.[7] The above assertion resides in the realm of mimetic language to which de Man has given us the
key. One can read it by simply substituting "rhetoric" for "key" and "self" for
"lock." While de Man's language remains unproblematically representational,
what it speaks of is a rhetoric that may refuse access to a referent behind it. Yet
it is not quite that rhetoric refuses access to a self behind it; for to bypass the distressing absence of corresponding locks (selves), is it not rhetoric itself that would
have to invent them?

"Perhaps there are none," de Man continues, "and perhaps the most refined key
of all, the key of keys, is the one that gives access to the Pandora's box in which
this darkest secret is kept hidden" (AR, 173).[8] The "key of keys" is not simply
one key among others, but that which is the key to the functioning (or nonfunc-
tioning) of all keys. And what it reveals is the secret that the keys with which we
daily deal (rhetoric) have no corresponding locks. Yet to understand the passage
in this way, as the straightforward assertion of an absence, is to fail to read the
vacillation in the phrase "in which this darkest secret is kept hidden." Does the
key of keys (rhetorical analysis of rhetoric) give us genuine access to the secret,
or is it that we gain access only to a box in which the secret must, necessarily,
be *kept* hidden, even at the very moment when we think we are revealing it?
Surely this is the implication of the literary allusion to Pandora's box. In the myth
of Pandora, last in the box was Delusive Hope, and it was this hope that kept Pandora from committing suicide—a hope, then, in the service of preserving the very
self who revealed the self-threatening content of the box.

If the darkest secret of the absence of the self is *kept* hidden just at the moment
that one speaks it aloud, this is because that rhetoric which is the key of keys surreptitiously reintroduces the authority of the self, however deconstructive. But
if this is so, the structure of rhetorical control must come unhinged, and so it does.
"This would imply the existence of at least one lock worthy of being raped, the
Self as the relentless undoer of selfhood" (AR, 173). The "key of keys," the key
that implicitly turned all other keys to locks, has itself become a lock ("the Self
as the relentless undoer of selfhood"), for all there is, is rhetoric that now assumes
one role, now another. If before de Man spoke of a key that functions with
remarkable ease, if afterward of "locks worthy of being opened," the lock that
closes this difficult passage must be approached with violent force (as one "worthy
of being raped"). The movement is less one of opening locks than of their resis-

tance, less one of entering into a space of selfhood or reference than a displacement away from that delusion that nevertheless repeats it.

To be sure, keys are no longer simply keys (rhetoric) and locks are no longer simply locks (selves) since each key serves as a lock for the next. We can no longer read by the controlled substitutions of coded terms that are the hallmark of mimetic language. De Man makes this all the clearer in the last line we cited, a line he of course lifted from Alexander Pope: "This would imply the existence of at least one lock worthy of being raped." Here the substantial hardware of the previous imagery with all its implicit progress, ironized as it may be, gives way to the labyrinthine curl[9] of the allusion to "The Rape of the Lock," for when it is a question of metaphor, there is no telling where it may lead.

Where is all this insistence on de Man's irony bringing us if not to the end point of sorts that appears to close the volume *Allegories of Reading?*

> The anacoluthon is extended over all the points of the figural line or allegory; . . . it becomes the permanent parabasis of an allegory (of figure), that is to say, irony. Irony is no longer a trope but the undoing of the deconstructive allegory of all tropological cognitions, the systematic undoing, in other words, of understanding. As such, far from closing off the tropological system, irony enforces the repetition of its aberration. (AR, 300–301)

If *Allegories of Reading* ends with the ironization of allegory, how could it be insignificant that another text of de Man's, "The Rhetoric of Temporality," closes with the allegorization of irony?

In that earlier essay to which the last lines of the book apparently refer, if only by reversal, the trajectory to its end point has hardly been simple. In the context of critical studies on German, English, and French letters, "The Rhetoric of Temporality" tells of an abandonment of the arbitrary and rational allegory of the eighteenth century in favor of the symbol. The symbol promises a union between itself (the representation of experience) and experience (BI, 188), between subject and object. It displays the temptation of the self to "borrow . . . the temporal stability that it lacks from nature" (BI, 197). But de Man insists as well on the growth of another metaphorical style that arises just when the symbol is supplanting rococo allegory. This other style, a style that seems to constitute the blind spot of so many readings, de Man also chooses to call "allegory."

Tellingly enough, this other allegory, although outstripped by the symbol in the course of the nineteenth century, is able to account for the symbolic mode as a mere negative moment within its own structure. De Man arrives at this conclusion through a reading of Rousseau's *La Nouvelle Héloïse* where he juxtaposes two landscapes in the text, that of the Meillerie episode with Julie's garden, Elysium. In the Meillerie episode the analogical continuity among the style of Sant Preux's impassioned writing, the scenery he describes, and the emotion he experiences is exemplary of the coincidence between "mind and nature" (BI, 193) or language and its referent. But the novel, we are told, presents this episode as a scene of temptation and error by contrasting it with Julie's garden, which is not only an emblem of virtue but also, it would seem, an emblem of the allegorical. Thus the passages concerning the garden operate as allegorical language in that they place the symbolic thrust of the text in the proper perspective of error. For, in contrast to the symbol that appropriates temporal stability where there is none, allegory always involves a temporal discontinuity in which a renunciation of a previous symbolic moment takes place. This de Man calls the "unveiling of an authentically temporal destiny" (BI, 206). If "time is the originary constitutive category" of allegory, it is time as a medium of rupture, "distance," "difference" (BI, 207).

The temporal relationships in the example of Julie's garden would seem to cut in all directions. For these allegorical descriptions not only assert a negative *self-knowledge* on the part of the novel (with respect to Saint Preux's language), they also undercut any attempt to read this moment in Rousseau as confirmation of the other, to read it as a mirror of a world existing outside and prior to the text. It is not only that Rousseau refers to other texts rather than to a realm we tend to call "reality"; in elaborating the literary sources of the Elysium, de Man demonstrates that it is less the content of those texts to which *La Nouvelle Héloïse* refers than their "allegorical diction" (BI, 203). The allegorical text, therefore, refers to an outside only as a "previous sign" of which it is the "essence . . . to be pure anteriority" (BI, 207), a temporally distant sign, in turn emptied of its referent — the very inverse, then, of the symbol.

If we felt called upon to paraphrase the content of de Man's essay as he speaks of Rousseau, this is because it forms something of a commentary on de Man's own style. "The Rhetoric of Temporality" is divided into two sections concentrating, respectively, on the concepts of allegory and irony. Despite the apparent symmetry of the organization, the narrative modes of the inquiries prove to be critically dissimilar. The section entitled "Allegory and Symbol," as we have seen, tells a historical tale, that of a transition at the end of the eighteenth century from a concept of allegory as the key rhetorical term to that of symbol. The section on irony displays another narrative strategy, one that we will confront shortly.

Despite this disparity, allegory would seem to have a great deal in common with irony, for, as he nears the end of his essay, de Man has this to say:

Our description seems to have reached a provisional conclusion. The act of irony, as we now understand it, reveals the existence of a temporality that is definitely not organic, in that it relates to its source only in terms of distance and difference and allows for no end, for no totality. . . . The temporal void that it reveals is the same void we encountered when we found allegory always implying an unreachable anteriority. Allegory and irony are thus linked in their common discovery of a truly temporal predicament. They are also linked in their common de-mystification of an organic world postulated in a symbolic mode of analogical correspondences or in a mimetic mode of representation in which fiction and reality could coincide (BI, 222).

But, no sooner does de Man reach this "provisional conclusion," an apparent state of definitional wisdom, than he ironizes it by putting it into a historical frame. Might it not be possible, he suggests, just as he traced the historical regression away from allegory, to also trace a parallel historical literary development that abandons the notion of irony?

The regression in critical insight found in the transition from an allegorical to a symbolic theory of poetry would find its historical equivalent in the regression from the eighteenth-century ironic novel, based on what Friedrich Schlegel called *"Parekbase,"* to nineteenth-century realism.

This conclusion is dangerously satisfying and highly vulnerable to irony in that it rescues a coherent historical picture at the expense of stated human incoherence (BI, 222).

The irony is directed at the attempt to historicize the question of literature, an irony therefore directed at the entire first part of de Man's own "Rhetoric of Temporality" where he had spoken of the "need for historical clarification as a preliminary to a more systematic treatment of an intentional rhetoric" (BI, 188).[10] But it would be naive to take irony as a force that simply questions the particular historical scheme of the essay at hand. For, in a passage that is something of a turning point between the two sections of the essay, there is a certain laughter that reflects on and ironizes the text that precedes it in more ways than one.

In the case of irony one cannot so easily take refuge in the need for a historical de-mystification of the term, as when we tried to show that the term "symbol" had in fact been substituted for that of "allegory" in an act of ontological bad faith. The tension between allegory and symbol justified this procedure: the mystification is a fact of history and must therefore be dealt with in a historical manner before actual theorization can start. But in the case of irony one has to start out from the structure of the trope itself, taking one's cue from texts that are de-mystified and, to a large extent, themselves ironical. For that matter, the target of their irony is very often the claim to speak about human matters as if they were facts of history. It is a historical fact that irony becomes increasingly conscious of itself in the course of demonstrating the impossibility of our being historical. (BI, 211)

If the "mystification [about symbolic language] is a fact of history," one might add that history is a mystification about facts and, therefore, a language that shares all the delusions of the symbol about an organic connection between itself and reality, the representation of experience and experience (BI, 188). History, like allegory, implies a past, but hardly a pure unreachable anteriority. It is rather a past from which language borrows an unwarranted stability, a guarantee of its own significance.

But this is too obvious to be the crucial point at play here. What de Man also ironizes is what one might aptly call the allegorization of the question of allegory in part I of the essay—insofar as that spreading out in time was used to reach a satisfying historical conclusion. In question is not only the coherence of the historical picture but the implicit promise of moving away from the error of symbol to arrive at a coherence of a higher aletheic order. For while insisting on a regression in critical insight as conventional allegory gave way to symbol, de Man also speaks in that section of poetic figures such as Hölderlin, Wordsworth, and Rousseau who were at the same time producing a different sort of allegorical text.

Nor is it simply a matter of a blindness in de Man's writing that a later moment of insight is able to set straight. His text performs in this what it is unable to avoid. If we look to his reading of Wordsworth's "A slumber did my spirit seal," the strange temporality of the allegorical text becomes more comprehensible.[11] As in Rousseau's Meillerie episode, there are "two stages of consciousness, one belonging to the past and mystified, the other to the *now* of the poem" (BI, 224). "The stance of the speaker," de Man tells us, "who exists in the 'now,' is that of a subject whose insight is no longer in doubt and who is no longer vulnerable to irony. It could be called, if one so wished, a stance of wisdom" (ibid.). But wishing does not make it so. For the temptation exists to misunderstand the nature of that wisdom, as though it might belong to an undivided self writing within the temporality of actual experience. Yet "the 'now' of the poem is not an actual now, but the ideal 'now,' the duration of an acquired wisdom."[12] It is never open to a unified subject to overcome the state of error, to put it behind him in a moment of transcendent understanding.

> The fundamental structure of allegory reappears here in the tendency of the language toward narrative, the spreading out along the axis of an imaginary time in order to give duration to what is, in fact, simultaneous within the subject. (BI, 225)

If allegory can exist only within an ideal time and engenders a "duration as the illusion of a continuity that it knows to be illusionary" (BI, 226), if it is, therefore, never open to the individual to get beyond the moment of error, it is also never possible to avoid the attempt. Allegory is totally demystified as long as it remains within its language, but the writer is once again totally subject to renewed blindness as soon as he or she leaves that language for the empirical world, say, for the rhetoric of literary criticism. For the critical essay may recognize "inauthenticity but can never overcome it" (BI, 222). "To know inauthenticity is not the same as to be authentic [language]" (BI, 214).

Side by side with the satisfying history that culminates in such allegorical writers as Rousseau, there is, then, also that of de Man rewriting literary history to recognize and deconstruct a former state of error. The moment "The Rhetoric of Temporality" turns its ironical or allegorical structures into a desire for stable knowledge, it performs its necessary "interplay with mystified forms of language . . . which it is not in . . . [its] power to eradicate" (BI, 226).[13]

Thus, in de Man's essay we can repeatedly trace a movement from the recognition of a former state of inauthenticity to the fundamentally symbolic gesture of turning this negative insight into positive knowledge of various sorts,[14] or, at least, a vacillation between the two. When de Man describes the relationship between allegorical and symbolic language in *La Nouvelle Héloïse*, for example, we read the following:

> The tension arises . . . between the allegorical language of a scene such as Julie's Elysium and the symbolic language of passages such as the Meillerie episode. The moral contrast between these two worlds epitomizes the dramatic conflict of the novel. This conflict is ultimately resolved in the triumph of a controlled and lucid renunciation of the values associated with a cult of the moment, and this renunciation establishes the priority of an allegorical over a symbolic diction. The novel could not exist without the simultaneous presence of both metaphorical modes, nor could it reach its conclusion without the implied choice in favor of allegory over symbol. (BI, 204)

De Man speaks in terms of "tension," "contrast," and "conflict." There is a "triumph," but it is the triumph of the emptying gesture of renunciation. There is a "priority of an allegorical over a symbolic diction," but this asserts itself as an "*implied* choice" (my emphasis) in a novel that renounces, but never fails to insist on, and employ, symbolic diction.

As de Man continues to describe the tension between symbol and allegory, he reminds his reader once again of a constitutive distance within allegory.

> Whereas the symbol postulates the possibility of an identity or identification, allegory designates primarily a distance in relation to its own origin, and, renouncing the nostalgia and the desire to coincide, it establishes its language in the void of this temporal difference. In so doing, it prevents the self from an illusory identification with the non-self, which is now fully, though painfully, recognized as a non-self. It is this painful knowledge that we perceive at the moments when early romantic literature finds its true voice. (BI, 207)

But if the knowledge gained in the language of allegory is painful, the tale about that knowledge often appears remarkably satisfying. Thus, in the context of his own critical progress, de Man can speak of changing the historical and philosophical pattern such that symbolic diction becomes a mere negative moment, a temptation to be overcome (BI, 204–5). Writing from the perspective of his own conclusion, he can speak in the temporal framework of a "now" in which symbolic language "no longer" plays a role. He employs a rhetoric in which truth and lucidity are clearly distinguishable from regressive self-mystification.

> We are led, in conclusion, to a historical scheme that differs entirely from the customary picture. The dialectical relationship between subject and object is no longer the central statement of romantic thought, but this dialectic is now located entirely in the temporal relationships that exist within a system of allegorical signs. It becomes a conflict between a conception of the self seen in its authentically temporal predicament and a defensive strategy that tries to hide from this negative self-knowledge. On the level of language the asserted superiority of the symbol over allegory, so frequent during the nineteenth century, is one of the forms taken by this tenacious self-mystification. Wide areas of European literature . . . appear as regressive with regard to the truths that come to light in the last quarter of the eighteenth century. (BI, 208).

This is the voice of a self that has escaped its temporal predicament, the void of temporal distance, caught, as it appears to be, in a defensive strategy that hides from negative self-knowledge. For it is in such a rhetoric that claims to dispense with the symbolic—where time as rupture has given way to the "now" of conclusions, where other texts are read for a gain in knowledge rather than for a genuine recognition of their allegoricity—that de Man's diction presents itself at its most "symbolic."

This is why, as de Man's irony becomes increasingly conscious of itself, it demonstrates the impossibility of being historical. It rejects its own temporal movement of correcting error to produce (illusory) wisdom and recognizes it or rather performs it as a problem that exists within the rhetoric of temporality. In speaking of other critics and other theories of language, de Man necessarily spreads out along the axis of imaginary time what is, in fact, simultaneous within his text. This is what the passage we called something of a turning point in the essay ironizes, for that passage (cited on p. 114) goes on to say:

> In speaking of irony we are dealing not with the history of an error but with a problem that exists within the self. . . . [A] great deal of assistance can be gained from existing texts on irony. Curiously enough, it seems to be only in describing a mode of language which does not mean what it says that one can actually say what one means. (BI, 211)

If de Man's text means what it does not and cannot say, this is partly because his ironization of allegory as we have seen it to take place is also, necessarily, an allegorization of sorts. For those vertiginous, ironical lines we just cited might, ironically enough, be read as yet another attempt to move temporally from error to wisdom, this time from the error of the allegory[15] that makes up part I of the essay to the wisdom of irony. That is, we might read that ironization of allegory (ironized for its spreading out in time of what is actually simultaneous, for its conversion of allegorical duration into empirical knowledge, a conversion of time as distance into time as progress) we might read that ironization of allegory as itself an allegorization that privileges irony, one that must, in turn, be viewed ironically. Thus the movement of the literary text is restated and repeated on an increasingly conscious level by the critical reading that must, no less than irony, fail to overcome the inauthenticity of its own language. Things can never be left to rest at any point that one reaches, for the whole process takes place at an unsettling speed. One begins to experience a "dizziness to the point of madness" (BI, 215), a dizziness it would seem, that is unavoidable. For the "dialectical play between the two modes, as well as their common interplay with mystified forms of language . . . make up," de Man tells us, "what is called literary history" (BI, 226).[16]

They make up what is called literary history: that is to say, they are not simply forces at a particular moment of our historical past. De Man may speak of allegory coming into its own at "*the very* [historical] *moment*" (BI, 190) when symbolic modes were in full strength and go on to say "*Around the same time* that the tension between symbol and allegory finds expression in the works and the theoretical speculations of the early romantics, the problem of irony also receives more and more self-conscious attention" (BI, 208) (emphases mine). But, whatever evidence its "content" may offer to the contrary, however much the subject in question seems to be a particular moment in time,[17] the play of allegory, symbol, and irony constitutes not only the historical story one tells about romantic literature, but both literature in general and its theoretical (self-)commentary.

The kind of performance we have seen to take place in "The Rhetoric of Temporality" constitutes the movement of the Rousseau essays in *Allegories of Reading*. Time is an illusion created out of a series of repetitive reversals, for before the reversals can be recognized as such they seem to mark the progress of a gain in knowledge, however negative. This is the allegorical thrust of the text which is inevitably consumed by an irony that places the metaphor of time in perspective. That is to say, it collapses it, for de Man speaks of irony as "two irreconcilable . . . beings" "juxtaposed within the same moment" (BI, 226). Irony and allegory endlessly replace one another: this trajectory can be read as a text engendering other, critical texts or as a text reading itself, as a gain in critical knowledge or as an irresolvable split and endless vacillation.

After this long digression which was, of necessity, both a definition and transgression of de Man's text, we might return to the original crises, that of saying not only what de Man means but also what we mean when we say de Man. No doubt this essay, I confess, in de Man's own words, produces "a darkness more redoubtable than . . . [any] error . . . [it might] dispel" (AR, 217). To be sure, this is no excuse.[18] But, whatever I may have done in reading his text, if the reader will forgive the rhetorical question,[19] would it not still be possible to assert that it is "Ah! encore de Man"?

Buffalo, January 1985

Notes

1. De Man creates the sense of progress in this essay, ironically enough, by a movement that vacillates between vacillation and progress.

2. See de Man's essay on the *Social Contract*: "We call *text* any entity that can be considered from such a double perspective: as a generative, open-ended, non-referential grammatical system and as a figural system closed off by a transcendental signification that subverts the grammatical code to which the text owes its existence. The 'definition' of the text also states the impossibility of its existence and prefigures the allegorical narratives of this impossibility" (AR, 270).

3. The problem of teleological progression is raised in the chapter on "Self" with regard to Rousseau's play *Pygmalion*. "The provisional syntheses that are achieved along the way in the course of the action do not necessarily mark a progression and it is the burden of the reading to decide whether the text is the teleology of a selfhood that culminates in the climactic exclamation 'Moi!' or a repetitive vacillation" (AR, 176). But the question is, can "reading" ever be in a position to divest itself of this burden by making a definitive decision?

4. One can trace this general movement of revelation and recoil in other of de Man's texts. See, for example, "Literature and Language: A Commentary" (BI, 281, 289).

5. In ways that are too involved to outline here and for reasons that are all too easy to imagine, this evolutionary tale is almost a parodic recapitulation of the arguments of the first two chapters on Rousseau, "Metaphor" and "Self."

6. The "moi" functions both as a general Self that can bridge the gap and include the particular self of Pygmalion and as a self that marks the rupture between Galathea and Pygmalion as other.

7. In the opening essay of *Allegories of Reading* de Man writes: "The grammatical mode of the question becomes rhetorical not when we have, on the one hand, a literal meaning and on the other a figural meaning, but when it is impossible to decide by grammatical or other linguistic devices which of the two meanings (that can be entirely incompatible) prevails. Rhetoric radically suspends logic and opens up vertiginous possibilities of referential aberration. And although it would perhaps be somewhat more remote from common usage, I would not hesitate to equate the rhetorical, figural potentiality of language with literature itself" ("Semiology and Rhetoric," AR, 10). See also "Self," AR, 166ff.

8. Elsewhere de Man uses a simplified version of this metaphor to speak of false models of reading: "The attraction of reconciliation is the elective breeding-ground of false models and metaphors; it accounts for the metaphorical model of literature as a kind of box that separates an inside from an outside, and the reader or critic as the person who opens the lid in order to release in the open what was secreted but inaccessible inside" (AR, 5).

9. No sooner does de Man refer to "one lock worthy of being raped" than he goes on to speak of "the epistemological labyrinth of figural structures." The wit of the allusion to Pope can be found in canto II where a similar slide between lock and lock in the name of a labyrinth takes place. Here Belinda's ringlets become labyrinths that chain her admirers:

> This nymph, to the destruction of mankind,
> Nourish'd two locks, which graceful hung behind
> In equal curls, and well conspired to deck
> With shining ringlets the smooth ivory neck.
> Love in these labyrinths his slaves detains,
> And mighty hearts are held in slender chains.
> ("Rape of the Lock," canto II, lines 19–24)

10. In a 1980 interview de Man had this to say: "But irony is for me something much more fundamental than that. One gets beyond problems of self-reflection, self-consciousness. For me, irony is not something one can historically locate, because what's involved in irony is precisely the impossibility of a system of linear and coherent narrative. There is an inherent conflict or tension between irony on the one hand and history on the other, between irony on the one hand and self-consciousness on the other." "Interview with Paul de Man," *Yale Review*, Summer 1984, 580).

11. Ironically enough, this passage follows closely upon de Man's ironization of his own historicizing of the question of allegory.

12. Paul de Man, "The Rhetoric of Temporality," in *Interpretation: Theory and Practice*, ed. Charles Singleton (Baltimore: Johns Hopkins University Press, 1969), 206. (The phrase is inadvertently omitted in the reprinting of the essay.)

13. Walter Benjamin's *Ursprung des Deutschen Trauerspiels*, a text de Man invokes at the outset of his essay, distinguishes between what Benjamin calls the truth of the philosopher from mere knowledge which tries to stabilize and capture its object. "Truth, realized in the round dance of performed (*dargestellten*) ideas escapes being projected by whatever means into the realm of knowledge. Knowledge is a possessing. Its object itself defines itself as that which must become possessed by consciousness—even if it is transcendental" ([Frankfurt: Suhrkamp, 1963], 10, my translation).

14. The parallel insight in *Allegories of Reading* surfaces at any number of moments, say, for example, when de Man speaks of the subject, denied in the literary text by the author or reader, being "reborn in the guise of the interpreter" (AR, 174). "Is this not the best way to reintroduce the authority of a self at the far end of its most radical negation, in the highly abstracted and generalized form of a deconstructive process of self-denial?" (AR, 172).

15. See de Man's commentary on P. B. Shelley in a similar predicament: RR, 121–22.

16. Something similar takes place in the essay "Semiology and Rhetoric" in *Allegories of Reading* where the grammatization of rhetoric as an assertion of negative knowledge, of a deconstruction of metaphor, alternates with the rhetorization of grammar that brings us to a "suspended uncertainty" (AR, 16).

17. See the pseudomelancholic preface to de Man's *The Rhetoric of Romanticism*, where history, each time it is introduced, ironically gives way to phrases such as "a rhetorical analysis of figural language" or "theoretical inquiries into the problems of figural language" (RR, viii).

18. On the question of confessions and excuses, see the final chapter of *Allegories of Reading* entitled "Excuses."

19. On the question of rhetorical questions see the opening chapter, entitled "Semiology and Rhetoric."

Paul de Man's History
Kevin Newmark

Now that some of the urgency has dropped out of the polemics and panegyrics surrounding the name Paul de Man, a more sober attitude of critical assessment seems in order, and therefore it is not surprising to see the question of declaring *whether* Paul de Man's work is of importance turn into the necessity of determining just where that importance lies. The issue is essentially historical in nature, since it addresses the place of de Man's work in the field of literary studies, considered at a particular moment but also within an ongoing and more comprehensive process of continuity and change. Placing de Man in this kind of temporal scheme also represents the challenge of situating his writings with respect to ourselves, both as a reminder of part of our past and as a question addressed to our future. For this reason, references to his work tend these days to turn more and more insistently around overtly historical problems like ethics and politics. But before we attempt to assimilate de Man within the familiar literary and historical landscape that we inevitably bring along with such questions, we should recognize the possibility that *reading* de Man is also the possibility of questioning what place "history" occupies in his writings. For it may well be that it is only by *not* reading what place de Man's texts assign to history – that is, to us, our time, and our future – that we can so easily recuperate his work on behalf of a reassuring historical framework for our own self-image.

To some extent, the writings of de Man suggest that he is merely an opponent of history and historical modes of discourse. A gesture that returns in many of his essays is the summary dismissal of the usual terms of literary history. For de Man, the structures of ordinary historical discourse often conform to genetic patterns of filiation that are not confirmed by the texts they are being used to read, and de Man does not hesitate to criticize them for this. Conceptions of history such as these are based ultimately on *organic* (that is, nonlinguistic) referential models, and for this reason they turn out to be singularly inconclusive and inappropriate with respect to structures of meaning whose historical status is not given a priori. In an essay like "Sign and Symbol in Hegel's *Aesthetics*" (SS), there is a very strong sense of a rejection of just such history. At the end of the essay de Man identifies the disjunction he has been talking about as a disjunction between philosophy and history, which is also a disjunction between literature and history. And he concludes by saying, "The reasons for this disjunction . . . are not themselves historical or recoverable by ways of history. To the extent that they are inherent in language . . . the disjunction will always . . . manifest itself as soon as experience shades into thought, history into theory" (SS, 775). We get the impression here that there is something like a mutual exclusion between history and theory, and that eventually history will have to yield to ("shade into") theory for de Man.

But at the same time there are other references in de Man, particularly in the last essays, which go in a somewhat different direction and cannot be construed as a simple negation of history. Alongside what de Man himself would undoubtedly have called the *ideological* mystifications of literary history, which are to be criticized and resisted, there is another history, a history that is neither genetic nor empirical, but that also does not represent a refusal to acknowledge the complexities of language. And if we are to begin to understand anything like de Man's place *in* history, it will have to be on the basis of a reading of this "other" history, which is sketched out in his project for a critique of aesthetic and historical ideology and which is centered on writers like Kant, Hegel, Benjamin, and Baudelaire. A convenient, but by no means privileged, place to start asking about de Man's elaboration of such a nonideological concept of history is his essay on Baudelaire's "Correspondances" and "Obsession," called "Anthropomorphism and Trope in the Lyric." Not only does de Man complain in this essay about the recurrent strategy that pretends to situate this pair of texts "historically" in order to *avoid* reading them, it is also there, at the end of the essay, that we rather unexpectedly come across a most curious reference to another form of history. Within a general statement about generic and period distinctions, de Man states categorically that such terms "are always terms of resistance and nostalgia," and then goes on to add that they "[are] at the furthest remove from the materiality of *actual history*."[1]

The question is, where do we look for some kind of help in reading the term "history" as it is being used here? Earlier in the essay de Man makes reference to what could be considered a necessary first step in reading what is "actual history." Noting the reversed symmetries between "Correspondances" and "Obsession," de Man suggests that the relationship between the two poems can in fact be approached from a historical point of view, provided certain allowances are made in such a terminology. Putting texts side by side in order to describe and interpret historical relationships of before and after, says de Man, one is bound to notice and react to patterns of difference and complementarity. But these patterns of part and whole (where "Correspondances" comes out and names nature in its totality, "Obsession" builds up a list of forests, seas, and sky), of reversals (the serenity of the first poem turns into a torment in the second), and of complementarities (the Greek temple of "Correspondances" is balanced and rounded off by the Christian cathedral of "Obsession") are not themselves functions of chronology, since they not only cut across a single proper name, but also can occur heterogeneously within one and the same text. Rather, they are tropological relationships of similitude and difference that are essentially linguistic. As such, these patterns are produced by rhetorical figures like synecdoche, chiasmus, and metaphor *prior* to their determination in a meaningful historical scheme. Thus, "the terminology of traditional literary history, as a succession of periods or literary movements, remains useful only if the terms are seen for what they are: rather crude metaphors for figural patterns rather than historical events or acts" (RR, 254).

In the kind of move that has become habitual with de Man, historical terms, then, turn out not to be really historical after all, but rather are metaphors, and crude ones at that, for *figural* relationships. But if historical terms refuse to tell us about history and end up being disguised as metaphors, then perhaps reading metaphors will turn out to be our only reliable means of learning something about history. And what, after all, is de Man's reading of "Correspondances" if not a reading of metaphor—and not a crude one this time—if not in fact a reading of the metaphor *of* metaphor, that is, the verb "transporter" that serves to link the sensory and intellectual orders and that appears in the last verse of the poem:

> *l'expansion des choses infinies . . .*
> *Qui chantent les transports de l'esprit et des sens?*

> [*the expansiveness of infinite things . . .*
> *Which sing the transports of the mind and the senses?*]

What this means is that in order to read what history is all about we should exercise all possible restraint in talking about romanticism, classicism, or deconstructionism, and turn our attention instead to reading the metaphors, or the *transports* from rhetorical to historical discourse that such crude terms in fact are.

By now, the thrust of de Man's reading should be well enough known to allow us to dispense with all but a cursory summary of its principal moments. First of all, like any text, "Correspondances" is an answer, a *response* to the question necessarily represented by any reading of the text and which, in the case of this particular poem, can even be heard in the letters of its title. The implied question to which the reading of "Correspondances" seems always to reply takes the form: What is nature, and what is man's place there? The first lines of the poem respond by affirming that nature is a temple in which man is as at home as he is among his own kind. The fact that the glances bestowed on man in verse 4 are *"familiers"* rather than, say, *méfiants*, reinforces the suggestion that the relationship between man and nature is not only not antithetical, but that there is indeed a kind of *family* bond or resemblance at work here. The culmination of the poem, then, the mutual *transports* or exchanges between the mind and the senses, between man and nature, is already prefigured in the first lines of the text. What de Man is at pains to show here is that the link that will work to create this impression of a family resemblance between man and nature is a self-consciously *verbal* one, as is made explicit by the fact that man's relationship to nature is set up in this opening stanza by a reference to "confuses *paroles*" and then further mediated in the following verse through the "forêts de *symboles*." Man may be related to nature as in a family, but this relation is itself established only on the basis of linguistic structures like *paroles* and *symboles*.[2]

It is thanks to the mediations of these symbols, thanks to the verbal relays that progressively link man and nature, that the text is finally able to assert the possibility of amalgamating varying orders of difference and raising them ever higher into an ultimate synthesis of mutual transports.[3] And it is easy enough for de Man to identify the symbolic or tropological principle that propels the poem to its natural conclusion as being metaphor, or simile, since the number and importance of substitutive comparisons here based on a linking *comme* can hardly escape the reader's notice. Thus, and in spite of any logical difficulty involved, the poem moves through its ascending stages with the utmost assurance, suggesting along the way that sounds are "like" smells, that the vastness of light is "like" the vastness of night, or that the expansive activity of such an intangible thing as the mind can be "like" the ascending movement of a cloud of burning incense. The architectural emblem for this process of combining appears in the construction of the temple in the first verse, a construction built on the borders of finite and infinite space, between the heavens and the earth. Made by the piling of stone upon stone, the temple eventually encloses an airy space that seems limitless in its power to suggest the transcendence of a supernatural entity. And we should note that it is only within the ecclesiastical space of the temple here that it would make sense to bring together the different orders of sound and smell in a kind of liturgical service where expanding layers of incense can finally accede to the entirely new register of song or chant, as when it is stated in the last stanza that "le benjoin et l'encens / . . . *chantent* les transports de l'esprit et des sens" ("benjamin and incense / . . . *sing* the transports of the mind and the senses").

However, complications on the level of the rhetoric of the poem, though not necessarily apparent on the level of its theme, are seen by de Man to contaminate the key word *comme* near the end of the text. And one of the most memorable moments of de Man's reading occurs when he is able to identify a syntactical ambiguity that leaves open the possibility that the text's so-called symbolist pretensions to totalizing expansion may in the end fizzle out in an aimless stutter of enumeration. After demonstrating how the initial *comme* that links the various senses of sound, color, and scent is able to achieve a figure of speech by calling their relationship to one another a form of "echo" or "response," de Man comes to the following verses:

> *Il est des parfums frais* comme *des chairs d'enfants,*
> *Doux* comme *les hautbois,* verts comme *les prairies,*
> —*Et d'autres, corrompus, riches et triomphants,*
>
> *Ayant l'expansion des choses infinies,*
> Comme *l'ambre, le musc, le benjoin et l'encens . . .*
>
> [*There are scents fresh* like *the skin of children,*
> *soft* like *the oboe, green* like *the prairies,*
> —*And others, corrupt, rich, and triumphant,*
>
> *Having the expansiveness of infinite things,*
> Like *amber, musk, benjamin, and incense . . .*]

Just before the expanding tropes of comparison allow the incense to turn into song, the *comme* in verse 13 seems to hit a false note. For while it is clear that *frais* can be used here to link both scent and touch, that *doux* is meant to cross from scent to sound, and that *verts* is meant to mediate between scent and color, how are we to read the final *comme* in the poem?

In other words, by asking *how* to read we are also asking about the place of articulation of this particular "like" or "as"; what is its *syntax?* Does the verse that contains these scents relate to the *expansion des choses infinies* of the preceding verse, thus preparing the final synthesis of mind and matter by suggesting to us that the experience of infinity can be understood *by analogy with* the seemingly infinite expansiveness of finite things like amber, musk, and incense? In this case, the syntax would require a reading that at least implicitly would be something like, "l'ambre, le musc, le benjoin et l'encens sont [*comme*] des choses infinies." And while it is clear that these scents are not actually infinite substances—like the human mind or soul—the property of expansion that is common to them both and that grounds the figure of metaphor here can certainly be used to help us imagine the activity of such nonsensory phenomena.[4] On the other hand, the text simultaneously contains another possibility. The place or syntax of the *comme* makes it necessary to ask whether the figure of comparison comes apart here in a lifeless enumeration of smells. These verses can also be read in such a way that the quality of infinite expansion, which should occupy the position of analogical meditation and exchange, becomes purely appositive here, making the final *comme* depend exclusively on the species noun *parfums* in verse 9. Thus, we should be reading:

"Il est des parfums frais . . . / —Et d'autres . . . / Comme l'ambre, le musc, le benjoin et l'encens." In this case, there would be no comparison being made by the poem's key word, *comme*; rather than functioning as a prepositive conjunction of comparison that is able to link two orders of experience, as would be dictated by the symbolist ideology of the text, the *comme* here would be merely the adverbial preposition of exemplification, a kind of "such as" serving only to introduce a tautological list of perfume names and linking what follows artificially by the intervening and potentially endless commas.

It is all a question of deciding between the conjunctive and adverbial value, but nothing in the text read can allow us to make this choice with certainty.[5] What hangs in the balance of this decision is nothing less than a coherent reading of the poem, for it is one thing if the experience of infinity is being likened to familiar physical substances such as amber and musk, since then we would have the metaphorical linking of two distinct regions that can eventually come together in what the text itself refers to earlier as "une ténébreuse et profonde unité." But it is quite another if, in addition or between the lines as it were, we are also reading a monumental text that finally tells us that there are perfumes and then there are perfumes. Such a possibility, which is introduced by the adverbial *comme* of enumeration and which remains irreducible with respect to the actual syntax of the poem, would hardly permit the kind of unilaterally transcendental reading that is usually put forward for this text. Nonetheless, it is not a question of erasing one of the possibilities in favor of the other, of claiming that Baudelaire "meant" this or that, or stating univocally that the *comme* of exemplification does away entirely with the *comme* of analogy. The fact that two incompatible readings can exist side by side is what makes "Correspondances" into a text in the first place.

At any rate, it is at this point that de Man turns his attention to those all-important *transports* of the final verse, and he does so by claiming that the unexpected possibility of reading a tautological list of smells in line 13 allows in turn for the concluding transports to become literalized in a curious way. What interests us here is that it is also at this point that de Man once again makes reference to a vocabulary heavily invested with historical implications. Playing on the fact that "transports" can legitimately be read as a translated version of *metaphorein*, a Greek word that can be used to designate the mundane transfers or *correspondances* of an urban system of public transportation as well as the more strictly metaphorical substitutions that are supposed to occur between the mind and the senses, de Man asks whether the interruption of the transcendental ascension of "Correspondances" by the enumerative adverb *comme* in line 13 should be understood at the end of the poem as a prosaic, i.e., *empirical*, literalization of the ecstatic "transports" of lyrical poetry into the economic code of "transports" that take place in daily city life. If the *comme* of line 13 cannot guarantee the vertical substitutions that promise an ascension from the earth to the heavens by way of the hallowed monuments, or temples of lyric poetry, perhaps the horizontal churning of enumeration, like the stops along the Paris métro, can be used to take us along a more solidly earthly path. Such a reading would be a form of ideology critique and would move along the lines of debunking the extreme aestheticism that is usually considered the necessary corollary to symbolism in favor of a more aware discourse of history and economics.[6] What de Man is again hinting at here, of course, is that whereas the naively historical terms of traditional literary criticism turn out to be crude metaphors for figural patterns, the possibility remains that a rhetorically aware reading of metaphor might prove to be a reliable means of uncovering and diagnosing ideological tensions between aesthetics and politics, or between literature and history. A reading that could disclose the urban subway system lurking beneath the lyrical transports of symbolist poetry would clearly be a first and important step in such a direction.

But de Man goes on to point out that at this stage of the game such ideological demystification is in appearance only, for the vertical transcendence of metaphysics or aesthetics and the horizontal connections implied by an economically based sociopolitical system actually share the same presuppositions. Of these, undoubtedly the most important would be the unquestioned presence of semantically determined substitutive transfers between different orders. Whether we transfer from finite to infinite, or simply from the Porte d'Orléans line to the Porte d'Auteuil line, we are still operating within the same kind of unified system of motion and circulation. And since this sort of prosaically economic reading is no less dependent for its results on figural relationships and intersections produced by rhetorical exchanges—or metaphorical "transports"—than is the lyrical reading of "Correspondances," it cannot be considered a priori any more "historical" than the pseudohistorical terms of canonical literary history. In slightly different terms, then, we could say that all particularities notwithstanding, the *transports de l'esprit* and the *transports des sens* are both "transports" that seek to *merge* two distinct realms, whether they be heaven and earth or merely the arcades and barricades of Paris. Hence, de Man's further suggestion that a straightforward application of ideology critique "is not by itself disruptive with regard to the claim for transcendental unity." By subscribing uncritically to the same tropological patterns, this kind of reading will establish only its own "correspondence" with the original metaphysical ideology of the poem.

For this reason, the literalization de Man refers to, and which he also insists is a consequence of the syntactic ambiguity in "Correspondances," cannot be reduced to a simple turn from metaphysics to economics, or aesthetics to politics. And it is also clear that this literalization will have to be far more "historical" than any of the previous moments of the reading since, unlike the lyrical or prosaic transfers of metaphor that are stymied by the repetitive list of verse 13, not only is it beyond doubt that such a literalization actually does take place, it is also what threatens to prevent all else in the poem from happening. In other words, the disruption at issue here will not be simply a matter of substitution *between l'esprit* and *les sens*, between a transcendental and economic reading, or to put it in a more technically precise way, between figural and literal *meaning*, but rather a disruption, or literalization on the level of the *letter*, of what organizes meaning itself, including all subsequent distinctions and syntheses of the figural and the literal. Rather than being a question of one kind of meaning and another—poetic or political, lyrical or prosaic—the literalization de Man is talking about would be something like the literalization *of* meaning into its constitutive parts, the literalization of the lyrical or prosaic *word* into mere *letters*.

That this is indeed the case can be confirmed by way of a remark de Man makes earlier in the essay concerning the three orders of language that function side by side in "Correspondances." After pointing out that the dialectical process of the poem is self-consciously verbal, de Man adds, "Language can be the chain of metaphors in a synesthesia, as well as the oxymoronic polysemy of a single word, such as 'se confondent' (or 'transports' in line 14) or even, on the level of the signifier, the play of the syllable or the letter" (RR, 245). What de Man has in mind in this reference to a third dimension of language is the possibility of breaking apart semantic units into subsemantic particles in order to allow for substitutions and reversals that by themselves could never occur on the level of the signified, either synesthetically between different senses or polysemantically between various meanings of a given signifier. And he offers as a most remarkable example of this third dimension the poem's title itself, "Correspondances," which, he says, "is like the anagrammatic condensation of the text's entire program: 'corps' and 'esprit' brought together and harmonized by the *ance* of assonance that pervades the concluding tercets: from *ayant, ambre, chantent* to *expansion, sens, transport*, finally redoubled and re-echoed in *encens/sens*."

The remark that the poem's entire aesthetic program can be found embedded in its title is a striking one indeed, and the test of de Man's own rhetorical powers is the extent to which one is willing to assent to the demonstration that follows. Whatever else, though, "the anagrammatic condensation" in question should also give us pause, for it is about as reliable from a strictly philological or epistemological point of view as the commonest pun or wordplay. In adducing a purely poetic effect (paronamasia) to further his exegetical argument, de Man is following a long tradition, whose most famous examples would have to include Hegel, who makes the crucial argument about the essence of being and its necessarily mediated development through time depend at least to some extent on the fact that in German the essence, or *Wesen*, is already visible in the past participle of the word for "being" (*sein*), which just happens to be *gewesen*.[7] The fact that in French the word for "correspondences" already contains both the "body" and "soul" whose harmonious union the poem of the same name will eventually sing is nothing more than an accident, as can be proved by translating the same title into English or German. And once de Man has successfully traced what he has been calling all along the poem's tropological "program" of analogical substitutions to the random play of the subsemantic syllables "cor," "esp," and "ance," how can we tell whether the poem that then goes on to celebrate the "seamless articulation" of the mind and the senses is being determined by the cognitive principles of a mind or by the purely chance encounters of written signs?

At any rate, like the somewhat more playful discovery of "mind," "body," and "assonance" in the title, "Correspondances," the "sobering" literalization of "transports" underscored by de Man with the help of the dysfunction of the synthesizing *comme* near the end of the poem is not due merely to the oxymoronic polysemy of metaphysical and economical "transports," or metaphors. In other words, it is not like the juxtaposition of incompatible *meanings* that we previously observed in the word *se confondent*, which, as de Man points out, "can designate the bad infinity of confusion as well as the fusion of opposites into synthetic judgments." When de Man finally declares that the problem with "metaphor" in this text is not so much centered on *phorein* as on *meta*, he has left questions of semantically determined incompatibilities or polysemies far behind. For a look at any dictionary will tell us that *metaphorein* can easily *mean* both an ecstatic movement beyond thought and sensation in a common transcendental realm, and a spatial movement beyond some particular place to another in an industrial city, but how could it ever *mean*, in the words of de Man, "a state that is beyond movement entirely"?[8]

When de Man asks the question about how this "beyond," which by definition posits and names movement, could ever take us away from what it posits, he is literalizing the word "metaphor" into the play of its syllables. He is literally taking the word "transport" apart, breaking it loose of any prior semantic determination, and asking about the relationship of the letters, or syllables among themselves. "Transport," of course, comes from the Latin roots *trans* and *portare*, and the etymology of the word, which is still a semantically determined category based on substitutions and reversals occurring within an unreflected (that is, ideological) concept of temporal development, ensures the order here, ensures that the word, even when broken into its constitutive parts, still manages to *mean* a kind of carrying from one place to another, or a movement beyond any such place of origin. The etymology of the word can be used to ask whether and to what extent the "transports" of the mind are linked to the "transports" of the senses; that is, it can be used to ask about whether "transports" is a metaphysical or an empirical concept. But in neither case is the word's capacity to signify a "movement beyond" radically disrupted. Things are otherwise with the actual *order* of the word, however. For the literal syntax of the syllables of the written word, before they are organized according to semantic principles of etymology, can just as easily be read in such a way that they are made to ask about a beyond of movement, thus putting into question our ordinary conception of movement, whether as metaphysical transcendence or political change, that is, of movement as it is generally used to understand the successive or simultaneous motions of history.

In order to appreciate the theoretical significance of de Man's reading, we should recall that what allows for this bizarre ordering of the word "transport" in the first place, what allows for its literalization into the play of the syllable, is itself a principle of ordering, is the undeterminable *syntax* of the word *comme* in line 13, "Comme l'ambre, le musc, le benjoin et l'encens." De Man says that this *comme* "relates to the subject 'parfums' in two different ways or, rather, it has two distinct subjects." By making us aware of the syntax of *comme* in line 13, de Man reminds us of the syntax, or the disposition of the letters and syllables of the word "transports" in line 14. And by pointing out that *comme* in line 13 actually does have two subjects, de Man reminds us that on the level of the letter, on the level of syntax prior to any semantically overdetermined decisions, it is always possible to read two subjects.

For what syntax in fact names is a disposition of letters that is capable of *carrying* meaning (a kind of *portare*, then, as in the word "transports") without itself originally *being* meaningful. This carrying property of syntax can be seen to relate to the meaning produced beyond it in the two radically different ways that the *portare* of metaphor relates to its qualification *trans*, or as de Man says, "It has two different subjects." It all depends on what kind of reading any text as such receives and whether the focus, or subject, is the meaning (*logos*) or the production of meaning (*lexis*). If the carrying of *portare* is already understood as a preliminary form of meaning, then the focus will be on the ultimate accomplishment of this *movement*: "carrying" will be its own subject and "beyond" will merely be its somewhat redundant attribute. Such a movement is truly dialectical; that is, it progresses by a series of discrete negations, beginning with the negation of syntax, and manages at once to have itself as subject and to move continually beyond itself as it enters the semantic field of tropes that initiates the upward motion of expansion implied in any transcendental meaning. In this case, the syntax would read, "movement beyond," and would in fact be naming the traditional concept of "metaphor." By way of a dialectical reading, the surface order of syntax merges with or turns into the semantic depth of metaphor.

But if the carrying of this form of *portare* has its focus elsewhere, if its own movement is truly based on something that is itself not yet meaningful as dialectical movement, then the *trans* here has to be taken seriously. Read now with *trans* as its subject, i.e., as a purely lexical element whose relation to the movement of meaning has not yet been established, the text prevents the carrying from going on its predetermined path, prevents the carrying from ever becoming a homogeneous movement and cuts itself off from its own meaning as metaphor. And it does this by restricting the carrying to being an objective predicate of "beyond," which then simply marks itself as such as the place that actually is "beyond," or more precisely, "other than" movement. In this case, the text would have to read, "beyond movement" and would inscribe in an ironic way the text's most meaningful word for "metaphor," "transports," as the place, or the site of its other, that is, syntax. But the fact that in the one case "syntax" turns into "metaphor" and in the other "metaphor" turns into "syntax" cannot be taken as evidence of any kind of symmetrical reversal here, since in the first instance the "turning" is capable of merging the two categories into a kind of meaningful unity, while in the second case the turning of "metaphor" is drained of all predetermined meaning despite its continued presence as text. For these two radically heterogeneous readings of "metaphor," the whole question comes down to how we can determine the "subject" of its syntax, how we can determine the meaning of that which subsequently allows for meaning to be determined. Is the subject of syntax a movement that is already meaningful in itself, or is its subject just another syntactical component that is "beyond" meaning altogether? By allowing the syntactical aberration of *comme* in line 13 to literalize the "transports" of line 14 into a state that is beyond movement, de Man opens the way for what we might call a "syntactical" reading of "transports," or in other words, a figural narration or allegory of syntax that is inscribed in the key word for metaphor, "transports," and that disrupts both the aesthetic and historical ideology of the text.

In its turn, this allegorical reading of "transports" as "metaphor," which is subsequently literalized by the syntactic excess of *comme* into the impossible alternative between metaphor as meaning and metaphor as syntax, becomes crucial for de Man's reading of the gnomic figure of the temple in the first line of "Correspondances." The classical temple that seems to lie beyond tension and beyond motion is thus the analogical emblem for the syntactical reading of *metaphorein*, since in this text at least it stands all by itself and functions as a concrete figure for that which is indeed "beyond movement." As such, it is what subtends but does not take part in the movement of infinite expansion detailed in the rest of the poem. And by the same token it also becomes an emblem for the random play of the syllable in the title "Correspondances"—as opposed to the semantically determined transfers of tropes in the first stanzas—that helped to reveal the [syntactic] possibility of being beyond [semantic] movement in the last line of the poem. In other words, "temple" already names in the first line the ritual space where man's *corps* and *esprit* can be brought together by the syntactical incense (*ance*) that sings the end of the poem. So when de Man finally states that "within the confines of a system of transportation—or of language as a system of communication—one can transfer from one vehicle to another, but one cannot transfer from being like a vehicle to being like a *temple*, or a ground" (RR, 252), it seems that he is merely reallegorizing in the thematic vocabulary of the poem's own decor the nonthematic relationship between "metaphor" as semantically determined vehicles or tropes (which can also be understood as "movement beyond," or as a certain form of *comme* or "transports") and "metaphor" as semantically undetermined ground or syntax (which should be read as "beyond movement," or as other, nondialectical forms of *comme* or "transports"). The temple is the metaphorical figure for this syntactical excess of both *comme* and "transport" which, read with the help of de Man, translate into nonmetaphorical "stuttering enumeration" and "beyond movement." It is on the basis of this excess, or under the portal of this motionless temple, that the poem's infinite expansion of tropes is built and eventually undone.

Now, this temple that stands apart in the first stanza of "Correspondances" is an exceedingly curious and potentially misleading edifice. For if the ideology of metaphor — and all that such an ideology entails with respect to pseudohistorical gestures and claims of mastery — is what is being read in this poem, then how is it that a reading of metaphor *as* syntax produces only another metaphor *of* syntax? Even though it be of syntax, can the metaphor of the temple be anything other than a temple dedicated ultimately *to* metaphor and its correlative aesthetic and political ideology? Such a temple, were it simply metaphorical, would in fact be yet another in the series of what de Man dismisses as "terms of resistance and nostalgia, at the furthest remove from the materiality of actual history" (RR, 262). It is certainly true that when de Man first makes reference to it in the essay, he calls the temple a "verbal building," and this seems to follow logically enough from the previous paragraph where he had already alluded to architectural constructs as "icons" or metaphors for the way tropes can be used to build structures that reach higher and higher. Unpacking the figure, we would say that the temple is a verbal building insofar as it is an architectural construct (building) that works *like* and therefore *represents* rhetorical figures (verbality).

This would make the actual building into a figure for figure, perhaps just another metaphor, and in the end perhaps just another of those *chambres d'éternel deuil* built out of pathos and the resistance to reading. But there is another way to read this "temple" as a verbal building, one that is no longer a figure strictly speaking and that brings us much closer to de Man's remarks on "the materiality of actual history" at the end of the essay. The verbality of the temple in line 1 is not only based on substitutive tropes of resemblance like metaphors and icons. Its role in the poem is not restricted to figuring metaphorically the figurative or disfigurative power of language. There is a power of language that is inscribed in the temple in a wholly literalized way. A temple is a *verbal* building because it stands on consecrated ground, on ground that has been marked out *verbally*, a building carved out by the words of a duly empowered representative of a linguistic community. A rose may be as fair by any other name, but a temple is holy only so long as it is verbally marked as such and such a temple. In other words, there can be no temple without an *act* of language that marks out its ground as the site for a temple, and some form of *memory* or text in which the act is inscribed. Such an act which, like the temple, establishes the limit for all else in the poem, and because it is indisputable and infinitely iterable, is the only thing in the poem that is truly *historical* in the sense of being an actual occurrence necessary for any reading of the text. But it is not a priori based on a resemblance or an exchange with nature or anything else. Nature can become a temple, but a temple could never be natural. Which means of course that history itself is not natural but rather linguistic, and potentially violent, like the making and making over by reconsecration of Louis XV's Abbaye de Ste-Genviéve into the *temple de la renomée* or Panthéon. History is a linguistic event, the arrangement of verbal buildings, a syntax of inscriptions that exists to be memorized and then read.

A temple is also a verbal building, then, insofar as it is necessarily based on an inscription. De Man's assertion that a temple is a verbal building calls attention to the fact that the power of inscription that marks out the ground of a temple—or to write this in somewhat less metaphorical fashion, that puts into place the order of a syntax, which is the order of language itself—is not primarily a figure, a vehicle, an exchange, an icon, or a meaning. It is as silent, as invisible, as immobile as the impositional construct of verbality that is forever inscribed in the word "temple." For these same reasons, it is also not human, phenomenal, or temporal. It happens, but it happens originally with the blind necessity of impersonal and involuntary memory; as such it is a text that is forever beyond the power of a self, and the dimensions of time and space implied by it. Unlike all the other examples in this text, moreover, the trace of this inscription, the putting into place or marking out of a syntactic ground on which to build a verbal temple that will later be inhabited by man as both spirit and matter, is indisputable as long as there is a text to read, is neither checked nor interfered with the way that subsequent moments of the poem are. This verbal building, which can be read neither wholly independently of nor in subservience to the tropological movements of meaning it makes possible, is what de Man has been calling the materiality of actual history.

But will the temple that eventually comes to be built on this spot of marking, or of syntax, inevitably reenter the system of tropes it helps to produce, and in the reassuring figures of religious belief or conscious political action, or as we have just seen, even as a metaphorical figure for something that could disrupt them both, such as syntax itself? This sort of refiguration by means of successive negations, in fact, seems as unavoidable as de Man's own long list of "nons" that cascades at the end of his essay. The kind of specular misreading that de Man takes such pains earlier in the essay to undo in his rewriting of the verb *metaphorein* is once again suggested by the (negative) symmetry of his characterization of "true 'mourning' ": "the most *it* can do is to allow for *non*-comprehension and enumerate *non*-anthropomorphic, *non*-elegiac, *non*-celebratory, *non*-lyrical, *non*-poetic, that is to say, prosaic, or, better, historical modes of language power" (RR, 262). For once a syntax has been put in place the figural chain of dialectical substitutions engendered by it will follow as if by nature: the "noncomprehension" of true "mourning" is on its way toward comprehension as soon as it is named as such. It is all too easy to imagine how de Man's undoing of genetic history could itself be reincorporated into a genetic scheme whose final challenge would be to refashion his name in our own image. The work on allegory and irony, the readings of Rousseau and Nietzsche, are merely preparatory to a genuine confrontation with historical discourse that begins to take place in the last works on Kant and Hegel and that would undoubtedly have culminated in the announced readings of Marx. History, we like to think, occurs in the work of de Man right now, with us, and only "after" an intermediate moment of purely linguistic analysis.

No matter how convincing or attractive such a scheme, it risks falling back into a specular form of genetic understanding that is anything but "historical" in de Man's sense. And to the extent that it takes this "after" to be somehow "beyond" the moment of language and the rhetorical analysis of texts, it is not certain that it will be any more free of pseudohistorical complications and delusions than were the metaphorical figures *comme* and *transports* in Baudelaire's text. In the end such figures cannot really be said to occur at all in the full sense of the term since "before" they can complete themselves, they always get stuck in the enumerative syntax from which they proceed; in de Man's case, the figure of a developmental history that leads from questions of language to questions of history would never be able to master the way that his own historical discourse is inscribed ironically, that is, rhetorically, in an aimless stutter. These figures are merely the incomplete narratives, or allegories, of a purely nonfigurative occurrence that remains beyond them and their pseudomovement, and when they are read, such figures always and again tell the story of their impossibility to occur historically. What does occur, what is not impossible, what is actual history, and what takes place in de Man's own text with a regularity that is truly disruptive, is what de Man calls the language stutter that interrupts, marks, inscribes, reads, and writes that impossibility in a way that is incontrovertible, and because it is itself not a figure, an icon, a vehicle, or an exchange, promises to remain wholly inaccessible to us and our subsequent attempts to recognize ourselves in it.

Notes

1. "Anthropomorphism and Trope in the Lyric" (RR, 262; my emphasis).
2.   La Nature est un temple où de vivants piliers
                 Laissent parfois sortir de confuses paroles;
                 L'homme y passe à travers des forêts de symboles
                 Qui l'observent avec des regards familiers.

I leave aside for the sake of economy de Man's discussion of whether anthropomorphism is involved in this description of nature, for while the question does serve to introduce an element of ambivalence at the very beginning of the poem, not all of its implications are pursued by de Man at this point.

3. Although it is certainly more rhetorically precise, de Man's reading is anything but new up to this point. Marcel Raymond's remarks about Baudelaire and the role of modern poetry, while not derived explicitly from a reading of "Correspondances," certainly proceed from a familiarity with the text and thus may be taken as representative of the *idées reçues* surrounding it: "A l'aide de ces matériaux en désordre . . . le poète va créer un ordre qui sera . . . l'expression infaillible de son âme. Et cette expression—bien que les éléments dont elle se compose paraissent se rapporter aux choses de la *nature*—n'en sera pas moins essentiellement *surnaturelle*. Car l'âme . . . ne trouve sa vraie

patrie que dans l'au-delà spirituel où plonge la nature. La mission de la poésie est d'ouvrir une fenêtre sur cet autre monde . . . de permettre au moi d'échapper à ses limites et de *se dilater* jusqu'à *l'infini*. Par ce mouvement *d'expansion* s'ébauche ou s'accomplit le retour à l'unité de l'esprit" (*De Baudelaire au surréalisme* [Paris: José Corti, 1940], 22–23, my emphasis).

4. Since this is the syntax that is most compatible with an unquestioned thematic understanding of the "transports de l'esprit et des sens" in the final verse it is not surprising that it turns out to be the reading of choice, as is readily apparent in the English translation of the poem by Richard Howard:

> There are odors succulent as young flesh . . .
> while others . . .
> possess the power of such infinite things
> as incense, amber, benjamin and musk.

5. There also seems to be a good deal of uncertainty as to the exact grammatical status of "like." English prefers to distinguish between the conjunctive and all other uses in order to condemn it, but a trace of conjunction is often present anyhow. Whether the distinction goes between conjunction and preposition, or even extends to the level of adjective and adverb, the syntax of "Correspondances" will still be ambivalent in a radical way since, whatever the grammatical appellation, one reading allows for a comparison ("infinite things are *more* like musk than they are like benjamin") while the other reading does not ("there are other perfumes *like* benjamin, musk, etc.").

6. De Man's implicit reference here and elsewhere in this essay is to Walter Benjamin; *Charles Baudelaire: A Lyric Poet in the Era of High Capitalism*, trans. Harry Zohn (London: Verso Editions, 1983). The "spatial displacement" de Man mentions with respect to the verbal ending of meta-*phorein*, as well as the reference to a colder form of "analytic self-consciousness," recalls Benjamin's discussions of the Baudelairean *flâneur*, himself a kind of peripatetic philosopher. Similarly, de Man's description of the prosaic transposition of ecstasy into economic codes sounds very much like another version of Benjamin's account of how Lamartine's heaven collapsed once and for all into the marketplace of Baudelaire. However, rather than simply borrowing the terms of his reading of Baudelaire from Benjamin, it is much more likely that de Man is also reading Baudelaire at least in part in order to set up the possibility of later reading Benjamin, and in particular the uneasy relationship in Benjamin between economic and allegorical discourse. For the first part of such a reading, see de Man's " 'Conclusions': Walter Benjamin's 'The Task of the Translator,' " in *The Resistance to Theory* (Minneapolis: University of Minnesota Press, 1986).

7. For Hegel's own version of this "proof," see the section on the "Doctrine of Essence" in both the *Encyclopedia* and the *Logic*. It would perhaps be going too far to suggest that de Man's use of the anagram in the poem's title invalidates his argument, since his reading is much sooner an example (or *mise en abyme*) of this argument than an explanation for it.

8. Although the very question of such an attentive reading of the word "metaphor" may at first seem willful or of rather limited interest, we should recall that, in differing guises, the possibility of an unproblematic "moving beyond" is a familiar topos in philosophical discourse. In an overschematic way, we could say that it is precisely this question that determines the possibility of any form of dialectical thinking, including such representative instances as Pascal's "l'homme passe l'homme infiniment," Rousseau's concept of perfectibility, or Hegel's own *Aufhebung*. Nietzsche and Heidegger continue to reflect on this question while taking their distance from it. Within this "tradition" of texts, any reading of the "transports" in Baudelaire will lead inevitably to questions of metaphor, transcendence, and history. To this extent, then, the title of de Man's essay is itself somewhat ironic, since the real interest of his reading does not lie in the generic status of the lyric, or the possibility of determining what is lyrical by defining and delimiting trope and anthropomorphism. What is of genuine theoretical import in the lyric is its relationship to what de Man himself calls the "*motion* of understanding." And it is the question of this motion as the possibility of history and hermeneutics that is condensed in de Man's reading of "transports."

Pieces of Resistance
Peggy Kamuf

Teaching Resistance

A text such as the *Profession de foi* can literally be called "unreadable"
in that it leads to a set of assertions that radically exclude each other.
Nor are these assertions mere neutral constations; they are exhortative
performatives that require the passage from sheer enunciation to action.
They compel us to choose while destroying the foundations of any
choice. They tell the allegory of a judicial decision that can be neither
judicious nor just. . . . One sees from this that the impossibility of
reading should not be taken too lightly. (AR, 245)

These sentences conclude chapter 10 of *Allegories of Reading*, a chapter that
is itself titled "Allegory of Reading." The repetition of the title suggests that the
Profession de foi is exemplary of the allegorization of reading as both a necessary
and impossible task—necessary because it is impossible. It would be reassuring
to think that "unreadability" affected only the rare occurrence of a "text such as
the *Profession de foi*," or that it could be isolated within the limits of particular
authors' works—Rousseau's, for example. It would be reassuring but, like whis-
tling in the dark, perhaps a benighted attempt to keep the shadows at bay. Better
not to take the impossibility of reading "too lightly," warns de Man in the last
sentence.

But just how lightly is too lightly? While the question may be unavoidable, the
answer is bound to fall short, leaving readers with a puzzle not unlike the one that
confronts them on the page displaying, in epigraph to *Allegories of Reading*, this

phrase from Pascal: "Quand on lit trop vite ou trop doucement on n'entend rien" (When one reads too quickly or too slowly, one understands nothing). The phrase suggests that whoever would understand what she reads must find the *juste mesure* of reading: neither too fast nor too slow but, in the self-satisfied words of Goldilocks, "just right." Such a reading of the phrase, however, may itself have gone too fast, neglecting to notice that this rule does not set the speed for its own reading and thus carries over the possibilities for error or misunderstanding it is designed to warn against. Likewise, how lightly is one to take de Man's warning that "the impossibility of reading should not be taken too lightly" given that any reading—including the one just completed of the *Profession de foi*—will at some point have to cast off the burden of its own impossibility and leap out, no doubt too heavily, over the abyss of understanding? Is there not, as in Pascal's rule, a double error that has here been abbreviated into the more commonly occurring of the two: reading too fast, taking the impossibility of reading too lightly?

That reading, as de Man teaches it, always negotiates with a doubled possibility of error is confirmed by some lines we elided above from the concluding paragraph of "Allegory of Reading":

> If after reading the *Profession de foi*, we are tempted to convert ourselves to "theism," we stand convicted of foolishness in the court of the intellect. But if we decide that belief, in the most extensive use of the term (which must include all possible forms of idolatry and ideology), can once and forever be overcome by the enlightened mind, then this twilight of the idols will be all the more foolish in not recognizing itself as the first victim of its occurrence. (AR, 245)

The second error identified here is "all the more foolish," which could be taken to mean that it is more foolish than the first error, more foolish than the blind conversion to belief in an ordered meaning of the world. It is not more or less in error but rather more foolish to *believe* that belief can be overcome. In either case, reading, it would seem, leads to foolish behavior. While serious readers might understandably be expected to reject such an intimation, this reaction cannot disguise how the study of literary language installs a critical relation to the *institution* of all serious values—that is, to their interiority to themselves, to their self-evidence. It is this critical relation that institutions, naturally enough perhaps, resist and, to the extent that literary study has come to identify itself with the stability, or even the growth of institutions (particularly the teaching institution), one should not be surprised to find so many literary scholars reproving with one hand the critical enterprise that, with the other hand—the hand guided by a text's demand for reading—they endeavor to carry out.

The uneasy relationship between literary study and pedagogical institutions is one that interests de Man repeatedly but nowhere, perhaps, so distinctly as in the essay titled "The Resistance to Theory" (RT, 1–20).

One of the starting points of the essay (for there are several) is an empirical knowledge enunciated by a certain "we": "we know that there has been, over the last fifteen to twenty years, a strong interest in something called literary theory and that, in the United States, this interest has at times coincided with the importation and reception of foreign, mostly but not always continental influences. We also know that this wave of interest now seems to be receding as some satiation or disappointment sets in after the initial enthusiasm" (RT, 5). This general address, this "we know that there has been," is, we know, meant for scholars in modern languages and literatures in North American universities. We know this from the essay's contextual introduction, which will be taken up below. For the moment, we need only remark an address that institutes a knowledge, a ground on which to let stand or fall a theoretical movement of thought beyond what it thinks it already knows. This ground, however, displays at its edges "an ebb and flow," a differentiated movement of forces. "Such an ebb and flow is natural enough, but it remains interesting, *in this case*, because it makes the depth of the resistance to theory so manifest" (my emphasis). In this ebb and flow movement of overturning, there appears a figure that has title to theory's interest and is here titled: the resistance to theory. Having started out from the *terra firma* of what we know, we have come upon something that remains to be read and that interests whoever who would speak of literary theory as a critical relation to institutions, the relation that has been made manifest in a figure. Resistance to theory thus engages an act of reading that oversteps whatever established formal limits usually or by convention contain that activity. This because the ebb and flow of the figure concerns precisely the movement of inscription and erasure that underlies ("the *depth* of the resistance to theory") any formalization of limits: those of an institution or those of "something called literary theory."

But reading the figure of resistance encounters at the outset an ambiguity of reference. What is interesting "in this case" is filed under the name – the resistance to theory – which is also the title of the essay. The deictic "this" of "in this case" points in two directions at once: to this essay and to the apparent phenomenon to which the essay refers. Thus, when the phrase "the resistance to theory" occurs in the body of the essay, one cannot be sure whether it appears there as a citation of the title or whether one should read the title as already itself a citation of the phrase from the essay.[1] This undecidability keeps the figure from closing off too quickly in an illusion of reference since the gesture of pointing to some referent cannot exclude its own act of pointing with which it exceeds the whole to be pointed to. Such is, of course, the case of any text,[2] but the traces of a supplementary resistance to which the essay or its title cannot be said simply to refer have been reinscribed in this case.

Its case, that is to say its falling or befalling like an accident, the occasion of its falling and the coincidence between the falling that befalls it and the falling it describes. All of these terms – case, accident, occasion, coincidence – draw on the same Latin root: *cadere*, to fall. As does the word "chance,"[3] so we will not be surprised to find that the essay's chances of success — its chances of being read and understood — are bound up with a certain failure or falling before its occasion.

The rising and falling of "The Resistance to Theory" is briefly recounted in some prefatory paragraphs. This account seems to fit easily enough into the genre of the preface or introduction and thus to require little more than the minimal attention of any reader who is only passing through on the way to the essay "itself." Yet, to read these paragraphs as preface — standing before and outside the essay they point to — is perhaps to miss the point. Not just because one could justifiably speak here of a postscript rather than a preface but more importantly because these paragraphs, set off by a blank from the main body of the essay, allow one to question what are usually thought of as the limits of a textual body. Where exactly the text of the essay begins and ends, where it starts or stops falling are questions that the initial paragraphs render unavoidable.

That is, one cannot avoid noticing how the essay is made to double back on itself in these initial lines as the result of a resistance to "The Resistance to Theory." Here is the story, an allegory of reading the resistance to reading, as de Man tells it:

> This essay was not originally intended to address the question of teaching directly,[4] although it was supposed to have a didactic and an educational function — which it failed to achieve. It was written at the request of the Committee on the Research Activities of the Modern Language Association as a contribution to a collective volume entitled *Introduction to Scholarship in Modern Languages and Literatures*. I was asked to write the section on literary theory. Such essays are expected to follow a clearly determined program: they are supposed to provide the reader with a select but comprehensive list of the main trends and publications in the field, to synthesize and classify the main problematic areas and to lay out a critical and programmatic projection of the solutions which can be expected in the foreseeable future. All this with a keen awareness that, ten years later, someone will be asked to repeat the same exercise.[5]
>
> I found it difficult to live up, in minimal good faith, to the requirements of this program and could only try to explain, as concisely as possible, why the main theoretical interest of literary theory consists in the impossibility of its definition. The Committee rightly judged that this was an inauspicious way to achieve the pedagogical objectives of the volume and commissioned another article.[6] I thought their decision altogether justified, as well as interesting in its implications for the teaching of literature.

These paragraphs recount a pedagogical failure but one that "remains interesting in its implications for the study of literature." It is therefore not, strictly speaking or exclusively, a pedagogical failure because in falling short it keeps an interest for the theory of teaching literature or the teaching of literary theory. The interest may be seen to reside in a resistance that rejects an *inauspicious* reading of theory's chances for producing a positive discipline of reading. This is interesting because it implies that, according to a widely endorsed program, the teaching of literature would measure its success by the capacity to turn a student reader's attention away from signs that cannot be made to submit to reassuring definition and that are therefore, by definition, programmatically, judged to be "inauspicious." As de Man remarks toward the end of the essay, this interesting problem "quickly becomes the more baffling one of having to account for the shared reluctance to acknowledge the obvious," the rhetorical dimension of any text called "literary."[7]

The turning aside or turning away in an avoidance of reading the sign's rhetorical component is itself a trope to which de Man gives form in the words "resistance to theory." As we have seen, the figure points both to an obvious, albeit slippery, referent (what "we know there has been," the ebb and flow of interest in literary theory, the depth of resistance to theory made manifest) and to itself in a turning aside of reference, citing its title as the name of a figure. The turning of the figure is not arrested when it turns back on itself. Rather, it names "itself" as the error inherent in all proper names (and a title is also a proper name), their improper or rhetorical relation to a particular referent. Neither does the text "The Resistance to Theory" close itself off as a proper name having a known, historical referent. The empirical, referential meaning of "resistance to theory" is perforce turned aside when the phrase is used as the title of the essay and when, in referring, it also refers to itself.

The essay proceeds, then, as a deconstructive reading of its title, just one more reason one cannot bypass it reading by way of paraphrase. One cannot bypass reading, but of course neither can one overlook the fact that immense institutional programs function, precisely, to turn away from reading, to turn away what turns away itself, of itself or in itself. Each of these two imperatives which seem to exclude the other, is in fact leaving or inscribing its mark on the other in such a way that neither can emerge in its pure form or in a purely formal way. On the one hand, that the "main theoretical interest [of literary theory] consists in the impossibility of its definition" will continue to manifest itself in institutional resistance. And, on the other hand, because the institutionalization of literary theory in this country has tended to follow the way in which it can be made to serve an overarching pedagogical program[8] and because literary theory, when it pursues its main theoretical interest, has to question the defining limits of any such program when applied to literary language, institutionalization can be made to appear in its effects—the marks it has left—on the movement of theoretical thought. "The Resistance to Theory" inauspiciously resists this program and thus bears the mark of a certain institutional closure.

Self-Resistance

Given the deconstructed exteriority implicit in the title, questions such as "What is it that resists or threatens?" or, in the passive voice, "What is it that is being resisted or threatened?" are bound to encounter the complication or the coimplication of the supplemental mark of resistance from which the essay proceeds. Because they are so bound, the essay comes to speak of "the displaced symptoms of a resistance inherent in the theoretical enterprise itself" (RT, 12) and finally of the language of theory as "the language of self-resistance" (RT, 20). In the course of an analysis of this self-resisting movement, what will have become apparent is a limit on the validity of the subject-object, active-passive mode of positioning any truth about resistance.

Yet when de Man speaks of "displaced symptoms" of resistance, his choice of words seems designed to remind one of the key use of the term by psychoanalysis. Such echoes (for there are many in the essay) might even be heard as early as the title since "The Resistance to Theory" does not specify what theory is at issue.[9] The title, in other words, can be read as citing some relation to psychoanalytic theory that the text of the essay hints at but never makes explicit. One may be sure, however, that the supplemental resistance complicating rhetorical theory's relation to itself will also divide and render complex whatever relation could be installed with a theory that is itself constructed or that constructs itself around the concept of resistance. As we shall see when we try to discern at least an outline of this complexity, it is once again through the institutional effect that one may be able to read a supplemental line of resistance dividing theory from its own constructions.

But first, it may be useful to recall that the concept of resistance has traditionally taken shape along the line of contact between the conceptual faculty and some exteriority. The concept, in other words, shows a double face, turned inward and outward, along the line presumed to divide consciousness from its outside or its other. The *Vocabulaire technique et critique de la philosophie*, for example, defines resistance as a "primary quality of bodies":

> Resistance: the quality of sensible matter by which it is perceptible to touch and muscular activity. "The sensation of resistance, in particular, would have a real privilege over all others for proving that matter exists in itself; for, as the partisans of this doctrine argue, *we observe directly* the existence of that which resists us and whatever resists us is necessarily outside of us since it knocks up against us and stops us. This reasoning, as one may easily see, comes down to saying that resistance is a primary quality of bodies." (Dunan, *Essais de philosophie générale*, 532; my emphasis)[10]

The definition situates resistance in the "outside of us" ("that which resists us is necessarily outside of us"), which is to say outside a consciousness that has a direct or unresisted knowledge of material existence in itself and not only in consciousness. But this direct awareness depends on an ambivalent intervention of a body through "touch and muscular activity," ambivalent because it can be neither wholly assimilated nor rejected by consciousness. The notion of direct observation bypasses the necessity of this ambivalence (represented by the double sense—touching/touched—of the sense of touch) and thereby a body of resistance, the resistant body within the body of knowledge.

What is on the line here, in other words, are the conditions of certainty; for Descartes's subject of knowledge, the subject presumed to be sure of at least one thing: the difference between the thing it touches and the thing it only dreams of touching. Without this construction of difference, the subject simply will not stand up to its own rigorous scrutiny. It is not, however, just that the subject risks falling if it sees its construction dismantled, but that the fall takes down with it the distinction between standing and falling on the basis of which one could speak of a fall in the first place. The fall into uncertainty cannot even be certain that it is a fall. Such a formulation will return us to the final lines of "Resistance to Theory" where, as often in de Man's writing, it is a question of falling:[11] "Yet literary theory is not in danger of going under; it cannot help but flourish, and the more it is resisted, the more it flourishes, since the language it speaks is the language of self-resistance. What remains impossible to decide is whether this flourishing is a triumph or a fall" (19–20).

Insisting on the undecidability of the theoretical enterprise, de Man seems to neglect altogether the anxiety induced by not knowing what, above all, one needs to know: whether one is falling or standing. If, as we have suggested, there is a subtext in this essay whose title would be something like "Resistance to Psychoanalysis," then the bracketing of anxiety as a source of "displaced symptoms of resistance" would constitute one of its essential gestures. This subtext resembles most closely another brief text of de Man's, his review of Harold Bloom's *The Anxiety of Influence*.

There, the errors of an anxious selfhood or subjectivity are set over against the necessity of a "truly epistemological moment" that alone can make a literary theory possible. Resistance to theory, in other words, is seen here to occur in the form of self or subject and its intentions. Although to be sure *The Anxiety of Influence* does not propose a theory of poetry based on naive intentionality (for Bloom, as de Man notes, "influence can emanate from texts a poet has never read"), it nevertheless fails, according to its reviewer, "to free poetic language from the constraints of natural reference" and instead returns us to a scheme that "is still clearly a relapse into psychological naturalism." De Man even traces a regression from Bloom's earlier work to *Anxiety* where "[Bloom] becomes more dependent than before on a pathos which is more literal than hyperbolic." This regression displaces theoretical concerns from poetic language to self or subject, a displacement that puts at risk the "truly epistemological moment" necessary for poetic theory:

> From a relationship between words and things, or words and words, we return to a relationship between subjects. Hence the agonistic language of anxiety, power, rivalry, and bad faith. . . . [Bloom's] argument is stated in oedipal terms and the story of influence told in the naturalistic language of desire. . . . His theoretical concerns are now displaced into a symbolic narrative recentered in a subject. *But no theory of poetry is possible without a truly epistemological moment when the literary text is considered from the perspective of its truth or falsehood rather than from a love-hate point of view.* The presence of such a moment offers no guarantee of truth but it serves to alert our understanding to distortions brought about by desire. It may reveal in their stead patterns of error that are perhaps more disturbing, but rooted in language rather than in the self. (BI, 271–72; my emphasis)

The "truly epistemological moment" cannot occur, de Man suggests, between subjects who are, inevitably, subjects of desire. The identification of the poetic text as a subject constitutes, in Bloom's case, a relapse or a regression. In another context, de Man has given a specifically historical sense to this regressive turn when, in the opening paragraph of "The Rhetoric of Temporality," he implies a continuity between "the advent, in the course of the nineteenth century, of a subjectivistic critical vocabulary" and the romantic eclipse of all other rhetorical distinctions behind the single, totalizing term "symbol." If, however, subjectivistic criticism like Bloom's is to be understood in its continuity with romantic theories of poetic imagination (and this historical/rhetorical scheme will be more or less sustained through the latest essays collected in *The Rhetoric of Romanticism*), then in what sense can this continuity also be termed a relapse or a regression?

Referring to Bloom's subjectivism or romanticism, de Man writes that the "regression can be traced in various ways." The example he chooses concerns the use of Freud:

> It is apparent, for example, in the way Freud is used in the earlier as compared to the later essay. Bloom, who at that time seems to have held a rather conventional view of Freud as a rationalistic humanist, respectfully dismisses him in *The Ringers in the Tower* as the prisoner of a reality principle the romantics had left behind. In *The Anxiety of Influence* Bloom's reading of Freud has gained in complexity, yet he is still, in principle, discarded as "not severe enough," his wisdom outranked by "the wisdom of the strong poets." Still, his argument is stated in oedipal terms. (BI, 272)

The regression traced here in relation to Freud shows a contradictory logic since, in the later work, Freud is dismissed but as a weak son who cannot stand up to his stronger poet/fathers—he is dismissed, that is, in the oedipal terms of Freudian theory. This move is regressive (and not merely contradictory) because the dismissal of Freud ends up repeating the weak or later poet's oedipal impasse. And thus, notes de Man, "Bloom has become the subject of his own desire for clarification."

But it would seem that de Man is also pointing to a regressive reading of Freud, one that remains governed by the anxious desire for clarification in the face of precisely that impossibility as concerns unconscious desire. That is, the regressive or anxious resistance to reading may be understood to include a resistance to the psychoanalytic theory of the unconscious and thus as a defense of the ideological fiction of an unobstructed, unresisted self.[12] Clearly, however, this resistance can itself be overcome only in a regressive direction whenever literary theory leaps over its object and heads for the cover of the oedipal narratives with which Freud has enriched the supply of psychological naturalism. By the same token, no literary theory that would be "progressive" can avoid the evidence that "progress" also remains almost wholly to be read as a fictional narrative with a large network of roots feeding the same ideological functions as are fed by psychological naturalism. If it thus remains "impossible to decide whether this flourishing [of literary theory] is a triumph or a fall," then the question of whether one is regressing or progressing, falling or triumphing in the sight, on the site of theory will have to become, instead, one of how to keep one's anxiety about an answer to the first question from precipitating a decisive fall into interpretative readings based on defensive ego identifications.

Overwhelming Resistance

"The Resistance to Theory" manages to remind one of the important use psychoanalysis has made of the term "resistance" without all the same taking up an explicit discussion of it. One effect of this gesture is to position the essay as a reading *en blanc* or between the lines of Freud's essay with the echoing title "The Resistances to Psychoanalysis" ("Die Widerstände die Psychoanalyse"). Without presuming to fill in this blank, I want nevertheless to turn now to several details from the end of Freud's essay. I will suggest that one might recognize in Freud's rhetoric a scene of confrontation that de Man has analyzed elsewhere quite explicitly and, indeed, more than once.

These details, which are rhetorical figures, are also what allow that text to narrate an end to the self-resistance installed by the confrontation with the truth of resistance to some truth. When, toward the end of the essay, Freud recapitulates his account of the resistance encountered by psychoanalysis, he shifts to the past tense, which, in the context, can only be read as a hopeful anticipation of the future defeat of that resistance.

The strongest resistances to psycho-analysis were not of an intellectual kind but arose from emotional sources. This explained their passionate character as well as their poverty in logic. The situation obeyed a simple formula: men in the mass behaved to psycho-analysis in precisely the same way as individual neurotics under treatment for their disorders. It is possible, however, by patient work to convince these latter individuals that everything happened as we maintained it did: we had not invented it but had arrived at it from a study of other neurotics covering a period of twenty or thirty years.[13]

We will come back to the two complementary terms that supply the "simple formula" of the central analogy here—a totalizing figure ("men in the mass") and a figure of sheer repetition ("in precisely the same way")—when they recur in another arrangement in the text. As for the emotional source that overpowers logic, Freud has earlier identified this to be fear (*Angst*) in a passage that again sounds a hopeful, but perhaps not fearless, note: "psycho-analysis is regarded as 'inimical to culture' and put under a ban as a 'social danger.' This resistance cannot last forever. No human institution can in the long run escape the influence of fair criticism; but men's attitude to psycho-analysis is still dominated by this fear, which gives rein to their passions and diminishes their power of logical argument" (*Standard Edition*, vol. 19, 220). Freud's conviction that "resistance cannot last forever" may be read as a submission to that greater truth according to which nothing lasts forever. But, in that case, what of psychoanalysis itself as an institution? This question is not posed explicitly by Freud; however, because the essay concludes, as we shall see, by pointing to the recent foundation of the Berlin and Vienna psychoanalytic institutes, the question may be heard all the same adding an anxious note to this account of the defeat of resistances to psychoanalysis.

This defeat follows a certain narrative order—"everything happened as we maintained it did"—the order that psychoanalytic observation has uncovered through years of patient observation of its patients. Overwhelming evidence, however, may also show a tendency to overwhelm in an alarming way. Thus, having set out the simple, analogical formula ("men in the mass behaved to psycho-analysis in precisely the same way as individual neurotics"), Freud then comments:

The position was at once alarming and consoling (*etwas Schreckhaftes und etwas Tröstliches*): alarming because it was no small thing to have the whole human race as one's patient (*das ganze Menschengeschlecht zum Patienten zu haben*), and consoling because after all everything was taking place as the hypotheses of psycho-analysis declared that it was bound to.

This note of alarm is sounded in the presence of a figure—"the whole human race as one's patient"—a synecdoche that, more dramatically than the preceding figure of "men in the mass," identifies a collective entity of staggering proportions. This same figure, however, is given another face that consoles rather than alarms. It consoles by confirming and consolidating a certain narrative and a certain narration: "everything was taking place as the hypotheses of psycho-analysis declared that it was bound to." The figure has the effect of consolidating psychoanalysis with itself, joining it as a narrative whose end is already present in its beginning. Thus, "the whole human race" lends consistency to that other whole called psychoanalysis, the latter realizing itself or completing itself in the fulfillment of a narrative. The analogical formula that leads to the alarming/consoling figure also tends to reduce the plural resistances of Freud's title to a same resistance but one that has been distributed between the inside and the outside of the practice of psychoanalysis. "The whole human race as one's patient" would serve, then, to erase even this topological distinction by uniting all resistance behind the representative guise of a single patient whose treatment can be made wholly internal to the analytic process from where it can be overcome. No doubt, the idea is not meant to be taken seriously or literally; nevertheless, as the text continues, it seems to struggle to make good on its spontaneous figure, to comprehend the sum total of resistances to psychoanalysis and thus to take in the totality of its outside. Or, to put this another way, the sentence that both alarms and consoles from the position of psychoanalysis can perhaps be likened to a moment of gagging on the enormity of the thing. How does Freud swallow this huge morsel in order to bring his essay to some conclusion?

He first weighs what he calls "purely external difficulties" that "have also contributed to strengthen the resistance to psychoanalysis." These are enumerated beginning with the difficulty of an independent judgment with regard to psychoanalysis: "It is not easy to arrive at an *independent* (*selbstständiges*) judgment upon matters to do with analysis without having experienced it oneself or practiced it on someone else" (my emphasis). The difficulty these sentences would point to referentially, in some pure exterior, remains caught within a syntax that illustrates rather than situates the problem of resistance, and this because it is far from self-evident how the lack of an independent or external place from which to judge something can also be termed a purely external difficulty. In the succeeding sentences of the paragraph, however, the so-called external difficulty will be drawn into the more purely internal question of analytic technique: "Nor can one do the latter [that is, practice psychoanalysis on someone else] without having acquired a specific and decidedly delicate technique."

If one reads this movement inward as making good on a totalizing figure, then unmistakably technique becomes the key to translating rhetorical overstatement into something closer to referential accuracy. In effect, the resistant figure's alarming proportions are scaled down by the institution of technique and with that comes a marked improvement in the position of psychoanalysis: "until recently there was no easily accessible means of learning psychoanalysis and its technique.

This position has now been improved by the foundation (in 1920) of the Berlin Psycho-Analytic Clinic and Training Institute, and soon afterwards (in 1922) of an *exactly similar institute* in Vienna" (222; my emphasis). The exact similarity of these institutes, guaranteeing the repetition or reproduction of a technique, seems to advance the position of psychoanalysis beyond the stalemated encounter with a figure of overwhelming resistance. But there has been in fact no improvement in the *rhetorical* position, which remains as tenuous as ever in its promise to deliver one from the alarming figure of the opposition of the "whole human race." This is because only another trope, the powerful trope of mimesis, can allow one to say that institutes of whatever sort are *exactly* similar. The mimetic institution, the institution of mimesis as technique, appears to solve a difficulty, but actually it swallows that difficulty whole.

A Reading Lesson

The narrative elements we have been considering in Freud's essay are assembled in a similar sequence by Rousseau's account of the necessary primacy of figurative over denominative language. Both Jacques Derrida and de Man have made this episode from the *Essay on the Origin of Languages* justly famous, the latter even returning to the text a second time.[14] First, let us briefly recall the passage in question from Rousseau's essay:

> Upon meeting others, a savage man will initially be frightened. Because of his fear he sees the others as bigger and stronger than himself. He calls them *giants*. After many experiences, he recognizes that these so-called giants are neither bigger nor stronger than he. Their stature does not correspond to the idea he had initially attached to the word giant. So he invents another name common to him and to them, such as the name *man*, for example, and leaves the name *giant* to the fictitious object that impressed him during his illusion. This is how the figurative word is born before the literal word, when our gaze is held in passionate fascination.[15]

From de Man's reading of this passage and the consequences that must follow from it through the *Discourse on Inequality*, we lift the sequence that shows certain parallels with Freud's essay: (1) the fearful face-off with an overwhelming figure; (2) the reduction of the figure through a technical or empirical operation; (3) the substitution of a literal metaphor for the first, wild metaphor; (4) the institution or repetition of the mimetic figure as a proper denomination that can found a science: anthropology, sociology, political science, psychoanalysis.

De Man's rhetorical analysis of this sequence is laid out in two different essays: "The Rhetoric of Blindness" in *Blindness and Insight* and chapter 7 in *Allegories of Reading*. The second of these is said to have been written to "cope" with the "inadequacies" of the first (BI, xi). In both essays, the "giant" narrative is read in the sense of a demonstration of "the priority of metaphor over denomination." What shifts from one essay to the next, however, is the understanding of Rousseau's choice of fear as the passion with which to illustrate this priority. In the earlier essay, this reaction is aligned on the side of need rather than passion, a situation that places Rousseau in a certain contradiction with his assertion that it is the passions that produce the first metaphors. Thus, Rousseau would have made a mistake.[16] In the second essay, de Man realigns his own earlier reading when he addresses the choice of fear to illustrate the figurative source of denomination:

> [Fear] can only result from a fundamental feeling of distrust, the suspicion that, although the creature does not look like a lion or a bear, it nevertheless might act like one, outward appearances to the contrary. The reassuringly familiar and similar outside might be a trap. Fear is the result of a possible discrepancy between the outer and inner properties of entities. It can be shown that, for Rousseau, *all passions* — whether they be love, pity, anger, or even *a borderline case between passion and need such as fear* — are characterized by such a discrepancy; they are based not on the knowledge that such a difference exists, but on the hypothesis that it might exist, a possibility that can never be proven or disproven by empirical or by analytical means. A statement of distrust is neither true nor false: it is rather in the nature of a permanent hypothesis. (AR, 150; my emphasis)

In this passage, a shift can be seen to occur that moves the reaction of fear from the side of need to which it was consigned in the earlier essay. But this shift does not cross all the way over to the side of passion: it stays its movement at the borderline between the two. What, in the first reading, had to be termed a "mistake" so long as fear resided simply with other needs is not here corrected by reversing the distinction and calling fear a passion, although that might seem to offer the most obvious solution to the problem. By stopping *between* Rousseau's distinction of need from passion, de Man's reading, in effect, suspends the textual metaphors in several senses at once. First, what is called fear is suspended in the hypothesis of "a possible discrepancy between the outer and inner properties of entities." That is, when the metaphor "giant" accuses the possible discrepancy between the other's familiar exterior and bearlike or lionlike interior, it does so as well from a suspended position between the "exterior" and "interior" motives for the subject's acts, otherwise called need and passion. This is not all, however: the discrepancy is itself two-faced since it applies to *both* entities as they confront each other, the "creature" to be named no less than the naming subject. Thus, the series of conceptual distinctions structuring this encounter — need/passion, outside/inside, other/self — are all suspended in a "strange unity."[17]

The shift onto the border between these suspended oppositions also brings into focus the other encounter in progress here, not between two men but between an act of reading and a text. Fear or anxiety provides a pivot on which the text can turn from the action represented to the action of representing, from, in other words, one act of naming to another. The identification of the fearful reaction supplies something like a hook on which the reader can hang on identificatory interpretation of the text. At the same time, however, it is just such a precipitous identification or equalization of the two parties of the encounter that is denounced by the allegory as a wishful but unreliable mode of reading. Reading by identification precipitates the same leap into the reassuring generality of "man" and the same forgetfulness of the metaphoric substitutions that allowed one to arrive there. Most important, such a reader forgets that he[18] has substituted the model of an intersubjective, face-to-face encounter for this other encounter with metaphor that, precisely, has no model. This substitution reverses the order of substitution recounted by the allegory—the category of number or measure (a knowable, "externalizable" quantity) for the category of intention (an unknowable, interiorized quality)—that allows for the crucial passage from metaphor to concept in the allegory. Reading reverses this pattern when it reassures itself of its own understanding by interiorizing, turning the text's exterior into an intentional design of a subject: the text's author. The allegory positions the necessary priority of an encounter with metaphor over any concept of subjectivity or intersubjectivity, showing, indeed, that metaphor gives the model to understanding based on intersubjective identifications. Nevertheless, a profound reading habit inverts this insight and misses the point of the allegory.

We can consider, through one brief example, how de Man's commentary effectively recovers the point that has been blunted by nonreading, or rather how it sticks the point to that nonreader par excellence that is the overarching subject of identification.

The passage we are concerned with sets a trap for this subject by means of its assumption that, in encounters with "giants," it is "we" men who have everything to fear. This assumption is vulnerable precisely in its quick identification with the word "man" in the allegory, a move that erases the metaphorical interchangeability with the other word, "giant." It begins thus: "The word 'man' is the result of a quantitative process of comparison based on measurement, and making deliberate use of the category of number in order to reach a reassuring conclusion." This reassuring process is then illustrated with recourse to the first person: "if the other man's height is numerically equal to *my own*, then he is no longer dangerous" (my emphasis). It is the words "my own" that form the hook for the reader's identification. Once hooked, this reader is caught in the trap to be sprung in the final sentence, which returns to the mode of commentary: "The conclusion is wishful and, of course, potentially in error—as Goliath and Polyphemos, among others, were soon enough to discover" (154). The reader, in effect, has been tricked into identifying with the overconfident calculations of the doomed giants. Like a rat in an experimenter's maze, he receives a shock that sends him back to find a safer exit. These sentences, in other words, perform an object lesson in the perils of hasty reading which would be any reading that supplies an extratextual reference for the textual first person. That operation conceals a potential for error demonstrated in the very sentence one reads to its stinging conclusion. There, the names Goliath and Polyphemos, rather than the categories of giant or man, suddenly assume the force of proper names the reader has been led to substitute for "my own" name. The point of the allegory will thus have been brought home: names are properly metaphorical, which is to say monstrous in their potential unreliability.

This reminder of the differences subsumed through a conceptual, categorical operation depends for its effect on a certain reversal of the substitutive process of generalization, a falling back into proper names. De Man recommends reading the allegory in this sense of the fate of proper names in a note that precedes the demonstration: "The actual word 'giant,' as we know from everyday usage, presupposes the word 'man' and is not the metaphorical figure that Rousseau, *for lack of an existing word*, has to call 'giant.' Rousseau's 'giant' would be more like some mythological monster; one could think of Goliath and Polyphemos" (AR, 153; my emphasis).[19] To accept this suggestion entails certain consequences for Rousseau's tale of man's name. When these myths are superimposed on the allegory, another moral can emerge beside the one that appears to lift the word "man" out of a gigantic error: it is not just that one man's triumph is another man's fall, but that the same name has to be made to stand for one and the other sense. The measure of this predicament is taken by Rousseau's allegory when, "for lack of an existing word" to represent properly the impropriety of names, it falls victim to the categorical error which it also identifies.

Pièce de résistance

Rousseau's choice of fear should perhaps be read as the fear of never owning "my own" name. Such is also the anxiety that fuels resistance to a theory whose "main theoretical interest lies in the impossibility of its definition." Faced with an insistent reminder of the name's unreliability, one may, like Rousseau's man when faced with the "giant" or like Rousseau himself when faced with the deviations of his signature, alternately magnify and minimize the risk posed by the unnameable other. "It is," writes de Man, "a recurrent strategy of any anxiety to defuse what it considers threatening by magnification and minimization, by attributing to it claims to power of which it is bound to fall short" (RT, 5). De Man then proceeds to illustrate this assertion in a manner that I cannot help wondering how to read:

> If a cat is called a tiger it can easily be dismissed as a paper tiger; the question remains however why one was so scared of the cat in the first

place. The same tactic works in reverse: calling the cat a mouse and then deriding it for its pretense to be mighty. Rather than being drawn into this polemical whirlpool, it might be better to try to call the cat a cat and to document, however briefly, the contemporary version of the resistance to theory in this country.

It would be foolish, no doubt, to take such a light moment too seriously. But how seriously is too seriously? We are still trying to read in the absence of a measure of too fast or too slow, too big or too small. Since the passage in question qualifies such alternative errors as the recurrent strategy of anxiety, a mimicking effect is set off between the cat as metaphor *in* the text (which someone with an irrational fear of cats calls a tiger) and the cat as metaphor *of* the text one is trying to read. One's anxious question about how to read the cat in the text or the text in the cat already figures there precisely as the motive of rhetorical distortion. Whatever check the question seemed to offer on excesses of interpretation is overturned, mocked by a doubling reversal.

Like all acts of denomination, calling *the* cat *a* cat remains a figure that substitutes for the concept of difference (the singularity of the thing named) the concept of similarity (resemblance within a class or species). It would thus be sheerest delusion to believe that, having called the cat a cat, one has corrected the fundamental error of denomination. What is more, although the illustration moves to correct aberrant metaphors that try to pass themselves off as referential, this adjustment can only occur by leaving untouched the initial aberration that consists in giving that "something called literary theory" the other name of "cat." The thorough arbitrariness of this substitution (it is the substitution of allegory, or, if you prefer, of cat-egory) is not hidden behind any appeal to some natural resemblance between cats and theories, which is precisely why it is hard to take the example seriously.

Finally, however, the evident arbitrariness of the latter substitution (cat for theory) undoes the apparent tautological self-evidence of the former one (the name cat for the thing cat). It does this when it suspends at the limit of the example the question of why one was so scared of the cat in the first place. Not only, then, does the example illustrate the decision of the suspended state of anxiety through aberrant acts of naming; it remarks as well that an essentially linguistic predicament—the impossibility of proper names—has been displaced onto the psychology of a subject. Since replacing the aberrant metaphors of tiger and mouse with the referential figure that calls the cat a cat can hardly be of any comfort to whoever is scared of cats, the suspended question can be answered only by an identificatory leap of some sort. But precisely, this unnamed, unnameable cat poses the limit of reading by identification. Like a signature—a *griffe*—its mark retracts from conceptual measure.

Unmanned Resistance

In tracing the pattern of reading by identification, we spoke of "the reader . . . he." Is there a reason for this deliberate sexism? There are two ways of answering that question.

1. "He" remarks the mark of gender on the general concept "man." If we choose to read Rousseau's (or de Man's) allegory of man's name as an allegory of reading by identification, with all of the potential for error that it entails, than we also take it as pointing to a crucial condition of that reading habit: the exclusion of sexual difference. The exclusive condition is confirmed by the patterns that have determined literary study in the age of its institutionalization where the two parties to the encounter—reader and text—largely continued to play out the allegory of primitive man meeting other men and measuring himself through identification. On the one hand, even after women were finally admitted to these institutions as coequal students of reading, the grid of a presumed transparency between subjects identified as men remained in place as the unacknowledged prescriptive filter of measured understanding. On the other hand, the same prescriptive grid continued to shape and select the canon of texts to be studied according to the privilege granted men's signatures. This exclusive pattern of identification can be made to appear as so much playing with mirrors when a critical stance steps to one side of the mirrored field, into the beveled edge where the identificatory path is distorted or deflected. To read as a woman is to remark this unreflecting frame of reflection, to uncover its limits, and to overturn its exclusions.[20]

2. "He" effaces the mark of gender on the reader by identification. It insists, in other words, that whenever reading projects a model of identification, the model is masculine—not, obviously, in an empirical sense but in a structural one. To retain this structural sense means to recall that the effacement of difference is a conceptual violence whose effects can be all the more insidious when they are too quickly denied any political pertinence.[21] Because it leaves intact the identificatory structure, the program of "reading as a woman" *in itself* cannot end conceptual violence, but only redistribute its effects more equitably. The preserved structure presents little resistance to the institutionalized model of reading. Resistance, in other words, that takes the form of identifying (with) some feminine essence puts nothing essential at risk and even provides the reassuring comfort of an essential likeness with already institutionalized methods of reading.

Far riskier, it seems, would be reading in the absence of a model subject engendered by the *classification* of differences. This is not, however, to suggest a program to be institutionally adopted—for the obvious reason that reading in the absence of a model cannot, by definition, supply a model. But also for the equally undeniable reason that no reading is possible in the absence pure and simple of identificatory impulses. It is still a problem of reading too slowly or too quickly, resisting either those patterns of metaphorical sameness that allow reading to take some shortcuts or the marks of sheer difference that slow reading down and can bring it to a standstill altogether. This suggests that the pedagogical enterprise will remain a critical one only so long as it is practiced within the space of a double stricture where both the conceptual generality of the text and the singular difference of the reader can encounter their limits.

Notes

1. This is but one of the possible complications in the relation between title and text that Jacques Derrida discerns in Blanchot's *La Folie du jour*; see "Title (to be specified)," *Sub-Stance*, no. 3 (1981): 5–22.

2. See Rodolphe Gasché's commentary on *La Double Séance*: "The supplementary mark, instead of closing the text upon itself, in lieu of reflecting it into its own as a totalizing image is supposed to do, illustrates nothing but what Derrida calls 'the general law of textual supplementarity.' The surplus mark re-marks the whole series of the double marks of the text by illustrating what always exceeds a possible closure of the text folded, reflected upon itself. In excess to the text *as a whole* is the text 'itself.' " In "Joining the Text," *The Yale Critics: Deconstruction in America*, ed J. Arac, W. Godzich, and W. Martin (Minneapolis: University of Minnesota Press, 1983), 169.

3. On these words, see as well Jacques Derrida, "My Chances/*Mes Chances*: A Rendezvous with Some Epicurean Stereophonies," in *Taking Chances: Derrida, Psychoanalysis, and Literature*, ed. Joseph H. Smith and William Kerrigan (Baltimore: Johns Hopkins University Press, 1984), 5.

4. This is a reference to the *Yale French Studies* issue (63) titled "The Pedagogoical Imperative: Teaching as a Literary Genre" in which the essay was first published.

5. This predictable obsolescence is confirmed by Joseph Gibaldi, the editor of the volume referred to, whose preface recalls the success of the two previous volumes in the series (published in 1952 and 1970) and then comments: "By the end of [the 1970s], however, the time was right once again for a new collection of essays by a new group of authors." *Introduction to Scholarship in Modern Languages and Literatures* (New York: MLA, 1981), v.

6. This article, "Literary Theory" by Paul Hernadi, follows the "determined program" in the first two of the three requirements de Man discerns, wisely stopping short of a "programmatic projection of the solutions which can be expected in the foreseeable future." Despite its recognition that "quite a few critics even doubt the feasibility of defining literature on any grounds whatsoever" (100), the essay does not attempt to account for the resistance to theory, which may be a sign that its obsolescence is ahead of schedule.

7. To be sure, the MLA Committee on Research Activities is but one locus of this shared reluctance; yet, by virtue of its representative function and structure, this locus also serves to represent what *should* be the interest of literary theory to modern language and literature scholars in the United States.

8. This point is specifically made in de Man's review of Riffaterre's poetic theory in "Hypogram and Inscription: Michael Riffaterre's Poetics of Reading," *Diacritics*, 11 (1981): 18–19, and again in "Aesthetic Formalization in Kleist's *Über das Marionettentheater* (RR, 272–73).

9. In this regard, it is interesting that the bibliography in *The Yale Critics* lists this article under the erroneous title "The Resistance to Literary Theory."

10. André Lalande (ed.), 9th ed. (Paris: PUF, 1962), 925.

11. Falling is an insistent condition in de Man's writings and may even be one reason they have elicited such resistance. In "The Resistance to Theory," for example, a brief reading of Keats's two titles *Hyperion* and *The Fall of Hyperion* at one point poses the question: "are we telling the story of why all texts, as texts, can always be said to be falling?" (17). As well, in "The Rhetoric of Tem-

porality," it is Baudelaire's example of a fall from "De l'Essence du rire" that provides the key text for the discussion of irony; see BI, 213–14.

12. I am not suggesting here that one can ignore de Man's more or less systematic replacement of psychologistic terms with rhetorical ones. Rather, I would argue that the necessity of this replacement can in part be traced to Freud's break within traditional epistemology and that nothing in de Man's work prohibits making such a connection, while there are a number of moments, such as the one examined here, that encourage it. Geoffrey Hartman observes in his essay in this volume that "despite the antipsychologistic bent of de Man's practice," one may observe certain "alliances" between that practice and psychoanalysis. For another assessment of de Manian deconstruction in its relation to psychoanalysis, see Richard Klein's "The Blindness of Hyperboles: The Ellipses of Insight," *Diacritics*, Summer 1973.

13. *Standard Edition*, vol. 19, 221.

14. See Derrida's *Of Grammatology* (Baltimore: Johns Hopkins University Press, 1976), 275ff.

15. Translated by John H. Moran, in *On the Origin of Language: Two Essays*, ed. John H. Moran and Alexander Gode (Chicago: University of Chicago Press, 1966).

16. "In Rousseau's vocabulary, language is a product of passion and not the expression of a need; fear, the reverse side of violence and aggression, is distinctively utilitarian and belongs to the world of 'besoins' rather than 'passions' " ("The Rhetoric of Blindness," 134). De Man's revision of this distinction recalls Derrida's effacement of the limit between need and passion; see note 17.

17. The term is Derrida's to describe the effaced limit between need and passion: "This incoherence would apply to the fact that the unity of need and passion (with the entire system of associated significations) constantly effaces the limit that Rousseau obstinately sketches and recalls. Rousseau *declares* this backbone, without which the entire conceptual organism would break up, and *wishes to think it* as a distinction; he *describes* it as a supplementary difference. This constrains in its graphics the strange unity of passion and need." *Of Grammatology*, p. 238.

18. Or she? On the question of the gender of the reader, see the final section of this essay.

19. De Man's substitution of a proper name for the common noun "giant" as the instance of metaphoric or improper denomination allows for the description Derrida has made of this moment in the "Essai": "What we interpret as literal expression in the perception and designation of giants, remains a metaphor that is preceded by nothing either in experience or in language. Since speech does not pass through reference to an object, the fact that 'giant' is literal as sign of fear not only does not prevent, but on the contrary implies that it should be nonliteral or metaphoric as sign of the object. It cannot be the idea-sign of the passion without presenting itself as the idea-sign of the presumed cause of that passion, opening an exchange with the outside. This opening allows the passage to a savage metaphor. No literal meaning precedes it" (*Of Grammatology*, 276). "Goliath" or "Polyphemos" would be something like the improper name of the self as outside itself.

20. In a chapter titled "Reading as a Woman" in his *On Deconstruction: Theory and Criticism after Structuralism*, Jonathan Culler chronicles three moments in the development of American feminist literary criticism each of which is formed around the experience of woman reading. Culler's synthesis is especially valuable in that it isolates the ambiguous place of this appeal to experience: "It has always, already occurred and yet is still to be produced – an indispensable point of reference, yet never simply there. . . . The noncoincidence reveals an interval, a division within woman or within any reading subject and the 'experience' of that subject" (Ithaca, N.Y.: Cornell University Press, 1982), 62.

21. I would thus disagree with Jane Marie Todd ("Framing the *Second Discourse*," *Comparative Literature*, 38, 4) when she attaches a political label to de Man's insistence on this conceptual violence and concludes that by "identifying the conceptual with the political," de Man endorses Rousseau's "politically conservative stance" (310). The conservative label is entirely inadequate to account for the institutional *effect* that Todd herself notes in passing: "It is de Man's claim to institutional legitimacy that the institution has found threatening" (316).

"Reading" Part of a Paragraph in
Allegories of Reading
J. Hillis Miller

Any reader of Paul de Man's work is likely to be struck by certain aphoristic formulations that seem deliberately provocative in their all-or-nothing generality and
in their slightly defiant irony. Examples are the following: "Conceptual language,
the foundation of civil society, is also, it appears, a lie superimposed upon an error" (AR, 155). "One sees from this that the impossibility of reading should not
be taken too lightly" (AR, 245). "We never lie as much as when we want to do
full justice to ourselves, especially in self-accusation" (AR, 269–70). Among
such sentences is the one in "Allegory (*Julie*)" that says, "The paradigm of all texts
consists of a figure (or a system of figures) and its deconstruction" (AR, 205).
I want to try here to "read" this sentence and the remaining part of the paragraph
in which it appears (it comes in the middle) – in defiance of de Man's demonstration that reading is impossible.

I was led to this attempted act of reading as a preparation for reading what de
Man says on page 206 of *Allegories of Reading* about the necessary ethical moment in all allegories, that is, in all texts, since for de Man all texts are allegories
of their own unreadability. "Ethicity," like other forms of reference to the extralinguistic by way of the linguistic, occurs for de Man not at the beginning, as
a basis for language, and not at the end, as a final triumphant return to reality that
validates language, but in the midst of an intricate sequence. The sequentiality
of this sequence is of course only a fiction, a convenience for thinking as a narrative what in fact always occurs in the tangle of an "all at once" mixing tropological, allegorical, referential, ethical, political, and historical dimensions. I have

discussed the ethics of reading in de Man elsewhere. Here my focus is on part of page 205.

De Man has been reading the second preface to *Julie*, which leads him to the assertion that as soon as any document is seen as a text, that is, "questioned as to its rhetorical mode," "its readability is put into question" (AR, 204). An example is the way the second preface "puts into question" the readability of *Julie* by indicating that it is impossible to know whether Rousseau made it up or whether it is a collection of "real" letters. In the context of this discussion, de Man draws himself up and makes a series of apodictic statements about the rhetorical makeup of *all* texts. It is a good example of the way the theoretical generalizations he makes always occur within a specific context and have a somewhat different meaning when they are abstracted from that context, even though they affirm their independence of any context in that all-encompassing "all." Here is the series of generalizations that forms the essential preliminary presupposition for de Man's assertions about the ethical moment in reading:

> The paradigm for all texts consists of a figure (or a system of figures) and its deconstruction. But since this model cannot be closed off in a final reading, it engenders, in its turn, a supplementary figural superposition which narrates the unreadability of the prior narration. As distinguished from primary deconstructive narratives centered on figures and ultimately always on metaphor, we can call such narratives to the second (or the third) degree *allegories*. Allegorical narratives tell the story of the failure to read whereas tropological narratives, such as the *Second Discourse*, tell the story of the failure to denominate. The difference is only a difference of degree and the allegory does not erase the figure. Allegories are always allegories of metaphor and, as such, they are always allegories of the impossibility of reading—a sentence in which the genitive "of" has itself to be "read" as a metaphor. (AR, 205)

This series of sentences says a mouthful, as they say. Much of the de Man of *Allegories of Reading* is compactly folded together here. The reader who can understand these sentences will have gone a long way toward understanding *Allegories of Reading* as a "whole," though unfortunately the sentences cannot be "understood," if that word applies at all here, without a careful reading of that "whole." The confident absolutist tone of de Man's assertion, with its "all's" and "always's," is likely to lead the reader who is at all inclined to skepticism to raise questions: "All?" "Always?" Is de Man perhaps guilty of that tyrannical absolutism of the "one" on which Hölderlin pronounced his malediction in an epigram: "Whence comes among men the cursed wish that there should only be the one and that everything should come from the one?" It is a familiar reproach to deconstruction that it finds always the same thing in every text and that it finds, moreover, what the deconstructor has gone to the text expecting to find. Is de Man guilty of this crime? Is it possible not to be guilty of it? Do those who reproach deconstruction in this way mean anything more than that they prefer their own version of the "one" to that of deconstruction? How could one simultaneously re-spect the particularity of a particular text and at the same time respect the law which that text exemplifies? This is in fact, is it not, just what is always in question in any speculation about ethics, including no doubt the ethics of reading? Each ethical situation, including each act of reading, insofar as it involves ethical judg-ment or responsibility, is unique, but how can it be truly ethical if it is not in re-sponse to an unconditional law? And surely each reader would wish to be ethical in his or her reading![1] De Man is no doubt, like everyone else, faced with the necessity of somehow fulfilling this double obligation, and as for always finding the same thing, I defy any reader to predict beforehand exactly what de Man will find to say about a given text, any more than the reader of Henry James's *What Maisie Knew* can predict exactly what Maisie is going to say and do when she makes the crucial decision of her life. De Man, like Maisie, seems to be subject to a law, in this case a law of reading, to which only he has access.

There is a further problem, related to this one. The use of the terms "meta-phor," "narrative," "reading," and "allegory" in the passage I am discussing is id-iosyncratic, to say the least. At any rate the terms are puzzlingly opaque when taken out of the context of, for example, the essays elsewhere in *Allegories of Reading* on metaphor in Nietzsche and in Rousseau, and on reading in Proust. When de Man says the paradigm for all texts consists of a figure (or a system of figures) and its deconstruction, the reader must have in mind the radical theory of figure worked out with the help of Nietzsche and Rousseau. For de Man (or for Rousseau and Nietzsche as he reads them) the act of literal denomination is already an (aberrant) metaphor, blindly imposing a word brought from another realm to cover an ignorance that can by no means be turned into certain knowl-edge. In the example from Rousseau that de Man discusses at length, a primitive man in his fear names another man he encounters a giant, but since the correspon-dence of outside appearance and inside nature can never be verified, the metaphor remains suspended, aberrant. That error is further compounded when I deliber-ately invent the conceptual word "man" to cover my initial uncertainty. The word "man" is for de Man a metaphor over another metaphor or, as he puts it in the intransigent formulation I have already cited, "Conceptual language, the founda-tion of civil society, is also, it appears, a lie superimposed upon an error" (AR, 155). It is because all language is made up of metaphors of this sort, or a system of them, that the paradigm for all texts is a figure or system of figures. Since such figures are always unstable, any text "deconstructs" its metaphors at the same time as it asserts them. Deconstruction, as the reader can see from de Man's formula-tion, is not something the critic does to the text from the outside in the act of "read-ing" it, but something all texts inevitably do to themselves. It is a built-in fatality of language that any text must not only posit a figure or system of figures but must at the same time dismantle it, bring its aberrancy into the open.

For de Man this process can never be closed off in the triumphant mastery of the text by itself in its revelation of the erroneous figures on which it is built. In the act of deconstructing itself a text commits again another version of the error it denounces, and this means that all texts are a potentially endless series of repetitions of the "same" error only arbitrarily brought to closure. To put this another way, any text is a narrative that has no ending: "A narrative endlessly tells the story of its own denominational aberration and it can only repeat this aberration on various levels of rhetorical complexity" (AR, 162). All texts, in de Man's somewhat idiosyncratic nomenclature, are narratives, in the sense that they are the serial presentation, as if it were a story, complete with implied protagonist, narrator, and reader, of what is in fact the synchronic positing and deconstruction of a figure or system of figures. Any figure is deconstructed at the same moment it is posited. The positing contains the deconstruction.

It might be noted in passing here that though the example of the man named a giant is Rousseau's, the fact that the "figure" in question is also implicitly a prosopopoeia, a "disfiguring" of the face and figure of the other, or the ascription of a consciousness like my own or different from my own to an appearance in the perceptional field, prepares for the concentration on the figure of prosopopoeia in de Man's later work, from the essay on Shelley's "The Triumph of Life" on. De Man's work develops, but in retrospect it appears to have a remarkable consistency and focus, though of course that may be an illusion generated by the reader's inveterate habit of making a consistent story out of what may in fact only be a random series. De Man's notion of the impossibility of closing off any text in a final reading, especially any final reading of the text by itself, should give any reader pause who is tempted to see something in de Man's later work, for example, his theory that the fundamental trope of lyric poetry is prosopopoeia, as the teleology of the early post-1950 work. For him no such closure is possible, only the endless repetition of different versions of the same error.

De Man's formulation of this, in the passage I am trying to "read," needs to be looked at closely. The "paradigm" of a figure or system of figures and its deconstruction is spoken of as a "model." Presumably "paradigm" and "model" mean more or less the same thing: a schematic outline of universal applicability within which a limitless variety of different texts may be fitted. Of all of these it may be said that the illumination provided by the act of (self-)deconstruction coincides with a repetition of another version of the linguistic error that the deconstruction denounces. In fact, the deconstruction is at the same time a committing again of the error. This seems to be the logic of the "But since . . . , it engenders" in de Man's formulation. It is because a final reading is impossible, because the closure of a final illumination and mastery of language can never occur, that a secondary narration is superimposed on the first one, a third one on that, and so on, in the endless repetition of different versions of the same cycle: *"But since this model cannot be closed off by a final reading, it engenders, in its turn, a supplementary figural superposition* which narrates the unreadability of the prior narration" (my italics). The "unreadability" is not located in the reader but in the text itself, though the text's inability to mastery itself "engenders" in the reader a corresponding inability to master the text.

De Man's rather odd name for this "supplementary figural superposition" is *allegory*. I say "odd" because de Man's use of the word here seems to correspond neither to ordinary usage nor even quite to his own (also at first sight idiosyncratic) definition of allegory in "The Rhetoric of Romanticism." Here, again, is the formulation in "Allegory (*Julie*)": "As distinguished from primary deconstructive narratives centered on figures and ultimately always on metaphor, we can call such narratives to the second (or the third) degree *allegories.* Allegorical narratives tell the story of the failure to read whereas tropological narratives, such as the *Second Discourse*, tell the story of the failure to denominate." *Why* can "we" call such second- or third-level narratives *allegories*? In what possible sense or senses is that the right word? Why is it that texts can never "read themselves"? In any case, to speak of the relation between one part of a text and another as its reading of itself or as its failure to read itself would seem to be no more than a transparent trope for the activity of the author in writing the book. Replacing this trope by its commonsense literal meaning displaces the puzzle or even apparent absurdity of what de Man is saying to another level, where its implausibility is even more obvious. Surely an author is in control of what he or she writes and is able to read what he or she has written! What fatality is it that forces Rousseau, for instance, in the example de Man gives later on in "Allegory (*Julie*)," to commit again or have Julie commit again another version of the linguistic error (deification of Saint-Preux) she so lucidly denounces and demystifies in letter 18, part III? "In this text," says de Man, " . . . darkness falls when it becomes evident that Julie's language at once repeats the notions she has just denounced as errors. . . . If this is so, then it can be said that Julie is unable to 'read' her own text, unable to recognize how its rhetorical mode relates to its meaning" (AR, 217). A footnote to this passage convincingly argues that Julie's blindness is not compensated for by Rousseau's lucidity but is, as de Man would say, the allegory of it: "By the play of notes which allows him to acquire a distancing perspective with regard to Julie, Rousseau may seem to escape from this obfuscation at the expense of his character. But this pattern is anticipated in Julie herself, whose lucidity with regard to her past experience is never in question and who is capable of the same distance toward herself as Rousseau allows himself towards her, yet remains entirely unable to avert the repetition of her errors. R.'s statement, in the Preface, of helplessness before the opacity of his own text is similar to Julie's relapse into metaphorical models of interpretation at her moments of insight. The manipulation of point of view is a form of infinite regress inscribed within the metaphor of selfhood" (AR, 217).

Why this "helplessness"? It seems entirely inexplicable. The most obvious explanation, that it is a defect of memory, is explicitly rejected by de Man. It would be tempting to say that for de Man no one can remember long enough the difficult and painful process of rhetorical deconstruction to avoid committing again the same linguistic mistakes that have just been deconstructed. Certainly the difficulty of remembering the intricate argumentation of one of de Man's essays and making the displacements necessary to apply that argumentation to a different text (supposing someone should want to do such a thing)[2] would support the idea that de Man is talking about a defect of memory, a kind of fatal amnesia perhaps especially likely to occur with insights into the role of language in individual and collective human life so painful as those de Man offers the reader. We have every reason to want to repress and forget. But no, de Man explicitly forbids this interpretation of what he is saying. Julie is entirely lucid with regard to her past experience and Rousseau remembers and understands everything he has written. This comprehensive and comprehending memory nevertheless in no way mitigates the "helplessness," which means that both author and character are unable to avert the repetition of errors that are both remembered and understood. Why is this? It is not too much to say that getting a clear answer to this question is the key to understanding all of de Man's work, if the word "understand" is still in any way appropriate here, since part of de Man's point is that this insight is not open to understanding in the ordinary sense. Even though we can grasp what de Man is saying with total lucidity, we are still helpless before the opacity of the text of de Man's essays, just as Rousseau (or "R.") remains in a state of "helplessness before the opacity of his own text."

The reason for this impotence must be that the fatality in question has nothing to do with the psychological categories of memory, lucidity, insight, and blindness. It is a linguistic necessity that no amount of intelligence, memory, and vigilant insight will avail to avert. The harder I try to remember, even the more successful I am in remembering, the more certain I am to forget. It seems as if my insight must not ever have been "present" in the sense of being a possession within my consciousness in its self-presence. Therefore it is in principle not something I can "remember," nor forget either, for that matter. What de Man says about the failure to read even one's own writing must apply also to me as a reader (which is a metaphor for this essay as an act of reading). It must also apply to de Man himself, which is to say, to de Man's essay, though his work is peculiarly resistant to such demonstrations. What appears an example of self-opacity is often the object of lucid insight elsewhere in the text of *Allegories of Reading*. It would be a bold reader who would try to second-guess de Man and claim to make a move beyond the last move he has already made. He is pretty certain to have been there before and already to have surveyed the topography, mapped the terrain. In this case, de Man's peculiar use of the term "allegory" will help the reader to "understand" the irresistible coercion toward error that de Man sees in human beings' subjection to language.

"We can call such narratives to the second (or the third) degree *allegories*," says de Man. An allegory is therefore for de Man a narrative. It tells a story, but as opposed to primary narratives centered on the deconstruction of metaphor that tell the story of the failure to denominate, allegories tell the story of the failure to read. The term "degree" here is slightly odd, as is the addition in parentheses of "or the third." By "or the third" I suppose de Man means that the deconstruction of the initially asserted figure or system of figures could already be thought of as a second narrative superimposed on the first, so that the allegory of the failure to read can be thought of as already a third narrative posited over the first two, while if the positing of the figure and its deconstruction are thought of as a single story, then the allegory is only the second narrative. As for the word "degree," this makes an important assertion and forestalls what would be a serious mistake, namely, thinking of allegories of the impossibility of reading as being fundamentally different in kind from "tropological narratives," which "tell the story of the failure to denominate." No, de Man is anxious to have us understand that the rhetorical ingredients of both kinds of narratives are the same, able to be marked out on the same scale, measurable by the same standards. I take it he means that both kinds of narrative are made of the same universal narrative ingredients of figurative language taken literally and then shown to be aberrant. In one case the story is oriented toward the "real world," the object of "denomination." In the other case, the allegorical narrative at second (or third) degree, the story is oriented toward another story, namely, the story of denomination, but as de Man categorically asserts, "The difference is only a difference of degree and the allegory does not erase the figure." The word "erase" is also important here. It is a word de Man uses occasionally to name an (impossible) obliteration, as when, discussing in the preface to *Allegories of Reading* his use of the now polemically charged word "deconstruction," he says that he got the word from Jacques Derrida, "which means that it is associated with a power of inventive rigor to which I lay no claim but which I certainly do not wish to erase" (AR, x). In the present case, to say that the allegory does not erase the figure is a way of asserting the positive side of the linguistic operation called "deconstruction." Deconstruction reaffirms at the same time as it puts in question, which means that the whole chain of positings and putting in question remains unerased to the end, however many new layers of allegorical narrative are superposed on the original figure or system of figures: "the allegory does not erase the figure."

But why should de Man call this second or third degree of narration *allegory?* The appropriateness of the term "allegory" will become apparent if the reader remembers not only the etymology of the word but also the specific definition of it de Man gives in "The Rhetoric of Temporality," now reprinted in the new edition of *Blindness and Insight*. *Allegory*: The word means to say it otherwise in the marketplace, in public, as an exoteric expression of an esoteric wisdom. As in the case of parable, for example, the parables of Jesus in the Gospels, this is a way of revealing it and not revealing it. If you have the key to the allegory, then the esoteric wisdom has been expressed (otherwise), but then you would not have needed to have it said otherwise. If you do not have the key, then the allegory remains opaque. You are likely to take it literally, to think it means just what it says. If you understand it you do not need it. If you do not understand it you never will do so from anything on the surface. A paradox of unreadability is therefore built into the concept of allegory from the beginning.

This is not enough to say, however. For de Man, allegories are always temporal, that is, spread out on a diachronic scale, which is to say that allegories are always narratives. As opposed to symbols, which are synchronic and presuppose the similarity of the symbol and the symbolized within a spatial array, the symbol being a sign, the symbolized a thing, allegories are a matter of before and after, a matter of a sign-sign relation rather than a sign-thing relation. The relation between sign and sign within the allegory is always a matter of distance, difference, and discrepancy. The allegorical sign is unlike the sign it refers to, stands for, or substitutes for. Here is de Man's formulation of all this in "The Rhetoric of Temporality": "In the world of the symbol it would be possible for the image to coincide with the substance, since the substance and its representation do not differ in their being but only in their extension: they are part and whole of the same set of categories. Their relationship is one of simultaneity, which, in truth, is spatial in kind, and in which the intervention of time is merely a matter of contingency, whereas, in the world of allegory, time is the originary constitutive category. . . . It remains necessary, if there is to be allegory, that the allegorical sign refer to another sign that precedes it. The meaning constituted by the allegorical sign can then consist only in the *repetition* (in the Kierkegaardian sense of the term)[3] of a previous sign with which it can never coincide, since it is of the essence of this previous sign to be pure anteriority" (BI, 207). More pages of commentary, not entirely relevant here, would be necessary to elucidate that concluding phrase about "pure anteriority." Suffice it to say that de Man means here a pastness that was never present or presence and that therefore can never be reached as such by any remounting of the stream of time, for example, in recollective memory.

In the light of these definitions one can see why *allegory* is the right word for the universal linguistic structure of all texts de Man is describing in "Allegory (*Julie*)," and why all allegories are "always allegories of the impossibility of reading." If the allegorical sign repeats the earlier sign, then it repeats also the error inscribed in that earlier sign, which was always a figure or system of figures and its deconstruction. The error inscribed in the earlier sign is, however, repeated in the allegorical sign in a blind form, that is, in the form of an unrecognizable difference, or in the form of a difference that can be recognized only by those who have the key to the allegory. In that blindness, difference, and discrepancy between one part of the text and another, along the temporal and narrative line, lies the text's inability to read itself. The example de Man gives in this essay is Julie's repetition in her relation to God of the aberrant metaphorical structure she has first yielded to and then lucidly deconstructed when it was applied to Saint-Preux. The impossibility of reading is inscribed in the text in that allegorical relation between Julie's relation to God and her relation to Saint-Preux. De Man's logic seems clear enough, and it is airtight, irrefutable. It is just *because* all texts are a figure or system of figures and its deconstruction followed by a "supplementary figural superposition" "engendered" by the first, but engendered in the form of an allegory, that the story told is the story of unreadability. The new figure or system of figures refers to the first, but in a way that is based on difference and dissimilarity, so that the relation between the second "sign" and the first "sign" of which it is the allegory is both necessary, fatal, with the fatality of an unavoidable "engendering," and at the same time blinded, esoteric, not immediately apparent as a new version of the first. As de Man says in the definition of allegory in "The Rhetoric of Temporality," "The relationship between the allegorical sign and its meaning (*signifié*) is not decreed by dogma" (BI, 207). There is no available code by which the relationship can be made certain, masterable. It occurs, necessarily, but not in a predictable or rational way. It does not occur in a way based, for example, on the similarity between the allegorical sign and the earlier sign to which it refers. In allegory anything can stand for anything. No ground whatever, subjective, divine, transcendent, nor even that of social convention, supports the relationship. It just happens, by a linguistic or narrative necessity. Just go on talking or writing and you will be sure to narrate allegorically the impossibility of reading your prior narration. Since the allegory repeats the first error in this necessitated and yet not perspicuous way (in spite of the fact that the first error, the taking of a metaphor literally, was clearly deconstructed), this means that this second allegorical figural superposition "narrates the unreadability of the prior narration." It narrates it by showing that all the lucidity of the deconstruction of the first figure or system of figures has not in the least prevented the text from repeating another version of the same error. It is as if it could not remember from one moment to the next its own insights or perhaps were unable to recognize the allegorical similarity in dissimilarity. The supplementary figural superposition narrates the unreadability of the prior narration in the peculiar way allegories have of saying one thing and meaning another. The second part of *Julie* appears to narrate Julie's disenchantment with Saint-Preux and her subsequent turning to God, but what *in fact*, that is, allegorically, Julie's turn to religious devotion means, narrates, tells, is, by the fatality of a necessary engendering, the text's inability to read itself. Julie's failure to be able to "read" her own earlier letters to Saint-Preux (letters that, one would think, ought to prevent her from making the "same" mistake again) is the allegory of what the text is "really about," namely, its inability to read itself. The same thing may be said of Rousseau's inability to read what he has written. This is dramatized in R.'s stubborn refusal to say whether or not he has made up the letters of *Julie*, just as "our" inability to read *Julie*, yours, mine, de Man's, is another allegory of the text's inability to read itself. This intratextual unreadability is what all texts are "really about," the story they all really tell.

All this seems, as I said, clear enough. De Man's lucid formulations are a triumph of his methodological rigor and clarity. He lucidly expresses as knowledge or lucidly expresses knowledge *of* what he calls a perpetual and entirely irremediable "state of suspended ignorance" (AR, 19). But is that entirely the case? The reader may still have some nagging doubts, since certain aspects of what de Man says do not quite make sense, not at least from the point of view of ordinary logic and reason. Why in the world is it that a "text" cannot remember in one place what it so penetratingly knew in another place. Why can the text not read itself? The reader may have at this point the feeling that perhaps he or she has not been able to read de Man, has missed something vital in spite of having pored over and over this brief series of sentences in an attempt to defy de Man's claim that all texts are unreadable. As the beginning of an attempt to answer these troublesome questions, several preliminary observations may be made:

1. As opposed to the deconstructive procedures of Jacques Derrida, with which de Man's work is of course often paired, de Man has a tendency, in spite of the fact that each of his essays is the "reading" of a particular text, to move to levels of absolute generality and to say, for example, that *all* texts narrate the allegory of the impossibility of reading. Derrida, on the other hand, seems more interested in what is irreducibly idiomatic, both in the sense of belonging to a particular language and in the sense of belonging to a particular semantic region, about each one of the terms he interrogates, *différance, hymen, glas, pas,* or whatever—the list gets longer with each new essay he writes. In a recent essay, for example, "Des tours de Babel," Derrida makes a point of the fact that the word "Babel" expresses a general structure in a way that is unique, irreplaceable, "almost untranslatable": "En ce sens il [la tour de Babel] serait le mythe de l'origine du mythe, la métaphore de la métaphore, le récit du récit, la traduction de la traduction, etc. Il ne serait pas la seule structure à se creuser ainsi mais il le ferait à sa manière (elle-même *à peu près* intraduisible, comme un nom propre) et il faudrait en sauver l'idiome."[4] The relationship between the particular example and the universal law it exemplifies seems to be different in de Man from what it is in Derrida.

2. Another (different) way to put this would be to say that language appears to be the ultimate court of appeal for de Man, the place where the buck stops, so to speak. The end point of each of de Man's rigorous argumentations or readings is another demonstration that what appeared to have to do with selfhood or

society or history or ontology "really" is another manifestation of the implacable laws of language. This cannot quite be said for Derrida or cannot be said in the same way. There is the difference between them, even though it may be a difference no further away than the two sides of the same coin. It would be a mistake to make too much of the difference at the level of fundamental insight or presupposition between de Man and Derrida. The reader anxious to do that should remember Derrida's assertion in his book on de Man of entire allegiance to de Man's later work as a whole. Even so, it is unlikely that de Man would have written, for example, the following sentences in Derrida's recent book on Joyce, *Ulysse gramophone: Deux mots pour Joyce*, where there is a formulation of something almost prelinguistic that motivates the linguistic and makes it that the word "oui" or the word "yes" is presupposed by any act of language, even the first, and so is not a word at all in the ordinary sense. Or at any rate, it is that "place-no-place" of perpetual *différance* where the linguistic and the nonlinguistic converge. There is always a yes before the first yes: "Le discours sur l'être suppose la responsibilité du *oui*: oui, ce qui est dit est dit, je réponds ou il est répondu à l'interpellation de l'être, etc. Toujours en style télégraphique, je situerai alors la possibilité du oui et du oui-rire en ce lieu où l'égologie transcendentale, l'onto-encyclopédie, la grande logique spéculative, l'ontologie fondamentale et la pensée de l'être ouvrent sur une pensée du don et de l'envoi qu'elles présupposent mais ne peuvent contenir."[5] Although to say "oui" is an act of language, it always presupposes a "oui" before the first "oui," which can hardly be said to be language in the ordinary sense and to which the first "oui" responds, whereas for de Man it appears that there is nothing before language, though there is the darkness of the "other" of language itself within any text (a formulation in which de Man no doubt would have seen the trap of an undeconstructed metaphor in "other": other either as another person or as a name for a transcendental ground).

3. The figure or system of figures on which the passage in de Man I am discussing depends (and which it inevitably uses again even though it has lucidly deconstructed it) is personification, prosopopoeia. This is, as I have said, the trope to which he turns his attention in a series of brilliant essays written after the publication of *Allegories of Reading*. About personification in the passage I am reading there is, however, more to say.

Prosopopoeia has already been de Man's implicit target in the essay that immediately precedes "Allegory (*Julie*)" in *Allegories of Reading*, namely, "Self (*Pygmalion*)." The first person pronoun is used rarely and sparingly by de Man (though we have seen an example in the preface to *Allegories of Reading*.) This goes along with an austere rigor that makes his essays sometimes sound as if they were written by some impersonal intelligence or by language itself, not by someone to whom the laws of blindness and the impossibility of reading also apply, as they do to the rest of us. To put this another way, de Man is unwilling, perhaps on principle, to apply overtly to himself the insights into the necessity of error that he nevertheless formulates as universal. The "principle" in question may be the fact that on principle each reader must be blind to his or her own blindness. Attempts to recognize it or to formulate it would be futile gestures, merely compounding the error. This may be an area where it is better to keep silent, as de Man does.

To put this yet another way, de Man clearly recognizes or recognizes clearly that the self is a metaphor, moreover a metaphor without particular authority. Especially does the self not have authority in that attractive form of a return of the self beyond its deconstruction, as the wielder of the instrument of deconstruction. In "Self (*Pygmalion*)" de Man somewhat scornfully gives short shrift to the notion present in Heidegger and in a different way in Paul Ricoeur's interpretation of Freud that "the subject is reborn [beyond its deconstruction] in the guise of the interpreter": "Our present concern is merely whether Rousseau, like Ricoeur's Freud, reclaims a measure of authority for the self, grounded in its ability to understand its own failure to make such a claim" (AR, 174, 175). That would appear to describe exactly the authority that de Man seems to claim for himself throughout *Allegories of Reading*, the ironic authority to assert a lucid insight into ignorance, the authority of a self that can assert that the self is only a metaphor. But no, this recuperation of the self beyond its deconstruction is an illusion, another error, no doubt a particularly attractive one to the deconstructive critic, who needs all the comfort he can get and would like to find it in the assurance that "he" is the master of the technique of deconstruction. De Man deprives his readers (and himself) of even this paradoxical survival of the self as a substantial point of authority outliving the demolition of everything else but language, even itself: "From the point of view of truth and falsehood, the self is not a privileged metaphor in Rousseau" (AR, 187). Nor is it for de Man himself. What is described in terms of Rousseau, Proust, Nietzsche, or whoever is in fact an impersonal and universal operation of language, spoken of only "par la commodité du récit," as "Proust" puts it, in terms of this or that proper name.

Nevertheless the use of some proper name or pronoun, or at least the barely visible traces of some almost effaced prosopopoeia, seems to be another of those irresistible necessities of language, perhaps one of the most important, in the sense of having far-reaching consequences. The presence of this trope in de Man's most impersonal and universalized formulations, such as the ones I am discussing here, in spite of de Man's "deconstruction" of the idea that selfhood is a privileged ontological category, is evidence that he is unable to avoid using it in his own language. It could be said to be the example in my passage of each text's inability to read itself.

How does this occur? A text does not "read itself," except metaphorically. Reading is a word that applies literally only to the activity of some conscious reader, however metaphorical the existence of the self of that reader may be. Although he can scrupulously avoid, for the most part, speaking of himself as an

"I" or speaking of the operations performed by the critical texts he has written as products of a masterful subjectivity, all insight and no blindness, nevertheless it seems impossible even for a reader of "de Man's" rigor to avoid talking about the impersonal relations between one part of a text and another as if they were acts involving a self. The text tells the story of its failure to denominate. It brings lucidly into the open like a masterly detective the errors in its own metaphors. Then this narration "engenders," as if it were capable of sexual reproduction, a supplementary figural superposition that narrates its inability, in spite of its deconstructive insight into the aberrancy of its own metaphors, to read itself. This allegory, or narration at the second or third power is a demonstration that reading is impossible. This demonstration remains entirely intratextual, in spite of its applicability to the author, narrator, or critic as readers. It has nothing to do with any of them as selves.

The prosopopoeia in "engenders" is crucial here, since it personifies as a natural temporal process, one with the organic continuity and necessity of conception, gestation, and birth, what is in fact a very different kind of temporal necessity. The metaphorical word "engenders" names an impersonal linguistic necessity, a necessity marked, as de Man's theory of allegory insists, not by organic continuity, but by disconnection, contingency, and dissimilarity. The word "engenders" makes the strange linguistic process de Man is describing sound as if it were a story with beginning, middle, and end corresponding referentially to events in the historical world. In fact, de Man of course wants to affirm the reverse, that the "materiality of history," with all its violence and injustice, is determined not by human will, but by impersonal laws of language over which we have no control and which we cannot even clearly understand, since our understanding always contains a residue of misunderstanding.

The prosopopoeia in "engenders" and in the strange idea that a text reads or fails to read itself is far from innocent. It covers over and gives an appearance of plausibility to what remains, for "me" at least, the inexplicable mystery of why language behaves the way de Man says it does, that is, why it "engenders," by an unavoidable fatality, the two forms of incoherence de Man indentifies: the deconstruction of its own fundamental metaphors and then their reassertion in a different, disguised form, but in a form that may still be detected behind the mask of an apparent dissimilarity. Why does language behave *as if* it were a person? Since language is, as I have said, the court of final appeal for de Man, there seems no answer to this. It does because it does. "The error is not within the reader," says de Man at the end of "Promises (*Social Contract*)." Language itself dissociates the cognition from the act. *Die Sprache verspricht (sich)*: de Man's witty subversion of Heidegger's celebrated formulation means both "language promises (itself)," and "language makes a slip of the tongue, a *lapsus linguae*." "To the extent that is necessarily misleading," he continues, "language just as necessarily conveys the promise of its own truth. This is also why textual allegories on this level of rhetorical complexity generate history" (AR, 277). "Generate" here echoes "engenders" in the earlier passage. It insinuates the same idea of a genetic causality, borrowing a term from the conception of history that is being contested to name the very different idea that language, with the unhappy peculiarities de Man identifies, blindly makes history happen as it does happen.

As I said earlier, however, de Man is almost certain to have been there before we arrive and to have anticipated any "deconstruction" of his own text we may perform. The example of that here is the final phrase of the last sentence in the paragraph in "Allegory (*Julie*)" I have been reading. After having asserted that all allegories are "always allegories of the impossibility of reading," de Man adds, apparently as a kind of thought-teasing afterthought, the following, after a dash: "—a sentence in which the genitive 'of' has itself to be 'read' as a metaphor." What, exactly, does this mean? What does it mean to take the word "of," used as a genitive, as a metaphor? There are three "of's" in this sentence: "allegories *of* metaphor," "always allegories *of* the impossibility *of* reading," and presumably de Man's stricture must apply to all. A similar "of" of course appears in the title of the book: *Allegories of Reading*. The reader's first inclination may be to think that de Man is referring to the notorious doubleness of the genitive "of," the way it may go both ways and mean both "out of" and "about or concerning." An allegory of reading is both an allegory about or concerning reading and an allegory that is generated out of the act of reading. It is possible that de Man means that each of these versions of "of" is the metaphor of the other. To say "allegory of reading" or "allegory of the impossibility of reading" is to say simultaneously that a narrative is the oblique or hidden story of the impossibility of reading and to say that the allegory is generated out of the impossibility of reading or that the impossibility is generated out of the act of reading. Such a double reading of the genitive would not, however, be metaphorical at all, since it would leave intact the literal genesis of the allegory from the impossibility of reading the impossibility of reading from the allegory. A metaphor is a substitution, a transfer from one realm where it is legitimate to another realm where it is "only figurative." We know that for de Man all metaphors are always in error, aberrant, the covering over of an irremediable ignorance about what is "really there," for example, what it is really like inside that creature who looks like another me and to whom I give the name first of "giant" and then of "man." When de Man says the genitive "of" must be taken as a metaphor, he must want to break the literal line of generation and make it fictive, aberrant, figural.

In this case, it is clear what must be the metaphorical substitution, as is its motivation clear. To speak with the genitive "of" of "the impossibility *of* reading" or of allegories *of* that impossibility or of "allegories *of* metaphor" is to insinuate within the apparently abstract formulation just that covert prosopopoeia, that affirmation of a natural, organic, generative, genetic causality that I have identified in "engenders" and in the figure of the personified text reading itself. An old, crumbling *Webster's* (1898), the only English dictionary I have here where I am writing this essay, defines "of" as a preposition meaning "from or out of; proceeding from, as the cause, source, means, author, or agent bestowing. . . . Hence *of* is the sign of the genitive case, the case that denotes production; as, the Son *of* man, the son proceeding from man, produced from man." Old Noah Webster or whatever sons of Noah wrote this entry chose with admirable insight a Biblical example where the capitalized *S* indicates that the Son of man in question is really Christ, the son of God, divine as well as human, the logos itself or himself, therefore in a sense the father of all mankind, or at least the model on the basis of which God the Father produced all mankind. The example shows that theological issues are never very far from explicit in that genitive "of," along with a metalepsis reversing the order of temporal priority. The genitive "of" involves characteristically an inextricable mixing of metaphysical or theological categories (logos as ground of being), personal and genetic categories (logos as mind, as self, as father or son), and linguistic categories (logos as word or Word).

In any case, to "read" that "of" in de Man's sentence not literally but as a metaphor is to see the whole latent personification governing the passage as an error, an aberrancy. The metaphorical "of" covers a relationship that is not genitive or genetic but linguistic, and for which there is no name. If "of" is a metaphor here, what literal formulation could be substituted for it? No such alternative literal word exists. One may therefore say that the genitive "of" read as a metaphor is, like all primary aberrant failing denominations, strictly speaking a catachresis. It is another example of what de Man elsewhere observes, the overlapping, but not total symmetry, of prosopopoeia and catachresis. The metaphorical, personifying, catachrestic "of" is a placeholder brought in to cover over an irreducible ignorance about why language works as it does work. De Man's enigmatic phrase about reading the genitive "of" as a metaphor shows his awareness of this fact, or his text's awareness, as well as its awareness that the evidence of its own failure to read itself is the covert reintroduction of the category of selfhood that has already been denounced as an aberrant metaphor, without authority.

No doubt de Man's clarity about the impossibility "of" reading, his reading of the impossibility of reading, "engenders" new repetitions of the aberrancy it so clearly identifies, for example, in my persistence in referring to what is only a text, words on the page, as if it were a person, "de Man," with whom I might have a conversation or toward whom I might have ethical obligations.[6] As de Man makes clear on the page following the one I have been trying to read, ethics or "ethicity" is a linguistic necessity or imperative, not a subjective one. "Ethics," says de Man, "has nothing to do with the will (thwarted or free) of a subject, nor *a fortiori*, with a relationship between subjects" (AR, 206). Just what is de Man's conception of the necessary ethical dimension of language, and therefore of reading, I have elsewhere attempted to identify.[7]

Notes

1. For an attempt to avoid the totalitarian tyranny of the one in a theory of judging and of justice see J.-F. Lyotard and Jean-Loup Thébaud, *Au juste* (Paris: Christian Bourgois, 1979), and the discussions of Lyotard by various scholars in *Diacritics* 14 (Fall 1984) and in *La Faculté de juger* (Paris: Minuit, 1985).

2. It should be remembered that if this is to be done at all it has to be carried out all the way to the end, or even beyond the end. Nothing could be more futile and feeble than an intermittent or partial application of de Man's insights into language in a critical essay that remains nevertheless in its fundamental procedures blithely thematic, psychologistic, or referential.

3. Whatever *that* means; the allusion to Kierkegaard invites pages of discriminations, which cannot be added here.

4. Jacques Derrida, "Des tours de Babel," in *Psyché: Inventions de l'autre* (Paris: Galilée, 1987), 205.

5. Jacques Derrida, *Ulysse Gramophone: Deux mots pour Joyce* (Paris: Galilée, 1987), 132.

6. For another reading of "of" as figurative, see the paragraph about "of" in Keats's title, *The Fall of Hyperion*, in de Man's "The Resistance to Theory," *The Resistance to Theory* (Minneapolis: University of Minnesota Press, 1986), pp. 16–17.

7. In the chapter entitled "Reading Unreadability: de Man," in *The Ethics of Reading* (New York: Columbia University Press, 1986), 41–59. This present essay was written in 1985, before the discovery of Paul de Man's early writings and the ensuing outpouring of writings about those writings. My reading of the paragraph in *Allegories of Reading* still seems to me just, and I have made only two changes, necessary for clarification. On p. 158 a reference to de Man's "early work" now reads "early *post-1950* work." The sentence about Derrida and de Man now reads "entire allegiance to de Man's *later* work as a whole." The French version of Derrida's book on de Man, *Mémoires*, will contain an augmented version of his essay on the early writings of de Man, "Like the Sound of the Sea Deep within a Shell: Paul de Man's War," *Critical Inquiry*, 14 (Spring 1988): 590–652. I have had my own say about de Man's early writings and about their relation to his later writings and to "deconstruction" generally in an untitled article in *The Times Literary Supplement*, June 17–23, 1988, pp. 676, 685, and in "An Open Letter to Professor Jon Wiener," forthcoming in a volume of essays on de Man's early writings to be published by the University of Nebraska Press. I add here that the juxtaposition of de Man's early and late writings is a starkly dramatic way to confront the fact that the triumph of Nazi totalitarianism in Germany, the Holocaust, and the Second World War were a decisive transformation of Western culture and even a break in world history. Whatever we say, do, or write, do by writing, thereafter takes place against the background of those events, whether or not we know it or wish it. This was always true in a special way of Paul de Man's later writings, and now we have a way to know that. It may not be so easy to remember that whatever anyone writes henceforth is also in one way or another inscribed on the same background.

LECTIO: de Man's Imperative
Werner Hamacher

Translated by Susan Bernstein

It is not certain that there can be a science of literature.

If the goal of literary criticism[1] is determined as the systematic clarification of all the specifically literary aspects of literature, then one treats this specificity like a riddle that can be solved by the translation of the figures of literature into the generally comprehensible language of science. Literary language is thus declared to be a systematic distortion of a normal language with literary criticism operating as its orthopedic agent. Should failure occur in the process of decoding, a process that epistemologically presupposes the general validity of linguistic rules of composition and their use, the positivistic ideal of knowledge sees only a momentary hesitation within the course of enlightenment that can be made good by technical refinement or by further perfections of the decoding cutlery. Pursued in this way, literary criticism is essentially a business of rehabilitation, striving to recuperate all deviants — whether historical or formal — within the *ratio* of the present or of a more enlightened future. Its fundamental premises — the epistemological assumption of general rules of comprehensibility, and the corresponding historiographical view that the use of language in accordance with these rules must be promoted — these premises in fact exclude the possibility of the knowledge of literature *as* literature. This kind of literary criticism is not a science of literature, but rather, more or less clandestinely, science against literature.

That type of literary criticism concerned with literature as a specifically aesthetic phenomenon shares at least one fundamental trait with the structural and historicizing philology aimed at explication, namely, the conviction that literary texts are the sensible presentation of a meaning or a meaningful structure. This literary criticism gives its attention not so much to the meaning of a text and the possibility of its general mediation as to the constitution of linguistic images and figures in which meaning is supposed to have attained concrete form. But if the meaning is visibly given in the works themselves, then for this kind of scholarship nothing remains but to revel in the works in a hedonistic cult of images or to offer itself as the *maître de plaisir* to a weekend public. Not only in the now suspect idealist systems of aesthetics that center on the sensible appearance of the Idea, but also in the semiologically cultivated aesthetics of the most recent times, the pleasure of the text, guaranteed by the imaginary correspondence between the movement of meaning and its linguistic articulation, plays a dominant role. This role is all the greater the more the literary text, relieved of the burden of the Idea and the weight of referentiality, is declared in an extremely diffuse sense to be a "free play" of signs, the volatility of which is claimed to evade any rigorous determination. If seduced by the aesthetic reduction of its objects, literary scholarship ceases to be scholarship and becomes impressionistic literature.

It is not certain that there can be a science of literature. The ground of its possibility would have to lie this side of the norm oriented and the aestheticizing reduction of literature by means of the concept of a scientific discipline, modeled either on natural science or edifying discourse. This ground would have to lie in the texts of literature themselves. But in its texts, this ground cannot simply lie as mere passivity, as the abstract possibility of its explicit concretion in knowledge that would offer itself without resistance to the will to knowledge or to aesthetic pleasure. Rather, this ground must be laid in them in such a way that a dimension of critical knowledge of their constitution is proper to these texts themselves *as texts*. Only if literary texts are marked by the articulation of a knowledge of themselves can a science of literature have an objective foundation. But the knowledge of itself that literature articulates can provide a legitimate basis for a literary criticism laying a claim to objective understanding only if it has itself the affirmative and unproblematic structure of an objective knowledge. What knowledge, then, speaks in literary texts, and in what figures? Is this knowledge of such a kind that it speaks at all, and unequivocally? Or is it a knowledge that negates its universality and its own internal coherence? What does scholarship have to look for in the domain of literature? And from what must it flee? What is the law of literature's relationship to itself, and what law determines the relationship of reading to it?

These questions can be posed with the prospect of an answer in terms of only a single contemporary literary theorist. Only Paul de Man has exposed himself in his works to the demands of these questions. Here, these questions and the answers he has formulated will be traced and discussed through some of his texts. These are not de Man's questions, but rather questions that literary theory has to ask itself with regard to its own possibility. And they are questions that can be deciphered in the very texts to which de Man's studies are devoted; for otherwise they were vain questions whose authority would be exhausted by the personal authority of the one who tried to pose them. For only if it can be shown that these questions expose a dimension of literary texts themselves, that these texts are themselves concerned with the possibility or impossibility of understanding and of their knowledge and their activity—only then can one measure the proximity or distance between literature and its science. Only then is it possible to determine whether, and in what sense, literary criticism can have its basis within literature.

With an admitted naïveté, de Man first localizes the problem of the comprehension and the pleasure of literature at the thematic level. The essay whose original title provided the name of de Man's second book, "Proust et l'allegorie de la lecture"—in *Allegories of Reading* the title dryly reads "Reading (Proust)"—seeks an answer, in the scene of reading in the first part of Proust's *Recherche*, to the question: "What does *A la recherche du temps perdu* tell us about reading?" (AR, 57). The same question—a question that seems to pave the way for a movement of reflection, but will in fact reveal itself as a *mise en abyme*—reemerges in the Rousseau part of *Allegories of Reading* in the chapter complementary to the Proust essay entitled: "Allegory (*Julie*)": "What does the *Nouvelle Héloïse* have to tell us about the problematics of reading?" (AR, 193). The Proust essay, initiated by the question of reading as a theme of the *Recherche*, ends with the conclusion that a text, whether it is classed within the genre of literature or of literary criticism, can only thematize reading under the sign of the impossibility of thematization. Thematization presupposes the possibility of an unambiguous referential relation of literary language; but since the theme "reading" can always be used in a text as a metaphor for something else that would not be "reading," it is impossible to ascertain whether or not reading really is in fact thematized. Because no text can provide the criterion for the distinction between the literal and the figurative meaning of its elements, every reading is exposed to the unensurability of the referential relation. Its uncertainty is intensified when "reading" itself becomes an element of a text, be it a literary or a theoretical one, for referential ambiguity then becomes a distinguishing mark of reading itself, which can no longer be sure of either the meaning of the text or its own operation. However much reading finds itself thematized, it can never be certain of its own thematic content, of itself. Reading must—if only for the sake of the foundation of literary criticism—but it cannot be read. The specular structure of self-reflection, in which the text strives to assure itself of its own understanding and in which reading seeks the guarantee of an objective basis, is broken by the impossibility of determining without any doubt the referential status of the bond by which reflection and what is reflected could cohere. In "Allegory (*Julie*)," de Man draws the consequence: "Reading is a praxis that thematizes its own thesis about the impossibility of thematization and this makes it unavoidable, though hardly legitimate, for allegories to be interpreted in thematic terms" (AR, 209).

In every case, the referential intention of a text can be denied by the indication of the possibility of its merely figurative status. If literary language differs from the language of science and from everyday language, it is in its exposition of the unsublatable internal contradiction that cleaves asunder the semantic functions of every language. This exposition does not appease the antagonism between these functions, but rather intensifies it through repetition. For literary exposition also lacks the power to hold fast, secure, and control meaning: in this case, that is to say the meaning of understanding itself. The unensurability of meaning is not an effect of the temporal succession in which the text unfolds, as phenomenological and historicist hermeneutic approaches would happily assume, nor is it a consequence of the historical distance between the text and its understanding. On the contrary, time and history are first opened up by the semantic indeterminacy of language. In the last sentences of "Reading (Proust)" de Man writes:

> As a writer, Proust is the one who knows that the hour of truth, like the hour of death, never arrives on time, since what we call time is precisely truth's inability to coincide with itself. *A la recherche du temps perdu* narrates the flight of meaning, but this does not prevent its own meaning from being, incessantly, in flight. (AR, 78)

De Man does not speak of the meaning of meaning. He speaks of the flight of that meaning in which the flight of meaning is thematized. This flight of flight first opens up time and with it a world that, torn apart by the rifts between the various signifying functions of language, can in no instant coincide with the concept of the world that a thematizing consciousness forms for itself. This consciousness is a thematizing consciousness only because it itself takes flight from the tautologies of its own self-confirmation and, as in the formulation of the "unavoidably thematic interpretation," de Man insists here as well on the vocabulary of necessity: because this consciousness *must* take flight. In the Proust essay, de Man writes in the paragraph devoted to the ambiguities of consciousness: "it seems that the language of consciousness is unable to remain . . . ensconced and that . . . it *has to* turn itself out" (AR, 70; my emphasis). The epistemological meaning of this movement of consciousness into the external world lies in the fact that consciousness could find a guarantee for the truth of its experiences only outside itself. Only in the external world can the referential intention of language be verified and one of its possibilities, the capacity to refer, be assured. "Like Albertine," de Man writes, "consciousness refuses to be captive and *has to* take flight and move abroad" (AR, 71; my emphasis). The flight of consciousness into a world not mastered by its projections and independent of the schemata of its language is subject to an imperative, an obligatory constraint that is not made less harmful by the assumption that only an entity that suffers anxiety and knows the existential need for self-affirmation can be subject to it. But the imperative of flight is not a command of animalistic self-preservation, for consciousness is subject to it only as to the imperative of its own linguistic character: language *has to save itself* by seeking to assure its ability to mean within a sphere posited as independent of language. The imperative of language thus commands—and this constitutes its profound paradox—the abandonment of the uncertain basis of language in order to seek within a region, itself no longer language, the stable ground of its capacity for truth and the reliable confirmation that language really and indeed is language. The discussion of this region can only be problematic, for within language it can be encountered only as a theme, that is, only under an untenable premise, and therefore no longer as a possibility of verification. But nor can this region that is not language and cannot be represented in the phenomenalizing figures of discourse be definitively excluded from language without hypostatizing language as a self-related play of signifiers, extinguishing its capacity to refer in the unthreatened success of its play. That which is not language, which is not the expository and phenomenalizing language of representation, announces itself categorically, however, in the command to abandon the "intratextual closure" of figures and representations and "to move abroad" (AR, 70). This command is neither a constraint of material reality, nor is it conferred by the language of representation. Belonging neither to the one sphere nor to the other, it speaks out of the possibility of the rift between the two, and out of the impossibility to affirm with a priori certainty the homogeneity of these spheres and, with it, the referential content of language. The imperative articulates the difference between language and its meaning. It articulates this difference with a view to its reduction, but the necessity of the imperative already signals the impossibility of completing the task it poses. Every science of literature or, since we cannot assume that one is possible, for the moment, every critical reading is subject to this imperative, since the structure of linguistic signs and their concatenation can never exclude the possibility that, as the mere effects of chance, they are without meaning, so that all attempts to understand, to recognize, or to know are dismissed as empty pretense.

The imperative "to move abroad" is thus not an epistemological one, but rather issues from the unreliability of knowledge attained through language. It is an imperative in the strict sense, a practical imperative, commanding that the lacunae in the structure of knowledge be filled by the turn to the world of action. In his Proust essay, de Man points resolutely to the ethical dimension that opens up in a short sentence in the passage on reading—probably one of the shortest sentences in the *Recherche* that may not have drawn the attention of any other reader. If one skips over the temporal, that is, the climatic determinations, the sentence reads: "Mais ma grand'mère . . . venait me supplier de sortir" (Pléiade I: 83). The first time he mentions the grandmother's request, de Man already intensifies its emphasis by writing that the grandmother forced him to go outside, *"forcé à sortir"* (*Movements Premiers* [Paris: José Corti, 1972], 232), while the English version runs: "his grandmother *orders* him to go outside" (AR, 58; my emphasis). In the second, more detailed reference to this phrase, the grandmother's mode of language being "correctly" reproduced—though we are concerned here not with "correctness" but rather with what de Man perceived in this sentence—de Man emphatically throws into relief the imperative gesture this sentence is about. In the French version of the essay, de Man writes: "Contre l'impératif moral de la bonne conscience, *representé* ici par la grand'mère qui 'supplie Marcel de sortir,' Marcel doit justifier son refus de 'renoncer à la lecture' avec tout ce qu'elle comporte de joies secrètes" (*Movements*, 237; my emphasis). Here, the moral imperative that, like the imperative of consciousness, orders to go outside is presented *as represented* by the grandmother; in contrast, the representability of the imperative has become a problem for the English version, which speaks only of a speaking of the imperative itself for which the grandmother has become the means: "Against the moral imperative *speaking through* the grandmother who 'begs Marcel to go outside,' Marcel must justify his refusal to give up his reading" (AR, 64; my emphasis). So for de Man, it is not an empirical grandmother whom Proust may well have had in mind when he wrote this sentence; rather, it is the grandmother as a figure of the text, speaking as the agent of an imperative that the movement of the text itself brings forth. Contrary to the thematic suggestion of the narrative, this imperative is not the imperative of a morality Nietzsche often characterized as the morals of convention and Kant as a merely ritual morality ("Moral der Observanzen"); it is not an imperative of habits and dominant values, but a more compulsory imperative, independent of the intentions of an agent and the contingent pressure of its historical or social position, given as the commandment of language, the command of the decision about its semantic status. No empirical or historical authority—whether the psychic authority of the Grand Mother, or the authority of the grand institutions of state, church, and diffuse ideology—can adequately represent the force of this imperative. These empirical and thematic authorities, as figures of representation and normative instances, conceal precisely that aspect of themselves that is the work of the imperative, which for its part withdraws from representation and figuration. Its structure becomes apparent only at the point of failure of all attempts to grasp it conceptually or figuratively, to localize it in institutions and to bring it into consistency with a determinate type of language and its technical application. The imperative of language speaks only in the break of language.

De Man describes this failure through the particular turns of the reading passage and its metafigurative self-commentary. Here, Marcel suggests that the act of reading, experienced in a particular atmosphere at a particular time, can synthesize the interiority of subjectivity with the external world into which his grandmother sends him—the world of imagination with the world of reality, the sphere of passivity with that of action. The synthetic totality would preserve the opposing elements in a form more pure than their appearance within the separated spheres. Proust writes, according to the translation de Man offers in "Semiology and Rhetoric" (in which he once again discusses the same passage): "it gave my imagination the total spectacle of the summer, whereas my senses, if I had been on a walk, could only have enjoyed it by fragments" (AR, 14). The synthesis of imagination, which for Proust and for a long history of Western aesthetics possesses a totalizing power greater than the synthesis of the senses, finds its figurative correlative in the trope of metaphor: "It was hardly light enough to read, and the sensation of the light's splendor was given me only . . . by the flies executing their little concert, the chamber music of summer" (AR, 13). Synesthesia, grounded in the substitution of light by the chamber music of the flies, that is, in the language of metaphor, is the condition of reading: only in the light that the music of the flies sheds on the pages of his book is Marcel able to read, understand, and bring into harmony the divided realities of his world of experience. Reading itself becomes for him the event of metaphor. In this event, the contingencies of space and time within which it occurs disappear and are replaced by a necessary and essential relationship, lasting and immediate, between the external world of sound and light and the inner world of fantasy. Thus through the metaphor of the chamber music, reading is "connected to summer by a more necessary link: born from beautiful days, . . . containing some of their essence, . . . it guarantees their return, their actual, persistent, unmediated presence" (AR, 13). This necessary bond that metaphor—and with its help, synesthetic imagination—establishes between the internal and the external world makes reading into an act of subjective synthesis through which the whole world of appearance and activity is supposed to convene in a single moment of sound, and also makes reading into that experience through which the world's permanence, reality, and the immediate presence of its meaning, beyond its aesthetic character, ought to be secured. Reading, this inconspicuous activity, becomes a fundamental ontological operation. A long aesthetic and literary tradition has contributed to this hypostasis; and that kind of literary scholarship participates in it as well that sees in texts like Proust's the presentation of the self-realization of subjectivity, and strives to put through a corresponding feat of self-affirmation in its public by means of conceptual explication. In a critical stance closer to the French and Anglo-Saxon traditions of literary criticism than to the German tradition of literary science, de Man remains aware of the difference between the theoretical statements of the text and its rhetorical praxis. The text—and, like this one, every other text as well—does not do what it claims to do: "the figural praxis and the metafigural theory do not converge" (AR, 15).

In Proust's text, metaphor can succeed in its suggestion of a phenomenal presence, of the immediate meaningfulness and necessity of the totality it generates, only at the cost of severing itself from the determinations of its context, by forgetting the contingency of the specific situation that gives rise to it. De Man shows that it is precisely at the point at which the metaphorical structure—and with it, reading as an operation of metaphor—claims to reconcile the most extreme opposition, between meditation and activity, that the linguistic forms of its contingency infiltrate the language of metaphor and obstruct the work of totalization.

De Man cites the following as such a point in Proust's text: "The dark coolness of my room . . . matched my repose which . . . supported, like the quiet of a motionless hand in the middle of a running brook the shock and the motion of a torrent of activity" (AR, 13–14). The metaphorical intention of this sentence fails by the fact that the coolness of the brook is opposed to the heated activity with which it is supposed to coincide; and the *torrent d'activité* that the motionless hand of the reader is supposed to support does not comply with the establishment of a necessary bond between rest and motion. For although the literal sense of this expression connotes coolness, the figurative meaning of a great deal of activity, adhering to it not as a metaphor but rather as a cliché, in fact connotes the opposite quality of heat, intensified by the association with *torride* (hot) (AG, 66). Grammatical contiguity, figurative ambivalence, and the merely conventional, in no way essential, character of the cliché dissolve the unity of the metaphor, undermining its supremacy over the merely external, accidental nexus produced by metonymy. The connections that Marcel's text establishes between the competing forces of his world are not necessary, but only contingent, not essential, but accidental, not paradigmatic, but rather syntagmatic and, moreover, atagmatic—if not asthmatic. Like the reconciliation of these powers, the attempt to appease the imperative to go out into reality and thereby resolve the ethical conflict also fails.

Reading, as a process of knowledge and aesthetic experience and their synthesis is under the sign of metaphor, breaks down because the disparate elements it tries to bring together in a closed figure, structure, or form belong to a system of articulation different from the one in which figures of totalization can be constructed. De Man's rhetorical analysis remains largely determined by Jakobsen's distinction between the paradigmatic and syntagmatic levels of language, despite important additions, radicalizations, and hints of a fundamental critique. But within the Proust essay and in several other texts in *Allegories of Reading*, in opposition to Jakobsen's privileging of metaphor, the linguistic field is dominated by the metonymic relations of contiguity and contingency. Their fleeting and accidental character and their unreliability deny every figure promising the permanence, necessity, and immediacy of meaning and intuition. The element of chance in the concatenation of signs is the unreliable and uncontrollable ground of the metaphor that disowns it. Even in terms of the linguistic structures claiming to be paradigmatic, like *torrent d'activité*, one can distinguish a figurative and a literal meaning, related to each other not paradigmatically but syntagmatically. Even in the name and in the atom of the word, the sentence is at work, shattering their unity. If reading is only possible under the assumption that it can successfully restore the meaning inherent in the sign, then the fundamental contingency of the relation between sign and meaning condemns its effort to failure and deprives the reader of the illusion that he, too, could experience the world of reality and of action in the synthesizing of reading. This is why in Proust's text, the sentence, "mais ma grand'mère . . . venait me supplier de sortir," immediately follows the failed metaphor of the *torrent d'activité*. The imperative to go outside and discover truth in action is governed by the law of metonymy, of the external and contingent bond, inconstant and momentary, sanctioned by no higher law, between language and its meaning, between reading and writing. Although the imperative declares itself in the rhetorical (and also grammatical) figure of the grandmother, which gives the imperative a definite form and direction, and to that degree, the illusory promise of a possible reconciliation, the law ruling both this imperative itself and the figure of its agent is the law of the irreconcilable disparity of the figurative and literal meaning of linguistic signs: the law of the impossibility of identifying any epistemological instance that could secure the meaning of language and even its very capacity to mean. It is the imperative of disintegration, of impropriation, effective only as the dumb and lusterless defacement of linguistic figures. It is not dictated by a transcendental subject; it cannot be exhausted by figures, nor can it be accomplished by any acts of consciousness. The law to which the imperative is subject—the law of the law—makes the imperative a linguistic event susceptible of occurring in the world of figures oriented toward synthetic totality and rational necessity only as contingent force: as chance, as a meaningless mechanical repetition, as groundless positing, as the failure and the disruption of the intentions of a will that wills itself. Only in this sense does the imperative have necessity: not the internal necessity demanded by a consciousness, a will, a subject, or other transcendental instances; but rather the necessity of an accident annihilating any hope of the security of a transcendental foundation. The imperative, insofar as through it the unification of intuition and meaning proves to be illusory, is the imperative of deaestheticization. Insofar as the unensurability of meaning speaks through it, it is the imperative of disinterpretation. If it is still possible to read, then only in the aporia of unreadability articulated by literary texts themselves. In all writing and in all meaning is read the imperative: *Sors de la lecture. Sort.*

Literary texts, characterized by the dissolution of their figurative, and more precisely, metaphoric structure, attempt to recover the place of the certain existence of a referent by the pathos of their negativity. In "Allegory (*Julie*)," de Man describes this movement of the restitution of meaning through the power of its negation:

> The very pathos of the desire (regardless of whether it is valorized positively or negatively) indicates that the presence of desire replaces the absence of identity and that, the more the text denies the actual existence of a referent, real or ideal, and the more fantastically fictional it becomes, the more it becomes the representation of its own pathos. . . . pathos is itself no longer a figure but a substance. (AR, 198–99)

In the passage in the "Seconde Préface" to the *Nouvelle Héloïse*, to which de Man turns his attention in the discussion of the interrelationship between pathos and language, Rousseau writes: "L'amour n'est qu'illusion; . . . il s'entoure d'objets qui ne sont point, ou auxquels lui seul a donné l'être; et comme il rend tous ses sentiments en images, son langage est toujours figuré" (Pléiade II: 15). The language of love does not correspond to any object that it itself has not already projected through its tropes. Its images and turns of phrases, its sentences and words refer to something that does not exist and that they cannot wholly produce because they lack the ability to say it completely and effectively. A letter dictated by love, as Rousseau writes, "redit toujours la même chose, et n'a jamais achevé de dire." The language of pathos does not speak but, almost in a stammer, only repeats its own incapacity to speak. Its figures are not figures of an objective reality located somewhere beyond language, but rather are figures of the incompleteness of all objective worlds that could occupy the position of a referent. They are figures of the impotence of their own claim of referentiality. However much its essence lies in illusion, the language of pathos — of love, longing, of desire, or of anxiety and suspicion — is a language of disillusionment about the referential capacity of language. It obeys the imperative of metonymy that dissolves the metaphoric pretension of the unification of reality and knowledge, of language and action. In de Man's formulation, this negative activity renders pathos a "figure that disfigures, a metaphor that confers the illusion of proper meaning to a suspended, open semantic structure" (AR, 198). His language, no longer referential, but self-referential, demonstrates and unveils its own illusory character; it is "the monster of its own aberration, always oriented toward the future of its repetition" (AR, 198). But the power of disillusionment belongs to the language of the affects only because this language no longer seeks to say anything, but only to present its own speaking, to present not representations, but only the very form of representing itself. To this extent, the figure of pathos is no longer a figure *of* pathos, but pathos itself; the figure is the substance and subject of language, substance and subject are nothing but figures. Because to this language, as the pure speaking of gliding metonymy, every referent must appear as illusory, as an always transgressed limitation, and because for the language of pathos the infallible ground and the abiding meaning of its speaking appear to be given only in themselves, the language of pathos is not merely the referent and the figure of its own discourse; it is the referentiality, the figurativity of speaking itself.

Pathos, denuded of all empirical, individual affectivity and positive meaningfulness, is sheer intentionality. In the texts of both Rousseau and Proust, pathos pretends to a transcendental function; the energy of intentionality is hypostatized not only as the organizing principle of its texts but, beyond that, as the only trustworthy ground of their comprehensibility — not only as the form of its speaking, but also of its being heard and perceived independently of any acts of consciousness. In the "Seconde Préface," Rousseau writes: "Si la force du sentiment ne nous frappe pas, sa vérité nous touche, et c'est ainsi que le coeur sait parler au coeur" (Pléiade II: 15). Not the power but the powerlessness of emotion—its truth, that it is not the master of language and that no language could ever correspond to it— links the subject of the discourse and the subject of understanding. The substantial figure of pathos, the figure of subjectivity itself, by denying all deviating media-tion by figures, is also the figure of immediate communication. The language of pathos would thus be the language of pure understanding. In it, not a determinate intention but rather intentionality itself would be spoken; no determinate content would be communicated, but pure communicability; no empirical subject would articulate itself, but only its subjectivity. Every imperative that negates the figura-tive synthesis on the grounds of the pathos of negativity is an imperative of subjec-tivity. It makes no restitution for language's pretension to refer to real representa-tions, but rather speaks as the language of referentiality itself. The imperative of pure subjectivity is at the same time the imperative of universal communicability in the medium of the negative. But to precisely the same degree, it is no longer an imperative. Its negativity already appeases the tensions between what the im-perative demands and what it, as this demand, already fulfills, between that which it asserts and its asserting, and generates a homogeneity more powerful than the synthesis of metaphor.

De Man did not succumb to the seduction of negativity and was able to see through its apparent status as the substratum of the subjectivity of the subject of language. In this negativity he recognized instead one of the generative functions of texts destined to disavow their own contingency. He writes: "Contrary to received opinion, deconstructive discourses are suspiciously text-productive" (AR, 200). To be sure, this productivity of negative pathos is not that of organic extension and fulfillment, but rather of the mechanical repetition of one and the same, as it were, grammatical pattern. If literary texts unfold themselves both the-matically and in their rhetorical structure as forms of disillusionment and unveil-ing, of critique and self-critique, it is because they can promise themselves and their readers a greater certainty in these forms than in affirmative statements and reassurances: they offer the certainty of the unreliability of the world and of all assertions that can be made about it. In this negative certainty, critical literary scholarship, too, communicates with its objects. The pathos of destruction is just as suspiciously productive for scholarly as for literary texts; one can read the trace of this pathos especially clearly in the Anglo-Saxon concept of literary criti-cism and even more in its praxis. As de Man states, scholarly texts, too, are characterized by that "negative assurance that is highly productive of critical dis-course" (AR, 16). Any kind of literary studies that assigns itself to this sort of *docta ignorantia* and erects upon it the system of a negative epistemology, a nega-tive hermeneutics, or a negative dialectic of literary works and their communica-tion, no matter how sober, pragmatic, and free of illusions it pretends to be, will cultivate a theology of pathos, a pathology that, uncritical toward its own concept of critique, itself merely repeats the movement of subjectivity and its intentionality rather than analyzing it and reading it analyzed by their texts. If the pathos of defiguration were actually the determining trait in the structure of literary texts, then paradoxically, the reading that would correspond to its metonymic movement would be its metaphor. The text and its science would converge in a figure — the figure of defiguration — whose universality would delete its figurative character and, in pure mediation, sublate both the text and its science: both "a text of desire as well as a desire for text" (AR, 289).

But the will to the text, the text that wills itself — another version of the will to power — when it articulates itself in the text, is no longer sheer referentiality, no longer the mere figurativity that it thematizes itself as ("L'amour n'est qu'illusion"), but a figure that must be submitted to the decision about its referential status in order to be understood. For the assertion that love is merely an illusion able exclusively to speak in figures because its objects possess reality only as generated by itself — this assertion, however radical the theory it enunciates about literature as the language of love may be, is above all a statement in a literary text, a sentence that can just as well be a strategic fiction in the service of the argumentative consistency of this text as a serious statement of the author intended to designate the real character of love. While there is no definite criterion for the decision about these alternatives, no more can we name any ultimate ground for determining the intentions of the author, who may have meant these statements seriously, but might just as well have limited this seriousness to the field of a particular text or to particular cases of its application. There is no word, no sign — from whatever conventions of language or action it may originate — that does not forfeit its semantic orientation in the instant it is posited and exposed to the possibility of being understood. But it is not thereby disburdened of its semantic gravitation, as de Man has most strongly underscored. For although the referential content of an utterance is unreliable and cannot be assured by any dialectically impassioned device, the contention that the utterance was liberated from all referential possibilities, a free play of signifiers, would itself necessarily be referential. No text has the power to exclude the possibility that it says the truth, or at least something true; but no text can guarantee this truth because every attempt to establish its certainty must proliferate the indeterminacy of its meaning. Since understanding — at least the kind that science depends on — is impossible without the strict determination of the semantic status of statements, no text can be understood *strictu sensu*. But the great texts of literature know this and do not cease to deal with it in one way or another. The defiguration of figures, trying to constitute itself as the *ultima ratio* of literary discourse — the infinite suspension of reference toward pure referentiality, the sublation of subjective intention in the general structure of intentionality, negative totalization — because it is primarily nothing but an element or a structure of a literary operation, is exposed to a semantic indeterminacy that no longer obeys any *ratio*, neither of rhetoric nor of hermeneutics. The structure of pure subjectivity is shattered, the transcendental function of the negative figure founders, the text as the will to itself and to its unrestricted communication is splintered. Pathos—including the pathos of an imperative of which the mere perception would already be its pure fulfillment, which would pronounce itself without a shadow of doubt as the imperative *itself* and the imperative of the self—this pathos can never evade the possibility of being read as a *pathos affecté* (Rousseau, Pléiade II: 18), as a pathos that, however seriously it is meant and however painfully it is experienced in its effects, can never contain the guarantee that it is anything more than a linguistic fixture. So this imperative of negativity, too, cannot be read. No more than the figures of totalization does the command of their subversion, which calls for an even more powerful, negative totalization beyond figures and language, offer any prospect of coming to a halt for understanding.

The literary texts devoted to this tension are not exhausted in figurative—and in the last analysis, this means metaphorical—discourse and its destruction, but rather, by reiterating its aporia, at the same time they expose another way of reading them: they are allegories.[2] In "Allegory (*Julie*)," de Man writes:

> The paradigm of all texts consists of a figure (or a system of figures) and its deconstruction. But since this model cannot be closed off by a final reading, it engenders, in its turn, a supplementary figural superposition which narrates the unreadability of the prior narration. As distinguished from primary deconstructive narratives centered on figures and ultimately always on metaphor, we can call such narratives to the second (or third) degree *allegories*. Allegorical narratives tell the story of the failure to read. . . . [They undo] both the intelligibility and the seductiveness that the fiction owed to its negative rigor. (AR, 205)

With the "supplementary figural superposition" that allegory presents, the literary text does not attain a genuinely new dimension, structurally superior to the prior ones, but rather expounds and repeats the aporias of the previous levels: "the allegory does not erase the figure. Allegories are always allegories of metaphor and, as such, they are always allegories of the impossibility of reading—a sentence in which the genitive 'of' has itself to be 'read' as a metaphor" (AR, 205). We can read this genitive to mean: allegories are always allegories of the metaphor "metaphor" and thus allegories of the translation of that which precisely must resist all attempts at translation because there is no certain criterion for its translation into a proper or a literal meaning. Allegories are always allegories of the untranslatability, the unreliability, and the unreadability of that which, as a translation, asserts its pure readability, and thus they iterate the very hermeneutic error they discredit.

But this iteration—and this is the decisive difference between allegory and the mere mechanical execution of the metonymic model—can only succeed because an alteration, both thematic and tonal, migrates into the texts. For the work of negation, carried out on the figures by pathos and on pathos by its figures, is always already subject to a linguistic imperative demanding the proof of its own truth value in the sphere of practical action. *Although* the decision about this truth value must remain suspended, it is "the way abroad"—for both Rousseau and Proust—which makes this epistemological imperative also a practical one. But *because* the epistemological decision must remain suspended, the practical intention is loosened from the intention toward truth and establishes its independence in allegory: it becomes ethical discourse. Allegorical texts are imperative.

In one of the central passages of *Allegories of Reading* in "Allegory (*Julie*)," de Man writes:

> The concatenation of the categories of truth and falsehood with the values of right and wrong is disrupted. . . . We call this shift in economy *ethical*, since it indeed involves a displacement from *pathos* to *ethos*. Allegories are always ethical, the term ethical designating the structural interference of two distinct value systems. . . . The ethical category is imperative (i.e., a category rather than a value) to the extent that it is linguistic and not subjective. . . . The passage to an ethical tonality does not result from a transcendental imperative but is the referential (and therefore unreliable) version of a linguistic confusion. Ethics (or, one should say, ethicity) is a discursive mode among others. (AR, 206)

Allegories do not merely thematize the inability of language to verify its assertions by its own means; rather, with the characteristic gesture of the "nevertheless," they suspend all epistemological uncertainties and become demands: demands which themselves do not yet correspond to any existing reality, but the fulfillment of which is supposed to confirm their truth value and legitimate them. Allegories are not epistemological figures, for they yield no knowledge and in fact originate in an epistemological obstacle inherent to the structure of language; but they are figures organized with a view toward possible knowledge and possible verification. Nor are allegories moral figures, for they do not necessarily preach determinate conventions of behavior and values as if they were already thematically performed within them; but they are figures constructed within the perspective of the formal possibility of a universality of action. And above all, what first determines the gesture of allegory is this: they *must* be constructed, they are not random depositions of an empirical or a fictional subject, but rather *necessary* expositions of a determining trait of language itself. This trait is the referential function. No statement can exclude the possibility that with it, something is meant. Where the unensurability of the semantic content of language itself becomes the theme of statements, as occurs in allegorical texts, its referential function is not extinguished but rather is related to the possibility that what is said is not said, that it is not yet or not sufficiently said. In this relation to its possible not-being, the referential function of language, emptied of all thematic content, steps forth as a barren formal constraint. This referential constraint without a referent, proper to all language, is isolated in the imperative of allegory. It is not because allegory makes demands that it is an ethical figure, but rather the reverse: the language of allegory is a language of ethical requirements because it itself is requisite and indispensable; it is a language of constraint because it is itself necessary; a language of coercion, because it itself is governed by the structural coercion of language. "The ethical category," de Man writes, "is imperative . . . to the extent that it is linguistic." The ethical character of language, its allegorical quality, is not due to a speaking subject prior to language, nor to historically determined conventions of speaking; its ethical character is not something that could just as well not be at all, that could be restricted to a merely conditional, empirical validity. This ethical character is unconditional—and this is why de Man rightly calls it categorical—and is a character of language itself, that is, a necessary trait that first makes language language at all. Language is imperative. It is imperative because its referential function gives the directions for possible reference, even if no referential meaning answers to it and even though it corresponds to no referent. And only because language itself is imperative, there can and indeed must be imperatives in language, in its figurative structures and its thematic content. And only because language itself is imperative can and must there be the categorical imperative. The law of action formulated in the imperative is itself subject to the law of language.

To *one* of the laws of language. Language is imperative, and only under its coercion can there be categorically imperative utterances. Nevertheless, language is not a thoroughly ethical entity able to fulfill its own demands—including the unconditional demand of making demands. Thus we can understand de Man's assertion, lapidary but uncommonly rich in its consequences: "The passage to an ethical tonality does not result from a transcendental imperative but is the referential (and therefore unreliable) version of a linguistic confusion" (AR, 206). Transcendental, resulting not from a transcendent power but from a structural constraint within language upon which every will, every subject, and every merely transcendent instance depends, the imperative of the language of allegory is surely transcendental in this Kantian sense. For this reason, the validity of de Man's concluding consideration remains, for the moment, problematic: "Ethics (or, one should say, ethicity) is a discursive mode *among others*" (AR, 206; my emphasis). The ethical character of language—and *a fortiori* of the language of literature—is not an arbitrary mode of language, its function interchangeable with others; for it is indissolubly bound to that function of language that alone comprises the directions for meaning and thus makes language into language at all: the referential function. We find another sentence in *Allegories of Reading* about this function a page after the one just quoted in which at least one expression contains a remarkably parallel formulation, but also one with an opposed sense. The sentence refers to Rousseau, but its similarity to a whole series of statements in de Man's texts suggests that it simultaneously expresses an insight of de Man:

> His radical critique of referential meaning never implied that the referential function of language could in any way be avoided, bracketed, or reduced to being just one contingent linguistic property *among others*, as is postulated, for example, in contemporary semiology which, like all post-Kantian formalisms, could not exist without this postulate. (AR, 207; my emphasis)

But if the referential function of language does not number among its contingent properties but is rather a constitutive structural element of all language, that is, if it is not simply a function "among others," then its ethical function, characterized by de Man as a "referential version of a linguistic confusion," cannot issue in a "discursive mode among others" (AR, 206). Ethical propositions and, even more, imperatives are not incidental contents of language that are "also" possible within it "among others"; rather, they appertain indissolubly to the occurrence of language itself. But the law of language out of which ethical imperatives arise, its referential function that cannot be erased, is not the only law; its validity is continuously contested by the other law: that of language's figurality. As little as the referential meaning of statements can be secured, no more can the directions for reference contained in the referential function ever be converted into an imperative that would correspond to these instructions without residue. There can be an imperative only because the referential function finds no correspondence in that imperative; but because the referential and, moreover, the ethical function of language is thwarted by its figurative function, not exhausted in its referential and moreover in its ethical function, it can never be determined with certainty that this imperative (and even the categorical imperative) is unconditional, and consequently whether it is imperative at all. Therefore every imperative must remain exposed to the question of whether it is not merely in the service of contingent authorities and ephemeral experiences. For this reason, the problem of the imperative, which de Man places in the center of one of the central concepts of his work, in the center of allegory, must remain exposed to the suspicion that the demand enunciated within it is merely onomastic, that all fundamental obligation and commitment are the bare effects of his name. And in fact, one of the statements in "Promises (*Social Contract*)" devoted to the problem of property and its relation to the name reads: "There can be no more seductive form of onomastic identification . . . it satisfies semiological fantasies about the adequation of sign and meaning" (AR, 262). And in the passage about the imperative character of allegorical language de Man writes: "Morality is a version of the same language aporia that gives rise to such concepts as *man*" (AR, 206; my emphasis). Insofar as the figurative function of language excludes all certainty about whether an imperative is an imperative, de Man validly asserts that "ethics (or, one should say, ethicity) is a discursive mode among others" (AR, 206). The reliability of the one linguistic law is rescinded by the other, though the latter is itself no more reliable than the first.

Since allegory is always an allegory of unreliability, even of the unreliability of its own epistemological and ethical meaning, it cannot be forced into a closed system of judgments; and since the effectivity of its function is not interrupted, allegory speaks and works effectively as praxis (AR, 208–9). The language of allegory relates itself to language not reflexively but rather as an epistemologically uncertain praxis: language relates to itself in the mode of possible unrelatedness. If allegory thematizes the unreadability of texts, it can do so only because, in an epistemological paradox, it becomes the praxis of reading, of an other reading, of allegorical reading. It can make clear their intransparency only to the degree that it increases their readability. Allegories as de Man describes them are the texts of literary criticism that literature itself contains. If there is to be a science of literature in a genuine sense, it can have no other *fundamentum in re*, no other objective basis in literary texts than the ground of allegorical praxis, in which they explicate the unensurability of their own operations. Literary scholarship cannot hope mimetically to assimilate its statements to those in the text and become their metaphor any more than it can make itself into the unleashed metonymy of these texts. In correspondence to the referential moment at work in both of these modes of relating to the text, literary scholarship must comply with the imperative of referentiality that commands it to relate every textual element and every text in its entirety to a possible meaning. At the same time, literary criticism has to consider this imperative of referentiality, which alone contains the promise of a common ground between scholarship and its texts, under the reservation of its possible figurality that robs it of every prospect of attaining certain knowledge and becoming a science. For the sake of its scientificity, literary science must give up its claim to scientificity. It must understand itself as the agent of the logical aporia according to which the figurative function of language—of the language of science, too—thwarts its referential function in every one of its movements. The science of literature, if it remains true to its own claim and follows the aporetic logic of literary language—and of language in general—can be nothing but the allegory of the impossibility of its own project. As science, it obeys the imperative to assign meaning—knowingly or unknowingly, willingly or unwillingly; but this imperative, which it *must* obey, never offers itself in any other form than allegory. This imperative is the allegory of an imperative that can never proffer itself as such, never in its purity and as the certain basis of scientific operations. Only in this way, as allegorical, unfulfilled in its offering, is it an imperative demand. That which obeys this order, whether in literary or in scholarly language, always says not only something other than what it means, but in fact something other than what it *can* say. It speaks beyond the limit of its own possibility.

Language speaks only in exposing itself to the possibility of its own impossibility. Language itself has no ground and the ground that it is able to offer, by positing imperatives, for example, bears the mark of possible contingency, possible groundlessness, possible impossibility.

It is not certain that there can be a science of literature because it cannot be certain that it can comply with the imperative of language, nor that this imperative is an imperative at all, and because it cannot even be certain that language makes ascertainable meanings possible: that language makes language possible at all.

A number of consequences result from the allegorical constitution of the imperative to which literary scholarship is subject. Four of them shall be briefly sketched here.

Because the imperative of the assignment of meaning arises from a law of language—namely, its referential function—but yet is thwarted and suspended in each of its moments by another law of language, the law of its figurality, there is no reliable criterion for the distinction between referentiality and figurality. The imperative, however much it may be set up to establish the legitimacy of certain interpretations and the illegitimacy of others, is itself illegitimate insofar as it cannot correspond to its own foundation, the referential function of language. Contrary to all intention, especially the intentions connected with a curtailed concept of science, the imperative is also always the imperative of figurality and therefore always in the service of two antagonistic principles. In opposition to its totalizing tendencies, it is therefore also always the imperative of disintegration, of defection from that principle, an imperative of hermeneutic apostasy. Since the figurality of language holds the latitudes of its meaning open to the power of sheer contingency, every hermeneutic imperative[3] subject to its law must necessarily be contingent, an accidental imperative. Not only the connection established between the literal and the figurative sense of an utterance, or the one between a text and each of its readings, but also the internal structure of every reading falls under the law of contingency that never allows its elements to converge in a systematic unity. No history of interpretation, of hermeneutic principles or exegetical "methods" can constitute a reliable basis of unity or a teleological orientation in the interpretations of literature that would be able to emancipate them from their erratic character. Every history of literature that nevertheless attempts to do so acts as the agent of law and order. But if it is to be scientific, its task is precisely to articulate this erratic character, which is just as much its own character as that of literature. The imperative is an imp of the erratic. The entanglement of its imperative in the figures of contingency has above all the consequence that as an imperative it puts forth a command that, as a mere figure, it revokes. There is no possibility of distinguishing between this demand and this countermand, no possibility of deciding between them. De Man has pronounced the consequence with an emphasis free of illusions: "the intolerable semantic irresolution" that properly inheres in allegory and its imperative is "worse than madness" (AR,

202). Like the categorical imperative, the imperative of literary scholarship—and we are reminded once more that without this imperative, it has no possibility of becoming a science of literature—is, monstrously enough, a demented demand. It is an excessive demand because it is perhaps no demand at all. We must speak under the rule of this imperative, and every gesture that literary scholarship can make is subject to it.

A second consequence of the aporetic structure of the imperative concerns what we may provisionally term the communicative structure of reading. If the referential movement of language is thwarted in each of its moments by its contingency, the imperative can only be universal insofar as it is the imperative of the universality of its singularization. This not only means that this imperative has a unique tone in any particular case and can make valid demands only for this case at best; foremost, it means that the imperative, torn within and from itself, is an imperative of difference and departure from itself. Despite its intention toward unity and universality, in accordance with its own structure it can command only an infinite diversification. It is one of the trivia of literary criticism that every text is open to an illimitable abundance of interpretations, applications, and reactions; but most crucially, this manifold of interpretive possibilities does not indicate a lamentable insufficiency of the interpreters that could be healed in a messianic moment; rather, it is a structural effect of the constitution of language itself that every project of literary scholarship must take into account. The structure of language does not simply make different interpretations of texts possible, but it does so with necessity. Polysemy is a necessary possibility of linguistic utterances. Now this possibility is necessary because the figurative connotations of utterances are not reducible to a single meaning, and moreover because—perhaps—they have no such meaning. Only the guaranteed unity (even of a manifold) of meaning could ground the universality of the imperative of understanding. As a result of the circumstance that no such unity is given, or if it is, it cannot be perceived, the imperative of interpretation is the imperative of the unlimited alteration of meaning with neither beginning nor end. Furthermore, a text can impart itself only by virtue of its internal partition and as partitioned. In the *com-* of any communication this partaking partition must already be at work, and only in the partitioning of communication can the meaning and the interpretation of a text communicate.[4] They communicate, then, not at the locus of their convergence, but rather at the place of their contingency, which can be localized within no order and which can never be ascertained or secured. Self and other are first constituted in their partition of communicative language, both par-taking and taking apart, which robs them of their independent standing and their internal coherence. Reading, therefore, is never an intersubjective process in which two or more already constituted subjects could come to an understanding on the common ground of language. Much more, it is the uncontrollable process of the partition of communication that pervades every language along with everyone who uses it. Reader and text meet in the pause of meaning: where every possible communication is interrupted. When de Man speaks of the text as an allegory of unreadability, perhaps it should be read thus: it is first and foremost this unreadability, namely, the impossibility of verifying and universalizing the text's meaning, that compels that it be read in always differing ways, and that it be read at all. The imperative governing literary scholarship is not the imperative of communication, but rather of par-taking. The imperative is impartive. Only under its command can scholarship take part in literature, and avoid succumbing to the illusion that it could ever grasp literature as a whole, or as what it is.

A third consequence of the imperative character of allegory concerns its position vis-à-vis what de Man calls aesthetic ideology. Because allegory thematizes the unreliability of its own statements and the impossibility of the distinct thematization of its own structure, an ideological moment will always inhere in it. In "Allegory (*Julie*)," de Man writes: "The question is not the intrinsic merit or absurdity of these pieces of good advice but rather the fact that they *have to* be uttered" (AR, 207). Independently of the intentions of its author, allegory *has to* repeat its claim to refer to an extralinguistic world, although it itself rejects this claim as untenable. But the compelling repetition of allegory is a constraint of language. In the same context, de Man writes: "The reintroduction of the intentional language . . . into the allegory is not itself intentional but the result of a linguistic structure. The entire assumption of a nonverbal realm . . . may well be a speculative hypothesis that exists only, to put it in all too intentional terms, *for the sake of* language" (AR, 210). De Man answers the question of why the language of intentionality must be repeated in allegory, itself essentially a critique of intentionality, thus: it is in this repetition that language seeks to preserve itself as language. Moreover, it is the referential function of language that strives to maintain itself in the hypostasis of the intention and its corresponding referent. Every literary science that confounds a linguistic possibility with its unrestricted realization corroborates this hypostasis, that is, the illegitimate inference from a function to its successful functioning. Literary scholarship thus serves as the agent of an ideological moment within the structure of language itself. In "The Resistance to Theory," de Man writes: "What we call ideology is precisely the confusion of linguistic with natural reality, of reference with phenomenalism" (RT, 11). Instead of succumbing to this ideology, literary criticism must learn from the allegorical structure of literature that the referential function of language provides no guarantee that "language functions according to principles which are those, or which are *like* those, of the phenomenal world" (ibid.). Literary criticism has to learn from allegory that neither it itself nor literature operates in accordance with the laws of the world of appearance, for example, the laws of cause and effect (thus the legitimacy of any kind of sociology of literature or aesthetics of effects is questionable). It has to learn from allegory that literary texts, conceived under the pressure of a long philosophical tradition as aesthetic, that is, as the phenomenalization of a substantial reality, cannot be grasped under the category of the aesthetic. But literary scholarship also has to learn—and what is of concern here is not to be, *sondern / Zu lernen*—that as long as it proceeds in accordance with the prescription of allegory, a residue of the phenomenalistic misunderstanding of literature will live on in it as well. It has to consider the liberation of its imperative from its phenomenological implications: for example, no longer to consider it teleologically as a commandment that could be fulfilled successively in the extension of natural time, even if only approximately; no longer to see it as a demand that makes itself generally and clearly perceptible and comprehensible, as if with a truly penetrating perlocutionary force; it has to cease to consider the imperative as the cause of an effect that can persist in the normative apparatus of a science of literature as long as the cause is sufficient. The imperative of literary scholarship can no more be the object of knowledge than the movement of literature it orders to read, for all knowledge depends on the unrestricted functioning of linguistic phenomenalization. But it is still imperative—not because it could be secured, understood, and presented as universally operative, but because the imperative is the mode in which language relates itself to the possibility of its eclipse. Since this possibility can never come up in language except as a possible reality, there are no means for staving off the delusive effects of the imperative. Even the language of denomination, still in use when we say "demand," "law," "imperative," ideologically suggests the existence of an essence that is disavowed by this very demand, this law and this imperative. Reading is never in the stance of truth, not even when it is certain of its own imposture. However great the dephenomenalizing force of an analytic reading may be, it is never sufficient to prevent itself from making ideological suggestions. But reading does have the power to analyze the constraints of language even as it submits to them, and to distance itself from them through its analysis. Only in this permanent distantiation can reading become experience of language.

The fourth and most important consideration, no longer really a consequence, concerning the imperative gesture of allegory has to do with its performative character. The imperative comes to light in the failure of reference. It is the imperative of interpretation because meaning can no longer prevail as given, but only as given up, as given as a task. Referentiality persists in the imperative, but no longer as a natural or technically installed relation of language to a phenomenal object, rather as the mere possibility of such a relation: but a possibility—and this is decisive—that is first *posited* in the imperative. But the act of positing, or, since it cannot be the positing act of the transcendental "I" as Idealism since Fichte has conceived it, more precisely: the linguistic event carried out in the imperative can be neither the expression of an already constituted subject nor the instrument of its self-constitution, and thus has no internal relation to its referential use. On the level of pure performance, language is prepredicative, with no subject or determination, language without language, the bare possibility of its determination as language, yet not already teleologically designed toward this determination. Connecting the indeterminate performative force of language with the possibility of a direction, an intention, and a telos, the imperative, itself still this side of a constituted language, projects the possibility of its constitution. Every question about the ground of this determination, a question about a *causa finalis*, already moves in the space first opened up by the imperative. The power of the performative function of language operates in a dimension different from the cognitive function of reference; but just as there can be no reference without this performative function, no more can the performative manifest itself without its diminution, distortion, and denial in the language of cognition. The imperative of interpretation is the place of arbitration of the tensions between these interdependent but incompatible linguistic functions: the function of unverifiable, nonreferential positing, and the referentiality that knows no more secure ground than that positing it disputes.

Every allegory—and in de Man's presentation, all are allegories of the indeterminability of language—makes manifest the negative insight that there is no constituted language. De Man writes: "The assumption of readability, which is itself constitutive of language"—leaving open an admirable ambiguity whether the assumption of readability or simply readability is constitutive of language—"cannot only no longer be taken for granted but is found to be aberrant" (AR, 202). If the assumption of readability and with it of an already constituted language is aberrant, then there is not yet language and there can never be language in any other mode than its aberrant assumption. The imperative of interpretation and of meaningfulness is above all the unreliable and epistemologically unfounded imperative that there shall be a language. It commands not only "read" or "write" or "understand" or "speak," but first of all, in all these demands: "There shall be (one) language." This Babylonian imperative, the only one that does not proceed from a previously given language or other already constituted essences, is the only one with which literary criticism, or more precisely, analytic reading, can project a common foundation to share with literature and with language at large. To be sure, as a science it can never grasp this ground nor, as knowledge, contain it; for no knowledge is possible without a closed and completed language, whereas this imperative first demands the constitution of a language. In always divers ways, de Man has indicated the efficacy of this imperative and its consequences for interpretation. In "Reading Proust," he writes: "no one can decide whether Proust invented metaphors because he felt guilty or whether he had to declare himself guilty in order to find a use for his metaphor. Since the only irreducible 'intention' "—note here the quotation marks around "intention"—"of a text is that of its constitution" (AR, 65). Despite all the reservations about the decidability of this problem, we read here that a text is not to be understood as an available linguistic tool destined to help this or that feeling—guilt, for example—come to expression. Rather, the text can be understood *as text* only as the direction toward its own constitution, drawing everything that touches it—experiences, emotions, cognitions—into the movement of its attempt at self-constitution. A text must be read as the project of its own constitution.

Language has to be understood not as a given structure or as a process under way, but as the imperative that there shall be a language. We are not using language, we are demanding it—and with it ourselves. The apparent fact, that we speak—but *do* we? and is it *we* who speak?—does not contradict this affirmation, for there is no way of ascertaining that we as autonomous subjects use language instead of being used by a linguistic function that would coerce us into its realization.[5] Referentiality is a function rather than a contingent possibility, which would allow us to leave it aside, for the very possibility of language depends on the imperative demand to engage in its referential project. However, as neither referentiality implies an ascertainable reference, nor figurality implies the reality of a figure, *linguisticity* does not imply an already constituted language or even the unrestricted possibility of its constitution. Language is not just possible, but it *has to* be. This imperative structure of linguisticity would be the principle and the very project of language itself, it would be its very possibility in the sense of a substantial form. It would be—if this demanding referential function would not be disrupted from the start by the figural, which does not allow for a strict determination of a referent: of language. The collusion rather than the collision of these two functions subverts the very possibility of language, of its substance, and of its project. Its imperative is unreadable. Language *has to* be, but it is not possible. Speaking of language—and we can never avoid speaking (of it)—we always are speaking off language.

A passage in "Excuses (*Confessions*)" again takes up the line of thought from the Proust essay:

> It is no longer certain that language, as excuse, exists because of a prior guilt but just as possible that since language, as a machine, performs anyway, *we have to* produce guilt (and all its train of psychic consequences) in order to make the excuse meaningful. Excuses generate the very guilt they exonerate though always in excess or default. (AR, 299; my emphasis)[6]

We have to: it is a law of language and therefore a law for all who are exposed to the capacity of language, to generate the possibility of its meaning; for otherwise there would be no language at all, but only a nonhomogeneous chaos of positing acts. But the meanings that must be assigned to the blind arbitrariness of these positings, no matter how consistent they may be, are erroneous, for they cannot have been "meant" by that arbitrariness. De Man, with a decidedness that could not correspond more exactly to its subject, writes in one of his most outstanding texts, "Shelley Disfigured": "language posits and language means (since it articulates) but language cannot posit meaning; it can only reiterate (or reflect) it in its reconfirmed falsehood" (RR, 118–19). But if the first meaning we can connect with the arbitrary acts of an absolutely positing language is the constitution of meaningful language itself, then not only any single meaning but the entire system of meaningful language is deceptive. For it is grounded on nothing but an incident, on what simply happens to come to mind, the breaking in of a random event that follows no intention, not even that of its own preservation. And if in the first instance the imperative—that is, any imperative—is the imperative of the constitution of a language, but for its part can take place only in the train of a linguistic function, which permits the generation of meaning, but does not itself mean and thus indicates the region of muteness within language; then it can never be the imperative, that is, the possible ground of the constitution of language, except insofar as it befalls from this muteness. It is constitutive for the imperative— of language, of meaning—that it is thwarted by the inconstituting trait of the incapacity for meaning.

The foundation of language projected by the imperative is permanently undermined by the performative force at work in the imperative itself. For this reason, intention toward language, which the imperative links with the uncodifiable act of positing is interrupted and ex-posed in each of its utterances, able only to reiterate its own alteration in each. There is no imperative—of interpretation, of language—that is not suspended by its intentionless power. It is posited as an imperative only where the operation of its meaning is ex-posed. Where meaning fails, a *must* enters into the field. Where there is no "is," it has to . . . For the relationship of understanding to language, especially to the language of literature, this means that the referential indeterminability of its statements is not an obstacle to knowledge. Rather, it is precisely at that point in the work of interpretation at which a logical aporia, a gap in language's capacity of determination, opens up that something of what is true of language communicates itself to interpretation. Independently of subjective motives and conventional rules, language's force of positing makes its first appearance in the miscarriage of the cognitive intention toward language—and with necessity, imperatively. And along with this force, piercing through all ideological distortions, a necessary, imperative understanding. In the foreword to Carol Jacobs's book *The Dissimulating Harmony*, after showing that all ethical and aesthetic premises of understanding must be epistemologically legitimated, while critical reflected understanding is "productive of its own ethical imperative," de Man writes:

> What makes a reading more or less true is simply the . . . necessity
> of its occurrence, regardless of the reader or of the author's wishes. "Es
> ereignet sich aber Das Wahre" (not *die Wahrheit*) says Hölderlin, which
> can be freely translated, "What is true is what is *bound to* take place."
> And, in the case of the reading of a text, what takes place is a *necessary* understanding. What marks the truth of such an understanding is
> not some abstract universal but the fact that it *has to* occur regardless

of other considerations. . . . Reading is an argument . . . because it *has to* go against the grain of what one would want to happen in the name of what *has to* happen. (xi; my emphasis)

The "freedom" of de Man's translation lies in his decision to translate the impact of Hölderlin's gnome into an imperative, into *is bound to, has to*, that is, into the formula of an internal necessity of language. This necessity is in fact problematic because it precedes all verification and is itself unverifiable. The imperative of interpretation has a *problematic* necessity, in the etymological sense of the word, insofar as what it imposes does not necessarily imply the possibility of its realization. The necessity of the imperative—of interpretation, of language—is the necessity of a demand for language, for interpretation, whose reality has no other guarantee than the incomplete facticity of this demand itself. The imperative commands, before all "real" language, that there shall be a language—a meaning and an interpretation. It does not speak properly. It is, in every sense, in advance of language. It is—and its being is—a *problem*.

The proleptic trait of the imperative makes it a law: a law of language, no longer simply the law of its referentiality or of its figurality, but rather the law of a specific performative mode. In "Promises (*Social Contract*)," de Man writes: "All laws are future-oriented and prospective; their illocutionary mode is that of the *promise*" (AR, 273).[7] Language itself is promised in this law of language. In the imperative, language is forespoken before it, as constituted, is able to speak. De Man did not always accurately assess this forestructure of language, which was perhaps first worked out in the romantic theory of irony. In his 1969 essay "The Rhetoric of Temporality," he writes of Starobinski's and Szondi's presentation of irony: "In temporal terms it makes irony into the prefiguration of a future recovery, fiction into the promise of a future happiness that, for the time being, exists only ideally" (BI, 219). While de Man aptly criticizes the assumption that romantic irony is a disguised form of messianism, yet the global nature of his critique does not do justice to Szondi's characterization of the temporal mode of irony, though it, too, partly misses its mark. In "Friedrich Schlegel und die romantische Ironie," Szondi writes: "durch Vorwegnahme der künftigen Einheit, an die er [the man divided within himself] glaubt, wird das Negative für vorläufig erklärt, damit zugleich festgehalten und umgewertet."[8] De Man translates: "the negative is described as temporary (*vorläufig*)," and gives the following commentary: "Contrary to Szondi's assertion, irony is not temporary (*vorläufig*) but repetitive, the recurrence of a self-escalating act of consciousness" (BI, 219–20). "Temporary" is certainly one of the possible correct translations of *vorläufig*, and corresponds exactly to the meaning the word takes on in the context of the sentence cited. But Szondi takes up this word again on the same page of his text in the appendix "Ueber Tiecks Komödien," furnishing it with another meaning that, although it gains no entry into de Man's translation and commentary, all the more legitimates the precaution with which he lets this word, decisive for him, persist in the original German even after he has translated it. Szondi writes:

> Die romantische Ironie fasst die Realität als ein Vorläufiges auf und bringt ihrerseits nur Vorläufiges hervor. In der dramatischen Formenwelt ist es der Prolog, dessen Sinn die Vorläufigkeit ist. . . . Zu zeigen ist das Leben in seiner Vorläufigkeit, gezeigt wird der Prolog in seiner Endgültigkeit. Die Frage, ob der Realität ihr Sinn immanent, ob sie schon ernst ist oder aber erst Vor-Spiel, ein Vorläufiges, das spielend auszuhalten sei, wird nicht in einer konkreten Situation besprochen, sondern der Ausgangspunkt ist bereits ein Prolog.

[Romantic irony conceives reality as something temporary and provisional (*Vorläufiges*) and for its part, brings forth only the provisional (*Vorläufiges*). In the dramatic world of forms, it is the prologue whose meaning is this provisionalness (*Vorläufigkeit*) . . . Life is to be shown in its temporary provisionalness, the prologue is shown in its finality. The question of whether its meaning is immanent in reality, if it is already serious or only fore-play (*Vor-Spiel*), something temporary that is to be endured playfully, is not discussed in a concrete situation; rather, the point of departure is already a prologue."—Trans.]

But if the fore-play (*Vor-Spiel*), which the prologue enacts as the dramatic form of the temporary and the provisional (*Vorläufigkeit*), is final, then the "future unity" of reality and fiction, of the subject and object of reflection, is possible exclusively in a mode of "anticipation" (*Vorwegnahme*) that is essentially ironic. The "fore-" has taken leave of all after, provisional temporariness is absolute, and the future of happiness is given nowhere but in the promise of it.

By uncovering the prestructure of language de Man in *Allegories of Reading* at the same time discovers the complicated rift between two functional traits of language: the sheer nonreferential speaking of language that in its positional violence rips apart the web of its meanings and even breaks open the system of that negative semantics that is crystallized in allegory; but these meanings, however negative they may be colored, are themselves there thanks to that nonintentional act that disrupts them. If meanings could be posited and positing acts as such could be meaningful, there would be a transparent, communicative, and universal language, thus there would no longer be *language*: not one in which figures would still be possible and not one in which meaning could be distinguished from what is said. Indeed, therefore, a momentary positing act is to be thanked for meaning—but such an act is to be thought without an intentional relation to this meaning. A meaning can only be tied to a positing subsequently, *post positionem*, and so it can never be epistemologically legitimated before the authority of the sheer speech act. The connection of a meaning to an act has no ground in this act itself. The synthesis between positing and meaning has the character of an arbitrary positing—an *imposition*, as de Man says, taking the word from Shelley—and this synthesis must therefore be compelled to renounce its own claim to epistemic certainty according to the measure of *homoiosis*.

All imperatives are at once positings and demands. As demands, they are oriented toward the future, intentional actions that include the means to measure their fulfillments and in this way present themselves as paradigms of a temporal sequence, be it finite or infinite. As positings, imperatives are linguistic events that are without intention; one can enter them neither into a temporal nor into a historical sequence, because they appear on this side of the polarity between chance and determination and consequently exclude every presumption to measure. As positings, imperatives therefore bring to naught the claim to correspondence that, as demands, they put forward. But since the claim cannot waive the positing moment, every imperative and furthermore everything that may stand under it and follow from it must carry with it the index of its impossibility.

It is this impossibility that in "Promises (*Social Contract*)" de Man elaborates in the figure of the law and its positing, thus in the imperative and the illocutionary mode of promise that is implicit in it. The imperative of language—of reading—considered as an act directed toward the future, contains the promise of a future language, a future understanding in such a way that the formal conditions of all individual acts of understanding are outlined in this project. It announces for the future what cannot be performed in the present. Now, however, a not inconsequential complication emerges because of the transcendental status of such a project: the performative act of promising a possible understanding must be structured as an epistemologically illegitimate rhetorical figure, as metalepsis, in order to be carried out. For what is announced by the promise only for the future—a possible understanding—is asserted to be already effective in the present. The rhetorical figure of confounding a future with a present, which is at work in every dialectic of presupposition and, in another way, also in the hermeneutic circle, is unavoidably a figure of deceit, insofar as that which it implicitly states to be present can be opened up only by the illocutionary act as futurial. So the constative moment of opening up a possible understanding is not only in constant conflict with its performative function—and thus makes the establishment of the law itself into an illegitimate act—but this unavoidable and irreconcilable conflict within the original constitution of understanding becomes valid throughout as an endless suspension of this constitution itself. The interlacing of constative with performative brackets both: the presupposition of a possible understanding could be formulated only under the condition that it is given, its being given only under the condition of this presupposition. Since neither of these conditions can be without the other and hence since neither of them can already be fulfilled when the presupposition is asserted, every project of a possible understanding remains a fiction that can be neither probed nor verified. The project remains, suspended, in the projection—and the fundamental operation of hermeneutics will never have offered a secure ground for individual acts of understanding, since it does not reach that ground that could only be given in the unity and verifiability of its performance. The promise as primordial project of understanding can always only promise its own possibility, but never carry itself out as a genuine promise. The performative act of the imperative — of language — and with it the corresponding constative forms of reading remain suspended.

The promise promises itself — that always means: the promise, in a not yet constituted language, does not yet promise anything other than its own future: the promise does not promise. Language for de Man is just such a promise. Heidegger's apothegm *Die Sprache spricht*, "language speaks," still courts the misunderstanding that there is already a constituted language and it could correspond to its own Being. In a highly ironic, yet necessary, combination of Heidegger's gnome and Freud's vocabulary, de Man writes at the end of his essay on promises: *Die Sprache verspricht* (*sich*) (AR, 277). As finite, language is never already constituted, language always is promised; but since its promise can never be fulfilled by itself as promised, this promise, at once the suspension of language, brackets *itself* — language — and confesses, since it, despite its endless suspension, thus despite its impossibility, is "effective," that it is a failed linguistic performance, a parapraxis, *lapsus linguae*. Language, since it can relate to its own operation only in the epistemologically illegitimate figures of prolepsis and metalepsis, is a *lapsus*. And since no imperative, at the very least the categorical imperative that a language has to be, can come out without the metaleptical suggestion that there is an already constituted language, every imperative is an epistemological parapraxis. The ground of meaning, the ground of understanding, the ground of the science of literature — a *lapsus*.

Every allegory, even that of unreadability, is still a figure of knowledge. Every imperative — and first of all: "Understand!" — is still a figure of incomprehensibility that, as a figure, remains inscribed in a system of negative certainty. This tropological system, however, wrenches apart whenever the known negativity encounters in the impossibility of its self-legitimation its barren, groundless positedness. Imperatives — and first of all: "Understand!" — can be meant and understood as demands only if they are already encountered as positings that are without intention. That they are posited, *hypothesin*, before all thematization, formalization, allegorization — such is their truth, their only unverifiable truth: "as a violent — not as a dark — light, a deadly Apollo" (RR, 118). A deadly clearing. Thus: *Es ereignet sich aber Das Wahre*. The imperative, the promise — no longer as the promise of a future truth but rather, here and now, as the promise in its truth: "to the extent that it is necessarily misleading, langauge just as necessarily conveys the promise of its own truth" (AR, 277). One cannot turn away from the violence of this truth, for every turn is already under its spell.

De Man has called this truth of language, the truth of its promise, irony. At the end of "Excuses (*Confessions*)," the concluding essay in *Allegories of Read-*

ing, he describes the grammatical figure of anacoluthon, which designates the gap between two different linguistic systems, as irony and, borrowing Friedrich Schlegel's definition, as "permanent parabasis": "the permanent parabasis of an allegory (of figure), that is to say, irony. Irony is no longer a trope but the undoing of the deconstructive allegory of all tropological cognitions, the systematic undoing, in other words, of understanding" (AR, 301). No allegory can grasp the incidences of irony by which it is disrupted, none can catch up with the positing violence of the imperative, but each one—for each one remains exposed to its positing—must undertake the attempt to translate it into a cognitive content. The allegory of the imperative is the endless labor of mourning the traumas inflicted by irony. But the imperative is, as positing, as exposed, itself the irony in whose light its allegory disintegrates.

The science of literature, if it is to have its justification in the structure of the literary text and in the structure of language in general, stands under this duplicitous imperative in every one of its operations: under that of allegory, to which it compels the confession of its foundering in always new figures and arguments, and under that ironical imperative that withdraws its every epistemic and legitimating ground under which there is no foundering and under which every word, however erring it seems, fits. Ironically, the imperative—of language, of understanding—allows no decision whether it is to be allegorical or ironic.

It is not certain that there can be *no* science of literature. But were there one, the science of literature itself could know nothing of it. That it is and has to be—this experience could be imparted to it always only on this side of the figure of understanding and its foundering. But no experience other than this and hence only the disfiguration of the science of literature itself could be its fundament. If there were one, then only as that permanent irony toward itself, which de Man associated just as often with Nietzsche's *gaya scienza* as with madness and death.

"Envy" and "Charity" are the two allegorical figures of Giotto, from the arena in Padua, to which Proust's Marcel compares the pregnant maid in his parents' house. Like Giotto's figures, so heavily weighted down by the burden of their emblems that they can no longer express the idea represented in them, the maid is so burdened by what Proust calls, oddly enough, "le symbole ajouté qu'elle portait devant son ventre," that she can no longer grasp its meaning, "sans avoir l'air d'en comprende le sens, sans que rien dans son visage en traduisît la beauté et l'esprit" (Pléiade I: 81). The same dyslexia that strikes the reader in the "Seconde Préface" of Rousseau's *Julie* (AR, 202) has befallen these figures too (AR, 74). Through the expressionless force of their mode of meaning, these allegorical forms lose all relation to the very things to which they have been determined to have the most intense relation, namely, their allegorical meaning. They remain readable only because their "proper meaning"—KARITAS, for example—is attributed to them by an authorial act. These allegories become unreadable because their material appearance always indicates some meaning other than the intended one, finally robbing them of all determinable meaning. "Proust may well spell out all the letters of LECTIO on the frames of his stories . . . , but the word itself will never become clear, for . . . it is forever impossible to read Reading" (AR, 77). The force of that which deflects from the understanding of the figure of understanding, from the reading of the allegory of reading and also of unreadability, "that sidetracks our attention" (AR, 74), is not a power of cognition or meaning, nor of language, but rather of their failure: "in the case of Envy the mind is distracted towards something even more threatening than vice, namely death" (AR, 75). The sentence in Proust to which de Man's paraphrase refers, without quotation, reads: " . . . cette Charité sans charité, cette Envie qui avait l'air d'une planche illustrant seulement dans un livre de médecine la compression de la glotte ou de la luette par une tumeur de la langue" (Pléiade I: 81–82). The cancer of the tongue, the language tumor, death, deflects meaning into a region where there is no more meaning. Language—of literature and of its science—"sans beauté et sans esprit," speaks only in this deflection, of its themes, its figures, its passions, and its errors. It is this deflection that brings about muteness: *tumeur de la langue*; but it is also that which attracts all speaking. What makes understanding necessary, and impossible. One could read this coercive deflection as the imperative of reading and as the ironic suspension of the imperative: *tu meurs*. Or as the provisional end of reading: *tu meurs de la langue*.

March–April 1985

Notes

1. The German term *Literaturwissenschaft* designates the scholarly field of literary studies in a form parallel to other "scientific" disciplines (e.g., *Naturwissenschaft*: natural science). *Wissenschaft*, built on the verb *wissen*, "to know," can mean both science and any kind of academic, scholarly knowledge. *Literaturwissenschaft* will be rendered as science of literature, literary criticism, scholarship, studies, etc., depending on the context. – Trans.]

2. One of the starting points of de Man's concept of allegory may well be the one developed by Walter Benjamin in *The Origin of German Tragic Drama*. Particularly pertinent are the ethical implications Benjamin touches upon in connection with a line by Sigismund von Birken: " 'Mit Weinen streuten wir den Samen in die Brachen und gingen traurig aus' [Weeping we scattered the seed on the fallow ground and sadly went away]. Allegory goes away empty handed. Evil as such, which it cherished as enduring profundity, exists only in allegory, is nothing other than allegory, and means something different from what it is. It means precisely the non-existence of what it represents" (trans. John Osborn [London: NLB, 1977], 233, translation slightly modified; – Trans.). Heidegger's formal characterization of the work of art as allegory also stresses that it says something other than the mere being of its representational, "thing-like" basis: "The art work is, to be sure, a thing that is made, but it says something other than the mere thing itself is, *allo agoreuei*. The work makes public something other than itself; it manifests something other; it is an allegory" ("The Origin of the Work of Art," in *Poetry, Language, Thought*, trans. Albert Hofstadter [New York: Harper & Row, 1971], 19–20).

3. "Es gibt einen hermeneutischen Imperativ" ("There is a hermeneutic imperative"), noted

Friedrich Schlegel, one of the literary theorists most valued by de Man, in *Zur Philologie II* (no. 95), *Kritische Friedrich Schlegel-Ausgabe*, ed. Hans Eichner (Paderborn: Schoenigh, 1981), XVI: 96.

4. For the notion of partaking see Jean-Luc Nancy, *La Partage des Voix* (Paris: Galilée, 1982), Werner Hamacher, "Das Beben der Darstellung," in *Positionen der Literaturwissenschaft*, ed. David Wellbery (Munich: Beck, 1985), and *The Second of Inversion: Movements of a Figure through Celan's Poetry*, in *The Lesson of Paul de Man, Yale French Studies*, 69 (1985).

5. See in the opening passage of "Self (*Pygmalion*)" these sentences that also contain an explication of one of Heidegger's well-known formulas: "But we do not 'possess' language in the same way that we can be said to possess natural properties. It would be just as proper or improper to say that 'we' are a property of language as the reverse. The possibility of this reversal is equivalent to the statement that all discourse *has to be* referential but can never signify its actual referent" (AR, 160).

6. This passage, to be sure, does not contain a pledge for the dissolution of responsibility, moral or political; on the contrary, it opens the possibility to think—and to practice—a responsibility that would not be confined to the realm of conventions.

7. In a note following this statement, de Man adds: "In the *Genealogy of Morals*, Nietzsche also derives the notion of a transcendental referent (and the specificity of 'man') from the possibility of making promises." I have tried to pursue this problem in my essay, "*Das Versprechen der Auslegung*—Überlegungen zum hermeneutischen Imperativ bei Kant und Nietzsche," in *Spiegel und Gleichnis: Festschrift für Jacob Taubes*, ed. N. Bolz and W. Hübener (Würzburg: Königshausen & Neumann, 1983). Since this text was written, Jacques Derrida has published his *Mémoires—for Paul de Man* (New York: Columbia University Press, 1986) with a meditation about de Man's promises in its third part: "Acts—The Meaning of a Given Word."

8. Peter Szondi, *Schriften II* (Frankfurt: Suhrkamp, 1978), 25.

Response to Paul de Man
Hans Robert Jauss

Translated by Andreas Michel

Dear Paul,

No name has been mentioned more often than yours in my seminars between Sather Tower and Wheeler Hall and none has been called upon more frequently in discussions among students, colleagues, and myself. While the debate in New York in 1973 was concerned with reception aesthetics and semiotics, in New Haven in 1976 with the tensions between the Konstanz School and the Yale Critics, the Berkeley debate in 1983 focused on the polarity of hermeneutics and "deconstruction." Thus, today, what better opportunity to end my third American adventure than to write a thank-you note for your introduction to *Toward an Aesthetic of Reception*. This belated thank-you has at least one positive side. Belatedness once again proves to be hermeneutically productive: it undoes the bias of immediate understanding and allows me, in view of the reaction to our common book (if you permit my saying so), to assess what of its impact may be due to its German origin and what of its American reception may be due to the extraordinary character of your presentation. It will hardly come as a surprise to the author of *Allegories of Reading* that time and again I found myself confronted with a specific "misreading," namely, that I was asked again and again what I thought of a presentation that—in opposition to the academic custom of *laudatio—*

This letter was written in Berkeley, California, on February 29, 1983, and was completed after the author's last conversation with Paul de Man, in New Haven on March 25, 1983. My references to Paul de Man's introduction to my book *Toward an Aesthetic of Reception* are now made to those pages in his *Resistance to Theory*, where it has now been collected.

included within the book to be prefaced its first American critique. Ought I not to have felt hurt, even altogether misunderstood? Would hermeneutics and deconstruction have to remain divided by an unbridgeable abyss? Would your critique not call for a reply and a countercritique that would renew the argument of *Blindness and Insight*, the great debate that none other than Paul de Man, "much praised and much blamed," had brought about, having thus revitalized the discussions on methodology ever since the 1960s?

It is questions of this kind that I have been trying to answer ever since my arrival, but seemingly without being able to wholly convince my interlocutors. They do not seem to believe me when I maintain that, in general, I feel understood by you in my intentions and limits, in some positions even "better than I understood myself." This is also true for my research group, whose name "Poetik und Hermeneutik" has never been more accurately commented on than by you. Critics in this country do not seem to realize that there are more similarities between the schools of Konstanz and Yale than dogmatic supporters in both camps would like to admit. And they have difficulty believing that our remaining differences may not be the kind that can be definitively settled by a "right or wrong," for they spring from different interests that one need not share to still see and accept the ideas of the other. Gadamer's dictum according to which it is the advantage of hermeneutics to be able to understand the opponent is more than a ruse of liberal reason. . . . That is why I am now directing my answers to you as the absent-present third who, in the final analysis, "both praising and blaming," has judged my work strictly but always generously—and I hope, in my case, to dispel the myth that in a dialogue with Paul de Man, one should always keep in mind the old warning: "timeo Danaos et dona ferentes."

That the Yale Critics as well as the Konstanz School entered the discussions concerning methodology with a dismissal of logocentrism, the essentialism of traditional philology, and classical aesthetics, (represented by Curtius, Lukács, and also Gadamer), seems not to have been recognized by American critics as a position basic to both groups. Might this be due to the fact that in this country hermeneutics is readily equated with esoteric theology of the old exegetic style ("the ultimate aim of a hermeneutically successful reading is to do away with reading altogether" [RT, 56]) whereas the younger German hermeneutic tradition follows the Heideggerian maxim: "A right or a correct explanation never understands the text better than its author, but rather, differently"? Indeed, what unites me with Harold Bloom is the wish to oppose to the purportedly timeless presence of the classical a dynamic and dialectical process of a continuous building and rebuilding of the canon, except that his interests are primarily oriented toward the side of the aesthetics of production while mine are oriented toward the aesthetics of reception. As a result of my critique of Gadamer's "fusion of horizons," I have, in addition, developed a more sophisticated conception of the process of active historical understanding—that of a differentiation of horizons.

With your truly illuminating explanation of my theory of the horizon structure of understanding as a "complex interplay between knowing and not knowing" (RT, 58), you have brought to light a second similarity between the two groups: the insight into the epistemological ambiguity of historical consciousness and the ensuing "willingness to give up the illusion of unmediated understanding" (RT, 60).

I am in complete agreement with your description of the disjuncture between expectation and experience in the change of horizon of historical understanding as that of the relationship between the dominant convention and the individual work, its formal structure, and the concretizing interpretation ("in Jauss's historical model, a syntagmatic displacement within a synchronic structure becomes, in its reception, a paradigmatic condensation within a diachrony" [RT, 60]). And I am grateful when you ascribe to me the achievement of a genuine synthesis of reception and semiotics, though not without admitting that I did not have this consequence in mind when I began reading the Prague structuralists and discovered that Vodicka's notion of reception as concretization of a linguistic sign structure can be married to my model of a horizon of expectations, its disruption, and the reconstruction of a new horizon.

However, I cannot agree when you say that literary understanding, which always presupposes a horizon of expectations, is analogous to everyday perception, even imitates it and is therefore, in the final analysis, "mimetic" (RT, 67). Does this claim not run counter to everything you said before concerning the advantage of my notion of horizon: its ambiguity between the conscious and the unconscious (or: the not yet known) ("the historical consciousness of a given period can never exist as a set of openly stated or recorded propositions" [RT, 58])? In my model, the horizon of expectations of a literary work cannot at all be determined mimetically because it encompasses what can be perceived (in my terminology: the latent preunderstanding) as well as what cannot be perceived in the life world; indeed, it rather brings out, makes conscious, and allows us to reconstruct the difference that exists between self-understanding and preunderstanding of an experience in the world as distinct from simple everyday perception. It is for this reason that my model needs the hermeneutical tool of question and answer (a preunderstanding can only be questioned or inquired after, not immediately perceived), which, in its ateleological structure, you had fittingly described before ("the question occurs as an individual disruption of an answer that has become common knowledge" [RT, 59]). If I have to presume that you do not consider this hermeneutic tool (which is constantly used in deconstructionist criticism without, as far as I know, having been incorporated in its theory) capable of uncovering latent horizons of a literary work, of reconstructing the horizon of past experience, and of mediating it with the horizon of present understanding, then all I can do to fight this skepticism is to refer you to the practical application of my method, which you can find in my new book.[1]

If in the face of our fervent supporters as well as the opponents of the "hermeneutic mafia" we can appeal to a common ground (*Grundverständnis*) – the Yale Critics presupposing a theory of understanding, the Konstanz School presupposing the ambiguity of historical consciousness – the difference of our positions, in your presentation, becomes apparent only when (as in a real family quarrel when the elders get involved) we appeal to our philosophical authorities. This difference is evident wherever the category of the aesthetic comes into play, which you rightly single out as the *punctum saliens* of our differences (RT, 63–64). With the help of authorities one can argue exquisitely ("There are one and a half for each rogue," as a German proverb has it). You consider it vain, as I do, to hold up to each other philosophical predilections and dependencies (RT, 62–63). Since they have not been chosen arbitrarily and thus cannot simply be explained biographically, I shall complement your series with my own in order to render visible our different interests (*Frageinteressen*) – may the consuls of philosophy decide who relied upon whom with better judgment and whose interpretations are "more correct." You appeal to the early Benjamin ("The Task of the Translator" from 1923, where reception is banned and translation alone accepted as the model of understanding) and I to the late Benjamin ("Eduard Fuchs, Collector and Historian" of 1937, where the turn to reception is accomplished – to the "now of knowability" ["Jetzt der Erkennbarkeit"], which, in the "Theses on the Philosophy of History" as well, cannot disguise its aesthetic origin in the "now of readability" [*Jetzt der Lesbarkeit*].[2] You prefer the late Heidegger of "Holzwege" (1950), who granted the great poet a personal relationship to truth, the work of art a "self-satisfying being" (which, in my rendition, you have to call a "simplification" [RT, 62]); I prefer the early Heidegger before the "turn to the history of Being," his book on Kant (1929) with its analysis of the transcendental imagination and, particularly, with its already mentioned hermeneutical maxim of the "necessary difference in understanding" (*notwendiges Andersverstehen*). You may enlist Kierkegaard, Nietzsche, and Adorno against my attempt of a rehabilitation of aesthetic pleasure (for me always already cognitive), whereas I can call upon the equally respectable authority of Kant, repressed in your tradition, and his analysis of the reflective judgment in the Third Critique in order to argue why the pleasure principle in the aesthetic experience can include – as you formulate so poignantly – a "eudaemonic judgment" (RT, 64).

In all this you opposed to the aesthetic the destructive power of the poetic, equated with rhetoric, and you make me curious as to why, for you, the aesthetic had to become the category of "blindness" par excellence (the "aesthetic idol" that you have hidden in note 26). Aren't you thus pulled into the secular tradition of rigorous puritans reaching from Plato to Rousseau and Adorno, a tradition in which you will hardly feel at ease. Are we not both positioned on the side of the *modernes*, who saw in the Platonic triad – "The truth which is the Father who engenders the good which is the Son from whom springs the beautiful which is the

Holy Spirit" (to do honor to the Neveu de Rameau) – the idol of the *anciens* that was to be deposed? The liberation from this Platonic heritage is, for me, the work of the aesthetic experience, as the chapter on the ambiguity and unruliness of the beautiful in my book tries to argue *expressis verbis*. If, for you, it is the work of poetic and rhetorical analysis, don't we mean practically the same thing under a different name? Indeed, wouldn't you agree with (or else on what grounds refute?) the latest thesis of Rainer Warning, namely, that "*imitatio* as a rhetorical use of language, i.e., as a definite form of semiotic praxis, always already implicitly denies its metaphysical foundation as a participating imitation of being. . . . that secretly, the poets always believed themselves to be questioning metaphysics," in other words: that, in the final analysis, the goal of deconstruction ought not to be the deconstruction of poetic texts "but the proof that poetic fiction itself is the systematic locus of all work of deconstruction."[3]

Doesn't this thesis, which represents the first explicit reception of deconstruction in the Konstanz School, offer, perhaps, a new chance for an accord with the Yale Critics? Having read *Deconstruction and Criticism*, I, for my part, would be able to underwrite without hesitation the final conclusions of Harold Bloom ("Poems instruct us in how they break form to bring about meaning") as well as of Geoffrey Hartman ("For [us] the ethos of literature is not dissociable from its pathos"). Thus, I leave it up to you, dear Paul, to place me in the future, if not in the purgatory of "boa deconstructors," at least in the limbo of the conservative wing of your "Bella Scuola" as a corresponding member. Remaining differences like our divergent interpretations of Baudelaire's "Spleen II" might be settled with the help of the maxim according to which it is "possible to understand a text differently" – a maxim that is most productive at the moment when it cannot be decided whether one interpreter understands the text better than the other. You begin on another thematic level, with the spirit as an empty vessel, place the decapitated painter there (Boucher/*débouché*), and establish an analogy between his metamorphosis into a voice and the *itinerarium mentis ad Aegyptum* (in the emblematic sequence of memory connoting death, pyramid, and sphinx). Then you refer to Hegel, for whom the pyramid ("within which a strange / foreign soul is placed and kept")[4] is the paradigm for sign in opposition to symbol. However, not the pyramid (line 6) but the sphinx (line 22) is the last form into which the I of "Spleen II" metamorphoses (*sich entäussert*). Since you mention Hegel, wouldn't you have to say something about the fact that the sphinx was, for him, the paradigm for symbol ("the symbol, so to speak, of the symbolic itself"),[5] more specifically the symbol for the Egyptian spirit ("as it begins to rise out of the natural, to tear itself away from it"),[6] in a final stage in which "the locked away, the spiritual . . . breaks out of the animal being as a human face,"[7] whereas in the new stage of the Greek myth of Oedipus, who kills the sphinx, "the riddle was solved thus: the content be man, free, self-knowing spirit"?[8] I cannot see on what grounds you could say, "But the sphinx is not an emblem of recollection but, like

Hegel's sign, an emblem of forgetting." Recollection or forgetting is not an issue in Hegel's distinction of sign and symbol. Baudelaire, however, turned the sphinx (in my terminology) into an "allegory of forgetting" when he most arbitrarily joined together the two Egyptian myths of the sphinx and the column of Memnon and interpreted (in your teminology, "deconstructed") them in contradistinction to their secular tradition. Whatever the merits of Hegel (we can now leave him aside), here our interpretations have obviously reached the same conclusions, although you don't say so . . .

The next difference concerns the line: "oublié sur la carte." You interpret it thus: "In Baudelaire's poem he is not just 'oublié' but 'oublié sur la carte,' inaccessible to memory because he is imprinted on paper, because he is himself the inscription of a sign" (RT, 70). You insinuate (what cannot be derived from Baudelaire's formulation) that the place of the sphinx was marked on the map and has simply been forgotten (although a sign imprinted on paper, and therefore published, is usually not per se inaccessible). Hence I believe my deconstruction of the myth to be more sharply argued when I—following the literal meaning—interpret it otherwise: Baudelaire's sphinx is irretrievably forgotten because its place is marked on no map (because someone forgot to mark it on a map). It is as these "memories for no one" that the sphinx is an "allegory of forgetting." For me too, the sphinx is, in the final analysis—after the "I" has reverted into the petrified non-"I"—"the grammatical subject cut off from its consciousness." The only difference is that I point out the destruction of the self as an inescapable process of the loss of memory within the movement of the poem itself and step by step—from "J'ai plus de souvenirs que si j'avais mille ans" to the "memories for no one"—while you wish to derive the destruction of self and world directly from the sphinx's sign character ("because he is himself the inscription of a sign"). The poetic instrument that allowed Baudelaire to represent this process of a destruction of self is for me, as it is for you, his modernized use of allegory so that I am taken aback to find myself relegated by you to a "classical position."

There remains as a last and—I fear—unbridgeable difference my final interpretation of the sphinx's song as "poetry of poetry" (*Poesie de Poesie*) that, folded back onto the genesis of the text, describes its own production. Here, only a Paul de Man can be so generous as to concede to the friend that he finds his interpretation "convincing" and the promise of aesthetic sublimation "powerfully argued" while he must, at the same time, disagree with him because he does not share Valéry's framework, to which I am indebted, and has declared unrelenting war on all forms of aesthetic sublimation. However, at issue is not really the appearance of the beautiful into which the process of deconstruction of self and world reverts in the end, for I also want to stress that the beautiful in "Spleen II" can no longer shine/appear in its classical transparency but only as an "allegory of uncomprehended beauty."[9] Rather, the point at issue is whether Baudelaire's poem, if it objectifies *Weltangst* up to its utmost horrors, can and may bring about its own catharsis through aesthetic sublimation. I see in the cathartic effect of poetry its power; you, however, its weakness. Even the shadows of Plato and Aristotle, which are customarily called upon in this situation, would be hard put to settle this last point of contention between hermeneutics and deconstruction. Let me therefore respond to your last question for me with a last question for you, which also leads into uncertain territory: what would be achieved if Baudelaire's poem withstood all aesthetic sublimation? Would it still be a poem? You seem doubtful yourself: "What he 'sings' can never be the poem entitled 'Spleen'; his song is not the sublimation but the forgetting, by inscription of terror, the dismemberment of the aesthetic whole into the unpredictable play of the literary letter" (RT, 70). But to what extent would this ("the forgetting, by inscription of terror") still be song? May the deconstructivist sphinx be allowed to sing at all if it denies the hermeneutic sphinx the right to sing?

This is where our dialogue ended—forever, as we could not know at the time of our last conversation. Nobody knew better and experienced more painfully than Paul de Man why any apology for poetry or why any friendship must remain fragmentary and therefore an unfinished and never-ending task to which he knew himself devoted with an unswerving passion. May this letter, which for me is the last sign of a happy understanding in dissension that grew over a great number of years, keep alive the spiritual stature of the friend and be understood as an allegory of the unforgettable, which his work has inscribed on the world map of the republic of letters!

Notes

1. "Rousseaus *Nouvelle Héloïse* und Goethes *Werther* im Horizontwandel zwischen französischer Aufklärung und deutschen Idealismus," in my *Ästhetische Erfahrung und literarische Hermeneutik* (Frankfurt: Suhrkamp, 1982), 585–653.

2. Hans Robert Jauss, "Spur und Aura: Bemerkungen zu Walter Benjamin's Passagenwerk," in *Art social und art industriel*, ed. Helmut Pfeiffer (Munich: Fink, 1987), 19–47, esp. 36.

3. Rainer Warning in W. Ölmüller (ed.), *Ästhetische Schein*, Kollegium Kunst und Philosophie, no. 2 (Paderborn: Schoenigh, 1982), 168ff.

4. G. W. F. Hegel, *Theorie-Werkausgabe*, 20 vols. (Frankfurt: Suhrkamp, 1969–71), 3:270.

5. Hegel, *Werkausgabe*, 13:465.

6. Hegel, *Werkausgabe*, 12:246.

7. Hegel, *Werkausgabe*, 12:263.

8. Hegel, *Werkausgabe*, 16:442.

9. Hans Robert Jauss, *Toward an Aesthetic of Reception*, trans. Timothy Bahti (Minneapolis: University of Minnesota Press, 1981), 179.

Aberrations: de Man (and) the Machine
Geoffrey Bennington

Techné belongs to bringing-forth, to poiesis, *it is something poetic.*
— Heidegger, *The Question Concerning Technology*

A letter of exhortation to a friend to encourage him to seek. And he will reply: but what use will seeking be, nothing appears. And reply to him: do not despair. And he would reply that he would be happy to find some light. But that according to this religion even if he were to believe in this way it would do him no good. And that this being the case he may as well not seek. And at this point reply to him: The Machine.
— Pascal, *Pensées*

In the complete works of Blaise Pascal, the famous arithmetical machine is the more-or-less absent referent of three texts, two of which are by Pascal himself.[1] The first of these is a dedicatory letter addressed to Chancellor Séguier, and apparently dominated by its addressee in the form of the pronoun of respect, *vous*; the second is an *Avis* (not quite an instruction booklet), destined to "those who will have the curiosity to see the said machine and to make use of it," again dominated by the addressee, but this time in the familiarity of the pronoun *tu*, designating the *ami lecteur*; the third text is the *privilège* or patent, granted and signed by the king, dominated this time by the addressor, marked by the *nous* of royal prerogative and power.

For reasons to which I shall return, detailed description of the machine is disappointingly sparse in these brief pages, and what description is provided is of the most general kind. In its minimal specification, the machine is intended to *perform* arithmetical operations in a mechanical manner, and to do so more quickly and accurately than someone working with pen and paper or with counters, the two alternative methods with which Pascal favorably compares his machine (189b). The attraction of the machine's performance of its operations is thus that it is, simply enough, *performante*, a high performer when measured against rival methods according to the criterion of an input/output ratio. This high performance is, however, not just a result of speed and accuracy; the essence of the machine seems rather to lie in its capacity to stand in for and render unnecessary a certain number of the mental operations required of a human calculator: "the most ignorant person finds in [the machine] as great an advantage as the most experienced; the instrument supplies [*supplée à*] the defect of ignorance or lack of habit, and, *by necessary movements*, it performs all alone, *without even the intention of the user*, all the abridgements possible to nature" (189b; my emphasis). It will do all the "borrowing" and "carrying" that normally tire the human calculator's memory: "it does of itself what he desires, without his even thinking about it" (190a). Earlier, in the dedicatory letter, Pascal suggests that the machine he is presenting to the chancellor is capable of doing, "with itself alone and without any work of the mind, the operations of all the parts of arithmetic" (188a).

This *facility* promised by the machine is not simple or absolute or free, but enters into an economy with complexity, depth of thought, and hard practical labor. In the dedicatory letter, Pascal presents with no small amount of pride and pathos (which go some way toward challenging the addressee's dominance over the text) a passably heroic account of his invention and realization of the machine. This *difficulty* in the production of *facility* is in fact figured in the machine itself, according to an opposition between its inside and its outside: preempting a possible objection that his machine is needlessly *composée* or complex, Pascal develops a nice economy that explains that such internal complexity is the necessary price to pay for external and operational simplicity—the simple and the easy are the effects of the difficult and the complex, the greater the one, the greater the other:

> in which you will be able to note a sort of paradox, namely that in order to make the movement of the operation the more simple, it was necessary that the machine be constructed of a more complex movement (190a).

In rudimentary form, Pascal's story of his machine appears to be a narrative of legitimation, and of legitimation by performativity, as Lyotard would say.[2] Here a generalizable facility is paid for, and paid off by, the quasi-heroic labor of the inventor, the genius. The performativity of the machine is ensured by its standing in for, as supplement or prosthesis, certain parts of the mind of its user: variously the memory, intention, expertise, and mental labor in general. But if the machine can do this, it is because something of the mind of the inventor has gone into it, possibly at the expense of his health,[3] but certainly to the benefit of his name, his renown. Once the machine reaches its user, its mechanical supplementation of the mind is, in principle, *euphoric*; for once the heroism of invention has paid off any debt owed for facility, the machine goes on performing for free, and, in principle at least, for good (part of Pascal's long and long-suffering period of invention was concerned with ensuring the solidity and durability of the machine). This free performance continues after the death of its inventor, to which it is indifferent, and regardless of the death of any particular user; and this would appear to be part of the essence of machines in general, which are the death of inventors and users alike.

But if this indifference to death is conducive to euphoria, it is also troublesome for any such euphoria, and generates aberrations in the text. So far I have analyzed the textual network of Pascal's machine in terms of description and performance, and neglected a whole prescriptive dimension. The smooth legitimation of technological advance is in fact constantly interrupted by a complex nexus of points for legislation, involving bodies and birth, orders, obligations and justice, legitimacy and falsification. In the terms of the dedicatory letter, Pascal may have "conceived" the machine, but it owes its "birth" to the chancellor's "commands": those commands can be modalized as praise or guidance, "seeing that in the young age in which I am, and with so little strength, I have dared to attempt a new road in a field bristling with thorns, and without a guide to open my path for me [*pour m'y frayer le chemin*]" (188a). Recompense for Pascal's time and expense is not in fact adequately provided by the narrative of technical legitimation, and is only satisfactorily achieved, beyond the mere approbation of experts, in the judgment of the chancellor, as "that same mouth which every day pronounces oracles on the throne of justice" (188b).

This irruption, into a story of legitimation by performance, of quite different codes, can of course be linked to certain conventions and to a historically bound rhetoric of flattery: but we cannot dispose of the matter so simply; there is here a political and ethical tension that it would be foolish, as Paul de Man might have said, to "historicize out of consciousness" (P, 3). This tension can be read as the conflict between *legitimation* and *legitimacy*, and it is in fact as much in evidence in the *Avis* as in the dedicatory letter. Here, having disposed of the first possible objection to his machine (that it is unnecessarily complex), Pascal moves to a second possible cause of "umbrage" to his addressee, and that is the existence of bad copies of his machine. These copies are described as "little monsters," "formless," "useless abortions," "little abortion[s]" (190a–191a). The "illegitimacy" of such pseudomachines would, one might think, be sufficiently determined by the fact that they simply do not work, fail to perform, but Pascal analyzes the question beyond this simple judgment (made within the discourse of legitimation by performativity) into a mythical romance about the marriage of theory and practice (*art*): monsters and abortions are the result of the presumption of the artisan to give birth *alone*, without the fecunding, prescriptive, intervention of theory. Whence the third text, the *privilège*, procured by the chancellor, signed by the king, which aims to prevent hasty condemnation by the public of "true originals" it mistakes for bad copies, or hasty approbation of bad copies it mistakes for true originals: according to Pascal, the privilege "stifles before birth all these illegitimate abortions which might be engendered somewhere other than in the legitimate and necessary marriage [*alliance*] of theory with art" (191a). Here then is a concern with paternity and signatures, property and propriety, apparently quite foreign to the technical legitimation of the machine in terms of its performativity. The *privilège* duly forbids anyone to make any such machine without Pascal's instruction or permission, on the grounds of an aberrant logic that states simultaneously that the machine is both easy to counterfeit (and therefore in need of legal protection) and impossible to counterfeit in such a way that it will perform as it should (and therefore in need of legal protection). And this protection of the inventor's rights and signature quite consequently extends beyond the death of the inventor or signatory of the machine, and implicitly confirms that in an important sense the signatory is *already dead*: the *privilège* is also a tombstone.

How are we to read this impression of overkill in the second aspect of these texts? Simply this: that the prescriptive elements of the text are not *simply* extraneous to, or superfluous with respect to, an essentially performative legitimation, but that the apparently disruptive language of justice, legitimacy, paternity, and signatures is in fact called up precisely by the apparent indifference of the logic of performativity to any such concerns. For the logic of the supplementary machine is that it must be able to work independently of inventor or father, that it is necessarily cut from any origin in Pascal's intentions or mental labor, that it can be reproduced ad infinitum and respond promiscuously in the hands of anyone at all. The "legitimate" machine has to have its legitimacy certified, signed, and sealed, precisely because in its essence it exceeds legitimacy: the father lays claim to it precisely because it is essentially a bastard. And just as the machine can be said to function prosthetically, *supplying* defects of memory, intention, and even intelligence, so it can be said to *dispossess* the user in general (including Pascal) of those same faculties.

Readers of Jacques Derrida will have recognized that the performing machine functions like the written text as described by Plato in the *Phaedrus*,[4] and gives rise to the same anxieties and prescriptive interventions: Pascal's myth of the marriage of "theory" and "art" is also the story of the *logos* reclaiming its own against the generalized threat of *techné*. And it will now come as no surprise that Pascal's "disappointingly sparse" description of his machine is justified by the assertion that "this doctrine [that of how to construct and use such a machine] is one of those that can only be taught *viva voce*" (189a)—the voice as protection against the promiscuous availability of machine and written text alike.

"Pascal's machine," then, performs arithmetical operations, but also performs as text, staging scenes of performance, description, prescription, proscription, signature, and so on. As supplement to the *logos*, it gives rise to facility only by opening up the possibility of uncontrollable mimetic doubling and degradation, and generates further apotropaic supplements to control and police that threat. The machine is thus both text and text-productive; conversely, the text is a machine and produces further machines. It follows that Pascal's machine is an "allegory" of writing and/or reading, that writing and/or reading involve a complex of conflictual components or nondialectizable "moments" that simultaneously dispossess the "subject" of writing/reading and set up the drive to signature as a means of legislating for that "subject" and its "legitimacy" against such dispossession. The text as machine is thus both the life and the death, the life-death of anything like a subject, be that subject determined as "author" or "reader," "inventor" or "user."

For this duplicity of the performance of the machine and the text clearly questions the pertinence of a number of the oppositions that have tended to dominate and confuse the questions of writing and reading. The recent enthusiasm for readers and reading in literary studies may have been beneficial in disrupting certain notions about the author, but has also brought with it at least as many regressive tendencies as it has afforded new insights. No sooner has the "death of the author" been proclaimed, than all sorts of reassuring surrogate sovereign subjects appear on the side of reception and reading: empirical, existential, phenomenological, psychoanalytic, individual and collective, strong and weak, politically activist—just waiting to *respond*. To assert, for example, that "the 'primal scene' of literature is always an act of a reader rather than a mysterious attribution of a text"[5] may well be no more helpful, and no less mysterious, than what it purports to attack, unless we are prepared to take the logic of "primal scenes" and *Nachträglichkeit* a good deal more seriously than has usually been the case in recent considerations of reading. It is the aim of the present essay to clear some ground toward suggesting why, when Paul de Man claims that "the systematic avoidance of the problem of reading, of the interpretive or hermeneutic moment, is a general symptom shared by all methods of literary analysis, whether they be structural or thematic, formalist or referential, American or European, apolitical or socially committed" (BI, 282), he is inviting anything but the return of the subject and the so-called act of reading. As is so often the case, the work of Jacques Derrida might have served as an early warning of the problems to come in this domain, although it would evidently be facile to assert that we could have avoided all manner of naïvetés if only we had been able to *read* statements such as those in "Force and Signification" on "the deferred reciprocity between reading and writing,"[6] or in "Freud and the Scene of Writing" on "the author who reads and the first reader who dictates":[7] facile because it would presuppose the problem of reading that is here at issue.

But it might be no accident that the second of these two comments from Derrida occurs in the immediate context of discussion of machines, of the "mystic writing pad," of *psyché* and *techné*, of life and death: "The subject of writing is a *system* of relationships between the strata: of the Mystic Pad, of the psychical, of society, of the world. Inside this scene, the punctual simplicity of the classical subject cannot be found. In order to describe this structure, it is not enough to recall that one always writes for someone; and the oppositions sender-receiver, code-message, etc., remain extremely coarse instruments. We would search the 'public' in vain for the first reader, i.e. the first author of the work. . . . The machine does not work all by itself, and this means something else: a mechanism with no energy of its own. The machine is dead. It is death. Not because we risk death playing with machines, but because the origin of machines is the relation to death."[8] Writing, reading, machines, and death: It would be hard to find a more apposite and emotive cluster of terms with which to approach Paul de Man. If de Man is dead (and they say he is), and if he remains so alive (for one who knew him only as texts), then that life-death is a question of writing, reading, and machines as the economy of life and death in life and death. The "aberration" of Paul de Man's death is also the aberration of a reading and writing machine, or reading and writing as machine. And only the machine (and therefore death) will allow us to avoid hasty assimilation of Paul de Man's work to the long *théorie* of theories of reading.

Traditional literary studies habitually use the language of machines in a negative way, deploring the mechanical and the technical as the death of the values attached to life, form, inspiration, and so on. At best, a "technical" use of concepts is accorded an uneasy neutrality, without ever being allowed to become the heart of the matter. Machines *repeat*, and repetition means danger—compulsion and death. No doubt even the most "technicist" forms of structuralism never simply escape this type of values. Some of this can be found in de Man's writing: *Allegories of Reading* claims to use the word "deconstruction" in a "technical" sense (AR, x), and refers to "the techniques of structural analysis refined to near perfection" (AR, 3). But elsewhere, as is also the case in Derrida,[9] this traditional system is disrupted: already in "Semiology and Rhetoric" there are references to "the programmed pattern of grammar," to "semi-automatic grammatical patterns," to "the impersonal precision of grammar" (AR, 16), where the "merely technical" or "mechanical" sense is suspended; this will be increasingly the case as syntax is thought to be prior to semantics, grammar to reference, and so on. By the time de Man is discussing and to some extent adopting Rousseau's language of the machine in the context of the *Social Contract*, the mechanical is becoming dominant, and the final essay in the book explicitly charts a move from text-as-body to text-as-machine:

The machine is like the grammar of the text when it is isolated from its rhetoric, the merely formal element without which no text can be generated. There can be no use of language which is not, within a certain perspective thus radically formal, i.e. mechanical, no matter how deeply this aspect may be concealed by aesthetic, formalistic delusions. . . . The text as body, with all its implications of substitutive tropes ultimately always retraceable to metaphor, is displaced by the text as machine and, in the process, it suffers the loss of the illusion of meaning. The deconstruction of the figural dimension is a process that takes place independently of any desire; as such it is not unconscious but mechanical, systematic in its performance but arbitrary in its principle, like a grammar . . . Far from seeing language as an instrument in the service of a psychic energy, the possibility now arises that the entire construction of drives, substitutions, repressions, and representations is the aberrant, metaphorical correlative of the absolute randomness of language, prior to any figuration or meaning. (AR, 294, 298, 299)

Other texts of the same period would confirm this displaced importance of the mechanical.

But if de Man's readings increasingly find machines in or as texts, what about those readings themselves? Here is a description by a reader of de Man of de Man reading:

One listens to him as one witnesses a performance: one has the feeling beforehand that one knows what de Man will do, yet one is still awed by the elegance, precision, and economy of his performance; one has a reluctant but solid conviction that one could not duplicate it. De Man is thought to be highly original, yet, in a sense, he does exactly what we expect him to do.[10]

This description is, in part at least, that of the performance of a machine. De Man reads like a machine. But he also reads machines;[11] and insofar as his readings are texts, they are machines too: "the punctual simplicity of the classical subject cannot be found." Paul de Man is dead: what remains in the repeated (un)predictability of performance is the tensions we noted in Pascal, between high performer and a signature, between the supplementation of our inabilities and the suspicion of dispossession—de Man's death guarantees him the *privilège* of being (in)imitable. The commonplace accusation that de Man's work is unduly "aestheticizing," and even the aesthetic sense of performance evident in Godzich's description, is secondary to this mechanical dimension.

The performativity of de Man's readings, as well as this secondary notion of performance, inevitably points to the importance of the performative "speech-act" in de Man's later writing.[12] It is this performative aspect of language that leads de Man to describe one aspect of textuality in terms of machines; and insofar as this machinelike performance is, in its disruption of cognition (in the guise of the referential dimension of descriptive or constative sentences), definitive of what de Man means by "text," and thereby of what "reading" might possibly mean, then it seems important to resist any temptation to read performance hastily in terms of the "aesthetic," and to clarify its link to the machine.[13] And following the chain of terms we have already established, it would seem that our ability to read the sentence "Paul de Man is dead," and *a fortiori* our ability to *mourn* his death, will depend on some such clarification.

There is a complication in the status of the machinelike performative that in fact depends on a principle of great generality that could no doubt be formalized: whenever one of a series of elements is also used transcendentally with respect to that series in order to totalize, dominate, or explain it, aberration begins. As a preliminary example of this principle we might take Fredric Jameson's argument in favor of Marxism in *The Political Unconscious*: Marxism is one of a series of rival theories in the intellectual "marketplace," but it is also the *best* of those theories because it is also the transcendental explanation and measure of the marketplace itself.[14] Or: Philosophy is one discipline among many, but it is the best of those disciplines because it can also explain and subsume the whole series of disciplines of which it is only one. Other examples would not be hard to find. This type of aberration seems to come from bogus reasoning and self-confirming claims. But now try this example: there are many sorts of language: constative, prescriptive, evaluative, interrogative, performative, etc. But just one of those elements also dominates the series. It is easy to imagine claims being made (and of course they always have been made) for one or other of the elements. Let us suppose that Austin's work amounts to saying that philosophy has always tended to assume that it is the constative that is dominant, but that in fact the performative deserves this privilege. Does such a claim give rise to the same sort of aberration as the previous examples? It seems clear that the answer is no, but perhaps less clear why that is the answer. I would suggest that *this* form of the question (which would have to be linked to Russell's set-theory paradox and Gödel's incompleteness theorem) leads us to de Man's own sense of "aberration," or "the impossibility of reading," and that the tension between the clarity of our no and the murkiness of its reasons is more a version of the problem than a mark of an inability to solve it. I would also suggest that the implication of de Man's work is that it is better to view this problem as an ethical rather than epistemological issue.

The generalized performative (as illocutionary force) that is the result of Austin's investigation has no more than a strategically privileged connection with the "performative" from which he begins. Even if we decide that any speech act is best discussed in terms of its "felicity" or "infelicity" rather than, say, its truth or falsehood, this "second-level" felicity or infelicity is quite different from that affecting "first-level" performatives. If a "first-level" performative "misfires" or is otherwise infelicitous, it is *not* in fact a performative, it fails to perform.[15] But this infelicitous act can be judged to be infelicitous only if there was nevertheless a performance of some kind. The nonperformance of a performative (the failure to bring off the marriage between theory and art, for example) presupposes performance at this generalized level. "First-level" performatives have only a heuristic privilege over constatives (for example) in this respect. Prior to any possibility of judgment as to felicity or infelicity, or prior even to any decision as to whether the "act" in question might, at the "lower" level, be considered a constative or a performative (for example), *there is* performance. Only this "primary" performance can account for the possibility of distinctions between types of acts. The constative "there is performance" presupposes and therefore cannot ground performance. It follows that this primary or archiperformance, of which there is no "first" performance, cannot be spoken or written as such, and therefore cannot itself be performed, which would imply that it is another, and equally improper, name for what Derrida calls (among other things) *différance*, and what Lyotard in recent work calls *présentation*.

This derivation of the archiperformance cannot be repeated with other elements of the series: any attempt to derive an archiconstative or even an archiprescriptive will presuppose performance. On the other hand, the fact that the archiperformance cannot be performed as such prevents it from falling into the simple aberration of earlier examples. But it brings its own sort of aberration, insofar as it would evidently be unreasonable to make it the basis for claims to truth or knowledge, for example. This would imply that the transcendence of the term "performance" with respect to the series of which the "performative" is one element cannot be simple or secure. And it further suggests that insofar as we are here working with something prior to distinctions between types of acts, then our suspicion of the "aesthetic" reading of de Man was justified.

This second type of aberration (one of de Man's favorite terms: it and its cognates occur at least fifty times in *Allegories of Reading*) is nonetheless intimately linked to de Man's new notion of the machine. Archiperformance *is* the machine, and is aberrant when approached in terms of secondary distinctions between different types of speech acts. The disruption of those distinctions is disturbing, insofar as it looks like a celebration of blind force (of the machine), which can modulate into either the so-called rhetoric of authority[16] or into so-called aestheticism. This disturbance is unavoidably political and ethical, in a difficult sense,[17] and so it seems reasonable to approach it by means of de Man's reading of overtly ethical or political texts. An obvious place to look would be the reading of Rousseau's *Social Contract* offered in the chapter "Promises" from *Allegories of Reading*, but as I have already had occasion to discuss this elsewhere,[18] I shall here return to Pascal and to a less well known essay by de Man, "Pascal's Allegory of Persuasion" (P).

The first part of this essay is a difficult discussion of nominal and real definitions in Pascal's theory of language, and of the heterogeneous status of the zero in his number theory: in the second part of the essay, which is more approachable here, de Man, with all the elegance, precision, and economy we have now come to expect, reads a number of the *Pensées* and reveals their "rhetorical machine" as "a fundamentally dialectical pattern of reasoning, in which oppositions are, if not reconciled, at least pursued toward a totalization that may be infinitely postponed, but that remains operative as the sole principle of intelligibility" (P, 20; see also esp. P, 13–19). Wondering whether any of the *Pensées* disrupt this pattern, de Man goes on to consider number 103 in the Lafuma classification, which reads as follows, in his own translation:

> It is just that what is just should be followed; it is necessary that what has the most power should be followed.
> Justice without power is impotent, power without justice is tyrannical.
> Justice without power is open to contradiction, because there are always wrongdoers. Power without justice stands accused. Justice and power must therefore be brought together, by making the just strong and the strong just.
> Justice is subject to dispute. Power is easily recognizable and without dispute. Thus it was impossible to give power to justice, because power has contradicted justice and said that it is unjust, and that it is itself just.
> And thus, not being able to make the just strong, one has made the strong just.

De Man wants to argue that whereas in his previous examples what was at stake was oppositions between two modes of cognition (or apparently contradictory constative sentences), here there is a disruption of that pattern because of the introduction of the performative dimension. Here is de Man's initial statement of the problem:

> The opposition is stated at the start in the contrast between "il est juste" and "il est necessaire," in which the first assertion depends on a propositional cognition, but the second on sheer quantitative power. . . . Propositional statements line up on the side of cognition, modal statements on the side of performance; they perform what they enunciate regardless of considerations of truth and falsehood.[19]

This analysis immediately calls to mind Godzich's characterization of de Man as machine: readers of *Allegories of Reading* both expect this type of distribution in terms of cognition and performance, and probably grudgingly admit that they would have had difficulty performing that distribution so powerfully and elegantly. It will be remembered, however, that the machine, in Pascal's description, works by "necessary" movements, and so if we accept this mode of reading de Man's reading we are curiously already implicated, in the terms of the passage, on the side of necessity, power, and indifference to truth and falsehood. Simply assenting to this reading is thus, in view of the passage read, a failure to read. It seems to follow that if we *are* to read this reading, we should ask the question, is it *juste*? This creates the problem of situating us, in de Man's terms, on the other side of the divide, on the aesthetically less attractive and technologically less powerful ground of cognition, and runs the risk of again failing to read. This seems to create a typically de Manian situation of aporia in which what his reading demonstrates is the impossibility of reading.

Luckily, things are not so simple. It seems plausible to argue, for example, that the statement "il est nécessaire" depends on what de Man calls "a propositional cognition" just as much, and just as little, as does "il est juste." "Il est nécessaire" performs what it enunciates just as much, and just as little, as does "il est juste": both are descriptives and can be the object of assent or disagreement. The contrast comes in the referents of these descriptives, that is, in the states of affairs indicated in "what is just should be followed," and "what has the most power should be followed." The first of these states of affairs involves a prescription of the type: "you should follow what is just" (*sollen*); the second a modal statement that is perhaps not clearly either descriptive *or* prescriptive, of the type "you must follow what has the most power" (*müssen*). The tension of the passage stems not from a distribution in terms of cognition and performance, but from a split in words and concepts such as "law" and "right" in their reference to both obligation and necessity.

De Man's reading is not unaware of this additional complication, which suggests a certain originality of prescription (of the question of justice, precisely), when it goes on to suggest that the adjective *juste* can be linked both to the cognitive value of *justesse* and to the juridical value of *justice* (cf. AR, 269); but this is rapidly reabsorbed into the familiar cognitive/performative distinction, for the importance of the juridical aspect for de Man is simply that it *weakens* cognitive claims and is the more vulnerable to usurpation by power.

Similarly, might here does not usurp "the consistency of cognition," as de Man has it, but the quite different order of obligation, by playing on the descriptive/prescriptive undecidability of "law" and on the sense of the verb *devoir*. The *coup de force* of force lies less in its claim to *epistemological* rightness, as de Man asserts, than in its claim to subsume the ethical under the epistemological. We might indeed accept that "force . . . is pure performance" (P, 22), but, as our earlier derivation of archiperformance suggests, there is no particular reason to oppose this to cognition (constatation) rather than to prescription (for example). De Man is right to suggest that the conclusion of this *Pensée* discomforts reading, but the fact that he refers to this as a "discomfort one *should* experience" (P, 22; my emphasis) shows the persistence of a prescriptive dimension that the analysis has not resolved. Pascal's text may well suggest that "the tropological field of cognition is revealed to be dependent on an entity, might, that is heterogeneous with regard to this field," but if this is something of a scandal, that scandal is ethical rather than epistemological. The discomfort provoked by that scandal does not depend on some moral judgment delivered from a position exterior to the struggle of performance and cognition, but from the elusive *involvement* of the ethical in the heterogeneity of might with respect to cognition.

This is not to suggest that de Man is wrong or even unjust, with respect to Pascal or anyone else. At this level of the machine, such judgments would simply not be pertinent, and presuppose what is at issue. But just as Pascal's machine failed to function without generating its accompanying and aberrant scenes of prescription, so de Man's readings generate ethical preoccupations that they cannot dominate: they do this not through any lack of rigor, but because of their rigor. To suggest that de Man's work is somehow reprehensibly apolitical is therefore blindly superficial, as is the idea that taking a "position" on ethical and political issues is, however necessary, somehow sufficient to come to terms with the nature of the ethical and political. De Man's apparent "neutrality" on such matters is no more and no less neutral than, for example, the question concerning technology. The unresolvable aporias revealed by de Man in terms of cognition and performance, the "aberration" he regularly produces as reading machine, signal the unavoidability of attempting to resolve ethical and political questions either cognitively or performatively, and the equally unavoidable irreducibility of such questions to the terms of truth or performativity. "Aberration" becomes a name for this type of situation, for the impossibility of constatives, performatives, prescriptives, and so on ever achieving purity or propriety, in the face of an unconditional demand that they nevertheless be separated and *respected* in their incommensurability.[20] The general milieu of this generalized aberration is what I previously called archiperformance. If the performative in the narrower sense is legitimated in terms of its performativity, the archiperformative is aberrant in its inaccessibility to any kind of legitimation. The blind performances of the archiperformance machine cannot be dominated by any language or by any notions of subjects, consciousness, life, or death that might attempt to contain them. The belatedness of language with respect to these performances not only marks a failure of cognition to be able to account for its own production,[21] but also underlies the possibility of any sort of distinction between justice, truth, beauty, performativity, and so on, while simultaneously leaving perilously and necessarily ungrounded the obligation to respect some such distinctions.

In one of the *Pensées* de Man does not discuss, we find the following: "The arithmetical machine produces effects that approach nearer to thought than anything animals do; but it does nothing that could make one say that it has will like animals" (Lafuma, 741). Let us read this as suggesting not at all some wonderful and mysterious quality of "life," and clearly not of "humanity," but rather as implying that nothing in the blind aberrant machine of archiperformance allows us the comfortable pathos of attributing any purpose or meaning to it: the machine has no will but generates what we call the will—before any specification as will to power, to truth, or to anything else, this "will" strives for and against its blind "origin" in the aberrant activity or passivity that opens the ethical. In this perspective, "reading" as much as "writing" becomes a matter of "doing justice" to this aberration, in the sense neither of speaking the truth about it nor of judging it to be good or evil, beautiful or monstrous, but of working with it, respecting it, and letting it be.

"Death is a displaced name for a linguistic predicament," wrote Paul de Man. (RR, 81). "Paul de Man," we might add, has become a displaced name for a set of machines and aberrations that are now as alive as ever. A signature, a tombstone, a text, a reading, a machine.

January 1985

Notes

1. Blaise Pascal, *Oeuvres complètes*, ed. L. Lafuma (Paris: Seuil, 1963), 187–192. The slightly less accessible edition of Brunschvicg and Boutroux (Paris: Hachette, 1908) gives some additional documentation and includes a letter from Belair to Huygens that provides fuller description of the machine itself (I:293–321).

2. See *La Condition postmoderne* (Paris: Minuit, 1979). Translated by Geoff Bennington and Brian Massumi as *The Postmodern Condition* (Minneapolis: University of Minnesota Press, 1984), esp. chapters 11 and 12.

3. See, for example, the remarks in Mme Perier's biography of Pascal, in the Brunschvicg and Boutroux edition, I:57–58.

4. As analyzed by Derrida in "La Pharmacie de Platon," in *La Dissemination* (Paris: Seuil, 1972), pp. 71–197. Translated by Barbara Johnson (Chicago: University of Chicago Press, 1982). When I wrote this essay I did not know of Derrida's "Psyché, Invention de l'autre," (in *Psyché. Inventions de l'autre* [Paris: Galilée, 1987], 11–61), which thematizes the question of invention, touches on de Man's text on Pascal, but, somewhat to my relief, does not discuss Pascal's arithmetic machine. *Ressentiment* pursues invention.

5. Bernard Sharratt, *Reading Relations: Structures of Literary Production. A Dialectical Text/Book* (Brighton: Harvester, 1982), 31.

6. Jacques Derrida, "Force et signification," in *L'Ecriture et la différence* (Paris: Seuil, 1967; reedited collection, "Points," 1979), 23. Translated by Alan Bass (Chicago: University of Chicago Press, 1978), 11.

7. Derrida, *L'Ecriture et la différence*, 335; English trans., 227 (translation modified).

8. Derrida, *L'Ecriture et la différence*, 335; English trans., 227 (translation modified).

9. A reading machine would be needed to read all the machines in Derrida's work.

10. Wlad Godzich, "Caution! Reader at Work!" introduction to BI, xv—xvi.

11. See Godzich, BI, xxvii: "De Man's rhetorical inquiry consists in recognizing the finiteness of the text and in bringing out its rhetorical machine"; and Rodolphe Gasché, " 'Setzung' and 'Übersetzung': Notes on Paul de Man," *Diacritics*, 11 (1981): 36–57, 41–42: "A rhetorical reading, then, sets out to explore the mechanics of grammar as well as of traditional rhetoric, the machinery that produces the effects of univocity and totality." Gasché further exploits the language of mechanics and machines (42, 43, 45, 51, 55).

12. Gasché's article provides a brilliant discussion of de Man's use of speech-act theory in general.

13. A full discussion of the relationship between aesthetics and the machine lies outside the scope of this essay: a starting point might be found in Lyotard's *Les Transformateurs Duchamp* (Paris: Galilée, 1977).

14. Fredric Jameson, *The Political Unconscious: Narrative as a Socially Symbolic Act* (Ithaca, N.Y.: Cornell University Press 1981); see my discussion in "Not Yet," *Diacritics*, 12 (1982): 23–32, 24.

15. Cf. Lyotard, *The Postmodern Condition*, p. 9.

16. This is the familiar charge brought by Frank Lentricchia in *After the New Criticism* (Chicago: University of Chicago Press, 1980).

17. Cf. AR, 206: "Allegories are always ethical." The present essay might be read as an attempt to understand the paragraph in which the assertion appears.

18. See my "Reading Allegory," *Oxford Literary Review*, 4 (1981): 83–93, and for a more detailed discussion, my *Sententiousness and the Novel: Laying Down the Law in Eighteenth-Century French Fiction* (Cambridge: Cambridge University Press, 1985).

19. P, 21: The printed text has "model" rather than "modal."

20. This is also the problem and the demand of Lyotard's recent work: see *Au Juste* (Paris: Christian Bourgois, 1979) and *Le Différend* (Paris: Minuit, 1984). *Au Juste* is now available as *Just Gaming*, trans. Wlad Godzich (Minneapolis: University of Minnesota Press, 1985).

21. AR, 300: "any speech act produces an excess of cognition, but it can never hope to know the process of its own production (the only thing worth knowing)."

The Deconstruction of Politics
Bill Readings

> *What importance, for example, had the power, merely formal up till now, which Klamm exercised over K.'s services, compared with the very real power which Klamm possessed in K.'s bedroom? So it came about that while a light and frivolous bearing, a certain deliberate carelessness was sufficient when one came in direct contact with the authorities, one needed in everything else the greatest caution, and had to look round on every side before one made a single step.*
> —Kafka, *The Castle*

At the Oklahoma Conference on Contemporary Genre Theory in 1984, Barbara Johnson, at the opening of a symposium with J. Hillis Miller and Louis Mackey, called for a dialogue between Marxism and deconstruction that would take the form of an interchange between the realm of "discourse" and the "realm of historical and political action":

> Deconstruction . . . has within it the creation of a feeling of imperative. . . . a feeling that if deconstruction can take you this far in the critique of power structures in discourse, then why not go further? Why not actually translate what deconstruction has done on texts into the realm of historical and political action?[1]

This then, would be the manifesto of the encounter between textual deconstruction and active politics. Its description of a possible relationship is shared both by those like Barbara Johnson who are identified as deconstructive critics, and by those like Said and Eagleton who attack deconstruction for having failed to effect such a shift from textual subversion to the subversion of power in the world of action, and who argue that deconstruction cannot perform such a shift.[2] I want to argue first of all that Said and Eagleton are correct in saying that deconstruction cannot provide a program of coherent action in a political sphere conceived as distinct from the textual sphere in which they think that deconstruction takes place, yet that, like Barbara Johnson, they are seriously in error in phrasing the question in these terms, in asking the question of deconstruction *and* politics. I shall consider what is at stake in the deconstruction *of* politics with regard to the three main charges laid against deconstruction: (1) that it preaches a pantextualism that infinitely regresses from the possibility of political action; (2) that deconstructive indeterminacy offers no criteria for political judgment; (3) that deconstruction's assault on traditional conceptions of subjectivity erases the possibility of a potent agent of political action.

Edward Said has joined Terry Eagleton in what has now become a standard attack on deconstruction as the privileging of textuality at the expense of the real world and its political imperatives, as the concentration on language to the exclusion of its referent, as the paying of attention to rhetoric so as to elide the literal, which is considered by them as the sphere of political action.[3]

Perhaps we should ask ourselves what the project of translating deconstruction into politics in the manner suggested by Johnson might resemble. Bluntly, it would not be deconstruction at all, because in the first instance, deconstruction would have to be reduced to a theory and its working to a process of *demystification*, a powerful mechanism of assault on texts, which could show the rhetorical (false) at work in phrases purporting to be literal (true), to describe the real world. Political action would thus be the insistence on pure literality, the annulment of the oppressive function of rhetoric when taken as literal. Johnson's political deconstruction would thus counter effects of power such as the metaphysical erection of property into the very ground of being itself, but in the name of an undifferentiated being, prior to any act of appropriation. In other words, deconstruction would be a souped-up version of the practice of Roland Barthes in his early work, with its distinction between denotative and connotative signifying practices, more sophisticated in that deconstruction extends the analysis to the subject as well as to the representation of which he or she is, for Barthes, the vanishing point.[4] Deconstruction according to Johnson's model would thus *preserve* the distinction and hierarchization of the literal over the rhetorical at the price of the infinite regression of the literal in the analysis of signifying practice, in its peeling away of the onion-skin layers of rhetoric. This would permit the belief in the political "application" of critical insight, and with it the grounding of critical insight as pure *knowledge*. The desire for a political *application* of deconstruction masks the desire to preserve deconstruction as a critical method *before* politics, and thus to guarantee its status as a critical method, to ground in some sense the insights that it offers as "real." Any attempt to get out of the problems of this model of deconstruction, to preserve a possibility of literal action through deconstruction by invoking the "strategic" rather than the homeomorphic as the groundless ground of agency, is redundant insofar as we continue to think strategy within the literal, as having a literal function, and hence a *literal telos*, which deconstruction must interrogate or refuse.

The attempt to lend deconstruction the status of demystification and then to seek to empower it for social change in a literal sphere of agency is futile.[5] This process becomes either nihilistic or quietistically utopian, leading either to the complete negation of the possibility of political agency in the sphere of the literal (because of the impossibility of access to the literal except in a language conceived as secondary and as always already figural),[6] or to the renunciation of any contingent agency in attendance upon the point at which capitalism (the power structure governing historical and political action in the era of deconstruction) will be forced to face its own contradictions. Capitalism will then be forced to have recourse to the literal (and thus to know itself as terror) in order to reorder a paradigm of self-representation (capitalism's "image," if you will) that has become nonfunctional because of the deconstructive explosion of its rhetorical or superstructural contradictions. Deconstruction can produce no simple model for political action, as Spivak has recognized.[7] However, neither can it produce any possibility of political agency at all, either fully instrumental or contingent (strategic), within a sphere of political action conceived as literal, as functioning literally, as in any sense finally detached from the rhetorical sphere of signifying practice. Therefore, deconstruction cannot be translated into the literal, either as model or as strategy. As I shall argue, the force of deconstruction is the extent to which it forces a rethinking of the terms of the political.

The interrogation by the Left of deconstruction in terms of its political implications seems to me to be the product of a strange refusal to extend the operation of deconstruction to the manner in which the sphere of the political is conventionally thought (to risk using the term "thought" as a misnomer). This will not have been an analysis of deconstruction *and* politics, but the deconstruction *of* politics, or rather of the opposition of politics to textuality, an opposition traditionally conceived in terms of that of action to language, of the rhetorical to the literal.

To speak of deconstruction and politics would be to submit deconstruction to the law of analogy in its most undeconstructed form, to presume that a practice reserved to an isolated sphere of textuality might be lifted across, transported into, an isolated sphere of political action, so that we might practice our politics as if we were reading "texts," and vice versa. As Barbara Johnson put it, with a disregard for all the work deconstruction has done on the status of "translation" as a metaphor, as the metaphor of metaphor (metaphor may be "translated" by *translatio*), which is surprising in so fine a critic, "Why not actually translate what deconstruction has done on texts into the realm of historical and political action?"[8]

First, the division of the textual from the political is founded in an *undeconstructed notion of textuality*, a notion that has admittedly functioned in some of the manifestations of liberal pluralism that have been named under the name of deconstruction in the United States. Second, Johnson ascribes a neutral status to that act of transportation, as if the law of analogy, of the *as if*, were not itself a metaphor, which might in turn be deconstructed.[9] This implies a vision of politics as a pure metalanguage into which all theoretical dialects could be translated. Politics would be the horizon of action in terms of which competing theories could be judged, which is to lend metaphysical status to political action.

There are three common levels to the undeconstructed opposition of the textual to the world of action. Most simply, a real world of action is counterposed to a fictional world of books. The function of criticism is to judge those books insofar as they escape fiction to present as content the described world and thus the imperatives of the world of politics. The struggle of criticism is to produce practice by demystifying and reducing the ideological function of the literary. Political action is conceived as the escape from literary ideology. Second, if the Marxist insistence on the ideological functioning of the superstructure is admitted, a division is made *within* texts between the literal sphere of political activity and their rhetorical form. Literature itself becomes a field of ideological struggle as content. The function of criticism becomes itself an element of class struggle and criticism struggles to produce a revolutionary literature, a way of writing that will most literally communicate the political imperative of practice. The literary sphere is itself conceived as an instance of the political. Third, if literary form itself is admitted to have a political function, a division is made between rhetorical forms as politically acceptable or not, conceived in terms of the functioning of rhetorical form as *literal content* in the political sphere. The work of Eagleton or Said reaches this level, at which the rhetorical or formal aspects of literature are translated into the political sphere as the literal political content of literature: thus, formal or rhetorical analysis is proper to the criticism of Brecht, for example, insofar as it can describe a literary form that is its own (political) content.

This sketchy description of the development of the political criticism of literature—from philistine opposition to the bourgeois institution of literature, through the struggle to enlist literature for political practices, to the recognition of the ideological specificity of literary form—reveals the whole project of classical "political" criticism of literature as organized through an abiding opposition between the literal or contentual (the political) and the rhetorical or formal (the textual). Even the most sophisticated form of analysis, insofar as it continues to conceive the question as that of the relation between the political *and* the textual, performs the analysis of literary form solely in terms of its becoming-literal in the sphere of the political. The textual is implicated in the political only at the expense of its relinquishing the rhetorical for the literal: even if it may adopt or employ rhetorical forms, in the final (Althusserian) analysis political discourse or political action seeks to authenticate itself by appeal to the literal, gesturing to its concern with "real people" or "real struggles."[10] The conventional description of the political is always governed by the binary split of text from world. To put it bluntly, literature is political only to the extent that the political is in some sense the *referent* of the text, a referent that is conceived literally, as something exterior to the text. Nor is this attitude confined to Marxists: they share it with conservatives who attack the humanities as having nothing to do with the real world, or with deconstructors like Barbara Johnson who request a translation of deconstructive moves into the political sphere.

In seeking to provide a deconstruction of this classical opposition of the textual to the political, of the rhetorical or formal to the literal or referential, three moves are necessary. First, we shall consider the deconstruction of the relation of the political to the textual, following the hints thrown out by Derrida in his interview "Deconstruction in America." Second, we shall perform a reading of the law of analogy, of the representationality of law as analogy, the structuration of prescriptives by analogy with descriptives. A third move will sketch how a deconstruction of the opposition of action to texts would alter the conceptual structure governing the way in which the political is thought.[11] It will suggest that politics is always textual because the literal political referent is to be found only within the text, as a rhetorical form of textuality.

Textual Politics

Consider the reaction of Derrida to Said's criticism that deconstruction represents a limitless "discursivization" of the political, to the extent that any concrete political referent, and hence any possibility of political action, is lost. In "Deconstruction in America," Derrida resists the implication that deconstruction is an "enclosure in 'the prison house of language' " by saying:

> It is incumbent on you to try to see *why* it seemed strategically useful at a given moment to say, for example, "a body is text, the table is text, the market—Wall Street, etc.—is text." Or else "nuclear arms are text." That seemed strategically useful at a given moment. And I believe that it has in fact been useful. So, it's everything but a textualization in the sense that Foucault and Said want to represent it. . . . To say for example, "deconstruction suspends reference," that deconstruction is a way of enclosing oneself in the sign, in the "signifier," is an enormous naiveté stated in that form. . . . Not only is there reference for a text, but never was it proposed that we erase effects of reference or of referents. Merely that we re-think these effects of reference. I would indeed say that the referent is textual. The referent is in the text. Yet that does

not exempt us from having to describe very rigorously the necessity of those referents.[12]

Derrida's point is that to say that everything is text is not to say that everything happens in books, merely that there is no referent that is exterior to effects of textuality.[13] Deconstruction does not assert the primacy of the signifier, does not say that there is no escape from the prison house of language to the real world, but that the "real world" is itself a textual effect, rather than something outside textuality toward which we might be able or unable to move.

The deconstruction of politics would be the consideration of the politics of this move outside the text into "politics," outside the rhetorical into the literal, a project that the work of Paul de Man mapped out in the most rigorous fashion, the more rigorous in its studious avoidance of any recuperative claims to "strategy." De Man's work articulates most fully the deconstruction of politics in its scrupulous refusal to invoke the suggestion either of subjective generalship or the literal finality of "political ends" underpinning his rhetorical politics. *Allegories of Reading* enforces a reading of the politics of reference that avoids any easy deferral of the question of politics by the invocation of strategic claims that always tend toward transcendence. To pay attention rigorously to effects of reference is to think reference within the text, which deconstruction does by undermining the distinction of literal (reference-oriented) language from referential or figural language (see esp. AR, 103–18). Literary criticism draws the conventional formula of this description from a tradition at least as old as Rousseau, by which the rhetorical trope is seen as a detour in the field of meaning that is governed by literal reference, by reference either to the gaze of a conscious subject intending objects or to the prelinguistic presence of objects themselves.[14] Therefore rhetoric is anchored to intention or to expression, to a prelinguistic content ("what is, to be said") that finds itself outside itself in the literal. The literal is conventionally that which most properly respects the properties of things, of events conceived as either mental (intentions) or physical (the being of things), that which speaks them most properly, most cleanly.[15] Figuration is a secondary or mediating function ("how it is said, what is"), a detour within language, which departs from the literal in language in order to reveal what is most proper, most literal, in the proper. The conventional literary analysis of rhetoric is thus more literal than the literal in that it allows us to apprehend the hidden properties of things in themselves prior to their transportation into the purely denotative, closed order of a literal language. Thus literary critics can read menstruation, that for which the literal code of nineteenth-century narrative realism had no word, in George Eliot's metaphorical insistence on flooding.

Rhetoric, conventionally, considered, is the means by which the literality of being or of thought, the elementary being-literal of meaning itself, is preserved against the risk of the insufficiency of literal, denotative language, be it an insufficiency of content (the literal code has no word for it, as in the case of "menstrua-tion" in the nineteenth-century novel) or of form (meaning has an organic vivacity that would be lost in the systematic functioning of the code, meaning has a latency that would be betrayed by pure denotation, etc., etc.). Thus the literal governs the figural in that, even if language may be rhetorical, may turn away from the literal, meaning itself, prior to language, must always be literal. Prelinguistic meaning is governed, even before it comes to language, by a linguistic metaphor of literality. The referent's standing outside language, and the concomitant possi-bility of a purely literal use of language, is only guaranteed by a *linguistic figure*. The nonlinguistic meaning, the sense to which language refers, can only be in-itself before language as *prepared for literal speech*.

The referent is in the text in the sense that reference is a figural necessity of the fiction that language is the vehicle of a communication or an expression, a vehicle that can *transport*, can move outside itself to the properties of things (whether present to subjective consciousness in communication or present as ob-jects in expression), can function *literally*. The name of the figure of the referent is the literal, and this figure is the trope of a language that can erase its own metaphoricity. Yet the referent is in the text in an even stronger sense, in that this sublime dream, this transport (metaphor), which is at the same time the carrying off of language itself, is itself, as a transportation, a metaphor, a formal and "secondary" operation of language. The literal, in its most rigorous sense, is a metaphor, and in that branch of Western philosophy named positivism, it has be-come the metaphor of metaphors. The literal is thus a trope among tropes, which is not to erase literality but to insist that the literal be rhetorically rather than liter-ally described: that is, that the literal cannot ground itself outside rhetoric, in a referential real abstracted from the figural. Furthermore, the distinction between the figural and the literal must be read as a tropaic distinction in an order of rheto-ric, rather than as a literal one in an order of meaning. At this point we must signal a point of differentiation from the de Manian project, in *Allegories of Reading*, of reading the distinction of the figural from the literal, or the "grammatical" from the "rhetorical." De Man's failure lies in the fact that he continues to distinguish the literal from the rhetorical on grounds of a difference in semantic meaning (content) rather than trope (form): as he puts it, "Our recurrent question is whether this transformation is semantically controlled along grammatical or along rhetorical lines" (AR, 13). Even within a reading that refuses to subordinate the figural potentiality of language to grammatical literality, which questions "the reduction of figure to grammar" (AR, 7), the distinction between tropes (catachre-sis, literality) is illegitimately fixed as a *semantic* one, as a difference of content, rather than of form, if you like. That is, it is not enough simply to refuse to say which came first, the chicken or the coward, to refuse to apportion priority to ei-ther the literal meaning or the rhetorical swerve; one must, furthermore, refuse to think the rhetorical solely as a swerve away from literal meaning. The question of the separation of the rhetorical from the literal illustrates the point that it is not simply the hierarchization of literal and rhetorical but the descriptive order of the distinction between them that must be challenged: we must investigate what the politics of a literal distinction of figural from literal might be. The distinction of figural from literal must not be read as a difference *in the order of literal meaning*.

The referent is in the text in the same way as we have seen that the literal is a trope within rhetoric, rhetoric's trope of the absence of rhetoric. The referent is the text's fiction of the absence of text, the text's fiction of its own outside. This fiction of an outside is, of course, produced from the inside of the text. There is no pure exteriority, no referent outside the text. Nor, however, is there a pure interiority: the referent is not just a verbal fiction, it is not simply the case that everything happens in books, because the fiction of the real is a *necessary* or determining one. The fiction of the outside is a structural necessity of the inside. Deconstruction of the text/referent opposition does not replace the conventional primacy of the real over the text with a new primacy of the text over the real, or of signifier over signified, but reveals their interdependence and mutual contamination.

The possibility of a translation from deconstructive textuality *to* politics, from the figural to the literal, from the textual to the real, is founded upon this misrecognition of the figural status of the literal, and the correlative positing of an empirical real outside the text. The condition of the operation of power in Western society (the condition by which domination effects are invisible in the representation of democratic participation) is to think politics as empirical, as that which is self-evident, which makes its place as it takes it. That is, domination works by denying its politics, by establishing its particular politics as an empirical or prepolitical real, so that domination is invisible in that it takes place before what is named as the political. The operation of domination is in defining the political, so that power appears to operate in a political vacuum (that is, in no place, nowhere), a vacuum guaranteed by the notion of representation as transparency. Thus, what is at stake in the deconstruction of the opposition of the textual to the political, in the refiguration of the literal, is precisely politics itself, the terror of the real that governs the government and the argument (so that argument is limited to government) of Western politics in democracy or in its most extended form in totalitarianism, a terror that operates by grounding its prescriptive judgments as the descriptions of an empirical reality outside signifying practice.

The Rule of the Undetermined

Having seen how deconstruction undermines the binary opposition of text to referent, inside to outside, rhetorical to literal, in terms of which it is accused of pantextualism or nonengagement, I want to develop this argument by sketching a politics, a rhetoric, that would rigorously interrogate the opposition of real, literal, political content to the formal or rhetorical textual sphere.[16] To do so is also to confront the accusation that the deconstructive destabilization of the real leaves no grounds for political judgment. It is often argued that once rhetoric is no longer the determinate production of the literality of being, and the political is given up to the indeterminate play of a rhetoric within which the literal is a trope, the result must be vacuous relativism, a pluralism without criteria for discrimination between justice and injustice. Deconstruction undermines the possibility of determinant literal criteria, a literally representable law, but proposes a justice without criteria and proposes that justice (the possibility of responsible judgment as opposed to operation) in fact relies upon the absence of criteria. This judgment is not an undifferentiated pluralism, but is based in the most rigorous respect for difference.[17] Neither is it a reinscription of individualism, as will be shown.

The "real" is the accomplished ground of injustice in that it is always the assertion of the possibility of a nonmetaphorical voice, a pure literality. To appeal to the "real" is always to lend a voice to the state of things — what we do when we appeal to a "political reality" is to *personify* literality, to invoke a possibility of a purely literal voice that would provide the criteria of justice, in that it would speak a nature. Thus a literal voice would provide both the form and the content of justice: as mimetic adequation to a nature that would be just because it would be just nature (no rhetoric).[18] In rigorously thinking the metaphor of literality, deconstruction produces a justice *without* criteria.[19]

Injustice is an order of language, the possibility of purely literal voice, which is not, as I hope has become apparent, the same thing as saying that injustice is *only* in language, that it does not work. It is no longer only in language because language is no longer opposed to the real. The real is an order of language, which is unjust. It is an unjust order of language in that it claims to be not an order of language but the criterion of (mimetic) justice for all orders of language.

The possibility of relativism is elided in that this is a nonreversible proposition: there is an asymmetry that enforces a political resistance. To perform an operative justice in the realm of the real, a just literality, a mimetic justice, would be itself an injustice, a repose upon a language that claimed not to be a language. Injustice must inhabit the realm of the real, for a purely rhetorical injustice, in these terms, would not need to be brought to judgment, since it would make no claims about the real that is the tribunal of mimetic justice. The real is language's unjust fiction of an escape from rhetoric, from the linguistic, to the literal as the personified voice of the prelinguistic real itself. In an argument that identifies injustice as the invocation of the real, the reality of injustice is of course exactly what is to be combated, as I am sure my opponents would agree: the first step is to combat the injustice of reality.

The beginnings of an analysis of the injustice of reality seem to me to lie in the recent work of J.-F. Lyotard. Always proceeding with the reserve that one cannot hope to do justice to the complexity of his argument, Lyotard has sought to identify the problem of injustice in terms of the conflation of prescriptives with descriptives. That is, terror consists in seeking to establish the justice of an ethical judgment (prescriptive statement) by reference to a representable order of things (a descriptive statement). Lyotard stresses the impossibility of passage from the true to the just, the incommensurability of descriptive and prescriptive language games.

Any politics that seeks to unite the two seeks to establish a representable law, a determinant use of the Idea of justice, and thus leads to totalitarianism, the conception of society as totality that annihilates resistance as, by nature, unjust. This conception is founded in the conflation of description and prescription, "the deep conviction that there is a true being of society and that society will be just if it is brought into conformity with this true being."[20]

After Lyotard, then, we can identify the problem of the terror of the real as lying in the erection of the notion of a justice that might be justified, the confusion of prescriptive justice with descriptive *justification*.[21] That is, we must perform the difficult feat of thinking about justice without recourse to notions of mimetic adequation. To believe that there might be a representable reality of justice is to light the way to terror. The voice of pure literality, which might speak the law as such, always performs the operation of terror, in that to assert the law as literally representable is to silence its victims by relegating the operation of resistance to the condition of transgression. The binary functioning of the law through obedience and transgression has a double terror: it both silences resistance (turns the injured party into a victim) and confines resistance within itself.

The representable law, the literal *voice* of reality as prescriptive, silences resistance by victimization: those who lie outside the law (since the law is the justice of nonmetaphorical reality) are unreal, and cannot speak. If description is conflated with prescription, if justice can be justified, then those upon whom the law operates are not oppressed, they simply do not exist.

This is the weight of Lyotard's analysis of Faurisson's critique of the historical reality of the sufferings of victims of Nazi gas chambers in *Le Différend*. There he defines injustice as an "injury accompanied by the loss of means to prove the injury."[22]

The Holocaust is undescribable, in that to experience it is to be annihilated, to have "seen" a gas chamber work is to be deprived of the capacity to speak of it. This is a strong example of the injustice of reality as literally representable, of the insistence that justice can be justified, that law can become the referent of a literal discourse of description. Resistance becomes transgression of the real, the victim is silenced. Nor is the Holocaust simply a limit case. We might argue that the commodification of experience is the functioning of capitalist hegemony. It proceeds by the law of the market, which insists that everything is representable by money. In view of this, market research becomes important as one of the discourses by which knowledge can be gained about what it is to be under capitalism, a discourse of knowledge that is largely organized through the manipulation of statistics. A particular product will thus be advertised, a particular activity exhorted: in short, a prescription about life experience will be formulated, on the basis of a statistical description. "Eighty percent of all those interviewed in a representative sample" agreed that smoking is bad for you, or that Marlboros are the best cigarettes. The fear that animates the addressee of these prescriptions is deeper than that of nonconformity. In terms of the total representability of experience in the marketplace, the penalty for not heeding these prescriptions is nonexistence. The use of statistical description in formulating prescriptives works not solely to make it statistically improbable that one will not smoke a certain brand of cigarettes, but more deeply so as to make it statistically *probable* that anyone who does not make the prescribed "choice" *does not exist*. This is not to say that the penalty for not smoking a certain brand is death, but that the representation of existence under capitalism is structured by a binary opposition of inclusion/exclusion, which denies existence to the transgressor. A simple example of what is at stake in a law that conflates prescription and description would be the phrase "Nobody stays in Paris in August." To oppose the injustice of that statement by a quibble over terms in the presumption that a consensus might be reached about a literal sense of what it is to be "somebody" would be to miss the point: any description of what is to be "somebody" that could be the basis of prescriptions about life, the ground of a representable law, would always exclude somebody, though of course it would claim only to exclude nobody, to exclude only nobodies, only women, only blacks, only lunatics, etc., etc. Resistance is silenced.

The law would have to exclude somebody in that the representable law is terror in the sense that it establishes its rule over its victims, those who lie outside it, by establishing its victims of as the marks of its own beyond: "of course we are rational men, we are not women/apes/lunatics." In refusing the possibility of consensus, one is refusing mere pluralism, which is always mortgaged to a describable totality less relative than the preceding one. To recognize the nonrepresentability of law is to refuse undifferentiated relativism, which is the insistence upon the plural representability of law, a multiplicity of justices, in favor of a justice of multiplicity.[23] It is not to say that we cannot choose, but that we must choose, prudently, with the indeterminate law of indeterminacy as our only law. The question remains: who does the choosing? Who speaks? At this point my analysis might begin to look like a reinscription of classical subjectivity: prudent individuals making strategic choices within a sphere of political agency that has become an indeterminate series of rhetorical moves, subject to rhetorical analysis . . .

The Subject of Deconstruction

Politics itself is at stake in the deconstruction of politics in the sense that the work of deconstruction will refuse the conventional description of politics as the relation of a subject to a society (be that subject an individual, a class, or whatever).[24] At this conjuncture, the most useful way to think this shift is by replacing the traditional subject of politics with the subject of a tradition of ethical thought, that is, to think politics ethically, as it were. The tradition of ethical thought offers a displacement of the subject/object distinction that may produce a subject under deconstruction. The completion of this argument must rest in a redescription of agency in terms of a deconstruction of the subject/object distinction, a move that may handily be conceived as the thinking of *political* agency with an *ethical* subject.

The subject of ethics is the subject who judges without criteria, who practices a justice that cannot be justified. The just person cannot be described justly, since to describe his or her prescriptive function would be to fall in with the injustice of reality. This is no less true of a theoretical analysis than an attempt at empirical mimesis.[25] The ethical subject is displaced in the sense that choices are not made from a position of transcendent subjectivity that *precedes* or stands outside the judgments it makes.[26] Judgments, in that they are made without criteria, presuppose their own judgment. The justice of a judgment can only be judged, again, without criteria. Thus the just person, the judge, does not make judgments, but is made *by* them, is continually judged by and in terms of the judgments that the judge makes. Since those judgments are also made without criteria, the process is continual; the judge can never be finally judged as just (and therefore justified, described as just), since the process of judging can never reach the point where a final account can be given of it.

The redescription of political agency with a subject under deconstruction is not a simple process. The most obdurate attack on deconstruction from the position of political subjectivity has been advanced by Eagleton. In *Walter Benjamin or Towards a Revolutionary Criticism*, Eagleton claims that since deconstruction does not respect the political subject, it erases the possibility of political agency.[27] To speak of an ethics without a subject, however, is to run the risk of a misunderstanding. Rather we should address the question of an ethics with a subject under deconstruction. Perhaps the strongest recuperation of deconstruction for metaphysics has been the assertion that deconstruction *erases* the subject, rather than deconstructing it. As Derrida reminds his interviewers, "As you recall, I have never said that *there is not* a 'subject of writing.' . . . It is solely necessary to reconsider the problem of the effect of subjectivity such as it is produced by the structure of the text."[28]

To erase the subject is to think its place as an absence, while to subject it to deconstructive work is to displace the subject into indeterminacy, which does not deny the possibility of agency but merely disrupts its status in ways that precisely allow the possibility of a political resistance that might escape confinement to the field of a political real, which is always already defined by the State as the state (of things).

When Derrida seeks to deconstruct the binary opposition of the representation to the original, he does so by introducing a third term, the trace.[29] The third term or deconstructing trope ensures that his argument does not fall back into the hierarchical binary order of metaphysics by simply privileging representation over original, in place of the conventional priority of the original. The trace inhabits both representation and original, while being exhausted by neither. Nor, importantly (and the strategic significance of this point is often missed), is the third term equally balanced between the two: if it were it might fall easily into being a Hegelian synthesis, a sublation of the opposition as a higher unity, which would serve to *confirm* the binary opposition. Thus, in the case of the trace, the third term leans toward representation, as it were. In deconstructing the opposition of subject and object that governs conventional analyses of political agency, we require a third term that would be neither subject (inside) nor object (outside). The production of that third term is merely a heuristic device for untying the subject, and thinking the other at the heart of subjectivity, thinking the real as always already offered to the perception of a subject.

The recent history of deconstruction has not escaped a binary mode of representation, showing that the strategic choice of whether the third term should lean toward subject or object, toward inside or outside, is the grounds of an important tactical differentiation, which can roughly be characterized as the distinction between a rabbinical deconstructionist school (often named under the name of Geoffrey Hartman) or a more politically radicalized movement (often named as French deconstruction). If the third term chosen tends toward pure interiority, then a description is produced that places alienation as the ground and not the disruption of subjectivity, as the founding instance of subjectivity and not something that befalls the subject. This school of deconstruction has tended to lean toward negative theology, to the recognition of Judaism as providing a similar description of subjectivity. If that third term leans toward pure exteriority, toward a conception of the phenomenal as pure surface, in the metaphorics of the Möbius strip, then an alternative strategic emphasis comes into play. If deconstruction produces a trope as third term that leans toward interiority, then we will produce a deconstruction that is the *enfolding* of an alienated subjectivity, whereas a term that leans toward exteriority, a term such as I will propose, will lend its strategic weight to a notion of *unfolding*. This can be characterized as a choice between a deconstruction of *mysticism* and a deconstruction of demystification.

A de Manian and deconstructive consideration of this binary opposition between rabbinical mysticism and claims for demystification (such as those advanced by Spivak in her early article "Revolutions That As Yet Have No Model") leads to a new understanding of the ethical. For reasons given earlier, deconstruction is at odds with grand claims of demystification that reinscribe the knowing subject as implicitly as mystification does. This is not to say that the answer lies "in the middle," between mysticism and demystification; it is to insist on the *indeterminate* possibility for the trope produced by deconstruction between a term that leans toward pure interiority or pure exteriority. The choice of a third term is not the arbitrary act of will on the part of a writing or reading subject in that the work of deconstruction upon the binary oppositions underlying a text produces a third term that is situated in certain ways according to concatenations of substitutions determined by the text. The choice and politics of deconstruction come at this point, where deconstruction subjects its own tropes to deconstruction, producing a choice between a deconstruction that looks like mysticism or a deconstruction that looks like demystification, for deconstruction (at the risk of an oxymoron) precisely blurs the opposition of demystification and mysticism. The de Manian imperative of choice has the advantage of casting the play of deconstruction as, first, free of the risk of self-determination (priesthood) that must still inhabit the metaphorics of negative theology and, second, as implying a public availability of deconstruction that is not still mortgaged to classical conceptions of the societal (demystification). In deconstructive thinking about political agency, a third term between subject and object, between inside and outside, between agent and world, is necessary, and that term is necessarily asymmetrical in order to avoid a synthesis that might confirm the opposition being deconstructed. The decision as to this third term is necessary, yet it is also free in that it can have no *determining* relation over the opposition it deconstructs (if it did, it would reproduce the hierarchical order of metaphysical binary oppositions by privileging either pure interiority or pure exteriority). It is therefore an *ethical* decision in that we are forced to make a choice without criteria. which makes us as subjects of (subject to) that choice — a choice that is made for and by a subject under deconstruction — this choice is thus an agency, but not a pure determinant agency of a subject upon an object. It is further an ethical choice in that it is made without criteria, so that full responsibility must be taken for it. There is an apocryphal story told of de Man, that when asked what his "blind spot" was, after his statement that every discourse had an enabling "blind spot," he replied that he had none. To have claimed to know his blind spot, or even to have claimed to be aware of the possibility of such a blind spot, would always have been in some sense to have recuperated a *descriptive* subjectivity for himself, and therefore to have grounded his own discourse unethically, in describable criteria, rather than in the ethical destabilization of the subject beyond factual description (the judging subject can only be known to be just in terms of the judgment of his or her judgments, rather than by the possession of any determining describable features). I must therefore insist upon the choice of a third term that leans toward pure exteriority as *ungrounded*. To make that choice on the side of exteriority (in the sense that

Derrida's "trace" leans to the side of representation) is to identify a resistance that is *public*, a subject under deconstruction that is an enclave or fault within the surface of the public, a wound that punctures the public sphere without detaching itself from it or forming itself into its own interiority.

As an example of this, I wish to cite Barthes's last work, *Camera Lucida*, where he produces a subject under deconstruction in the viewing of photographs. To the conventional discourse of the photograph as an object of scholarly or social knowledge, of the *studium*, he counterposes what may appear a peculiarly subjective theory of the viewing of photographs. Barthes selects a number of photographs for study on the grounds of personal taste, and discusses them in terms of what he names their *punctum*, the detail that traverses, lashes, or stripes the "docile interests" of the *studium* so as to attract or distress the spectator. This individuality is not, however, a subjective hedonism, in that the force of the *punctum* is constituted through the *sacrifice* of subjectivity. The detail expands in the photograph as a wound, both in the surface of the photograph and in the docile gaze of the studious viewer. It thus disrupts conventional subject/object relations, and thus far (as the dedication of the work to Sartre suggests) might seem like phenomenology. But *Camera Lucida* moves beyond phenomenological accounts of perception in the recognition that the phenomenological dream of a universal subject cannot accommodate the privacy of desire and mourning: "Classical phenomenology, the kind I had known in my adolescence (and there has never been any other since), had never, so far as I could remember, spoken of desire or of mourning." The photograph is bound up with death in that the photographed person is viewed as if dead, and thus marks the death of the viewer: "each photograph contains the imperious sign of my future death." The *punctum* is the operation that marks this equivalence (it is not death as such), rendering the photograph as an excess over subjectivity or objectivity, engendering their loss. The catastrophic writing of photographs is thus read through a play of the public and the private rather than of subject and object: "I must, by a necessary resistance, reconstitute the division of *public* and *private*: I want to utter interiority without yielding intimacy." The interior is uttered, spoken out, becomes exterior, is no longer the detached site of knowledge itself, and the site of speaking is not the subjective but the intimate, the private. This is the intimacy of death, the freedom of suicide attached to a public image, not to a subjective will, the "site where my image is free (free to abolish itself)."[30] The private is different from subjectivity in that it is not folded in or back upon itself to produce a pure interior space *from* which the public is known as object. Rather, the public and the private are contiguously extended on the surface of the photograph, the private has no more depth than the public, is mere detail, is distinguished as *punctum*, a wound that does not penetrate to a depth beyond or behind the materiality of surface.

This is not the reinscription of classical subjectivity, it is not the return to bourgeois individualism that it might seem. The phenomenality of the photograph is experienced as a pure exteriority, but an exteriority that is always wounded or implicated with a subjectivity that the phenomenality of the photograph cannot exhaust (this is not phenomenology). Yet this privacy is not a classical subjectivity, in that the private is an enclave *within* the surface, which wounds the purity of the surface, yet *without* folding back upon itself to assume the depth of an interiority distinct from the surface, from which the outside could be viewed, perceived, or known.

The asymmetry of the third term has a resistance implicit in it, and to place that resistance in these terms is to produce a politics as deconstruction. This is neither a politics practiced by a political subject (a subject as agent upon a society or within a society enacted through his or her assent) nor a politics that would be the motor of a society constructing subjects as fictions (this would be totalitarianism, in which society produces the fiction of classes, but one class or *Volk* is the meaning of politics when it constitutes itself as the totality of society), but rather a politics practiced by an ethical subject or a subject under deconstruction.

The force of the activity of deconstruction lies not in the construction of new models of political activity but in a rigor that permits an interrogation of the structuring of the political as modular. The argument will continue, in books, on picket lines, in meetings, in bars, but the grounds of argument will not always already have been ceded. The real will not be the ground of judgment; we will not seek to defend our prescriptives by appealing to a descriptive function that is purely denotative. The real will no longer be a given by the standards of which all attempts to think outside the status quo will be silenced, forced to transgress the real, even as they seek to enter the argument. Instead of a description of political agency that must reproduce the law of Lampedusa's *The Leopard*, (namely, that "everything must change so that everything can stay the same," the proposition that is at the heart of capitalism), everything will be the same, but different. That is, by respecting (in the Kantian sense) forms of difference, a rhetoric of political argumentation will be produced that resists victimization, which will not be always already silenced before the law, a rhetoric of the unrepresentable that is not subjected to the authority of the literal voice.

Deconstruction breaches conventional descriptions of the political to produce a fully rigorous politics, which it does by thinking the politics of sociopolitical description which are conventionally considered as "politics" (the use of quotation marks will differentiate the undeconstructed notion of politics from the politics of deconstruction). The politics of deconstruction lies in the attempt to escape from the limitation of political argument to a literal sphere of sociality. A "politics" founded in an appeal to literality, to a real, always has as its full form an apolitical literality of being. This is the case in all totalizing thought about the political, whether repressive (Nazi) or libertarian (capitalist). In this sense, I would argue that American pluralism is as totalitarian as Stalinism, in that both seek to elide the possibility of differing (politics, in the sense in which I wish to use it) from the state, either by inclusion within, or exclusion from, a real that is the totality of the state determined as the literal ground of political existence. There is thus no politics in the totalitarian state, not because politics is repressed, but because the political *is* the polis, because the state becomes, or is defined as tending to become (on any side of a "political" argument), the realized referent of the political. *"Politics" is everything*, and hence *politics appears nowhere* (the polis cannot be resisted). The referent of "politics" has been, or will be, fulfilled as polis. This is the unified ground of all political thought, however much it may appear to differ, which is organized through an opposition of the rhetorical to the literal. The work of deconstruction is to think the function of reference itself as a rhetorical strategy, as itself political, a matter of difference of opinion. This releases politics from the law of representability by which it has heretofore been governed, limited to "politics," to produce a politics that *is nothing* and that is *apparent everywhere*.

Political argument can perhaps begin here, political argument that allows a clash of radically discontinuous structurations of law, a political argument that would respect multiplicity without becoming vapid pluralism, that would permit, in the fullest sense, the possibility of a difference of opinion while retaining the necessity of discrimination. Discrimination is precisely the necessity of political judgment rather than a falling back upon criteria that cannot themselves be thought as political because they are grounded as real. Deconstruction begins by insisting that strategic choices be made about differences of opinion on properly political grounds, that is, on grounds attentive to the politics by which, for example, the literal is detached from metaphoricity. Herein lies what now seems the only chance for a rhetorical politics that *works*, rather than a political rhetoric doomed only to speak (of) a reality that it must represent as finally alien to its rhetoric and politics and hence inviolable by them.

This is a large claim for the political, but it can only be made in such a way as to refuse totalitarianism (the totalization of the political as real) by a *withdrawal* of the political, a withdrawal I have characterized as the shift from politics as practiced by the social subject to politics as practiced by the deconstructed or the ethical subject.[31]

Notes

1. Barbara Johnson, symposium transcript in Robert C. Davis and Ronald Schliefer (eds.), *Rhetoric and Form: Deconstruction at Yale* (Norman: University of Oklahoma Press, 1985), 78.

2. Said attacks deconstruction because its "oppositional manner . . . does not accurately represent its ideas and practice, which, after all is said and done, further solidify and guarantee the social structure and the culture that produced them" (Edward Said, *The World, The Text, and The Critic* [Cambridge, Mass.: Harvard University Press, 1984], 159). His reflex use of the idiom "when all is said and done" betrays the desire of his argument for an escape from language into a pure realm of understanding, a detextualized sphere of knowledge the impossibility of which it is the purpose of this essay to mark. Eagleton characterizes deconstruction as a subversive textual practice that, for

reasons he does not analyze, functions "in ways that objectively legitimate bourgeois hegemony" (Terry Eagleton, *Walter Benjamin or Towards a Revolutionary Criticism* [London: Verso, 1981] 140). The strict division of theory from practice in this model of argument is a little strange in one concerned to defend a version of Marxism in the face of Stalinist manifestations.

3. Said (*World, Text, and Critic*, 292) attacks Derrida for an undifferentiated pantextualism, an argument that is concisely summarized in his conclusion, "Folding back upon itself, criticism has therefore refused to see its affiliations with the political world it serves, perhaps unwittingly, perhaps not."

4. See Roland Barthes, *Mythologies*, ed. and trans. Annette Lavers (London: Granada, 1973).

5. The only demystification that deconstruction can perform is the demystification of the literal as itself a figure among figures, which is to demystify the notion of demystification as a returning of things to their literal being.

6. This position is otherwise known as unreconstructed Lacanianism.

7. See Gayatri Spivak, "Revolutions That As Yet Have No Model," *Diacritics*, 10 (1980): 29–49.

8. Barbara Johnson in Davis and Schliefer (eds.), *Rhetoric and Form*, 78. In Johnson's defense, one should adduce the point made in "Apostrophe, Animation, and Abortion" (in Barbara Johnson, *A World of Difference* [Baltimore: Johns Hopkins University Press, 1987], 184–99) that "the undecidable *is* the political. There is politics because there is undecidability." Owing to the lack of theoretical elaboration in that essay, this interesting formulation unfortunately ends up sounding uncomfortably like a proverbial observation on the fact that some people will never agree, when much more could be made of it.

9. As Jean-Luc Nancy has pointed out, the *as if* is merely an inverted form of ontological realism. See Jean-Luc Nancy, "Dies Irae," in Jean-François Lyotard (ed.), *La Faculté de Juger* (Paris: Minuit, 1985), 14.

10. "The liberal humanists are right to see that there is a *point* in studying literature, and that this point is not itself, in the end, a literary one" (Terry Eagleton, *Literary Theory: An Introduction* [Minneapolis: University of Minnesota Press, 1983], 208). The point is, of course, a political one, a political point conceived as lying, in the last analysis, firmly outside the sphere of the textual or literary.

11. The nature of the preceding two moves in the strategy will, of course, render it impossible that this resemble a program of political action, conventionally considered.

12. Jacques Derrida, "Deconstruction in America" (interview with James Creech, Peggy Kamuf, and Jane Todd), in *Critical Exchange*, no. 17 (1985): 15–19.

13. As he has recently pointed out, "*Text*, as I use the word, is not the book . . . It is precisely for strategic reasons . . . that I found it necessary to recast the concept of text by generalizing it almost without limit, in any case without present or perceptible limit, without any limit that *is*" ("But, beyond . . . ," *Critical Inquiry*, 13 (1986): 167).

14. J.-J. Rousseau, "Essay on the Origin of Languages," in J.-J. Rousseau and J. G. Herder, *On the Origin of Language*, ed. and trans. J. H. Moran and A. Gode (Chicago: University of Chicago Press, 1986). Rousseau posits that figural language preceded literal language in its chronological development, but asserts that the literal is the true or proper form of language, the condition of meaning itself: "Figurative language was the first to be born. Proper meaning was discovered last" (12).

15. The literal is the *sens propre*, the clean or proper sense, that which presents the property of the referent cleanly.

16. The heading for this section is taken from the citation from Aristotle's *Nichomachean Ethics*, which stands as epigraph to J.-F. Lyotard and J.-L. Thébaud, *Just Gaming*, and marks the extent to which the argument here advanced depends on Lyotard's work. Lyotard and Thébaud, *Just Gaming*, trans. Wlad Godzich with afterword by S. Weber, trans. B. Massumi, Theory and History of Literature, vol. 20 (Minneapolis: University of Minnesota Press, 1985).

17. This is a respect for differences among things, not relativism's respect for things, which ultimately erases difference by making all things worthy of respect.

18. The necessity of deconstruction, the indeterminate rule of indeterminacy, consists precisely in the refusal to allow law to assume the status of a (literally representable) nature. The deconstruction of politics becomes the politics of deconstruction at the point where it undermines the authority of law as founded in its capacity to speak literally, refuses to personify the law as the voice of the nature of justice. In the words of Derrida, "Whatever the necessity of this question of the relationship between law and traces (or the *renvois* of traces, the *renvois* as traces), it exhausts itself perhaps when we cease representing law to ourselves, apprehending law itself under the species of the representable . . . perhaps the law itself manages to do no more than transgress the figure of all possible representation. Which is difficult to conceive, as it is difficult to conceive anything at all beyond representation, but commits us perhaps to thinking altogether differently." See Jacques Derrida, "Sending: On Representation," *Social Research*, 49 (1982): 325–26.

19. "The thinker I am closest to in this regard is Aristotle, insofar as he recognizes . . . that a judge worthy of the name has no true model to guide his judgments and that the true nature of the judge is to pronounce judgments, and therefore prescriptions just so, without criteria. This is, after all, what Aristotle calls prudence. It consists in judging without models" (Lyotard and Thébaud, *Just Gaming*, 25–26). The implication here is that politics as the search for social justice draws its rule of indeterminacy from ethics, something to which I shall turn my attention in the next section of this essay.

20. Lyotard and Thébaud, *Just Gaming*, 23.

21. To justify this page would be, after all, to line it up on the righthand side.

22. For the convenience of readers, I shall confine my remarks to translated extracts published in J.-F. Lyotard, "The Différend, the Referent, and the Proper Name," trans. G. Van Den Abbeele, in *Diacritics* 14 (1984): 5.

23. Lyotard and Thébaud, *Just Gaming*, 95–96.

24. The subject of deconstruction is, of course, the deconstruction of the subject.

25. As Geoff Bennington has phrased it, "Where description tries to move into and dominate the specific properties of the game of prescription, then there is injustice at best and terror at worst. One exemplary indication of this . . . is that Lyotard is not trying to write a new theory of justice, and that the author of *A Theory of Justice* is being unjust to justice on his title page" ("August: Double Justice" in *Diacritics*, 14 (1984): 66).

26. "He who states the just is himself as caught in the very sphere of language as those who will be the recipients of his prescriptions, and may eventually be judged by the judge. The judge is in the same sphere of language, which means that he will be considered just only by his actions, if it can be seen that he judges well, that . . . his actions are just. And his actions can be judged to be just only when one adds up all the accounts. But in matters of opinion there is no adding up of accounts, no balance sheet" (Lyotard and Thébaud, *Just Gaming*, 28).

27. "The nonsense of 'I killed myself is the nonsense of deconstruction . . . Deconstructionism, then, can salvage some of the dominant themes of traditional bourgeois liberalism by a desperate, last-ditch strategy: by sacrificing the subject itself, at least in any of its customary modes . . . a dispersal of the subject so radical as to render it impotent as any kind of agent at all, least of all a revolutionary one . . . it thus provides you with all the risks of a radical politics while cancelling the subject who might be summoned to become the agent of them" (Terry Eagleton, *Walter Benjamin*, 137–39). These brief quotations provide an example of the sloppy thinking that underlies Eagleton's attack on deconstruction. He proposes a distinction between French deconstruction and its North American formation, the one laudably engaged, the latter merely the ill-concealed desire of bourgeois liberalism for its own annihilation. Yet, having nowhere provided the grounds of an analysis of *why* Derrida's work is different, he uses the Yale critics' work as a stick with which to beat Derrida, who is targeted by the *ad hominem* epigraph to chapter 4 of section 2. In the quotations cited, we can see the lack of

rigor that considers a logically self-contradictory statement as self-cancelling, displaying an astounding inattention to the materiality of language in a proclaimed Marxist. The difference between silence and saying "I have killed myself" is precisely a mark of the extent to which the deconstruction of the subject/object opposition, of the classical description of agency, is not the erasure or cancellation of the subject but its displacement.

28. Jacques Derrida, *Positions*, trans. Alan Bass (Chicago: University of Chicago Press, 1981), p. 88. The attack on deconstruction as politically impotent because of its erasure of the subject has been most grindingly summarized by Barbara Foley in an essay entitled "The Politics of Deconstruction." Foley does at least make a serious attempt to suggest that her criticisms of North American deconstruction are not the product of a chance process of misappropriation, and devotes much of her argument to an attempt to find a link between Derrida's work and its American manifestations. Founding her argument in the claim that deconstruction erases the subject, she asserts that deconstruction cannot be a viable political praxis because its refusal to transcend binary oppositions is a neutralist refetishization of the metaphysical pain of operations. There is, according to Foley, no dialectical third term to deconstructive analysis, no "historically specific class-subject" to overcome the binary opposition. Deconstruction is trapped, she asserts, by its denial of either a knowing subject or the dialectical transcendence of a "reason of history," by its refusal of an epistemological breakthrough to a pure exteriority of positive mastery. It is thus caught within a static or immovable epistemological condition of binary oppositions, leading to a politics that is "little more than a rewarmed liberal pluralism." Foley's basic error is to read deconstruction's refusal to equate epistemology with ontology (meaning that there is no longer any epistemological condition as such) as synonymous with the erasure of the subject, just as she reads deconstruction's refusal dialectically to transcend the binary oppositions it identifies as necessarily confirming those oppositions (Barbara Foley, "The Politics of Deconstruction," in Robert C. Davis and Ronald Schliefer [eds.], *Rhetoric and Form: Deconstruction at Yale* [Norman: University of Oklahoma Press, 1985], pp. 119–21, 126–29).

29. The trace is merely one term among others, and it is necessary to note that third term does not itself have the operative function of a stable key in its destabilization of binary oppositions. As Derrida has noted, "The word 'deconstruction,' like any other word, draws its value only from its inscription in a chain of possible substitutions, from what is too easily called 'context.' As far as I am concerned, insofar as I have attempted and still attempt to write, it is interesting only in a certain context in which it substitutes, and lets itself be determined by, many other words, for example *écriture*, *trace*, *différance*, *supplément*, *hymen*, *pharmakon*, *marge*, *entame*, *parergon*, etc. By definition, the list cannot be closed, and I have merely enunciated the names, which is economical but is not sufficient. In fact, it would be necessary to cite phrases and concatenations of phrases which in their turn determine those names in my texts" (J. Derrida, "Pacific Deconstruction, 2. Letter to a Japanese Friend," *Rivista di Estetica*, 17 [1984]: 9; my translation). In this sense, we must think of the third term outside closure, beyond lexical de*term*ination, not as a literal essence or analytic tool, but as a trope, which changes from deconstructive work to deconstructive work, a migratory term that exceeds the binary opposition under deconstruction without ever fulfilling (confirming) it.

30. Roland Barthes, *Camera Lucida*, trans. Richard Howard (London: Fontana, 1984), 40, 21, 97, 98, 8.

31. Nancy Fraser, in "The French Derrideans: Politicizing Deconstruction or Deconstructing the Political?" (*New German Critique*, no. 33 [1984]: 127–54), has acknowledged the extent to which the drive to "deconstruct the political" supervenes over the demand for a "politics of deconstruction" (135). Her article does not so much examine what is at stake in this opposition as provide a competent summary of two texts, *Rejouer la Politique* and *Le Retrait du Politique*. While her paraphrase is lucid, it does not come to grips in a useful way with the central problem articulated by the books—the distinction of "politics" (*la politique*) from "the political" (*le politique*). She characterizes the force of the withdrawal of the political as failing to tolerate difference understood as political debate: "for there is one sort of difference which deconstruction cannot tolerate: namely difference as dispute, as good,

old-fashioned political fight" (142). This is completely at odds with the reading advanced here of politics as precisely the possibility of difference, as the site of a deconstructive agency of difference withdrawn from political totality.

Our variant readings of the project of the Cerisy Political Seminar proceed from her reductive and at times confused characterization of the opposition between politics and the political, which she views in terms of a theory/practice opposition, rather than a distinction of appearance from essence such as I have tried to install and deconstruct in these pages. The politics for which I call, the politics that *is* nothing and that *appears* everywhere, is distinguished from a totality (or partial totality) of the political in the form of its appearance, which is divorced from any grounding political essence. This is the force of the interrogation of the "essence of the political" that Fraser mentions on page 136, but the implications of which she never pursues. Fraser does not realize the extent to which "distinguishing between *le* and *la politique*" (137) inserts an ontological difference that precludes any passage from the theoretical to the practical or from the global to the specific.

Fraser closes her essay by seeking to return a deconstructed notion of the political as the sole conceivable grounds of an "engagement" (143). She therefore concludes by lamely suggesting that the force of the deconstruction of the political lies in a broader recasting of political essence, including a refigured socioeconomic or feminine-domestic dimension, to allow it to connect with "the specificity of the political" (153), which is Fraser's reading of *la politique*. Fraser paraphrases Fynsk: "when everything is political, the sense and specificity of the political recedes, giving rise to still another inflection of the expression le retrait du politique: the retreat or withdrawal of the political." This represents a blank misunderstanding of the force of the deconstructive decoupling of politics from the political. "Politics," in the sense in which I read it in opposition to "the political," is not the specificity of the political; it does not merely oppose totalization in the name of the local and tactical.

It is precisely the continuity of politics and the political, either as practice and theory, or as specificity and totality, that forms the grounds of terror. Fraser's article suffers from a failure to think the difference of the political from politics in terms of a disjuncture of essence from appearance (a withdrawal from a description of appearance as grounded in an essence of the political), which would be precisely the way out of the "dilemma" by which she claims Lacoue-Labarthe and Nancy are trapped (143).

Lessons of Remembering
and Forgetting
Timothy Bahti

Paul de Man was a man who is hard to forget, and whose remarks are often easy to remember. We are reminded of one of these in reading the revised second edition of *Blindness and Insight*, where the very earliness of the remark causes it to stand out as a reminder of what was to come in de Man's work. In the 1954 article entitled "Heidegger's Exegeses of Hölderlin," included in this revised edition, he writes of Hölderlin's manuscripts that "it is often impossible to choose between two possible lessons in the very places where explication is most necessary" (248). The formulation recalls similar statements that were to appear twenty or twenty-five years later, such as a characterization of "indetermination" as "a suspended ignorance that was unable to choose between two modes of reading . . . suspended in the ignorance of its own truth or falsehood" (AR, 16, 17), or one of "deconstruction" as "the impossibility to evaluate positively or negatively the inescapable evaluation it implies" (AR, x). But what is striking in the early remark is not only its anticipation of various statements de Man would come to make on impossibility, ignorance, and inescapability. Rather, Wlad Godzich's felicitous translation of de Man's *leçons* as "lessons" strikingly captures the situation of reading de Man's writings. This teacher and writer, above all, a teacher and writer of a theory of reading — how are his readings (lessons) to be read, and what are their lessons? At a moment when a life of reading tends to become monumentalized as a legend — a reading — of lessons, the question of reading his readings, and of the impossibility and necessity of choices of readings, poses itself as the question of how we remember and forget Paul de Man.

Remembering something that passes away, or that threatens to escape our mind's hold, most commonly takes the form of naming or labeling the tenuous object of our attention in the most familiar terms possible, as when we speak of the fleeting experience of a dream with recourse to the terms and names of our everyday, waking world. The periphrasis of labeling terms and proper names would link the unfamiliar to the familiar, the dissolving to the self-identical, even as the object in question may resist the generality of generic terms as well as the individual essentialism of single names, and so a first remembering of de Man's work within a category of names is perhaps as inevitable as it is suggestively inadequate. Such remembering recalls that, before he came to the United States, de Man studied philosophy alongside literature, and it further recalls that a repeated occasion for misunderstanding de Man has surely been when he is read by scholars of literature often ill prepared to notice and deal with the philosophical assumptions and terminologies he invokes. But the philosophical discourse is sometimes inexplicit, often unacknowledged, within de Man's writings themselves, and a thumbnail sketch of an itinerary—say, from early preoccupations with Hegel and Heidegger, through an interest in Nietzsche, to the treatments of Pascal, Kant, Hegel, and Benjamin toward the end—would leave one with a supposedly forbidding pantheon of prestigious philosophical names that might simplify matters far more than clarify them.

"The power of memory does not reside in its capacity to resurrect a situation or a feeling that actually existed, but it is a constitutive act of the mind bound to its own present and oriented toward the future of its own elaboration" (BI, 92): to recollect de Man situating the reading of literature alongside the study of philosophy is perhaps only to recollect our attention around the present site of his work and the future of its elaboration. There is no denying that de Man's work, above all his early work, achieved much of its didactic force from its reminder of philosophical assumptions and problems residing within literary critical methods or habits of mind. A prominent form that this teaching initially took was the reminder of problems of temporality.

A summary version of such reminders of temporality within literature and literary study might collect them under the rubric of time and truth. What could it mean, de Man's work seems to ask, for one to address the truth of literary language and its understanding under the sign of temporality? If we return to "Heidegger's Exegeses of Hölderlin," we find de Man writing of Heidegger's reading of Hölderlin's "poetic word" that "instead of stating Being, it can only state mediation. For man the presence of Being is always in becoming. . . . In its moment of highest achievement, language manages to mediate between the two dimensions we distinguish in Being. . . . Their unity is ineffable and cannot be said, because it is language itself that introduces the distinction" (BI, 259). Poetic language might mediate between being and becoming, and to the extent that it achieves this mediation, it might be coextensive with the experience of temporality that defines the possibility of mediation. This is one version of an attention to temporality that is even more explicit in "Form and Intent in the American New Criticism," for example, where the reminder of temporality would recall criticism to its present and its future elaboration: "the temporal factor, so persistently forgotten, should remind us that the [literary] form is never anything but a process on the way to its completion" (BI, 31).

De Man could remind us quite explicitly of what we could, and would, persistently forget. But toward what end were such reminders of forgetting uttered? Was the condition of temporality such that, in understanding literature, one might wholly remember what is otherwise forgotten? The same paragraph from "Form and Intent" continues: "Understanding can be called complete only when it becomes aware of its own temporal predicament and realizes that the horizon within which the totalization can take place is time itself. The act of understanding is a temporal act that has its own history, but this history forever eludes totalization" (BI, 32). The expansion from the object of forgetting — temporality — to the sphere of its remembering — also temporality — is evidently no simple reminder, if nonetheless a salutary one. As the indication of a horizon signals, time is not construed as a series of moments when one might forget temporality one instant and remember it (upon reminder) the next; the experience of critical understanding, like the experience of poetic mediation, reintroduces temporality as that which remains to be forgotten because it always remains on the way to remembrance.

The vocabulary of "experience," of being "on the way," indeed, of mediation and of being and becoming, is of a piece with the Heideggerianisms of many of de Man's early essays. It is no news that, for de Man as for Heidegger, temporality under the form of an anticipated horizon (one that "forever eludes totalization") itself takes the form of an understanding-toward-death. This vulgarly simple formulation of what is itself vulgarly Heideggerian should make us cautious. To return once more to "Heidegger's Exegeses," we find that de Man could write that "for us . . . the sorrow of mediation lies in finitude, and we are able to conceive of it only under the form of death" (BI, 262). With no less pathos, but clearer reference to our question of remembering and forgetting, he could write in "The Rhetoric of Temporality" that one of Wordsworth's Lucy poems displays "a grim awareness of the de-mystifying power of death, which makes all the past appear as a flight into the inauthenticity of a forgetting" (BI, 224). When death spells and guarantees finitude, and its remembrance casts a proleptically past life as one of death's forgetting, the form of temporality as an anticipated horizon is not a totalization but a deferral. That is, the mutation of Heideggerian temporality as being-toward-death into a construal of understanding's temporality as understanding-toward-death does not yield the "horizon" of a horizon-of-expectations in the sense that such a spatialization of the image might render it knowable and therefore totalizable (de Man criticized this Gadamerian version of horizonality, invoking Husserl's specifications to the contrary [RT, 58–60, 62–63]). Rather, temporality takes the form of an anticipated horizon against which knowing is partial, and its "collection" is only the deferred recollection of what has actually been forgotten—death. According to this understanding, death is the condition for the meaningfulness of temporal understanding of literature and its truth.

"Poetry is the foreknowledge of criticism," de Man writes in the same "Form and Intent" essay: "no fundamental discontinuity exists between two acts that both aim at full understanding; the difference is primarily temporal in kind" (BI, 31). Understanding is a common project, but temporality is a common difference or discontinuity within it. Could death then be paraphrased, and remembered in advance, as the foreknowledge of life? At this level of reduction, which yields either more pathos or a *via temporaliter negativa*, something is being prematurely straightened out, or totalized as linearity. For there is no straight line from life to death, or from remembering back to what had been (and would no longer be) forgotten, when the second point that would define a line remains deferred. Understanding-toward-death, which names the essential futurity or proleptic character of understanding, is no more stable than the ongoing, lived, that is to say, *historical*, effort of understanding a past. In an early essay on romanticism entitled "Wordsworth and Hölderlin," de Man argues that the act of which we would have knowledge—here, the historical activity of romanticism—is one that we ourselves participate in, but only in the mode of a departure that is our interpretation; interpretation falls away, or forward, from its past just as a future falls away, or forward, from its present: "The future is present in history only as the remembering of a failed project that has become a menace" (RR, 58, 59). Death as a possible understanding or remembering of a life of forgetting is, when turned inside out, life as the future "death" or the deferral of its own understanding.

In either version, death names a necessary but necessarily missing act of consciousness. Our focus has been the relation between poetic language and its possible understanding, construed as the dédoublement of a lived activity such as writing or reading and its anticipatory interpretation as understanding-toward-death. The temporality of falling toward a future that remains deferred, or falling away (and forward) from an immediate past that is remembered as forgetting, is itself a version of this dédoublement. "This temporal doubling of the act and its interpretation . . . discloses a general structure of poetic temporality: it lends duration to a past that otherwise would immediately sink into the nonbeing of a future that withdraws itself from consciousness" (RR, 64). Doubling and duration name and institute what is missing, or threatening to become so: temporality as an achieved condition, achieved as a straight line or a series of constant points, along which understanding and, especially, death could be located and remembered, even if only in anticipation. Were understanding-toward-death to be an understanding of death, were anticipation to be an achievement, death and its consciousness would emerge as a single, quasi-specular moment—"quasi" precisely because the temporal dimension that constitutes the speculation would be missing.

Instead of this seduction—an understanding of death as the death of understanding's temporality—de Man arrives at a different formulation of the problem in the essay "The Rhetoric of Temporality," where the language of temporality and understanding appears in the mode of a rhetoric in the terms of allegory and irony. For the kinds of literary criticism and consciousness that would "persistently forget the temporal factor," de Man recovers the term of symbol and wields it as an effective accusation and judgment at once: "an illusionary priority of a subject that had, in fact, to borrow from the outside world a temporal stability which it lacked within itself" (BI, 200). But what of those kinds that would remember it, either retrospectively or in anticipation? Allegory and irony reappear as versions of temporal understanding that are neither comfortably stable nor clearly distinct. Allegory "always corresponds to the unveiling of an authentically temporal destiny" in which "time is the originary constitutive category," but this mode of so-called understanding does not actually remember or recollect what are otherwise the dismembered or scattered moments and aspects of a consciousness in time. Rather, it *signifies* or represents the signification of the nonbeing of such achieved collection: "this [allegorical] relationship between signs necessarily contains a constitutive temporal element; it remains necessary, if there is to be allegory, that the allegorical sign refer to another sign that precedes it. The meaning constituted by the allegorical sign can then consist only in the *repetition* . . . of a previous sign with which it can never coincide, since it is of the essence of this previous sign to be pure anteriority" (BI, 206, 207).

A repetition of "pure anteriority" is neither an achieved remembering *back*—this would be the "originary" but illusory stability of the symbol—nor an anticipated retrospective memory, since the possible coincidence of signs is denied within allegory. "Allegory designates primarily a distance in relation to its own origin, and, renouncing the nostalgia and the desire to coincide, it establishes its language in the void of this temporal difference" (BI, 207).[1] Such temporal difference, or temporality as difference, can no longer be construed or formed as any kind of remembering, except perhaps as a remembering ineluctably accompanied by a forgetting. That is, allegory at once reminds of what it is *not*—coincidence in time, with an origin—and remembers this only in order to forget it: "a conflict between a conception of the self seen in its authentically temporal predicament and a defensive strategy that tries to hide from this negative self-knowledge" (BI, 208). One form of such knowledge together with its defensive occlusion is a certain understanding of irony.

If allegory for de Man designates an unremembering memory, irony displays a dismembering forgetting. This is to say that even as irony, in symmetrical opposition to allegory, forgets a prior remembering and always aims toward a future as the articulation of its understanding, this future and its understanding are described by de Man as "knowledge of inauthenticity," also as "unrelieved *vertige*, dizziness to the point of madness" (BI, 214, 215). Knowing and retaining memory of *this*, on the far side of a forgotten or abandoned "remembering" of a natural, self-coinciding or self-identical self that is an illusion of false consciousness, is either to know something that dismembers one, or to remember something that one would rather and will shortly forget. The knowledge of irony, de Man insists, is entirely on the part of "a self that exists only in the form of a language that asserts the knowledge of this inauthenticity" (BI, 214); this knowledge of a dismemberment into linguistic and empirical selves is then denied or forgotten, as the one "self" would cure or aid the other by way of a fall back into time and toward death: "The instant [irony] construes the fall of the self as an event that could somehow benefit the self, it discovers that it has in fact substituted death for madness" (BI, 218). Irony that remembers an authentically temporal predicament of noncoincidence — here called a mad, untenable knowledge — falls back into a forgetting that anticipates death. This could be called the allegory of irony, that it, too, would forget what it would remember, or remembers only in order to forget, just as the irony of allegory is that allegory persistently re-members or collapses what its memory of the repetition of pure anteriority holds apart.

The relation of allegory and irony, as the renunciation of nostalgia and desire for coincidence turning into and back away from "the prefiguration of a future recovery" (BI, 219), is itself a repetitive one that does not know any sequential series of instants from anteriority to anticipation to posterior achievement. Rather, it institutes a sheer series of recurrences that figures the forgetting or denial of these modes of knowledge in their conversion into either a prefigured retrospective (allegorical) misunderstanding of irony or a projective (ironic) transcendental misunderstanding of allegory. Short of these common modes of understanding's forgetting of what rhetorical language remembers, which de Man amply demonstrates through readings of critics on irony, there appears only his own ironic knowledge, which he modestly calls "provisional" without wishing it to be any more than repetitive: "Irony divides the flow of temporal experience into a past that is pure mystification and a future that remains harassed forever by a relapse within the inauthentic. It can know this inauthenticity but can never overcome it. It can only restate and repeat it on an increasingly conscious level. . . . The temporal void that it reveals is the same void we encountered when we found allegory always implying an unreachable anteriority. Allegory and irony are thus linked in their common discovery of a truly temporal predicament" (BI, 222).

The mediated character of knowledge and understanding by way of the mediating character of language, which de Man argues in "Heidegger's Exegeses" and reaffirms in the companion piece, "The Dead-End of Formalist Criticism" (BI, 232, 237, 242), has been transformed into mediations of temporal knowledge and understanding by way of the correlative rhetorical modes of allegory and irony.

What *they* know is what we and they can try to remember and restate or, more frequently, forget and misrepresent. In a piece from roughly this same period, "The Image of Rousseau in the Poetry of Hölderlin," de Man writes, apropos of Hölderlin but as if with ironic distance upon the dilemma with which his "Rhetoric of Temporality" leaves us, that "the worst danger . . . comes rather from an excess of truth which risks a forgetting of the mediated limits of the human" (RR, 41, 42). Knowing the truth about an authentically temporal predicament, even in the mode of a remembering that also forgets or will be forgotten, will in its very rhetorical forms preserve the mediation that stops short of excess. "Why, then," he continues, "does Hölderlin identify the moment of retreat in Rousseau with the act of forgetting? What is it one 'forgets' when consciousness bends back on itself in this way? It is not being, for it was never known in the first place." This much is entirely consistent with both the sympathetic critique of "Heidegger's Exegeses" and the austere critique of the symbol in "The Rhetoric of Temporality." "Rather, we have to forget the fullness of our thought itself when it has been put back on the path of truth—especially in its almost uncanny understanding of the past and its concrete anticipation of the future" (RR, 44, 45).

This uncanny understanding of the past—"that is pure mystification"?—and the concrete anticipation of the future—"that remains harassed forever by a relapse within the inauthentic"?—leaves an unfull present thought oscillating repeatedly between allegory and irony, and repeatedly being identified as a truly or authentically temporal predicament. If death appears to have any place in this story any longer, it is not as an anticipated horizon, but as a perpetually displaced and resituated moment within a—rhetorically designated—structure of remembering and forgetting. The moment is still one of understanding, or more specifically of reading, although its insight is increasingly linked to the blindness of a misunderstanding or misreading, a blindness that empties it of fullness and disabuses it of the temptations of totalization. In "The Image of Rousseau," de Man writes in a footnote that "death for Hölderlin—and for Rousseau—is not at all an absolute, but a moment in the dialectic of existence" (RR, 294). This nonabsolute, nonfull moment, which de Man repeatedly identifies as a true or authentic temporal predicament, predicts (*praedicere/praedicare*) what appears in the later "Autobiography as De-Facement" piece as the statement that "death is a displaced name for a linguistic predicament" (RR, 81). What is "said in advance" by a displacement of a rhetoric of death upon a rhetoric of rhetorical and linguistic modes, and what does a linguistic predicament continue to say in advance of us?

The language of the essays from the fifties was identified as Heideggerian; a more accurate identification would include the names of Hegel and Husserl, and perhaps emerge under the rubrics of phenomenology and existentialism. (Some have added the name of Sartre, and let the discussion of de Man's "existentialism" rest there.) But the matter at hand is not to settle a question under the category of names, but to notice a shift within the vocabularies used to discuss a problem. As a language of the temporality of understanding and of understanding-toward-death merges into one of a rhetoric of temporality as structures of remembering and forgetting, an authentically existential vocabulary of consciousness, authenticity, and inauthenticity may be retained even as a new focus upon different objects of knowledge is coming to the fore. De Man himself underscores such a shift when he writes retrospectively of "The Rhetoric of Temporality" that its "[rhetorical] terminology is still uncomfortably intertwined with the thematic vocabulary of consciousness and of temporality that was current at the time, but it signals a turn" (BI, xii).

The naming of de Man's problem of the temporality of understanding as "existential" mocks a fullness of understanding and blocks access to the path it was already on, or at least turning toward. For as if with reference to the nonfull, self-emptying moment of understanding at which the first part of my argument has left us, de Man has written that the literary imagination takes place "only after the void, the inauthenticity of the existential project has been revealed; literature begins where the existential demystification ends and the critic has no need to linger over this preliminary stage" (BI, 34, 35). What was existential was always already structural (not "structuralist") in the sense that literary and specifically rhetorical structures such as allegory subtended the thematics of a consciousness ahead of and forgetting, or behind and proleptically remembering its temporally conditioned situation.

My discussion of understanding, death, and memory thus far has allowed remembering and its correlative forgetting to appear as terms for a strategy of mind and discourse for treating what is missing-in-advance. The missing fullness of consciousness and of understanding, construed as an "initial" problem of death, appears to receive a response from a rhetoric of memory remembering what it would rather forget, or forgetting what it tries to remember. But if death as an anticipated horizon was never really a *terminus ad quem*, but a displaced name for a temporal predicament resituated as the rhetoric of temporality, the latter's authentic knowledge of the inauthenticity of being (BI, 214) is itself a displacement and deferral of a *structural* problem of language and understanding. "Authenticity" is a term that will come to be forgotten as the structural dimension is pursued down to the verbal material of remembering and forgetting. Not authenticity but veracity becomes the category at stake, from which perspective any treatment of memory as existential or historical might remain authentically human but would also be pathetically untrue; the retrogression of historical memory would occur precisely to the extent that it would recast memory as a natural fact or second-nature (social) experience instead of knowing it as an engagement between mind and language.

When death is displaced in de Man's writings, much hinges upon whether something replaces it or whether a gap or mark of sheer displacement is retained.

Death functions in an organizing way, not as a privileged moment of an end-of-time, a point of arrival at meaning, but as what is deferred; no on *experiences* it meaningfully—it cuts off experience from discourse and understanding—and that is why "experience" is a term to be left behind. Allegory becomes a privileged mode of understanding because it tries to put behind us the signification of nonbeing that is deferred, or displaced upon ongoing allegoresis. It "tells the story of" (or narrates) this failing or repeatedly failed effort, which is the irony of allegory. Allegory and its accompanying reading absorb the structure of deferral previously attributed to the relation between death and meaningfulness.

The privileged aspect of allegory emerges as the structure of deferral it carries and carries over (*metapherein*) or metaphorizes within itself. It is the mode of memory *as* deferral: to remember something is to put it off. Another way of saying this is that allegorical memory remembers nothing; the nothing is somewhere else. As such, temporality and meaning in allegory have come to be organized around an absence or a missing element. In "The Rhetoric of Temporality," de Man signals the two stanzas of Wordsworth's poem "A slumber did my spirit seal," with their corresponding stages of consciousness, and remarks that "the event that separates the two states is the radical discontinuity of a death." He first suggests that the stance of the poem, however, is not discontinuous: "The stance of the speaker, who exists in the 'now' ["No motion has she now, no force"], is that of a subject whose insight is no longer in doubt. . . . It could be called, if one so wished, a stance of wisdom. There is no real disjunction of the subject; the poem is written from the point of view of a unified self that fully recognizes a past condition as one of error and stands in a present that, however painful, sees things as they actually are" (BI, 224).

But this is to continue to speak apparently of a subject (or persona) remembering, and not yet of a structure displacing. De Man goes on: "The difference has been spread out over a temporality which is exclusively that of the poem and in which the conditions of error and of wisdom have become successive. This is possible within the ideal, self-created temporality engendered by the language of the poem, but it is not possible within the actual temporality of experience." With this turn, the allegorical structure of Wordsworth's poem is read as the displacement it always was: of subject onto text, with the consequent and ironic displacement in reading of the text back onto subjectivity. The present "now" that remembers actually re-members nothing because the "something" of this "now" is not actual; the temporal structure of the text displaced the Wordsworthian subject upon this rhetorical temporality, which reading then misplaces or misreads back upon a "real" now as if it could be experienced in a mode other than reading.

"The 'now' of the poem is not an actual now," de Man continues, "but the ideal 'now,' the duration of an acquired wisdom. The actual now, which is that of the moment of death, lies hidden in the blank space between the two stanzas."[2] The moment of death in Wordsworth's "A slumber . . . " has been written out of the poem, but marked as an absence – "the blank space between the two stanzas" – and then read back into it by de Man in his deconstruction of an ideal temporality ("the duration of an acquired wisdom") as one of forgetting and misremembering. The error of ideal temporality leads to the insight that the displacement of death leaves a blank mark of significant absence. The readability of the Wordsworth poem, which for de Man would otherwise remain unreadable or only misreadable, hinges upon the remarking of the significant textual passage and the movement it signifies: the blank space marked or framed in Wordsworth's text, and remarked or rendered conspicuously visible in de Man's reading as the locus of invisibility, of what "lies hidden."

To point to where an actual temporality of a moment of textual death lies hidden within or on the far side of an ideal temporality of "the duration of an acquired wisdom" is not to disclose it, let alone to reveal its meaning. It is to *mark* it, or to remark it as the mark of an absence. This absence is not forgotten just because it can be forgotten, for it can also be remembered. But it marks the point where reading de Man reading turns from one kind of privileging of forgetting to another. Forgetting begins to speak otherwise.

My discussion of discursive structures addressed by de Man has brought us to the point of analyzing those that necessarily constitute and represent (mis)understandings of the relations between temporality and meaning. In the instance of a Wordsworth poem, such relations obtain between a stabilizing remembering and a still-hidden or forgotten moment of death. More general terms may indicate such relations under the names of allegory and memory: the one that refers to what cannot be recollected, and therefore can only be forgotten or denied; the other that remembers nothing, a something that is no thing. In each case, what may be called "retrospective" verbal and rhetorical constructions appear to posit, as if "after the fact," meaning and understanding that are otherwise already missing or forgotten. But such discussion seems to accord all too well with our customary, quotidian understanding of the relations between remembering and forgetting, in which an apparent initial priority of forgetting always turns to reveal a real priority and victory of remembering. Our remembering what we forgot depends on a prior forgetting to remember, but the forgetting to remember can only appear under the sign of remembering: "I forgot to remember" always means "I remember," which means the forgetting of forgetting.

This memorial circle – a version of the hermeneutic circle – displays a structure of retrospection that manifests itself under various specifications. But is there a poststructure? Although I never knew Paul de Man to speak of "poststructuralism" (or "poststructuralists") with anything but ironic humor, I am tempted to call "poststructural" an effort within his work directed at understanding what comes "after" the retrospective move that always revalorizes remembering. What comes after the uncovering of a remembering dependent upon a forgetting that itself tends toward its remembrance? This is only another way of asking what it means to mark an absence.

In an essay entitled "Impersonality in the Criticism of Maurice Blanchot," after quoting from his *L'Espace littéraire* that "reading adds nothing to what was already there," de Man writes that "this 'nothing' that, in reading, we should *not* add to the work, is the very definition of a truly interpretative language" (BI, 64, 65). This nothing that is not, is not remembering so much as forgetting: not forgetting to remember—which can only be remembered—but remembering to forget (to add). Remembering to forget must be understood not as a retrospective act within a succession of moments, but as a simultaneous adding of subtraction; the tension within and against an allegorical succession of moments is what de Man indicates in "The Rhetoric of Temporality" as the Wordsworth poem's "spreading out along the axis of an imaginary time in order to give duration to what is, in fact, simultaneous within the subject" (BI, 225).

The simultaneity of remembering and forgetting, of adding a "not," is difficult to think, more difficult to sustain. If the locus of the discussion is reading, as it is with Blanchot, the sense of difficulty can be retained in language describing "the full ambivalence of the power contained in the act of forgetting . . . the paradoxical presence of a kind of anti-memory at the very source of literary creation" (BI, 66), language that accords well with that used to speak of "A slumber did my spirit seal." In a discussion of Nietzsche in "Literary History and Literary Modernity," however, where the locus is ostensibly life, de Man is critical in his insights into the attempt to move from reading history to living an unhistorical life. Nietzsche's "Vom Nutzen und Nachteil der Historie für das Leben" would oppose a vitalist forgetting against a kind of Hegelian absolute remembering: "Moments of genuine humanity thus are moments at which all anteriority vanishes, annihilated by the power of an absolute forgetting" (BI, 147). But this is an illusion, since life does not appear to be able to do without structures and experiences of retrospection; Nietzsche's text comes to display "a temporal experience of human mutability, historical in the deepest sense of the term in that it implies the necessary experience of any present as a *passing* experience that makes the past irrevocable and unforgettable, because it is inseparable from any present or future" (BI, 148, 149). The past cannot be called back, and neither can it be forgotten, as simultaneity yields duration and forgetting remembering. And yet after an appeal to forgetting, Nietzsche's appeal to a renewed remembering— he is quoted as saying, "But this very life that has to forget must also at times be able to stop forgetting"—leads only to dismembering and death. In the same paragraph from "Vom Nutzen und Nachteil der Historie," Nietzsche moves rapidly from remembering, to recalling injustice and the just deserts of destruction ("Then the past is judged critically, attacked at its very roots with a sharp knife, and brutally cut down"), to a latent fear of a suicidal self-dismemberment: "This is always a dangerous process, dangerous for life itself. Men and eras that serve life in this manner, by judging and destroying the past, are always dangerous and endangered" (BI, 149, de Man's translation).

Ironically, it is with reference to a text entitled "The Triumph of Life" that de Man returns to the simultaneity of forgetting and reading first posed with regard to Blanchot. In "Shelley Disfigured," he recharacterizes the problem of temporality and meaning, remembering and forgetting, in ways that avoid both the retrospective circular structure of forgetting (in order)-to-remember, and the correlative prospect of a lived dismembering by remembrance. "The structure of the text is not one of question and answer, but of a question whose meaning, as question, is effaced from the moment it is asked. The answer to the question is another question, asking what and why one asked, and thus receding ever further from the original query" (RR, 98). The terminology of effacing gives way to one of forgetting that denies any stance of retrospection, and the history of Rousseau that the poem narrates "tells of a specific experience . . . that can be designated by a single verb: the experience is that of forgetting" (RR, 103, 104). "What one forgets here is not some previous condition . . . we have no assurance whatever that the forgotten ever existed" (RR, 104); if we did, such forgetting would still be under the aegis of a remembering. Instead, this persistent forgetting seeks to become "aware of one's persistent condition of slumber, to be more than ever asleep, a deeper sleep replacing a lighter one, a deeper forgetting being achieved by an act of memory which remembers one's forgetting (RR, 105).

This forgetting, and remembering to forget, does not know something one forgot, but knows only the forgetting, and it is this "inability to know" that de Man calls "the form of a pseudoknowledge which is called a forgetting" (RR, 105). As he scrupulously respects the appearance of signs, shapes, and their articulation in Shelley's text, he insists upon what their marking or taking place takes away or effaces: "The repetition of the erasures rhythmically articulates what is in fact a disarticulation. . . . But since this pattern does not fully correspond to what it covers up, it leaves the trace which allows one to call this ambivalent shaping a forgetting" (RR, 107). The tracing, shaping, or marking of a forgetting yields the disarticulation, disfiguration, or *absenting* of those terms and shapes that otherwise mark and govern our reading of texts. Not the least of these is our otherwise nonallegorical understanding of understanding: "the shaped light of understanding is itself allowed to wane away, layer by layer, until it is entirely forgotten and remains present only in the guise of an edifice that serves to celebrate and to perpetuate its oblivion" (RR, 112).

The edifice that marks an absence of understanding and serves to perpetuate its oblivion is the signs of a text, Shelley's "The Triumph of Life." This series of brief and elliptical remarks on an essay that is at once one of the densest and most rapid in de Man's oeuvre cannot do justice to the problem his late work seeks to uncover: the disfiguration of understanding and meaning in the signs and figures of texts. Figuration is not thinkable without the design of signs: "it is the alignment of a signification with any principle of linguistic articulation whatsoever, sensory or not, which constitutes the figure. . . . Figuration is the element in language that allows for the reiteration of meaning by substitution . . . the particular seduction of the figure is not necessarily that it creates an illusion of sensory pleasure, but that it creates an illusion of meaning" (RR, 114, 115). At this juncture, the illusion of meaning is the perpetuation of the oblivion of understanding, its repeated substitution or reiteration into and as the memory of its forgetting.

Perhaps the most condensed appearance of the figure of understanding (questioning-and-answering, meaning, etc.) in the sign of forgetting occurs, somewhat unexpectedly, at the end of de Man's "introduction" to Hans Robert Jauss's *Toward an Aesthetic of Reception.* Writing against a certain understanding of Baudelaire, for which Jauss figures as an example, and toward a new one of Hegel, de Man remarks that "the sign, which pertains specifically to language and to rhetoric, marks, in Hegel, the passage from sheer inward recollection [*Erinnerung*] and imagination to thought [*Denken*], which occurs by way of the deliberate forgetting of substantial, aesthetic, and pictorial symbols" [RT, 69–70]. The figure of the sphinx in Baudelaire, then, is less an apostrophic figure of remembering than the sign of its deliberate forgetting: "the sphinx is not an emblem of recollection but, like Hegel's sign, an emblem of forgetting . . . inaccessible to memory because he is imprinted on paper, because he is himself the inscription of a sign" (ibid.). The status of the inscribed sign and the printed text resists memorialization (in the sense of interiorizing remembrance) because it preserves forgetting, and the material figure—the letter or sign—of the sphinx expands in de Man's analysis beyond the confines of a problem of remembering to forget: "He is the grammatical subject cut off from its consciousness, the poetic analysis cut off from its hermeneutic function, the dismantling of the aesthetic and pictorial world of 'le soleil qui se couche' by the advent of poetry as allegory" (RT, 70).

The return of the term of allegory brings us back to the problem of the temporality of its rhetoric: of its attempted remembering of the unrecollectible, its marking of an absence or blank of memory, and its insightful yet defensive interplay between the two. "At its apparent beginning as well as at its apparent end, thought (i.e., figuration) forgets what its thinks and cannot do otherwise if it is to maintain itself" (RR, 119). This statement from "Shelley Disfigured" marks a certain continuity within de Man's thought, between a language of disfiguration in the sign and one of forgetting in remembering. Where does this leave thought, especially the afterthought or *Nachdenken* that occurs after the death of Paul de Man? The conclusion to the introduction to the Jauss volume is linked to the Shelley essay in de Man's ruthless, even violent urge to sever poetics, as poetic-linguistic analysis, from any hermeneutics of understanding. But this tendency is also, when addressed to Hegel, a turn away from a monumentalizing tradition of "Hegelian" thought and comprehension, and a turn toward an acute analysis of thinking the memorial and the memorized in Hegel, who perhaps remained for de Man, as for others, the textual point from which "de mesurer en quoi notre recours contre lui est encore peut-être une ruse qu'il nous oppose et au terme de laquelle il nous attend, immobile et ailleurs."[3] In his late essays on Hegel one reads of thought, in a specified sense of memory (*Gedächtnis*) by now sharply distinguished from remembrance or recollection (*Erinnerung*), that "the progression from perception to thought depends crucially on the mental faculty of memorization. . . . Thought is entirely dependent on a mental faculty that is mechanical through and through . . . memory is a truth of which the aesthetic is the defensive, ideological and censored translation. In order to have memory one has to be able to forget remembrance" (SS, 772, 773). One also reads that "to read poets or philosophers thoughtfully, on the level of their thought rather than of one's or their desires, is to read them by rote. Every poem (*Gedicht*) is a *Lehrgedicht* whose knowledge is forgotten as it is read" (HS, 152)[4]

These are some of the last words; some of the earlier ones, on Blanchot, include the statement that "the remembrance of a forgetting can occur only while reading the work" (BI, 67). The simultaneity of remembering and forgetting is in de Man's work always linked to or instanced in the work of reading, and so it will be with the work of reading de Man reading. There is no question that in reading Hegel, he is reading the question of the possibility of truth, and there should be no less of a question that true reading is at stake in reading de Man. Those who would suggest that the true is bracketed in his work have not read it carefully, nor reflected on the fact that displacement, erasure, and forgetting are not the elimination of something true but the marking of its signs; his free translation of Hölderlin's "Es ereignet sich aber das Wahre" ("Mnemosyne") as "What is true is what is bound to take place," is followed by the statement that "no reading is conceivable in which the question of its truth or falsehood is not primarily involved" (F, xi).

I began with de Man's early essay, "Heidegger's Exegeses of Hölderlin," and I should like to return there. He writes critically that, in Heidegger's treatment of Hölderlin, "the witness is Heidegger's solution to the problem . . . : how to preserve the moment of truth. All Western metaphysicians, from Anaximander to Nietzsche, have forgotten the truth, according to Heidegger, by forgetting Being. . . . How are we to shore up our remembrance of authentic Being so that we can find our way back to it?" (BI, 252, 253). He goes on, in passages I cited earlier, to argue that Hölderlin's poetry states the mediation, not the immediate presence, of being, and that this leads to the finitude of mediation conceived under the form of death. Here, he is still retracing Heidegger's thought in its identification of Hölderlin as the speaker of truth: "The experience of Being must be sayable; in fact, it is in language that it is preserved. . . . then, the truth, which is the presence of the present, has entered the work that is language. . . . And the task that we, who, like Heidegger, cannot speak of Being inherit, is to preserve this language, to preserve Being. The preservation of Being is the commentary, the 'thinking-of' (*andenken*) Hölderlin" (BI, 253).

The *Andenken* of Hölderlin by Heidegger, generated from poems (including one entitled "Andenken") and yielding commentaries of thought, can also be translated as "remembrance." For and after de Man, the thinking of thought, generated from readings and yielding further ones, demands the forgetting of remembrance, or—the same thing—the remembering of a forgetting that occurs only in reading. De Man knows forgetting, but how will de Man be known? He associates understanding, meaning, thought, and figuration with the hardest thing to forget—substantialization—together with the hardest thing to read—the sheer materiality of the letter and the sign. To read without substantialization is to remember consistently to forget. It is to forget "life," and it is thus the transformation of a concern with death into one of the epistemology of remembering and forgetting: "a linguistic predicament." The veritable burden of remembering Paul de Man, of rereading the thinking of his texts, is to give shape to the weightlessness of forgetting he exemplifies.

Notes

1. For another version of de Man's critique of the nostalgic desire for the symbol's temporality, see his commentary on a line from Hölderlin's "Brot und Wein" in the essay "The Intentional Structure of the Romantic Image": "Hölderlin's phrase: 'Wie Blumen entstehen' is in fact a paradox, since origination is inconceivable on the ontological level; the ease with which we nevertheless accept it is indicative of our desire to forget. . . . it combines the poetic seduction of beginnings contained in the word 'entstehen' with the ontological stability of the natural object—but this combination is made possible only by a deliberate forgetting of the transcendental nature of the source. . . . The obviously desirable sensory aspects of the flower express the ambivalent aspiration toward a forgotten presence that gave rise to the image, for it is in experiencing the material presence of the particular flower that the desire arises to be reborn in the manner of a natural creation. The image is inspired by a nostalgia for the natural object, expanding to become nostalgia for the origin of this object. Such a nostalgia can only exist when the transcendental presence is forgotten, as in the 'dürftiger Zeit' of Hölderlin's poem which we are all too eager to circumscribe as if it were a specific historical 'time' and not Time in general" (RR, 5, 6).

2. I quote here from the first publication of "The Rhetoric of Temporality," in *Interpretation: Theory and Practice*, ed. Charles Singleton (Baltimore: Johns Hopkins University Press, 1969), 206, for its reprinting in the reedition of *Blindness and Insight* accidentally drops a line from the sentence in question (225).

3. Michel Foucault, *L'Ordre du discours* (Paris: Gallimard, 1971), 74, 75.

4. On this reading of Hegel, see also de Man, "Hypogram and Inscription: Michael Riffaterre's Poetics of Reading," in RT, esp. 42–43 ("Hegel, who is often said to have 'forgotten' about writing, is unsurpassed in his ability to remember that one should never forget to forget"), and Andrzej Warminski, *Readings in Interpretation, Hölderlin, Hegel, Heidegger* (Minneapolis: University of Minnesota Press, 1987). It should go without saying that there also remains the rereading of the problem of forgetting in *Allegories of Reading*, especially its second part on Rousseau, which exigencies of time and space have caused me to omit altogether.

In-Difference to Philosophy:
de Man on Kant, Hegel, and Nietzsche
Rodolphe Gasché

Since its incipience in Greece, philosophy has found itself in a relation of rivalry with rhetoric. Yet, as rivals, philosophy and rhetoric also have something in common, and make similar claims. What they share, and what thoroughly distinguishes them from the mode of discourse characteristic of the individual sciences, is their title to speak about everything, about all there is. Philosophy and rhetoric feel their competence to be excluded from no subject. But in spite of their common interest, rhetoric and philosophy are separated by an abyss. As Socrates' attempt to demarcate both discourses in the episode in the *Theaetetus* regarding the difference between the rhetorician and the philosopher clearly demonstrates, the difference between rhetoric and philosophy is rooted in incommensurable modes of object perception. Rhetoric is a type of discourse that services the self-affirming mortal human nature, and it is indeed its highest tool. Therefore, the rhetorician must perceive his object in the manner it presents itself to him in ordinary sense perception, that is, as a singular and concrete object. Yet, whereas rhetoric's activity takes place within anthropologically determined limits, philosophy relinquishes rhetoric's all-dominating motive of self-affirmation, and, eo ipso, rhetorical linguistic competence. In thus surrendering rhetorical and linguistic competence, philosophy, in distinction from rhetoric, acquires the chance to conceive objects in general, objects, consequently, that lack all common base with those of human life. Philosophy, as understood by Plato, is dependent on such a radical break with the necessities of life—a break based, as can be seen from the episode in the *Theaetetus*, and even better from the *Phaedo*, on the assumption that there is something worse than corporeal death. This distance from life radically distinguishes philosophy from rhetoric.[1]

According to a remark made by Plato in the *Theaetetus* — as well as by Aristotle at the beginning of the *Metaphysics* — philosophical questioning starts in *thaumazein*, i.e., in wonder, and marvel. In wonder, indeed, man stands back from the immediate and from his most elementary and purely practical relation to it, as Hegel explains at one point in the *Aesthetics*. In wonder, he is torn free "from nature and his own singularity and now seeks and sees in things a universal, implicit, and permanent element."[2] In other words, in the wondering retreat, difference irrupts into the world. It is a difference that not only opens up the world *as* world, viz., the world as a *whole*, but one that also constitutes that particular being who in the world, and in distinction from it, is capable of cognition. Because only through this difference does meaning come into a previously indifferent world of immediacy, it is a difference that cannot be explained by what is. As the opening itself of what exists in a meaningful manner, it is an absolutely irreducible difference. Because of its origin in wonder, in that sort of retreat from the immediate by which the immediate *as such*, in its totality, comes into view, philosophy has, from the start, been concerned with all there is, with the entirety of being, with being in general, as opposed to empirical particulars. This "all," however, is very different from all that rhetoric purports to speak about. It is not everything, each single item that exists, but the totality as such of what exists, in short, the whole of being, being *itself*. Philosophy, from the outset, has been concerned with the enigma that within being there is one such heterogeneous being for whom that which is can turn into an object of cognition. Such a being is clearly entirely different from the self-affirming mortal human being in whose survival rhetoric invests. The object of philosophy is a function of a cognizing subject, of a subject whose possibility presupposes difference, and whose object is the whole in its difference to what it is the whole of.

Philosophy must be radically distinguished from rhetoric not only on the basis of its objects and purpose, for philosophy is different from rhetoric insofar as it is a *discourse of difference*. It is rooted in difference, and reflects on that difference. It interrogates the difference that the thought of the *as such* (thought *as such*) or of the *whole* makes, in distinction from what is allowed to appear within its opening. Most generally speaking, philosophy, seen independently of its historical modifications must be said to be concerned with the enigma of difference — with the *essential* difference that is the general, the universal — in short, with an irreducible difference that cannot be explained by what is, since the empirically given is as to its meaning dependent on that difference. Philosophy is about a difference that makes all the difference, a difference that can only be accounted for in and by itself, in short, in difference from all other modes of existence.

Philosophy, in contradistinction from rhetoric, acquires the possibility of its object's generality by relinquishing the exigencies of mortal life, as well as the linguistic competence that survival requires. The philosopher gains this position through his retreat from language and speech as particular attributes of mortal human beings. (If he happens to be a powerful orator, it is certainly not *qua* philosopher.) But what does such a retreat from language and speech consist of, and what does it imply? Precisely because philosophy is concerned with the *as such*, with what as *thought* is in irreducible distinction from what it is the thought of, language in its concrete empirical reality is an obstacle, not by accident as it may be the case in the particular sciences or in rhetoric too, but *kath'auto*, in and by itself. Philosophy's relation to its objects is therefore always bent by the problematic of linguistic expression. This explains also why from its incipience, philosophy has been concerned with the possibilities and limits of language. Reflection on language is an integral part of the self-understanding of philosophy. It characterizes the philosophical enterprise as one that cannot be subsumed to any of the possible types of discourse that rhetoric may have distinguished. Concerned with the fact that the expression of a thought of general bearing is immediately and intimately linked to a problematization of language, the philosophical mode of discourse is characterized by a *know-how-to-speak-well — eu legein*.[3] This desire to speak well — contrary to the desire for efficient speech in rhetoric — prescribes that the objective problems arising from linguistic expression of general matters are made an integral part of these matters themselves, and radically distinguishes philosophical discourse from the use of language in the individual sciences, and in rhetoric as well. This desire represents the attempt to achieve, on the level of expression, the very difference itself that the subject matter of philosophy implies, and is, thus, in principle, irreducible to any empirical usage of language. Philosophical speech achieves the required transparency in language — its transempirical use — through a rigorous methodological practice of distinction. Indeed, philosophy is not only a discourse on the enigma of difference and, therefore, distinguished from all other modes of employing speech, it is also a discourse in which distinction becomes the major organon. As a strictly argumentative and reasoning practice that achieves cognition of what is as such and in its totality through a stating of grounds, philosophy hinges entirely on its sharp distinctions of levels and conceptual differences. Indeed, the considerable conceptual effort that philosophy demands of its reader and interpreter amounts to nothing less than an invitation to face its difference from other discourses and their objects, as a difference rooted in the difference that thought itself makes, and also, just as essentially, to a discourse that secures the difference of thought by a rigorous practice of linguistic and conceptual differentiation.

Philosophy comes into its own thus by separating itself from that other (anthropological, empirical) type of discourse — namely, rhetoric — that also claims for itself the right to speak about everything. Yet, at the very moment when philosophy reaches a certain fulfillment of its goal in a type of philosophy in which perhaps the most systematic layout of the totality of all thinkable differences is achieved—in Hegel's philosophy—early German romanticism, paradoxically enough, is becoming engaged in sketching a retrogression toward rhetoric. Friedrich Schlegel conceived of rhetoric not only as the reuniting of in an exclusively formal point of view but also as the annihilation of the differences between what he understood to be merely separate species of "literature"—poetry and philosophy. Despite some major differences to be emphasized hereafter, Paul de Man's linguistic or rhetorical reading of literature and philosophy continues, in a certain manner, that romantic project of dissolving the difference constitutive of both philosophy and literature, philosophy and rhetoric. In the following analysis devoted to de Man's reading of the philosophical texts of Nietzsche, Kant, and Hegel, we will attempt to make this point. As already indicated, de Man's reading differs from the manner in which the romantics aimed at bringing about an original indifference—the indifference of the *menstruum universale*. De Man does not reach back to a point of unity and presence that because it makes all the difference, remains intrinsically linked with the philosophical *desideratum*. On the contrary, as we will try to demonstrate, it is the unheard of attempt to think an indifference that makes no difference at all. A rhetorical reading, for de Man, is, indeed, a reading that seeks the transgression of philosophical difference in an indifference that is so radical as to become entirely indifferent—devoid of *all* relation—to the philosophical.

The Wild Card of Rhetorical Reading

Before establishing what a rhetorical reading means for de Man, and what it seeks to achieve, it may well be appropriate to first determine, as succinctly as possible, what he understands by "philosophy." The distinctive feature of a philosophical text is, according to de Man, its proclaimed property of unity. As his essays on Nietzsche reveal, such unity is a function of philosophy's conceptual, argumentational, and above all, developmental nature. A philosophical text, or discourse, is said to unfold in a process, built up from a beginning and proceeding toward a conclusive end. And because de Man considers all these characteristics meaningful only to the extent that they are supposed to demarcate philosophy from literature, they also establish what he calls philosophy's authority and centrality. De Man's rhetorical reading of philosophy purports to tackle "the perennial question of the distinction between philosophy and literature" (AR, 119)—a philosophical question par excellence, serving philosophy's attempt to establish its own authorial and authoritative difference—yet aims at nothing less than a questioning of the very possibility of such a difference. At stake in a rhetorical reading is philosophy's irreducible difference, the thought of difference, and difference as thought.

A rhetorical or linguistic reading or, for that matter, a literary, nonphenomenal reading, as it is also called, is a purely formal reading (see PM, 130). Although the essay "The Resistance to Theory" seems to link such a reading with the application of Saussurian linguistics to literary and philosophical texts, the Nietzsche essays in *Allegories of Reading* clearly suggest that purely formal linguistics is primarily indebted to certain romantic speculations on language. The linguistic theory of Friedrich Schlegel and Jean Paul, which is still "largely obscured by our lack of understanding," has demonstrated, according to de Man, "that the paradigmatic structure of language is rhetorical rather than representational or expressive of a referential, proper meaning" (AR, 106). In romantic linguistics, the trope is the linguistic paradigm, par excellence, and such privileging of figure over persuasion is said to correspond to the most typical romantic gesture (see AR, 106, 130). In short, a purely formal reading of philosophical or literary texts is in essence a tropological reading, since tropes are understood to characterize language in depth. Yet, when de Man refers to rhetoric and tropes, he does not think of mere stylistics and the linguistic art of representation. A linguistic or rhetorical reading, as de Man understands it, is essentially a nonphenomenal reading.

To understand what is meant by "nonphenomenal" and, thus, by a nonphenomenal linguistics, it is indispensable first to clarify what "phenomenal" means. Although de Man makes frequent use of the terms "phenomenalism," "phenomenality," "phenomenalization," etc., without clearly demarcating them, it is not difficult to see that these terms imply a meaning of phenomenon that stresses, in analogy (but in analogy only) to Kant's use of that notion, the object of cognition's appearing to the senses. Phenomenality for de Man denotes accessibility to the senses. A phenomenon is characterized by the fact that it is intuitable (*anschaulich*), imagelike (*bildhaft*). It contains an "iconic factor," and takes place through extension since it is constituted by the aesthetic forms of space and time (RR, 115, 127). Figures and tropes are phenomenal in that they appeal to the senses, and privilege a certain mode of cognition: that of the experience of the phenomenal world. A nonphenomenal linguistic reading is, thus, first, a nonperceptual or nonaesthetic reading. It centers not on images and tropes but on what de Man calls at one point the "para-figural" (RT, 15). For de Man, however, the phenomenal "implies the possibility of a determined totalization, of a contour," as well (RR, 127). It captures the meaning of texts not only as tangible figures but also as totalizing figures. A nonphenomenal reading, consequently, is a reading that reaches beyond the imposition—by a mode of experience in which the perceptual modes of cognition prevail—of unity upon the text. It extends beyond the totalizing function of figures or tropes. Yet, since intuition as *Anschauung* is that type of cognition that causes all experiences to be the experience of phenomena and also implies, to quote de Man, "perception, consciousness, experience, and leads at once into the world of logic and of understanding with all its correlatives, among which aesthetics, occupies a prominent place" (RT, 8), a nonphenomenal reading is also, necessarily, a noncognitive, or nonspecular (nonreflexive), reading.

Now, in Kant, "phenomenon" is used in contrast to what does not appear to the senses. But the nonphenomenal reading that we are here dealing with is not for that matter a noumenal reading. Although it aims at something nonperceptual, at "factors or functions that cannot be reduced to intuition" (RT, 13), phenomena, for de Man, are not in opposition to noumena. Until we are able clearly to pinpoint the exact nature of the "object" of a nonphenomenal or rhetorical reading, let us only say that it aims at "the modalities of production and of reception of meaning and of value prior to their establishment," or at "reference prior to designating the referent" (RT, 7–8). More simply put, a nonphenomenal reading centers on what de Man terms the "autonomous potential of language," on what foregrounds in language, and is prior to, the figural and the logical, in short, on "literariness" (RT, 10).

A reading that focuses on what is prior to the production and reception of meaning in a text is geared toward overcoming what de Man considers "the unwarranted separation between the way of reading and interpreting 'literary' as opposed to 'philosophical' or discursive texts" (AR, 226). In "The Resistance to Theory," he notes:

> By considering language as a system of signs and of signification rather than as an established pattern of meanings, one displaces or even suspends the traditional barriers between literary and presumably nonliterary uses of language and liberates the corpus from the secular weight of textual canonization. (RT, 9)

A reading based on a nonphenomenal linguistics not only erases the difference between literary and nonliterary texts, or between two types of critical reading that would take discursive differences into account, it also frees these discourses within themselves from all other "naive oppositions" (RT, 11). Such a reading intends to break down all differences as unwarranted distinctions and barriers. In thus subjecting philosophy to what the reading of its texts had until now been deprived of, namely, the "elementary refinements that are taken for granted in literary interpretation" (AR, 226), aim is taken at philosophical difference itself, i.e., at the possibility of a universal or general discourse. As we will see, the claim to such difference, and all it implies, is, for de Man, a sheer aberration, if not even a sort of *hybris*. Rhetorical reading sets out to demonstrate that difference cannot be made, that opposites remain undecidable and levels blend into one another, in short, that texts contain only a "potential confusion" (AR, 116). De Man's nonphenomenal linguistic reading, a reading that works at bringing about a systematic and generalized annulment of difference, would, consequently, seem to favor a "philosophy" of the same. Yet, whether or not this critique of philosophy (and of literature as well) really ends up in what Schelling called "indiffer-ence," remains to be seen.

In order to be able to reach beyond the difference that philosophy as such presupposes, a rhetorical or nonphenomenal reading of philosophy must neces-sarily transcend the literal meaning of the philosophical text as well as its canonized interpretations. Indeed, the work of differentiation in which philoso-phy is engaged becomes superimposed, in de Man's eyes, on the text as text by the philosopher's desire for meaning as well as by the tradition of canonized in-terpretation. De Man's manner of reading philosophical writings pretends to be-ing a reading "prior to the substance that such reading reveals" (CR, 384). It is an approach to the *texte brut*, to the text before it starts to signify and prior to the established meanings that the community of interpreters has inflicted upon it. It would seem, at first, that the possibility of such an approach to the text in its material and empirical immediacy is entirely unproblematic for de Man. But his repeated insistence that the necessity of such a highly prosaic reading—a reading "by rote," as he also calls it, that is, a reading that proceeds mechanically and unthinkingly—is inscribed in the philosophical text itself, considerably compli-cates the issue. When de Man remarks that "the necessity to revise the canon arises from resistances encountered in the text itself (extensively conceived) and not from preconceptions imported from elsewhere" (CR, 384), or that it springs forth from the disarticulating representation by the text itself of its own figuration, it becomes obvious that he is consistent in his attempt to debunk *all* differences. Indeed, if the necessity for a linguistic reading is prefigured in the text, it becomes eventually impossible radically to demarcate it from, say, philosophical models of reading. If the necessity of a nonphenomenal reading—one that centers on the text in its immediacy—"is itself phenomenally represented in the dramatic tension of the text," then the difference between such a reading and one centered on mean-ing fades away. Textual immediacy, consequently, cannot clearly be separated from the mediation owing to the philosopher's desire for meaning, or the cumula-tive interpretative work of the tradition. To "choose to hear," in a nonphenomenal reading, what a text or a philosophical sentence "actually says," in contrast to what it wishes to say, is not to choose between two absolutely distinct approaches. But, as will become evident hereafter, although both types of reading blend into each other, the necessity for reading in a nonphenomenal manner has a clear pri-ority over the other, and thus displaces the indifference into which both models of reading seem to have mingled.

The nonsymmetric priority of rhetorical reading can already be recognized by its claims to truth. It pretends to be a reading that allows for an adequate under-standing of the text, as opposed to the inadequate understanding that thematic reading provides (RR, 112). A reading such as de Man's aims at teaching what is true (RT, 4). It claims to be doing justice to the text under investigation. De Man contends that what he asserts about Hegel, for instance, is true in the sense of *adequatio*, because it "corresponds to an inexorable and altogether Hegelian move of the text" (CR, 387). Of the method of rhetorical reading in general, he writes that if it is technically correct, it is irrefutable (RT, 20). Yet, since he also asserts that the deconstruction of the aberrations of philosophy is not meant to "recover a measure of truth" (AR, 110), the truth yielded by rhetorical reading must be demarcated from philosophical truth. The deconstruction of philosophy as error takes place, indeed, in the name of the "higher" truth of "the untruth, the lie that metaphor was in the first place," as de Man puts it on one occasion. It takes place, in short, in the name of "the rhetorical, symbolic quality of all language" (AR, 111). Certainly, the truths revealed about the aberrations of philosophy eventually appear indistinguishable from these aberrations themselves. Still, the thrust of rhetorical reading, and of its claims to truth, remains unimpaired.

Contrary to readings within the confined polemical space of canonical interpretation, and centered on what a philosopher actually said or proclaimed, a rhetorical reading is interested in what the philosopher *qua* philosopher could never have admitted. The philosopher, writes de Man, could almost never be expected to be candid about the "threatening paradox at the core of his system against which his thought has to develop a defense," without stopping to be a philosopher (CR, 389). Such a rhetorical reading must necessarily be bold. It cannot indulge in "misplaced timidity" and the literalism of canonical reading. It should not shrink from tampering with the canon because the problems that it points at cannot be resolved by the canonical system itself (CR, 388, 389). But as de Man also insists, the rhetorical commentator "should persist as long as possible in the canonical reading and should begin to swerve away from it only when he encounters difficulties which the methodological and substantial assertions of the system are no longer able to master" (CR, 384). Such a rhetorical reading must, therefore, at least up to a certain point, remain accountable to the tradition of interpretation. It must measure up to the philosopher's intentions, the exigencies of philosophy as philosophy, and the demands of the history of canonical exegesis. In short, a rhetorical reading claims to be faithful to the texts it reads: it pretends an adequate understanding of the text itself. The production of such understanding must remain, at least to some degree, in touch with what traditional scholarship has established about the texts to be read. This is an indispensable rule securing a minimal intelligibility of the understanding that nonphenomenal reading is to produce.

But does de Man honor this self-imposed demand in his readings of the philosophical texts of Kant, Hegel, and Nietzsche? His constancy to this demand is indeed difficult to prove, not so much because a rhetorical reading (i.e., one that reaches beyond all canonized readings) would focus on "neglected corners in the Hegel canon," for instance, or because it would listen "to what is being said obliquely, figurally, and implicitly (though not less compellingly) in a less conspicuous part of the corpus" (SS, 774–75, CR, 390). The difficulty in question first arises from a systematic estrangement to which the philosophical texts are subjected in rhetorical reading. Indeed, from a traditional philosophical perspective, it is altogether incomprehensible why certain passages to which de Man refers in his readings are supposed to be "baffling," "surprising," "bewildering," or "startling," and thus taken as key passages. The philosopher also has difficulty realizing why certain philosophical movements are said to occur "somewhat abruptly," or why the introduction of certain specific statements is judged "unexpected" or "sudden." From an intraphilosophical perspective all these statements can easily be accounted for, as can the specific moment of their occurrence in the argumentative context. To give just one example: In "Phenomenality and Materiality in Kant," de Man contends that contrary to the illusion of clarity and control that seems to characterize the section on the beautiful in the *Third Critique*, the section that deals with the sublime is "one of the most difficult and unresolved passages in the entire corpus of Kant's works" (PM, 124). Yet, historically speaking, the "Analytic of the Sublime," however important its place may be in the total architecture of the *Third Critique*, is a concession to eighteenth-century aesthetics. In the "Analytic of the Beautiful," by contrast, Kant strikes new ground, and this section therefore reveals, as Ernst Cassirer among others has pointed out, a certain foreign quality as far as the subject is concerned, in spite of all the rigor and conceptual refinement invested in its developments. According to Cassirer, Kant moves "once again on terrain that is personally and genuinely his," when broaching the problematics of the sublime as the supreme synthesis between the basic principles of his ethics and his aesthetics. In contrast to the section on the beautiful, that dealing with the sublime is, from a theoretical perspective, excessively clear, indeed, of spotless transparency. It displays, says Cassirer, "all the moments of the Kantian spirit and all those properties indicative of the man as well as of the writer in genuine fulfillment and in the most felicitous mutual interpretation. Hence the trenchancy of the analysis of pure concepts is found united with the moral sensitivity that forms the core of Kant's personality; here the eye for psychological detail that Kant had already evidenced in the precritical *Observations on the Feeling of the Beautiful and the Sublime* is allied with the encompassing transcendental perspectives, which he had achieved since that time over the whole domain of consciousness."[4]

But, however disconcerting the affirmation of obscurity in the place of clarity may be, however incomprehensible it may be to the philosopher that certain statements made with full regard to the requirements of philosophical argumentation are called bewildering, the philosophically trained reader is certainly floored when he realizes that the rhetorical reading of philosophical texts not only completely disregards the literal meaning of texts, but proceeds by means of a *total leveling* of everything constitutive of the text's specificity. The nonphenomenal reading collapses all differences that serve as barriers between concepts and discursive levels, as well as between the premises and conclusions of the separate steps of argumentation, differences on which the whole argument and its movements are dependent. Such a reading pays no respect to the architecture of a work of philosophy, or to the differences between different works in the corpus of a philosopher.

That such an annulment of difference orients de Man's linguistic approach to philosophy can perhaps best be shown in the case of his readings of Hegel. Of the many examples one could summon to make a point in case, we choose de Man's interpretation of the symbolic in Hegel's *Aesthetics*.

For Hegel, according to de Man, art "belongs unreservedly to the order of the symbol" (SS, 766). "The theory of the aesthetic, as a historical as well as a philosophical notion, is predicated, in Hegel, on a theory of art as symbolic" (SS, 763). In his "Critical Response. Reply to Raymond Geuss," after having repeated that "the aesthetic sign is symbolic," he insists that this "is *the* canonical sentence of Hegel's Aesthetic, and any attempt to make it say something else is either false or, as I suspect is the case here [in Raymond Geuss's objections], says the same thing but in less precise terms" (CR, 386).

De Man's contention that, for Hegel, all art is in essence symbolic is based on his interpretation of the following passage from the *Aesthetics* that we quote here in his own translation:

In the case of art, we cannot consider, in the symbol, the arbitrariness between meaning and signification [which characterizes the sign], since art itself consists precisely in the connection, the affinity and the concrete interpenetration of meaning and form. (SS, 763–64)

Read in its proper context, the passage in question establishes that because all art *qua* art presupposes at least some form of connection and affinity between meaning and form, the symbolic—if it happens to occur in art—cannot have the structure of the sign. The fact that all art rests on a minimal relation between form and content does not, according to the terminology of the *Aesthetics*, make all art symbolic. Indeed, the symbolic is only one of the three possible relations between form and content in art, the other two being the classical and the romantic. Throughout the *Aesthetics*, the term "symbolic" designates that particular form of art in which the content, because still entirely abstract, stands in a relation of total inadequacy to its material form. It is certainly the case, as Peter Szondi (to whom de Man refers in his essays on Hegel with respect to other issues) has amply made clear, that this use by Hegel of "symbolic" is most unusual. Indeed, rather than stressing its etymological meaning as falling into one, or as throwing together, Hegel emphasizes the content's inadequacy to its form, and thus reduces the relation on which the symbol is based to that of a mere search for a mutual affinity between meaning and form.[5] Yet, this is the sense in which Hegel understands "symbol" in the *Aesthetics*. Instead of signifying the traditionally recognized natural kinship between its two parts, symbol in the *Aesthetics* only indicates the minimal relation between these two inadequate parts that thus can be said to be in search of adequation. As soon as full adequacy is achieved, the relation in question can no longer be termed symbolic. This is also true of the subsequent reseparation of form and content in the aftermath of classical art. In short, Hegel uses symbolic in his *Aesthetics* to indicate a form of art prior to both the classical—where the concept of art is fully realized in a perfect harmony between form and content—and the romantic, a reseparation of these two elements following the classical. The symbolic not only is one form of art among others, but is, in comparison to the classical, merely a pre-art (*Vorkunst*).

In his response to Geuss, de Man admits that his reading of Hegel never referred to that "more precise sense of the term [symbolic]" as "a historical term in a system of periodization," but rather to a purely linguistic sense of "symbolic" (CR, 385). Although de Man's essay did not demarcate his linguistic sense of "symbolic" from the technical sense in Hegel, he justifies his move in the "Response" by asserting that "the term 'symbolic' appears conspicuously in the *Aesthetics*, though it is not always used in the same sense." Hegel is said to also gloss "['symbolic'] in purely linguistic terms, by setting up a distinction between sign and symbol. This differentiation belongs to all language in general," de Man remarks, concluding that "the term 'symbolic' thus functions in a linguistic as well as historical register" (CR, 385).

In the following we must verify whether there is indeed another use of "symbolic" in the *Aesthetics*. As a matter of fact, one sees Hegel at times speaking of a "symbolic manner of representation and sensuous perception."[6] What Hegel means by this sense of "symbolic" is made explicit in the same part of the *Encyclopedia* to which de Man turns in his essay—not, as one would expect, to substantiate his interpretation of "symbolic" in purely linguistic terms, but to prove that "symbolic" implies reference to a linguistic *subject*. This part of the *Encyclopedia* is entitled *The Philosophy of Mind*, and is engaged in an analysis of the spirit's autointuition, wherein the spirit is shown to inquire into its own being alone and to relate exclusively to its own determinations; Hegel determines symbolic imagination as that form of imagination (*Vorstellung*) that allows the self-intuiting spirit to appropriate, that is, to universalize not the world (as de Man puts it) but the immediate datum in itself (*das in sich gefundene Unmittelbare*), by giving it the existence of an image, a *bildliches Dasein*. Imagination as symbol producing synthesizes the intellect's self-intuited immediacy with what it has found in perception. Because imagination, in order to achieve such representation, must choose material "whose *independent* meaning *corresponds* to the determined content of the universal that is to be rendered as image," Hegel can equate it with what is formal in art, for art, he writes, "represents the truly universal or the *idea* in the form of *sensuous existence*, of the *image*."[7] From this perspective, then, art in general can be called symbolic since it may choose only such material for its sensuous rendering of the idea that has some sort of natural relation to the content of the idea.

Throughout the *Aesthetics*, however, Hegel insists that he is concerned not with this sense of "symbolic" but only and exclusively with the symbolic as one among three *forms of art*. After having criticized the romantic attempt to extend symbolism to every sphere of mythology and art, he notes:

> Our task must therefore consist, not in accepting diffusion of the symbolic over the entire field of art, but conversely expressly limiting the range of what in itself is presented to us as a symbol proper and therefore is to be treated as symbolical.[8]

It has become clear that de Man considers all art symbolic because it implies a minimal (natural) relation between meaning and material form. In what comes closest to a definition, he writes that "the symbol is the mediation between the mind and the physical world of which art manifestly partakes" (SS, 763). Such a traditional understanding of "symbolic" also explains why de Man, in flagrant disregard of what Hegel wrote, can assert that because Hegel considers "the symbolic by way of an increasing proximity between sign and meaning, a proximity which, by principles of resemblance, analogy, filiation, interpenetration, and so forth, tightens the link between both to the ultimate point of identity," this identity would reach its climax in classical art: "Far from being nonsymbolic, classical art is the moment at which the semiotic function of language, which is, in principle, arbitrary and detached from meaning, is entirely transformed into a symbolic function" (CR, 386). Now although this sense of symbolic seems to correspond to what Hegel developed under the rubric of symbolic imagination, it is certainly not *the* canonical sentence of Hegel's *Aesthetics*. If there is such a sentence with respect to the symbolic in Hegel's work, it is one that stresses the relation of inadequacy between idea and natural form.

In addition to what has already been developed, it must be pointed out that "symbolic" in the sense of the universal images produced by imagination, is not, in essence, linguistic. To call it linguistic by arguing, as de Man does, that "we now associate [the term 'symbolic'] with linguistic structures," is merely to import a problematic into Hegel's text that reflects present theoretical concerns (SS, 763). The move is capital to de Man's whole argument, for it serves to suggest that an essentially Cratylian definition of language as symbolic sustains the whole of Hegel's *Aesthetics*. But, because of its imagelike products, symbolic imagination is still prelinguistic for Hegel. In symbols, the intellect only *looks at itself* in sensuous representations that are very distinct from the signs and words with which language begins. Hegel notes in the *Aesthetics* that "the symbol is *prima facie* a sign," only because it *designates* something, however inarticulately.[9] But such designation is not yet linguistic, and certainly not in the modern sense of that term. A full demonstration of this would require long detours through the *Ency-*

clopedia. Therefore, we will confine ourselves here to a number of points that indicate the direction such a demonstration would have to take. (1) It must be recalled that *within* the sphere of art, a movement takes place from the symbolic, which is essentially mute, to the sign and word in the last form of romantic art — poetry — which also brings about a passage to the higher spheres of the spirit. (2) As a whole, the sphere of art belongs to prelinguistic symbol-producing imagination. As soon as productive imagination turns into sign-producing imagination, that is, as soon as it becomes potentially capable of being linguistically expressed, the autointuiting spirit leaves the realm of art behind itself. (3) As Hegel argues in the *Encyclopedia*, imagination becomes sign-producing imagination when it gains greater freedom in the use of its interiorized perceptions for designating itself in its own immediate universality, or as *idea*. Such passage occurs where the spirit's perceptions *as* perceptions (perceptions belonging to the spirit alone) are put into relation with the spirit's *own* independent representations. Whereas the symbol's own content "corresponds, essentially and conceptually, to the content it expresses," signs have an arbitrary relation to what they refer to, because, in them, the intellect has annulled the immediate and proper content of the perceptions, giving them a meaning derived completely from itself.[10] Yet, what is true of the symbol is also true of the sign: it is not linguistic per se for Hegel. Not only are linguistic signs, or *words* merely one, however important, form of signs, but signs in general function at first only as mute representations of the spirit. Their linguistic articulation is still excluded. Signs, for Hegel, are only the mute foundation, or if one prefers, the condition of possibility of speech and language. (4) De Man refers to these parts of the *Encyclopedia* in order to prove that the problematic of the symbol, and especially of the sign, implies reference to a subject. It surely does, but the subject is here the self-knowing spirit, and not a linguistic subject engaged in speech acts directed at the world. If the foregoing points are carefully developed, they lead to the conclusion that the minimal relation between form and content that art generally presupposes cannot be called "symbolic" as referring to linguistic structures. If, however, de Man does so, if he subrepticiously turns Hegel's *Aesthetics* into a text based on and held together by a symbolic understanding of language, it is because for de Man, *all* "aesthetic theory, including its most systematic formulation in Hegel," is to be considered "as the complete unfolding of the model of which the Cratylian conception of language is a version" (RT, 10).

Rather than discussing the intriguing point of de Man's argument — an argument that extends Gérard Genette's contention that a "spontaneous belief in the resemblance of words and things, which is illustrated by a kind of eternal Cratylism . . . has always functioned as the ideology, or the 'indigenous theory' of poetic language," to the philosophical discipline of aesthetics in general — we would like to take de Man to task for his systematic leveling of conceptual differences and strata of argumentation in his own text.[11] Indeed, to argue that art in general is symbolic in Hegel's *Aesthetics*, de Man must disregard the difference between the symbolic as a *form* of art, and art as a function of symbolic *representation*, as well as confound symbolic representation with *linguistic* representation or speech act. Only by ignoring the difference in status between the developments in the *Aesthetics* and what takes place in the *Encyclopedia*, as well as the difference between certain parts of the *Encyclopedia* itself, can de Man's rhetorical reading arrive at the conclusion that the *Aesthetics*, as an aesthetic, is based on a metaphysical conception of language.

What is further revealed by this short analysis of an important segment of de Man's approach to a philosophical text is that the leveling of differences—the subversion of all possible development through an annulment of differences—is itself only one prominent effect of de Man's more general "methodological" procedure of analogizing. More precisely, his "method" is based on positive analogy, i.e., one that emphasizes the likeness among instances and moments of a text, or different parts of a work, while neglecting the differences. Such analogical inference allows for comparisons between truly incommensurable elements, or more precisely, between two incompatible types of relationships, or proportions. As a result of this procedure, de Man not only indefatigably points out mirror effects, close proximities, allusions, equivalences, resemblances, etc., between elements and movements in, or even outside texts, he also, and especially, draws similarities between relationships that because they are situated on completely different planes, or in entirely different corpora, are, in fact, uncomparable. Let us limit ourselves to two examples. In "Hegel on the Sublime," he notes:

> The relationship between pantheism and monotheism in the history of art and religion . . . is like the relationship between natural sciences and epistemology. (HS, 145)

Or, in "Phenomenality and Materiality in Kant":

> If critical philosophy and metaphysics (including ideologies) are causally linked to each other, their relationship is similar to the relationship . . . between bodies and their transformations or motions. (PM, 123)

Such analogies, according to de Man, do not operate solely on the semantic level of the text, but are also to be found on the level of enunciation, as well as between that level and the semantic level. In his essays on Nietzsche, he argues that one can draw similarities, in *The Birth of Tragedy*, between the theses stated there and the enunciatory text's level, between statement and what he calls, in one instance, "the *history* of the text," between its statements and its rhetorical praxis, between its semantic assertions and its rhetorical mode (AR, 116). He emphasizes that an analogy is to be found in *The Birth of Tragedy* "between genetic movements in history and semiological relationships in language" (AR, 102). Because such analogy produces "a potential confusion between figural and referential statement," and makes it impossible to distinguish the philosophical statements from the rhetorical figures on which they hinge, de Man concludes in these essays that the "textual authority" of the philosophical text is without all ground (AR, 116, 99).

Generally speaking, one can say that for de Man the very possibility of such analogy prohibits all clear and distinct establishment of levels and conceptual differences. As far as his own texts are concerned, this analogical reasoning also explains and accounts for the onionlike structure of his texts (especially his later texts), as well as for the relation of chiasmic inversion through which the various layers mirror each other into a certain identity or, rather, sameness.

Is one not, in light of the results produced by this truly systematic leveling of difference and positive analogization—a leveling that is clearly deliberate, and not attributable to mere oversight or philosophical naïveté in general—immediately reminded of Hegel's famous dictum concerning those philosophers for whom thought is a night in which all cows are black? Because of de Man's claim that his treatment of philosophical texts can at least up to a certain point be measured against the standards of the canon and the rules of interpretation, the philosopher's scorn about such a handling of philosophical difference is fully justified. Still, to become merely outraged at de Man's activity may well mean to become trapped and ensnared. A step-by-step refutation of all the gross, and almost too blatant, errors that de Man seems to entertain in his readings of philosophy may blind the critic, and disable him from grasping the uncannily coherent, if not cogent, "theoretical" project underlying all these flagrant violations. As said, de Man's work is involved in a rhetorical, nonphenomenal, literary, or linguistic reading of philosophical texts. Yet such a reading focuses on the "autonomous potential of language," and not, as a philosophical reading, on the transparent meaning that language purports to convey. The shift in focus to the autonomous potential of language, free of all relation to what is signified, causes language to turn opaque. Together with all the discursive differences of meaning, language, if thematized as such, loses all its previous semi-invisibility; it becomes objectified, and acquires an impenetrable opacity. Ultimately such analysis of the autonomous potential of language has no relation whatsoever to the meaning that this language appears to transport. Indeed, a rhetorical reading of a text is not geared toward revealing anything regarding the meaning of that text. It is not *about* a text, and thus cannot be measured against it. For such a reading, all the distinctive discursive moments and levels blend into one undifferentiated and nontransparent mass. But does this mass, therefore, correspond to that night of abstraction in which all cows are black? Although it is clear that such a reading does not contribute to the understanding of the text it deals with, de Man claims that precisely because such a reading is not *on* the texts it reads, it is *truer* to those texts (see RR, 123). De Man's readings make truth claims, but these claims do not concern the meaningful distinctions that literary criticism or philosophical canonical interpretation is concerned with. As far as philosophy is concerned, the truth that interests a linguistic reading of texts is not of the order of generality or universality. As seen, a linguistic reading is suspicious of the difference that philosophy makes, and of all the differences that it must set up to unfold and account for its own status. But such a reading remains concerned with a certain truth, and because this truth goes as far as to question the very possibility of abstraction, it does not seem to be a function of the black-on-black painting to which Hegel refers. But is it for that matter comparable to the gray on gray in which, according to Hegel, philosophy paints all things? Undoubtedly, de Man's enterprise presupposes, as does philosophy in general, a certain dusk—a "glimmering," in de Man's words—of meaning and difference. It also takes its flight with the oncoming of night, but it does not do so in order to reveal the thought of the world, the ideal, or the concept. The truth it summons is not one of difference, and its use of language in articulating that truth no longer yields to the philosophical imperative of speaking well.

Toward a Formal Materialism

In order better to circumscribe the sort of truth that a rhetorical reading is interested in, it is imperative to analyze in greater detail rhetorical reading's razing of philosophical difference. We return, therefore, to a discussion of de Man's essays on Nietzsche. As in his treatment of Hegel's *Aesthetics*, he sets out arguing that the illusion of coherence and of genetic development that *The Birth of Tragedy* displays, in spite of its obvious patchwork character of disconnected fragments, is an illusion rooted in a metaphysical assumption underlying that work. This assumption implies that all statements are grounded "in ontology and in a metaphysics of presence," thus securing "the possibility of language to reach full and substantial meaning." It is not without importance to mention that de Man neglects actually to prove that such "a deep-seated generative conception" controls all the levels of discourse in Nietzsche's early work (AR, 88). While de Man underpinned his assertion of the symbolic nature of Hegel's *Aesthetics* as a whole by reading "symbolic" in a nontechnical sense and according to the meaning that it has *now*, for us, the same assertion with respect to Nietzsche's text is taken for granted as having been proved by *recent* criticism on Nietzsche.[12] This assertion by de Man can be construed as one facet of a double strategy that organizes his readings of texts; this first movement consists of stating that the seemingly coherent and continuous nature of texts, as well as their referential properties, hinges on the symbolic and genetic model of language that sustains them. The second facet of the strategy of a rhetorical reading attempts to prove that a text inscribes reference to its nonphenomenal figuration. This reference is shown to take place in a twofold manner: through the text's thematic self-destruction of its own illusory continuity, on the one hand, and through thematic representation of the nonphenomenal and autonomous potential of language within the text, on the other hand. Such double reference, according to de Man, not only destroys the genetic continuity of the text, it also reveals the metaphysical assumption regarding language at the base of the text to be thoroughly erroneous.

It is certainly not insignificant that de Man does not find this inscription of the nonphenomenal power of language in the text of *The Birth of Tragedy* itself, but rather—already emphasizing in this manner the lack of phenomenal unity of Nietzsche's work—in the "discontinuous aphoristic formulations" not included in that work, and which feature Nietzsche's "main theoretical speculations on language and art at the time of *The Birth of Tragedy*" (AR, 101, 88). Yet what do these fragments, which are said to found the whole of Nietzsche's work on tragedy, establish? After having argued that in *The Birth of Tragedy*, unity and genetic unfolding hinge on the possibility of Dionysus's appearance as Apollo, on a will representing itself as music, on the authority of a human voice as the origin of the narrative, etc.—possibilities that, according to de Man, are all grounded in a genetic and symbolic model of language—de Man asserts that these fragments put the *possibility of such a passage or transition*—say, from the literal to the figural, from essence to appearance, from origin to representation, etc.— radically into question. De Man contends that these fragments contest "the will as the ontological category by means of which beginning and end, origin and purpose are united in one genetic pattern." By totally separating these instances, "all possible claim at genetic totalization" becomes undermined: "no bridge, as metaphor or as representation, can ever connect the natural realm of essences with the textual realm of forms and values" (AR, 99–100). The thrust of the second facet of the strategy constitutive of rhetorical and nonphenomenal reading thus serves to establish the complete impossibility of development, continuous construction, and unfolding of a philosophical argument.

As the essay "The Rhetoric of Tropes" holds, this impossibility of processlike development is a function of a structural aspect of language. In analyzing one passage from the *Will to Power*, de Man attempts to show that here the logical priority of one of the terms of the binary conceptual polarities in the history of metaphysics—the example is the priority of cause over effect—is always based on a "cumulative error" resulting from a linguistic event of erroneous substitutions, that is, without regard for truth, made possible by the rhetorical essence of language "as the play of reversals and substitutions." The logical priority of cause over effect thus appears to be a function of the rhetorical figure of metonymy or metalepsis by which cause and effect become interchangeable. But since according to that very figure, "the priority status of the two poles can be reversed," as well, there is, from a linguistic point of view, absolutely no intrinsic reason why one option would have to be privileged over the other (AR, 107, 108). As a consequence, all philosophical truths, and *a fortiori* all philosophical distinctions, are considered nothing but erroneous assumptions rooted in the figurative power of language. In the same essay, de Man also claims that although a philosophical text such as Nietzsche's may be critical of the category of self-hood, the critical discourse's own centrality and alleged self-identity is nothing but a metaphor of self, a displaced self never questioned, and based on an exchange made possible by the figural essence of language. In the same way as self-hood is an illusion, philosophy's centrality and authority are a lie, as a matter of fact, a cumulative lie because the lie of a lie, grounded in what de Man calls language's positional power (See AR, 111–12). All of philosophy's ontological claims as well are based on the linguistic "possibility of unwarranted substitutions," and on "misinterpreted systems of relationships." They are said to be, without exception, rooted in "the rhetorical substratum" of language (AR, 123). Yet, if this is the case, if, indeed, all philosophical truths and ontological claims are but the result of erroneously fixed exchanges or substitutions on the rhetorical level of language, then, instead of following from insight or genuine development, philosophical statements do nothing but *repeat* the figural properties of language as such. All philosophical cognition and its claims to truth stem from misinterpretations of the relations made possible by figures of exchange and substitution, figures that thoroughly undermine the very possibility of an unequivocal and continuous passage from one pole to another because the relations between them can always be inverted. From the perspective of de Man's linguistic or literary reading of philosophy, there can be no such thing as development, a continuous and articulated unfolding of an argument from a premise to a conclusion, or of a discourse from a beginning to an end. Indeed, in such a reading, the philosophical text *separates* into absolutely *unrelating* agencies, instances, levels, acts. The philosophical text becomes atomized in an out-and-out fragmentization against the backdrop of its rhetorical substratum.

In order to refine our analysis of rhetorical reading's dismantling of relations between terms, planes, and parts of a text, we now turn briefly to de Man's analysis of Shelley's *The Triumph of Life*. In this essay, de Man, following his double strategy of reading, first concentrates on what he calls a thematic or, rather, "specular understanding of the text." Such an understanding that coincides with a cognitive approach to the text—"in which the text serves as a mirror of our own knowledge and our own knowledge mirrors in its turn the text's signification"—is rooted, according to de Man, "in the illusion of doubleness," or of a split between self-contained unities that would make self-reflexive closure possible (RR, 112). A speculative reading bent on achieving self-reflective closure presupposes difference, more precisely, a difference in which the differents stand in a relation of duplication to one another. On the whole, "Shelley Disfigured" wants to demonstrate that such self-reflexivity is never attained because the text—in this case, Shelley's poem—does not produce the doubles required to achieve specular closure. De Man insists that all specular understanding becomes blocked already at its thematic level. Indeed, instead of providing answers to questions that punctuate the poem, answers that, as the doubles of these questions, would permit cognition, Shelley's poem only features further questions. De Man writes: "The structure of the text is not one of question and answer, but of a question whose meaning, as question, is effaced from the moment it is asked. The answer to the question is another question" (RR, 98). In the question that answers the first question, the initial question becomes forgotten because there is no answer that would still refer to it. In other words, with the mere occurrence of the second question all relation to the first question is cut off—it is literally forgotten. After having evoked the Platonic and Neoplatonic definition of forgetting as anamnesis, de Man notes that in contrast to the latter, "what one forgets here is not the previous condition, for the line of demarcation between the two conditions is so unclear, the distinction between the forgotten and the remembered so unlike the distinction between two well-defined areas, that we have no assurance whatever that the forgotten ever existed" (RR, 104). This is a radical forgetting that makes it impossible to distinguish something as preceding or following something else, since all relations are disconnected. Yet if that is so, it is already impossible on the thematic level itself to relate anything to anything, to tell the difference between one thing and another. Instead of giving way to symmetrical differents that could be related in a specular manner to one another, the text, already from a thematic perspective, appears to have a pulverizing structure that leads to hovering, or glimmering ambivalence, to use de Man's own terms. None of the images of Shelley's poem can be clearly determined with respect to (their) opposites, and hence the symmetry required by cognitive reflection is never attained. The poem's text is thematically disarticulated; nothing relates to anything, and this pointedly prevents the gathering of some unifying and totalizing meaning from the poem.

To understand adequately and truly why such a text as Shelley's poem allows understanding itself "to wane away, layer by layer, until it is entirely forgotten and remains present only in the guise of an edifice that serves to celebrate and perpetuate its oblivion," however, it is necessary to proceed with de Man to the second facet of rhetorical reading's strategy, that is, to its nonphenomenal phase. The necessity of such a reading is thematically, phenomenally, inscribed in a text. In the case of Shelley's poem, de Man locates it in the text's reference to "measure"—here understood as the figuration of "articulated sound, that is language," and not music, since "its determining property is an articulation distinctive of verbal sound prior to its signifying function." Indeed, if " 'measure' separates from the phenomenal aspects of signification as a specular *representation*, and stresses instead the literal and material aspects of language," then "measure," in the text of the poem, corresponds to a "thematization of language" (RR, 112, 113). With the term "measure," the text refers to its own linguistic figuration, to "the nonsignifying, material properties of language," signification, and figuration itself. De Man distinguishes at least three aspects of the literal and material properties of language; characteristics of all of these have a disruptive effect on the illusory continuity of the text and its meaning: (1) referring to the classical theories of the sign, he determines these properties to be relatively *independent*; (2) their "free play in relation to . . . (their) signifying function" shows them to be characterized by *randomness* and *arbitrariness*; (3) their representation or figuration in the text "disrupts the symmetry of cognition as representation," or to use more colorful terms, it extinguishes and buries all "poetic and philosophical light" (RR, 114, 113). These literal and material qualities of language are a first cornerstone of the very particular and extremely idiosyncratic philosophy that animates the nonphenomenal reading phase of texts. De Man calls it "formal materialism." As remains to be seen, it is a philosophy whose gaze traverses the substance of a text attending neither to the objectivity of its structures, nor to the spiritual activity at its base, but to qualities of the text that, as can already be seen from the nature of the material and literal properties of language, stand in no relation whatsoever to the text's figural and conceptual constructs amenable to aesthetic and nonaesthetic experience. Considering the sheer arbitrariness and intrinsic senselessness of the material and signifying agencies of language, the randomness of their individual occurrences, the relative independence of their play, and the opacity of their literal materiality, all experiencable meaning appears *superimposed* on them. But since these properties cannot, because of their material opacity and lack of meaning, relate to one another in any significant manner, all objective intelligibility, that is, the text's latent armature—its structure— seems to be the result of an imposition as well. As these literal instances become thematized in the text's inscribed reference to its own figuration, they tend to exhibit a sphere of irreducible heterogeneity characterized by the absolute impenetrability and material singularity of the linguistic sounds or letters that, therefore, do not lend themselves to any meaningful interaction. These instances form a chaotic sphere of radically fragmented material agencies between which no text can ever be woven.

In his readings of Kant and Hegel, de Man has made the attempt to conceptualize, so to speak, what must be viewed as the first element of the "ontological" base not only of all texts but of de Man's own highly disturbing practice of reading. Indeed, all his transgressions, whether related to the commensurability of concepts, levels of argumentation, parts of works, or works among each other, in short, all of his infractions against the philosophical law par excellence, the law prohibiting all *metabasis eis allo genos*, find their "ontological" justification in de Man's theory concerning the absolute heterogeneity and intrinsic meaninglessness of the linguistic signifier. This theory alone explains the coherent, if not cogent, nature of his infractions against the law of interpretation.

In order to situate and assess the nature of those literal and material properties of language, it is certainly appropriate to turn to de Man's essay "Phenomenality and Materiality in Kant," as well as to the (yet unpublished) article "Kant's Materialism." In the latter essay, de Man claims that "a materialism much more radical than what can be conveyed by such terms as realism or empiricism" inhabits Kantian idealism. What this materialism amounts to can best be grasped in "Phenomenality and Materiality in Kant." After having asserted that ideologies and metaphysics depend on transcendental philosophy, and that metaphysics and critical philosophy are interdependent as well, de Man raises the question of how transcendental philosophy can be said to be dependent on something metaphysical or empirical. In a more than questionable operation of analogy, that relation of dependence becomes conceptualized in terms of a causal link. The place where such causal relation can best be established, according to de Man, is the *Critique of Judgement*, which itself "corresponds to the necessity of establishing the causal link between critical philosophy, between a purely conceptual and an empirically determined discourse," that is, between the *Critique of Pure Reason* (in de Man's terms, a transcendental *philosophy*), and *The Critique of Practical Reason* (in short, "an empirically determined discourse," or what, for de Man, amounts to the same, an ideological or metaphysical *philosophy*; PM, 124). In total oblivion of the fact that the *Second Critique* is a critique and not a dogmatic philosophy, and that the category of causality is applicable to the realm of objects of nature alone, de Man turns the aesthetic—and above all one of its forms, the sublime—into the "phenomenalized, empirically manifest principle of cognition on whose existence the possibility of such an articulation" of the transcendental and the metaphysical depends. The privilege accorded to the sublime in this respect rests on Reason's involvement in the latter. In the sublime, the "noumenal entity" of Reason becomes phenomenally represented. Whereas "the beautiful is a metaphysical and ideological principle, the sublime aspires to being a transcendental one," writes de Man (PM, 125). Yet, the task of finding a phenomenal equivalent for a conceptually infinite notion turns out to be the real crux of the analytics of the sublime. Indeed, de Man notes, the model that Kant advances in answer to this problem, a model whose paradigmatic totalization leads to comprehension's discovery of its limitations regarding the noumenal entity of Reason, is, because of its economic pattern of loss and gain, "no longer, properly speaking, philosophical, but linguistic." Thus, instead of allowing for a transcendental determination, the sublime can only be formally determined. The model that Kant uses to phenomenalize Reason "describes, not a faculty of the mind, be it as consciousness or as cognition, but a potentiality inherent in language. For such a system of substitution, set up along a paradigmatic and a syntagmatic axis, generating partial totalizations within an economy of profit and loss, is a very familiar model indeed. . . . It is the model of discourse as a tropological system. The desired articulation of the sublime takes place, with suitable reservations and restriction, within such a purely formal system" (PM, 130). This purely formal system that animates aesthetic judgment in the dynamics of the sublime, and that under the guise of a philosophical argument produces a causal determination and a paradigmatic totalization of infinite Reason, is formal to the extent that it refers to language independently of all semantic depth, that is, to language in its purely material properties devoid as yet "of any reflexive or intellectual complication" (PM, 136). Yet the causal determination of Reason in the sublime thus brought to light—a determination of the transcendental by something metaphysical, that is, empirical and ideological in de Man's own terms—is based on a causation by something that, in the last resort, is accessible neither to the powers of transcendental philosophy nor, for that matter, to metaphysics or ideology. Hence, the materiality of the linguistic signifier radically disrupts the economy of interdependence, and of cognitive reflection in the play between transcendental philosophy and metaphysics, since the materiality in question, a materiality that does not illustrate or represent the infinite, is no longer of the order of metaphysics; rather, it stands in a relation of assymmetry to all the forms of cognition referred to, and their reflexive interplay.

This, then, is the status of the materiality of language in its unwrought, or native, state: it is a cause devoid of all meaning, of all semantic depth, which stands in a relation of excentricity to what it appears to effect. Because of its ultimate meaninglessness and its exorbitant situation, because of the absence of a (meaningful) relation between it and what becomes superimposed on it as its effect, this irreducibly formal materiality functions as "a break or discontinuity" at the heart not only of the *Third Critique* but, more generally, of thought itself (PM, 132). It disarticulates what it effectuates, says de Man. On the last pages of "Phenomenality and Materiality in Kant," he seeks this materialism "that Kant's posterity has not yet begun to face up to," in the very "dismemberment of language," in meaning's dependence on "the fragmentation of sentences and propositions into discrete words, or the fragmentation of words into syllables or finally letters." De Man goes as far as to ascertain that the very success of certain Kantian arguments, rather than resulting from philosophical development, is decisively dependent on "the play of the letter and of the syllable," in short, on elements that are in themselves without any meaning whatsoever. He writes:

> Is not the persuasiveness of the entire passage on the recovery of the imagination's tranquility after the shock of the sublime surprise based, not so much on the little play acted out by the senses, but on the proximity between the German words for surprise and admiration. "*Verwunderung*" and "*Bewunderung*"? And are we not made to assent to the more than paradoxical but truly aporetic incompatibility between the failure of the imagination to grasp magnitude with what becomes, in the experience of the sublime, the success of this same imagination as an agent of reason, are we not made to assent to this because of a constant, and finally bewildering alternation of the two terms, "*Angemessen(heit)*" and "*Unangemessen(heit)*," to the point where one can no longer tell them apart? The bottom line, in Kant as well as in Hegel, is the prosaic materiality of the letter and no degree of obfuscation or

ideology can transform this materiality into the phenomenal cognition of aesthetic judgement. (PM, 144)

But, although the prosaic materiality of the letter, the arbitrary element of the nonsignifying properties of linguistic articulation, undoes "the representational and iconic function of figuration," as de Man argues in his analysis of Shelley's *The Triumph of Life*, it "does not by itself have the power to break down the specular structure which the text erects" (RR, 114). The materiality in question disrupts only the figural, the sensory cognitive aspect of the iconic function. But figure, de Man adds, is not essential to figuration: "The iconic, sensory or, if one wishes, the aesthetic moment is not constitutive of figuration." Figuration creates the illusion of meaning neither merely nor primarily through sensory pleasure, but through signification rooted in the semiological possibility of substituting reiteration (RR, 114–15). We are told that this latter possibility is a function of the irreducibly mechanical rules of grammar and syntax. Functioning "on the level of the letter without the intervention of an iconic factor," these mechanical rules, whose repetitive senselessness constitutes the signifying function of language, are, because of their exorbitant position, disfigurative of figuration as the meaning-creating process itself. There is, however, a last nonsignifying aspect to language that serves as another essential disruptive ground of all linguistic figuration in that it concerns the act of the signifying function as such. If what we developed under the category of the literal and material dimension of language could be considered to be the "ontological" foundation of rhetorical reading, this last, and complementary, linguistic function bears on its "epistemological" foundation. Together these two aspects of formal materialism seem to represent a miniature philosophical system, one that combines an ontology with a theory of cognition. The formal materialism at the base of de Man's rhetorical reading is a philosophy, consequently, that in its own way lives up to the major standards and requirements of classical philosophy. But, as remains to be seen, this is not yet all. It is indeed a philosophy similar to all others in that it also submits to the aegis of *theoria*. Yet, before engaging in a discussion of what thus appears to be in nuce, at least, a comprehensive system of foundation, let us first establish the nature of that aspect of language, which according to de Man, radically disrupts figuration as a meaningful act.

What radically disfigures figure is nothing less than the fact that "the figure is not naturally given or produced but that it is posited by an arbitrary act," as de Man notes in his analysis of *The Triumph of Life*. In other words, de Man asserts that between the linguistic act constitutive of signification and meaning itself there is no relation of any sort. It is an arbitrary act that, by virtue of the total absence of continuity between itself and what it causes, is itself absolutely meaningless. But this blind, and in itself senseless, act is not only separated from what follows it as its effects, it is also preceded by nothing. We read that it "relates to nothing that comes before or after." It is "detached from all antecedents," and, consequently, an act in "its own right," absolutely singular and pointlike, "brusque and unmotivated." Or, to cite again: It is "a single, and therefore violent, act of power achieved by the positional power of language considered by and in itself" (RR, 116–17). This positing power of language, as de Man understands it, whose performative properties differ "considerably from conventional as well as from 'creatively' (or, in the technical sense, intentionally) constitutive" performance elaborated by speech-act theories, "is both entirely arbitrary, in having a strength that cannot be reduced to necessity, and entirely inexorable in that there is no alternative to it. It stands beyond the polarities of chance and determination" (RT, 19; RR, 116).[13] In the same way as the sun, which in the poem is said to spring forth of "its own unrelated power," free from all dependence on the agonistic pathos of the dialectical battle between the doubles or differents, the speculative play of cognition, and the self-reflexivity of the text—the *act* of linguistic figuration—is irreducibly singular and, because relating to nothing, instantly forgotten. A text is punctuated by its myriad positing acts. In a manner similar to the literal and material properties of the linguistic signifier, these acts form a chaos of opaque (since they are always unique and unrelated), linguistic events that in principle "cannot be made part" of the text (RR, 116). But, without these meaningless events of positing there would be, of course, no text.

A rhetorical reading, one that focuses on the nonphenomenal and autonomous potential of language, rather than producing noumena, exhibits a fragmentary chaos of meaningless linguistic matter, repetitive mechanical rules, and absolutely opaque linguistic events. The radically irreducible empiricalness of all these agencies and instances represents the truth about texts. It is the truth by which a rhetorical reading must abide. But one question remains: how can this truth be beheld? In short, it is the question of how the "ontological" and "epistemological" substratum of texts comes into view at all. We recall that a nonphenomenal, nonaesthetic linguistic reading is a reading that reaches not only beyond the aesthetic and sensuous categories but also beyond the intuitable as such. In this sense it is necessarily nonperceptual. What sort of gaze, then, animates a nonphenomenal reading? How is one to look at texts in order to bring that "ontological" and "epistemological" substratum to the fore, in whose light they revert into an uncanny opaqueness? To circumscribe this opacifying glance that stares at the incomprehensibility or chaos which Friedrich Schlegel considered the origin left in darkness, out of which the intellect constructed the entire unending world—to circumscribe this it is necessary to return once again to de Man's reading of the *Critique of Judgement*.[14]

The problem facing the *Third Critique* is, according to de Man, one of finding a representation for what in principle is unrepresentable—reason and the ideas. As we have already pointed out, de Man finds Kant's solution to this problem, in the part of the *Critique of Judgement* devoted to the mathematical sublime, unsatisfactory, obscure, and ridden by difficulties. He explains these difficulties by the constraints forced upon Kant to seek recourse under the guise of rigorous philosophical argumentation to something that is not philosophical at all, namely, to a linguistic and formal structure of substitution void of all content. Neglecting the fact that the two parts of the sublime—the mathematical and the dynamical sublime—represent symmetric possibilities of the sublime as such, de Man notes that rather than further developing, let alone solving, the difficulties apparent in the mathematical sublime, the chapter on the dynamics of the sublime only repeats, restates, and refines those difficulties. The obscurity and difficulty to which de Man refers, especially in the second chapter on the sublime, lie with Kant's reminder that if nature is to produce sublime effects, it must be experienced in an entirely disinterested manner, free of all teleological judgment. The starry heaven and the vast ocean are sublime only if we regard them "as poets do, merely by what strikes the eye [*was der Augenschein zeigt*]," in short, as "a distant, all-embracing, vault," or respectively as "a clear mirror of water only bounded by the heaven."[15] Yet, what is, according to de Man, so difficult and obscure about Kant's demand? Seemingly, it is the fact that the sublime as a representation of ideas is dependent on what de Man perceives as an irreducibly mindless act of ocular vision, a purely *material* vision, as he translates *Augenschein*. Now, before further analysis of what de Man means by such a vision, it needs first to be clarified whether one can, indeed, equate disinterested vision of objects of nature, that is, a vision free of all particular judgments of sense, of logically determinate, and of teleological judgment, with mere vision.

The question, first, is whether, in Kant, there can be a thing such as mere vision at all. Is regarding nature "just as we see it" really free of everything intellectual? Although de Man recalls that Kant speaks in his *Logic* of mere intuition (*blosse Anschauung*) as an intuition devoid of concepts, it is questionable whether mere intuition can be equated with mere vision in de Man's sense. One certainly remembers Kant's famous sentence from *Critique of Pure Reason* that concepts without intuitions are empty and intuitions without concepts, blind. The savage's observation of an object whose purpose he does not know—Kant's example is a house—is a blind perception for sure, since from a formal point of view it lacks all relation to consciousness. But Kant's limitation of the savage's perception to the matter (*Materie*) of perception alone is meaningful only insofar as the lack of determination of the matter of cognition immediately calls upon cognition's other facet, its relation to the subject. Even if the savage perceives without concepts, this very lack implies a negative relation to the formal aspect of cognition. The faculties never operate alone, absolutely independent of one another, in the last resort, because of the transcendental unity of apperception. The mere vision de Man speaks of cannot be identified with the mere intuition in question. By rights, it is asymmetrical to the amorphous sensation of the savage (which is not

even, strictly speaking, visual) whose lack of concepts is meaningful for Kant because it is counterposed to the formal categories.

The aesthetic judgment on the beautiful is excellent proof of this essential interdependence of the faculties, since it exhibits, in what is called the play of the
faculties, the minimal agreement between imagination as the highest sensible
faculty and understanding as the intelligible faculty of the concepts. By contrast,
the judgment of the sublime is witness to a play that implies a minimal relation
between imagination and the faculty of the ideas, i.e., Reason. In the same way
as the aesthetic judgment on the beautiful can be construed as the formal condition
of possibility, or the minimal synthesis required for there to be a cognition of nature, the aesthetic judgment on the sublime must be understood as the minimal
synthesis needed for there to be a mediation between concepts of nature and concepts of freedom. The sublime is, by definition, this relation *sine qua non*, without which no application of Reason to imagination could ever be envisioned. The
sublime, then, is at first a relation. Kant writes in the *Third Critique*: "The *Sublime* consists merely in the *relation* by which the sensible in the representation
of nature is judged available for a possible supersensible use."[16] Yet, what sort
of relation can the sublime be if one remembers that it is a relation between a sensible faculty (however elevated) and a supersensible faculty, the "faculty express-
ing the independence of absolute totality"?[17] Imagination is the faculty of *Darstellung*, that is, of the sensible presentation of the spontaneity of understanding and
Reason. Contrary to the beautiful, which must be understood as the direct presentation of the possibility of schematizing presentable concepts, the sublime takes
it upon itself to present what by rights is unpresentable. Thus, the task that seems
to be devolved upon it seems to be a variation of what Kant calls in §59 "symbolic
hypotyposis," a variation because Kant distinguishes only two types of hypotyposis, schematic and symbolic. Indeed, in the same way as symbolic presentation
presents only indirectly, the sublime renders the intelligible in an indirect manner. It does so by what can best be designated as a *negative* hypotyposis. As is
well known, the relation established between imagination and Reason in the judgment on the sublime is not a harmonious relation, but one of conflict. It is a relation, nevertheless, and as such a relation, the conflict (*Widerstreit*) staged between the two faculties does not exclude totality. On the contrary, totality is
presupposed by the conflict of the faculties: their severing takes place within it.
Yet, how does this negative presentation of the unpresentable take place in that
play of the faculties of imagination and Reason properly called "sublime"? It is
brought about, Kant tells us, by imagination's extension (*Erweiterung*). Imagination becomes extended as soon as it gives up its primary bias toward sensibility,
in short, as soon as it brings its presenting function to a stop. This interruption
occurs in an act of freedom and of self-determination. The extension of imagination, as Kant stresses, is the result of a self-violation and self-dispossession by
which imagination sacrifices its sensible nature, i.e., its destiny as a faculty of

mere presentation. Yet, in doing so, imagination submits to the rule of Reason, or what is the same, to the law of freedom as the law of absolute totality. Thus, in extending itself in an act of freedom, imagination turns *itself* into the subjective-purposive presentation of the unpresentable. In the context of Kant's treatment of the sublime, the reference to the Jewish commandment "Thou shalt not make thyself any graven image, nor the likeness of anything which is in heaven or in the earth or under the earth," as a command of Reason, leaves no doubt as to the necessity of imagination to give up its attempt to visualize Reason, to make an image of it.[18] But, by following this reasonable demand, imagination attains for itself a nonsensuous resemblance to Reason, that is, of the unpresentable totality itself. In short, then: In the sublime a minimal (and negative) presentation of the unpresentable, of the faculty of ideas that is Reason, takes place, which by the way is, in its very negativity, the matrix of all sensible actualization of these ideas in the ethical realm.

Let us now circle back to the problematics of the *Augenschein*. The philosophers immediately preceding Kant (those from Wolff to Baumgarten) make a strong link between the sensible faculty of imagination and eyesight. The specificity of the images of imagination consists, apart from their reproductive function, in conferring a sensible unity (individuality) upon appearances. What Kant calls "immediate intuition" or the "mere sight" or "what merely strikes the eye" is akin to Baumgarten's "dispositio naturalis ad perspecaciam," through which nature is perceived in its totality, not in a conceptual mode, however, but in a mode immanent to the being of nature.[19] The *Augenschein* is a synthesis of phenomenality in a minimally phenomenal manner. In Kant, this synthesis is made possible by the fact that the *Augenschein*, as soon as it enters into the service of the sublime, no longer sees anything determinate but the unseeable itself. What does the *Augenschein* refer to if not nature *as a whole*—the sky "as a distant, all-embracing, vault" (an example of the mathematically sublime), and the ocean as a similar totality—or to nature as a negative presentation of our incommensurable faculty of Reason in the image of the "abyss threatening to overwhelm everything" natural (an example of the dynamically sublime). In seeing nothing determinate but the unseeable par excellence, the *Augenschein* thus yields to the law of freedom and Reason. Free from concepts of understanding, and a sensuous presentation only to the extent that it is the faculty of eyesight itself, the *Augenschein*, because it does not see anything particular but the whole of nature or Reason, is itself an imageless image of Reason. But, ultimately, the unseeable revealed by the *Augenschein* as the *one* glance that embraces center and periphery at once, fails to show what it shows. It is, for Kant, an impossible endeavor to try to present the intelligible totality *as* the totality of nature, not only because that totality is by rights unpresentable, but also because no totalization of nature can be achieved. The *Augenschein*, however, while failing to present the intelligible, offers it to thought. Although the synthesis by imagination of the whole of nature fails, the *Augen-*

schein is sublime because it reveals "imagination in its greatest extension," that is, imagination as yielding to "the principles of the schematism of the judgement (being so far, therefore, ranked under freedom)."[20] The *Augenschein*, thus, shows imagination yielding to Reason; it is witness to imagination's minimal relation to that faculty. This conclusion springs forth, last but not least, from Kant's rather intricate statement that despite what the *Augenschein* shows, the ocean must (nonetheless) be judged sublime ("man muss den Ozean bloss, wie die Dichter es tun, nach dem, was der Augenschein zeugt . . . *dennoch* erhaben finden können").[21] Rather then being mere ocular vision, the "immediate intuition" of the *Augenschein* is immediate in a negative fashion through which it negatively presents the very faculty of the ideas. Instead of being an obstacle to the presentation of ideas, the *Augenschein* thus seems to be another name for the extended imagination itself and, consequently, the very presentation, however negative, of the faculty of absolute totalization.

By reading Kant by rote, de Man is compelled to understand the *Augenschein*, which confers sublimity on nature, as entirely destitute of all intervention by the intellect. He writes: "No mind is involved in the Kantian vision of ocean and heaven" (PM, 135). It is a "purely material" vision, "devoid of any reflexive or intellectual complication, it is also purely formal, devoid of any semantic depth and reducible to the formal mathematization or geometrization of pure optics." "In this mode of seeing, the eye is its own agent and not the specular echo of the sun" (PM, 136). According to de Man, this act of perception is absolutely unrelated, unique, entirely unintelligible in its singularity. Therefore, he can also hold that the perceptions of heaven and ocean as vault or floor, are not themselves of the order of trope or figuration: "Heaven and ocean as buildings are a priori, previous to any understanding," and inseparable from the material vision itself, which knows no duality (PM, 135). Now, in "Kant's Materialism," de Man speaks of the unity of *Augenschein* and Kant's architectonic world as a "stony gaze." This stony gaze is, for de Man, a moment of "absolute, radical formalism, that entertains no notion of reference or semiosis," and which lies forgotten at the heart of the *Third Critique*'s attempt to bridge Reason and the empirical. More precisely, the *Third Critique* is itself the result of a forgetting of its source in a purely formal, material, and mindless stare.

But this stony gaze of material vision, a vision in which the materiality of the letter and of the linguistic acts of positing are still one, in which no difference, and hence no substituting exchange between differents, is possible—this stony gaze is also what provides de Man's rhetorical reading with its theoretical thrust. In the nonperceptual perception of its frozen gaze, one indeed recognizes a formal and material act of synthesis—a transcendental apperception of sorts—in which both sides of de Man's enterprise, his "ontology" and "epistemology," appear still undifferentiated, one, and thus, absolutely impenetrable. But, obviously, this monstrous synthesis is also indistinguishable from the fragmentary chaos of the irreducibly singular material instances and purely formal acts of language.

At this point, one can no longer overlook the fact that de Man's destruction of philosophical difference, of the difference that philosophy makes by virtue of its claims to generality and universality, takes place in the name of a singularity so radical that it cannot be termed empirical anymore, a singularity that, in its irreducible idiosyncrasy, seeks to thoroughly foreground the possibility of intelligibility. But this extreme singularity that defies all comprehensibility also, by virtue of its fragmentary nature, appears to be a function of a very particular type of philosophy that can be construed as a "materialist" variation of the idealistic romantic project, the fragmentary chaos of progressive universal poetry. However, the elimination of all *differentiae* in the romantic medium of reflection takes on, in de Man's rhetorical reading, unheard of proportions. Instead of opening up to *one* universe of seedlike fragments susceptible of engendering worlds, de Man's philosophy emphasizes a much darker picture. His is a world of unrelated singulars, each so idiosyncratic that in it everything universal becomes extinguished; it is a world of heterogeneous fragments forming a whole only insofar as, by their mutual indifference and lack of generative power, they are all the same, endlessly repeating the punctuality of their lone meaninglessness. De Man's philosophy thus seems to invoke Schelling's originary indifference of the One, yet the connotations of indifference resonate here in a manner very different from that of the romantic philosopher.

Must we conclude, at this point, that the annulment of philosophical difference in nonphenomenal reading is a function of just another philosophy—of a philosophy that, in contradistinction to classical philosophy, would *not speak well*, and that by resisting the difference that philosophy makes, would relinquish universality for the sake of the absolutely singular? One might be inclined to think so, and explain the naïvetés to which such a philosophy would have to give in, as well as the insurmountable difficulties that it presents, by recalling the objections Sartre aimed at Bataille who, as one knows, was involved in a similar enterprise of recuperating a radical singularity, namely, that the neglect of philosophical difference and its exigencies inevitably results in philosophy's revenge: a philosophy of indifference as outlined suffers, indeed, from irreparable philosophical naïveté! But, rather than embarking on a discussion of the problems that such a variation on romantic thought may pose, we prefer to consider a variety of issues that, in the case of de Man, may severely limit the possibility of such criticism in the first place. Undoubtedly, the philosophy of formal materialism that we have shown to animate the nonphenomenal phase of de Man's reading of philosophy is one of this critic's major and consistent concerns. In literary theory it is the "necessarily pragmatic moment that certainly weakens it as theory but that adds a subversive element of unpredictability and makes it something of a wild card in the serious game of the theoretical disciplines," and upon this pragmatic moment de Man focuses his interest (RT, 8). When dealing with the philosophy of Kant, for instance, de Man brings a material vision into view that is said to remain external to the concept, while his readings of Hegel focus on the alleged dependence of thought as such on a material inscription and on the mechanical function of memory as *Gedächtnis*. De Man's reproaches of the tradition of Kant and Hegel exegesis for having "entirely overlooked what we call the material aspect" clearly demonstrate that his formal materialism comes closest to what could be considered his own "positive" philosophy (PM, 136). But the fact that this formal materialism is indeed a correlate of reading specific texts, and also primarily of rhetorical reading's second facet of nonphenomenal reading, should already be ample reason for caution against overhasty conclusions. Indeed, formal materialism as a philosophy is not de Man's last word.

Beyond the Pathos of Difference

By considerably simplifying the complex organization of de Man's critical operations, we were able to determine two major and juxtaposed moments of this operation: one that invalidates a thematic reading of texts by thematic means and another that reaches toward the text's inscription of its own figuration. As remains to be seen, these two approaches are superseded, so to speak, by a "third" facet of rhetorical reading.

Before we begin to develop this "third" overarching approach that supersedes the two facets of rhetorical reading, we must recall that de Man, in his nonphenomenal phase of reading texts, unearthed a formal materiality punctuating the texts that makes figuration as such possible. But since this materiality is without relation to the meaning that becomes superimposed on it, it is also immediately forgotten, and cannot be made part of the text. Yet, this meaningless cause of the text, precisely because the text cannot take in such a cause, also undoes the text's figuration, its meaning-producing activity. Although there would be no text without such a cause, the possibility of a meaningful text requires that the material and formal cause of the text recede into oblivion. Such constituting of forgetting is achieved by imposing on the material and formal linguistic event, and on the senseless power of positing language, the authority of sense and meaning.

In what precedes, we insisted along with de Man that the material and formal base of texts is absolutely indifferent to what comes before it and what follows it. It is irreducibly singular, destitute of all possible relations. But the following objections can be easily anticipated regarding the status of such singularity: if the material linguistic event has as such no relation whatsoever to a meaning intention, how then can it be said to make such an intention possible, or to subvert it? We have already stressed that meaning is the result of a forgetting imposition. What this means is that the act of sense creation itself corresponds to an act of positing, that is, to an arbitrary intervention that has no relation to the preceding linguistic act, and which is thus also immediately forgotten. The production of meaning occurs through an act of imposition, that is, through an act uncalled for by the material and linguistic stratum of an utterance or text. It is as singular, as devoid of all relations, as the act of linguistic positing itself. De Man writes: "Considered performatively, figuration . . . performs the erasure of the positing power of language," yet, since it has itself as a positing act no relation to the act that precedes it, "the initial violence of position can only be half erased, since the erasure is accomplished by a device of language that never ceases to partake of the very violence against which it is directed" (RR, 118–19). In other words, the act by which the event performed by language becomes forgotten, and by which meaning and cognition come into life, is itself a senseless act. It partakes in the very violence of mindless and absolutely singular positing of the "preceding" linguistic act. Thus, the production of meaning, or figuration, rather than being a beginning is nothing but a repetition of the material and formal linguistic act itself. It remains as punctual, as sterile, as the "first" cause.

For de Man, the semantic levels of a text, its strata of aesthetic or conceptual figuration, are nothing but the always already aborted attempts to cover up, or recuperate, the total lack of meaning at the base of the irretrievably singular linguistic events, by exactly repeating the originary act of violence. In his essay "Sign and Symbol in Hegel's *Aesthetics*," after having stated that Hegel's aesthetics is in essence an aesthetic of the symbol, he argues that the symbol and, *mutatis mutandis*, the whole of Hegel's science of the beautiful, is "an ideological and not a theoretical construct, a defense against the logical necessity inherent in a theoretical disclosure" (SS, 770–71). Referring in that same essay to Hegel's *Science of Logic*, he also claims that "an inescapable obstacle threatens the entire construction" of the logic from its very beginning, and that as a whole it represents the attempt to recuperate a "logical difficulty devoid of any phenomenal or experiential dimension," by staging that difficulty as if it were "an event in time, a narrative, or a history" (SS, 769). In short, the literary and the philosophical discourse are, for de Man, meaningful enterprises involved in forgetting or recuperating the nonphenomenal properties of the material and formal act of figuration, properties that come into view, as he insists, through figuration itself, precisely to the extent in which figuration is itself a repetition of the originary violence of positing. All there can be, consequently, is an endless series of acts of imposition that, because they lack all continuity with what precedes them, repeat, without ever lending themselves to any real discrimination, the "original" arbitrary act of linguistic positing. Ultimately, there is no difference between that act and the authority of meaning.

An additional consequence follows from the preceding developments, and this is of particular interest to us. As de Man has pointed out in his essays on Nietzsche, a philosophy geared toward spelling out the originary violence and arbitrariness of the irreducibly singular linguistic acts of positing—a violence that threatens, as we have seen, the closure and reflexive totalization of all meaning creation—remains as philosophy tangled up in what it denounces. To state philosophical aberration, says de Man, is deceiving, since by merely stating error and thus failing to apply those insights to itself, a critical philosophy such as Nietzsche's is ultimately indistinguishable from what it criticizes. It does not itself enact what it teaches. Yet this is a complication that is not attributable to some negligence of the thinker. It is not intentional but rather "co-extensive with any use of language," as de Man holds (AR, 125). The knowledge that a text gains of itself, of its own figuration—the link that it establishes with itself lifting its total arbitrariness in a remotivating act of self-reflection—is, as de Man asserts in "Shelley Disfigured," "a figure in its own right, as such, bound to repeat the disfiguration of metaphor" (RR, 120). In the same way as such a figure is deconstructed by the fact that it is itself a repetition of the singular and senseless act that it seeks to overcome through reflexive remotivation, a critical philosophy, which, as in the case of Nietzsche states the rhetorical origin of all truth, must let itself be deconstructed by the fact that such stating is, in essence, a repetition of the senseless act of linguistic positing. But since such deconstruction is, according to de Man, itself an act of cognition—that is, an act that pretends to speak *about* something, and to thus entertain a nonarbitrary relation to something—it always stages only a figure in need of further deconstruction.[22]

Such endless deconstruction is indeed, for de Man, the fate of all theory. Because theory is, as theory, a totalizing operation rooted in an all-embracing gaze and, ultimately, in the originary synthesis of transcendental apperception, it is, in de Man's own words, a figure. But as a figure, that is, as a totalizing and thus motivating device of everything arbitrary in language, it is put into question by the universals of the "consistently defective models of language's impossibility to be a model of language" (RT, 20). As he writes in "The Resistance to Theory," all theory, de Man's included, is a theory and not a theory; in short, it is the "universal theory of the impossibility of theory" (RT, 20). What follows from this is that no "positive" philosophy can emerge from a rhetorical reading. Such a reading cannot come to a final stop in what has been called the philosophy of formal materialism based on a disfiguring and disarticulating gaze that, however stony, constituted it into the figure of a theory. Precisely to the extent that such a theory or philosophy would be "positive," it would have failed to enact what it points out, and would have forgotten what it tries to recall: the irreducibly singular positing power of language. If a rhetorical reading proceeds by demonstrating first that a text on its thematic and semantic level already undoes what it weaves, and second, by showing that the inscription of figuration in the text itself points to the positing powers of language, disfiguring all meaning production, then the third facet of rhetorical reading will consist of deconstructing the latter's figural status—the illusion of having come to grips with the arbitrariness and the senselessness of the materiality of language and its acts of positing. Yet, such a debunking is not final. There is no end to it, since all deconstruction as de Man understands it, forgets what it is about. The third facet of rhetorical reading does not, therefore, supersede the first two. All it effectuates is thoroughly to strip the first and second phase of rhetorical reading of all their generalizing power, and to bring them to their status of hopelessly singular and unrelated acts in which the "originary" arbitrariness of linguistic positing becomes reenacted. Only by deconstructing the philosophy of formal materialism that emerges from the second phase of rhetorical reading, and thus enacting the rhetorical substratum of theory, can such a theory be faithful to what it is "about." Only by achieving idiosyncratic singularity, in short, by undercutting all motivating relation, does a theory concerning the formal and material substratum of discourses or texts achieve its goal.

Only by constantly offering itself to a singularizing deconstruction does a rhetorical reading live up to its task. The rhetorical substratum to which theories point becomes realized in the infinite series of deconstructed theories. But that series of repeated deconstructions, by which the conceptualization of the rhetorical substratum is endlessly deferred, has as such no generality or universality either. The endless repetition of the same figure or theory is for de Man a figure as well. In reference to Friedrich Schlegel, he calls it ironic allegory, that is, a figure in constant displacement. It is a figure in deconstruction. Hence, the series of theories in which the impossibility of theory becomes enacted also remains, in its totality, irreducibly singular. The thrust of idiosyncratic individuality or singularity remains unimpaired. It is, so to speak, the last word.

To draw some conclusions from these developments, we must circle back to the theoretical movements characterized earlier—the one concerning figuration's repetition of the senseless act of positing, and theory's need for (self-)deconstruction. As we recalled, Nietzsche's criticism of philosophy is a criticism that can never come to a halt. It is, therefore, in de Man's sense of that term, literary. But de Man says as well that the deconstruction of metaphysics, or philosophy, is an impossibility precisely to the extent that it is already literary (AR, 131). What follows from the crisscross of these two parallel arguments is that Nietzsche's critique of metaphysics and metaphysics itself are ultimately indistinguishable and, moreover, that there is no difference in principle between literature and philosophy. This conclusion is emphasized in the following passage:

> The critical deconstruction that leads to the discovery of the literary, rhetorical nature of the philosophical claim to truth is genuine enough and cannot be refuted: literature turns out to be the main topic of philosophy and the model for the kind of truth to which it aspires. But when literature seduces us with the freedom of its figural combinations, so much airier and lighter than the labored constructs of concepts, it is

not the less deceitful because it asserts its own deceitful properties. (AR, 115)

Although "philosophy turns out to be an endless reflection on its own destruction at the hands of literature," literature itself, to the extent that it "asserts its own deceitful properties," is philosophical, indistinguishable from philosophy, and also in need of a destruction (AR, 115). Or more precisely, in the same way as philosophy as aberration is put into question by the literary dimension of the linguistic signifier, literature as philosophy is constantly challenged by its own literary qualities. Philosophy and literature, the critique of metaphysics and metaphysics itself, are the same. For the same reason, distinctions such as linguistic and semantic, transcendental and empirical, distinctions that play a significant strategical role in de Man's analyses finally blur into total indifference, incapable of difference and, hence, of generality. But that blurring does not reside in a symmetrical canceling out. The conceptual oppositions, the sides of the arguments, the onionskin layers of de Man's text, are not abolished into one universal indifference, into the figure of the all-embracing essence of the medium of reflexivity. Since that stratum of a text that destructs its symmetrical opposite cannot itself escape destruction by what it points at, the thrust of deconstruction remains unimpaired. And since the series of the successive rhetorical reversals of the theories establishing the priority of formal materialism does not itself escape disfiguration, the negativity of the senselessness of the material dimension of language and its positing power remains unaffected. Yet does such an insight justify the conclusion that these properties of language are truly universal? De Man seems to say so at the end of "The Resistance to Theory." His radical empiricism—his stress on the arbitrariness, extreme singularity, and impenetrable materiality of the linguistic acts and signifier—appears to have gained such momentum here that its own generality and universality turn into a radical challenge to the generality of philosophical difference.

It must, however, be remarked that it is a longstanding philosophical truth that empiricism is capable of explaining everything except explication itself, that is, the difference that explication makes. Are the nonphenomenal material and formal properties really capable of putting into question—that is, accounting for— philosophical difference, the difference that thought makes with respect to what it is the thought of? If they are empirical qualities, pragmatic properties, they will never be able to elevate themselves to the thought of difference. If they are universal and general properties, then they are properties that make *the* difference, and all that has been achieved is a, perhaps, more sophisticated philosophical questioning of philosophical difference.

But must one not recall that de Man does not write *on* philosophy? His texts do not pretend to clarify philosophical problems, or to contribute to philosophical scholarship. Hence, de Man cannot be concerned with the *philosophical* problem of difference as such. His is not an approach that would recognize the legitimacy of such a distinction. Consequently, if the material and positional properties of language that de Man refers to were indeed capable of generality, it would be possible *truly to speak badly* from an empirical and pragmatic point of view, and thus to challenge from a however negative *philosophical* viewpoint, and in the name of another difference (that of the universal singular) philosophical difference itself. But the rhetorical substratum de Man speaks of is so destructive of generality that the theory of the universality of this substratum cannot but yield to its own singularizing effects. If one follows de Man's text to its logical conclusion, all that remains in the end of the rhetorical substratum's generality is the idiosyncratic singularity of such a contention. If the formal and linguistic properties to which de Man's texts have been referring have an assertable generality, it is a generality so particular that, ultimately, it must remain utterly incomprehensible. It is a generality that confounds with the unique and punctual proposition in which it becomes cast by de Man himself. It is a generality, then, that paradoxically makes no difference to philosophical difference, and that challenges it precisely by not challenging it.

What de Man has established as the lesson of his reading of Shelley's *The Triumph of Life* must thus be seen to apply to his own reading of philosophy as well:

> Nothing, whether deed, word, thought, or text, ever happens in relation, positive or negative, to anything that precedes, follows, or exists elsewhere, but only as a random event whose power, like the power of death, is due to the randomness of its occurrence. (RR, 122)

De Man's reading of philosophy is not *about* philosophy. It tries to show little or no concern about philosophy. It is a reading that challenges philosophical difference by not being about it, by not referring to it, by making no difference with respect to it. In contrast to philosophy, de Man's readings do not attempt to make any difference. In this sense they are "different," idiosyncratic to a point where, by making no point, they will have made their point—so singular as to make no difference but, perhaps, in that total apathy a formidable challenge to philosophical difference.

Notes

1. Heinrich Niehues-Pröbsting, "Die 'Episode' im 'Theaitetos': Verschärfung der Begriffe von Rhetorik und Philosophie," *Archiv für Begriffsgeschichte* (Bonn: Bouvier, 1982), vol. 24, no. 1, 16–23.

2. G. W. F. Hegel, *Aesthetics, Lectures on Fine Art,* trans. T. M. Knox (Oxford: Clarendon Press, 1975), I: 315.

3. Josef König, "Das spezifische Können der Philosophie als eu legein," *Blätter für deutsche Philosophie,* 10 (1937): 134.

4. Ernst Cassirer, *Kant's Life and Thought,* trans. J. Haden (New Haven, Conn: Yale University Press, 1981), 326–27.

5. Peter Szondi, "Hegels Lehre von der Dichtung," *Poetik und Geschichtsphilosophie* (Frankfurt: Suhrkamp, 1974), 11: 366–67.

6. Hegel, *Aesthetics*, 494–96.

7. G. W. F. Hegel, *Enzyklopädie der Philosophischen Wissenschaften*, Vol. II (*Werke in zwanzig Bänden*, Vol. 10) (Frankfurt: Suhrkamp, 1970), 269, 267.

8. Hegel, *Aesthetics*, 312–13.

9. Hegel, *Aesthetics*, 304.

10. Hegel, *Enzyklopädie*, 270.

11. Gérard Genette, *Figures of Literary Discourse*, trans. M.-R. Logan (New York: Columbia University Press, 1982), 120; in a manner very similar to Genette, de Man objects to the ideology of Cratylism on the basis that it dreams of language as motivated, i.e., as being in essence symbolic and, thus, as being (or having primitively been) a medium in which speech *is what it says*. As Genette, all differences respected, de Man also objects to the possibility of textual self-reflexivity, contending that it is a major form of sign motivation, ideologically oblivious to the founding arbitrariness of the linguistic signifier and act, and thus tributary to the dominating understanding of art as involved in a nostalgic misunderstanding of language as essentially symbolic.

12. De Man refers to the work of Sarah Kofman and Philippe Lacoue-Labarthe.

13. For de Man's demarcation of his own approach from speech-act theory, see my essay " '*Setzung*' and '*Übersetzung*': Notes on Paul de Man," *Diacritics*, Winter 1981, 36–57.

14. Friedrich Schlegel, "On Incomprehensibility," *Lucinde and the Fragments*, trans. P. Firchow (Minneapolis: University of Minnesota Press, 1971), 268.

15. Immanuel Kant, *Critique of Judgement*, trans. J. H. Bernard (New York: Hafner Press, 1951), 110.

16. Kant, *Critique of Judgement*, 107.

17. Kant, *Critique of Judgement*, 108.

18. Kant, *Critique of Judgement*, 115.

19. Alexander Gottlieb Baumgarten, *Aesthetica* (Hildesheim: Olms, 1961), 13.

20. Kant, *Critique of Judgement*, 109–10.

21. Kant, *Critique of Judgement*, 111.

22. For a precise account of how de Man understands "deconstruction" in counterdistinction from its use by Derrida, see my essay mentioned in note 13.

Notes on Contributors

Notes on Contributors

Timothy Bahti is Associate Professor of German and Comparative Literature at the University of Michigan. He is the author of the forthcoming book, *Allegories of History: Literary Historiography After Hegel*, and has also published articles on romantic poetry, German philosophy, and modern criticism.

Geoffrey Bennington teaches in the School of European Studies, University of Sussex, England. He is the author of *Sententiousness and the Novel: Laying Down the Law in Eighteenth-Century French Fiction* (1985) and *Lyotard: Writing the Event* (forthcoming). He is also an editor of the *Oxford Literary Review*.

Jacques Derrida teaches at the Ecole des Hautes Etudes en Sciences Sociales, in Paris, and at several American universities. Among his numerous works available in English the most recent are *Glas, The Postcard*, and *The Truth in Painting* (all published in 1987).

Deborah Esch is Andrew W. Mellon Assistant Professor of English at Princeton University. She is currently completing *The Senses of the Past*, a study of the rhetoric of temporality in James, and coediting Jacques Derrida's *The Institutions of Philosophy* and *Negotiations*. She has published readings of literary, philosophical, and theoretical texts in the romantic and postromantic tradition.

Rodolphe Gasché is Professor of Comparative Literature at the State University of New York at Buffalo. His publications include *Die hybride Wissenschaft*

(1973), *System und Metaphorik in der Philosophie von Georges Bataille* (1978), and *The Tain of the Mirror: Derrida and the Philosophy of Reflection* (1986). A new book, *Rethinking Relation: On Heidegger, Derrida, and de Man*, is nearing completion.

Werner Hamacher is Professor in the Department of German and the Humanities Center at Johns Hopkins University. His publications include an edition of G. W. F. Hegel, *Der Geist des Christentums*, with an accompanying book-length study, *"pleroma": zu Genesis und Struktur einer dialektischen Hermeneutik bei Hegel* (1978), and essays on Kant, Fichte, Schlegel, Schleiermacher, Kleist, Nietzsche, Benjamin, Celan, and others. He has edited *Nietzsche aus Frankreich* (1986), coedited *Paul Celan: Materialien zu seinem Werk* (1987), and translated and introduced the German edition of de Man's *Allegories of Reading*.

Geoffrey H. Hartman is Professor of English and Comparative Literature at Yale University. He worked with Paul de Man at Cornell and at Yale. His latest publications in criticism are *The Unremarkable Wordsworth* (1987), *Saving the Text* (1981), and *Criticism in the Wilderness: The Study of Literature Today* (1980).

Neil Hertz taught for many years in the Department of English at Cornell University. He now teaches in the Humanities Center and the Department of English at Johns Hopkins University. He is the author of *The End of the Line: Essays on Psychoanalysis and the Sublime* (1985).

Carol Jacobs is Professor of English and Comparative Literature at the State University of New York at Buffalo. She is the author of *The Dissimulating Harmony: The Image of Interpretation in Nietzsche, Rilke, Artaud, and Benjamin* and of *Uncontainable Romanticism: Shelley, Brontë, and Kleist*. She has also written many articles on literature and critical theory.

Hans Robert Jauss is professor of literary criticism and romance philology at the University of Konstanz, West Germany, and is founder and co-editor of *Poetik und Hermeneutik*. He has taught at Columbia, Yale, Berkeley, Los Angeles, and the Sorbonne. His writings include studies of medieval and modern literature as well as theoretical works (in English: *Toward an Aesthetic of Reception* and *Aesthetic Experience and Literary Hermeneutics*, both published in 1982).

Peggy Kamuf is Professor of French at Miami University in Oxford, Ohio. Her recent publications include *Fictions of Feminine Desire: Disclosures of Heloise* (1982) and *Signature Pieces: On the Institution of Authorship* (forthcoming).

J. Hillis Miller is Distinguished Professor of English and Comparative Literature at the University of California at Irvine. His most recent books are *Fiction and Repetition: Seven English Novels* (1985), *The Ethics of Reading: Kant, de Man, Eliot, Trollope, James, and Benjamin* (1986), and *The Linguistic Moment: From Wordsworth to Stevens* (1987). He is currently working on a continuation of *The Ethics of Reading* entitled *Versions of Pygmalion*.

Kevin Newmark teaches at Yale University and is currently at work on the status of symbolic language in French literature from Nerval to Proust.

Bill Readings is Assistant Professor in the Department of English at Syracuse University. He has previously held a teaching position at the University of Geneva. His *John Milton: The Restoration and the Fall of Language* is forthcoming; he is at present working on a book-length study of Lyotard's work.

Wlad Godzich is Professor of Comparative Literature and French Studies at the Université de Montréal. He is coauthor with Jeffrey Kittay of *The Emergence of Prose* (1987).

Lindsay Waters is General Editor at Harvard University Press, and the author of essays on Milton, Tasso, and Byron. He was an editor at the University of Minnesota Press from 1977 to 1984 and has edited the volume of Paul de Man's essays entitled *Critical Writings, 1953–1978* (forthcoming in the Theory and History of Literature Series).

Index

Index

Compiled by Hassan Melehy

Theory and History of Literature